SPORT IN CONTEMPORARY SOCIETY

SPORT IN CONTEMPORARY SOCIETY

An Anthology (Seventh Edition)

Edited by
D. Stanley Eitzen

Paradigm Publishers
Boulder • London

Copyright © 2005 by Paradigm Publishers

Published in the United States by Paradigm Publishers, 3360 Mitchell Lane Suite C, Boulder, Colorado 80301 USA.

Paradigm Publishers is the trade name of Birkenkamp & Company, LLC, Dean Birkenkamp, President and Publisher.

Library of Congress Cataloging-in-Publication Data

Sport in contemporary society: an anthology / [edited by] D. Stanley Eitzen. — 7th ed.
p. cm.
Includes bibliographical references.
ISBN 1-59451-047-4 (alk. paper)
1. Sports—Social aspects.   2. Sports—Social aspects—United States.
I. Eitzen, D. Stanley.
GV706.5.S733 2004
306.4'83—dc22
2004005610

Printed and bound in the United States of America on acid-free paper that meets the standards of the American National Standard for Permanence of Paper for Printed Library Materials.

Designed and Typeset by Straight Creek Bookmakers.

09 08 07 06 05
5 4 3 2 1

Contents

Part Seven
Problems of Excess: Big-Time College Sport 199

Part Eight
Problems of Excess: Sport and Money 225

Part Nine
Structured Inequality: Sport and Race/Ethnicity 257

Preface

Most North Americans are at least somewhat interested in sport, and many are downright fanatical about it. They attend games, read the sports pages and sport magazines, participate in fantasy leagues, and talk endlessly about the subject. But even those fans who astound us with their knowledge of the most obscure facts about sport do not necessarily *understand* sport.

Do sport buffs know how sport is linked to other institutions of society? Do they understand the role of sport in socializing youngsters in both positive and negative ways? Do they know that the assumption that sport builds character is open to serious debate? Do they know that racism continues in sport? What about the ways in which sport perpetuates gender-role stereotypes in society? How do owners, coaches, and other sport authorities exercise power to maintain control over athletes? These are some of the issues this book examines.

There are two fundamental reasons for the ignorance of most North Americans about the role of sport in society. First, they have had to rely mainly on sportswriters and sportscasters for their information, and these journalists have typically been little more than describers and cheerleaders. Until recent years journalists have rarely examined sport critically. Instead they have perpetuated myths: "Football helped a whole generation of sons of coal miners escape the mines" or "Sport is an island free of prejudice and racism."

The second reason for our sports illiteracy is that sport has been ignored, for the most part, by North American academics. Only in the past generation or so have North American social scientists and physical educators begun to investigate seriously the social aspects of sport. Previously, as with sports journalism, academic research on sport has tended to be biased in support of existing myths. In particular, the early research by physical educators was aimed at proving that sports participation builds character. In this limited perspective phenomena common to sport such as cheating, excessive violence, coaching tyranny, and the consequences of failure were, for the most part, simply ignored.

Today, however, not only academics but also a new breed of sports journalists are making insightful analyses of the role of sport in society. They examine the positive *and* negative consequences of sport for people, communities, schools, and nations. They demystify and demythologize sport. Most significant, they document the reciprocal impact of sport on the various institutions of society: religion, education, politics, and economics. There is no danger that sport will suffer from such examination. Critical reflection leads, sometimes, to positive changes. Moreover, the scholarly scrutiny of sport reveals a subject far more complex and far more interesting than what we see on the fields and arenas and what we read in the sports pages.

This book is a collection of the writings representing this new era of critical appraisal. It includes contributions from both journalists and academics. The overriding criterion for inclusion of a particular article was whether it critically examined the role of sport in society. The praise of sport is not omitted, but such praise, as with condemnation, must be backed by fact, not mythology or dogma. (Occasionally a dogmatic piece has been included to challenge the critical faculties of the reader.) The selection of each article was also guided by such questions as: Is it interesting? Is it informative? Is it thought-provoking? Does it communicate without the use of unnecessary jargon and sophisticated methodologies?

In short, the selections presented here not only afford the reader an understanding of sport that transcends the still prevalent stereotypes and myths, they also yield fascinating and important insights into the nature of society. Thus, this book has several groups of potential readers. First, it is intended to be the primary or supplementary text for courses in the sociology of sport, sport and society, and foundations of physical education. Second, the book can be used as a supplemental text for sociology courses such as the introduction to sociology, American society, and social institutions. A third audience for this book is general readers who wish to deepen their understanding and appreciation of sport.

The seventh edition of *Sport in Contemporary Society* has undergone extension revision. In fact, "Expanding the Horizons: Sport and Globalization" is a new section. Nineteen of the thirty-seven selections are new to this edition. In keeping with a major change to the previous edition, gender- and race-related articles are found throughout the collection, not just "ghettoized" in their appropriate sections. The result is a collection of lively and timely chapters that will sharpen the reader's analysis and understanding of sport *and* society.

I am indebted to the authors of the chapters in this volume. My thanks to them for their scholarship and, most significant, for insights that help us to unravel the mysteries of this intriguing and important part of social life.

D. Stanley Eitzen

PART ONE

Sport as a Microcosm of Society

The early part of the twenty-first century was a disheartening time in sports. Greed seemed to go unchecked. New stadiums were built at taxpayer expense *and the price of tickets went up.* Elite athletes were given astronomical salaries. Professional team owners threatened to move to different cities if they did not receive more subsidies. Parents were spending up to $100,000 annually to have their children groomed for the world of big-time sport. Scandals were commonplace in big-time college sport. Player and fan violence seemed rampant inside and outside the arenas.

> Against this tawdry backdrop we've again been forced to face up to the sad truth that sports isn't a sanctuary. It reflects, often all too clearly, society. And, yes, today greed and violence are a big part of society.[1]

My thesis is that sport is a microcosm of society. If we know how sport is organized, the type of games played, the way winners and losers are treated, the type and amount of compensation given the participants, and the way rules are enforced, then we surely also know a great deal about the larger society in which it exists. Conversely, if we know the values of a society, the type of economy, the way minority groups are treated, and the political structure, then we would also have important clues about how sport in that society is likely organized.

The United States, for example, is a capitalistic society. It is not surprising, then, that in the corporate sport that dominates, American athletes are treated as property. In the professional ranks they are bought and sold. At the college level players once enrolled are unable to switch teams without waiting for a year. Even in youth sports, players are drafted and become the "property" of a given team.

Capitalism is also evident as team owners "carpetbag," i.e., move teams to more lucrative markets. At the same time these owners insist that the cities subsidize the

1

construction of new stadiums, thereby making their franchises more profitable. The players, too, appear to have more loyalty to money than to their teams or fans.

Americans are highly competitive. This is easily seen at work, at school, in dating, and in sport. Persons are evaluated not on their intrinsic worth but on the criterion of achievement. As George H. Sage has written, "Sports have consented to measure the results of sports efforts in terms of performance and product—the terms which prevail in the factory and department store."[2]

Athletes are expected to deny self and sacrifice for the needs of the sponsoring organization. This requires, foremost, an acquiescence to authority. The coach is the ultimate authority and the players must obey. This is the way bureaucracies operate, and American society is highly bureaucratic whether it be in government, school, church, or business. As Paul Hoch has stated, "In football, like business . . . every pattern of movement on the field is increasingly being brought under control of a group of nonplaying managerial technocrats who sit up in the stands . . . with their headphones and dictate offenses, defense, special plays, substitutions, and so forth to the players below."[3]

Thus, American sport, like American society, is authoritarian, bureaucratic, and product-oriented. Winning is everything. Athletes use drugs to enhance their performances artificially in order to succeed. Coaches teach their athletes to bend the rules (to feign a foul, to hold without getting caught) in order to win. Even at America's most prestigious universities, coaches offer illegal inducements to athletes to attend their schools. And, as long as they win, the administrators at these offending schools usually look the other way. After all, the object is to win, and this mentality permeates sport as it does politics and the business world.

These are but some of the ways in which sport mirrors society. In this section we shall examine this relationship further through three selections. The first is from a speech by D. Stanley Eitzen that examines several paradoxes of American sport at the twentieth century's end: (1) While seemingly a trivial pursuit, sport is important; (2) sport has the capacity to build character as well as encourage bad character; (3) while the nature of sport is competition where ability tells, the reality is that race restricts; and (4) schools emphasize sports because of the personal and social benefits for participants, yet these same schools have generally resisted efforts by girls and women for participation and resources equal to those of boys and men.

The second selection, by Canadian cultural critic Varda Burstyn, is an excerpt from *The Rites of Men*. This segment examines the fascination that sport has for its fans and participants. She argues that the feelings and identification engendered by sport "approximate the experience of religion more than any other form of human cultural practice."

The final selection, by sociologist Jay J. Coakley, enhances our understanding of sport and society by elaborating on the two contrasting theoretical approaches—functionalist and conflict—that guide much of the work of sport sociologists. The understanding of both of these perspectives is vitally important to the analyst of society. Each approach offers significant insights about society. However, the theoretical approach guiding the structure of this book and the choice of selections is the conflict perspective. As I stated in the preface to Eitzen and Sage's *Sociology of North American Sport,*

> [the] goal is to make the reader aware of the positive and negative consequences of the way sport is organized in society. We are concerned about some of the trends in sports, especially the move away from athlete-oriented activities toward the impersonality of what we term "corporate sport." We are committed to moving sport and society in a more humane direction, and this requires, as a first step, a thorough understanding of the principles that underlie the social structures and processes that create, sustain, and transform the social organizations within the institution of sport.[4]

NOTES

1. E. M. Switch, "Giving His All," *Sports Illustrated* (December 19, 1994): 88.

2. George H. Sage, "Sports, Culture, and Society," paper presented at the Basic Science of Sport Medicine Conference, Philadelphia (July 14–16, 1974), pp. 10–11.

3. Paul Hoch, *Rip Off the Big Game* (Garden City, NY: Doubleday Anchor, 1972), p. 9.

4. D. Stanley Eitzen and George H. Sage, *Sociology of North American Sport,* 7th ed. (Dubuque, IA: Brown & Benchmark, 2003), p. xiv.

1

American Sport at Century's End

D. Stanley Eitzen

I want to examine sport by focusing on several paradoxes that are central to sport as it has come to be.

Paradox: While seemingly a trivial pursuit, sport is important. On the one hand, sport is entertainment, a fantasy, a diversion from the realities of work, relationships, and survival. But if sport is just a game, why do we take it so seriously? Among the many reasons, let's consider four: First, sport mirrors the human experience. The introductory essay in a recent issue of *The Nation,* which was devoted to sport, said this:

> Sport elaborates in its rituals what it means to be human: the play, the risk, the trials, the collective impulse to games, the thrill of physicality, the necessity of strategy; defeat, victory, defeat again, pain, transcendence and, most of all, the certainty that nothing is certain—that everything can change and be changed.

Second, sport mirrors society in other profound ways as well. Sociologists, in particular, find the study of sport fascinating because we find there the basic elements and expressions of bureaucratization, commercialization, racism, sexism, homophobia, greed, exploitation of the powerless, alienation, and the ethnocentrism found in the larger society. Of special interest, too, is how sport has been transformed from an activity for individuals involved in sport for its own sake, to a money-

Source: D. Stanley Eitzen, "American Sport at Century's End," *Vital Speeches of the Day* 65 (January 1, 1999): pp. 189–191.

driven, corporate entity where sport is work rather than play, and where loyalty to players, coaches, and owners is a quaint notion that is now rarely held. Also, now athletes are cogs in a machine where decisions by coaches and bureaucracies are less and less player-centered. I am especially concerned with the decisions made by big business bureaucracies (universities, leagues, cartels such as the NCAA, corporations, and sports conglomerates such as Rupert Murdoch's empire, which just in the U. S. includes ownership of the Los Angeles Dodgers, the Fox network, FX, 22 local cable channels, the *New York Post,* 20 percent of L.A.'s Staples center, a sports arena now under construction, and the partial rights to broadcast NFL games for eight years and major league baseball for five years). Another powerful sports conglomerate is the Walt Disney Corporation which owns the Mighty Ducks of Anaheim, 25 percent of the Anaheim Angels and the option to buy the rest from Gene Autry's estate, ABC-TV, ESPN, and, like Murdoch, partial rights for eight years of NFL games and five years of major league baseball. While we're at it, let's list the Time Warner sports empire, which includes ownership of the Atlanta Braves, Atlanta Hawks, Atlanta Thrashers, the Goodwill Games, World Championship Wrestling, Turner Field plus the Atlanta arena now under construction, *Sports Illustrated, Time* magazine, CNN, HBO, TNT, TBS, and Warner Brothers. They have a four-year deal as the NBA's cable partner. Obviously, sport is not a trivial pursuit by these media moguls.

A third reason why sports are so compelling is that they combine spectacle with drama. Sports, especially football, involve pageantry, bands forming a liberty bell or unfurling a flag as big as the football field, and militaristic displays with the drama of a situation where the outcome is not perfectly predictable. Moreover, we see excellence, human beings transcending the commonplace to perform heroic deeds. There is also clarity—we know, unlike in many other human endeavors, exactly who won, by how much, and how they did it.

Finally, there is the human desire to identify with something larger than oneself. For athletes, it is to be part of a team, working and sacrificing together to achieve a common goal. For fans, by identifying with a team or a sports hero, they bond with others who share their allegiance; they belong and they have an identity. This bond of allegiance is becoming more and more difficult as players through free agency move from team to team, as coaches are hired and fired, and because many times when coaches are successful they break their contracts to go to a more lucrative situation, leaving their players, assistants, and fans in their wake. The owners of many professional teams blackmail their cities for more lucrative subsidies by threatening to move, which they sometimes do, leaving diehard fans without teams.

Paradox: Sport has the capacity to build character as well as encourage bad character. On the one hand, sports participation encourages hard work, perseverance, self-discipline, sacrifice, following the rules, obeying authority, and working with teammates to achieve a common goal. Sport promotes fair play. . . . There are countless examples where competitors show respect for one another, where sportsmanship rules.

But for all of the honor and integrity found in sport there is also much about sport that disregards the ideals of fair play. Good sportsmanship may be a product of sport, but so is bad sportsmanship. Let me cite a few examples: (1) trash-talking and taunting opponents; (2) dirty play (a recent article in *Sports Illustrated* documented dirty play in the NFL, citing the ten worst offenders, saying that "there's a nasty breed of players who follow one cardinal rule: Anything goes, and that means biting, kicking, spearing, spitting, and leg-whipping"); (3) coaches who teach their players how to hold and not get caught; (4) faking being fouled so that a referee who is out of position will call an undeserved foul on the opponent; (5) trying to hurt an opponent; (6) coaches rewarding players for hurting an opponent; (7) throwing a spitter or corking a bat; (8) using illegal drugs to enhance performance; (9) crushing an opponent (a Laramie, Wyoming, girls junior high basketball team won a game a few years ago by a score of 81–1, using a full-court press the entire game); (10) fans yelling racial slurs; (11) coaches who, like Pat Riley of the Miami Heat, demand that their players not show respect for their opponents (Riley fines his players $1,500 if they help an opposing player get off the floor); (12) coaches who are sexist and homophobic, calling their male players "pussies" or "fags" if they are not aggressive enough; (13) a male locker room culture that tends to promote homophobia, sexism, and aggressive behaviors; and (14) coaches who recruit illegally, who alter transcripts and bribe teachers to keep players eligible, and who exploit players with no regard for their health or their education.

What lesson is being taught and caught when a coach openly asks a player to cheat? Consider this example. A few years ago, the Pretty Prairie Kansas High School had twin boys on its team. One of the twins was injured but suited up for a game where his brother was in foul trouble at half time. The coach had the twins change jerseys so that the foul-plagued twin would be in the second half with no fouls charged to the player's number he was now wearing. . . .

My point is that we live in a morally distorted sports world—a world where winning often supersedes all other considerations, where moral values have become confused with the bottom line. In this in-your-face, whip your-butt climate, winning-at-any-price often becomes the prevailing code of conduct. And when it does, I assert, sport does build character, but it is bad character. When we make the value of winning so important that it trumps morality, then we and sport are diminished.

Paradox: While the nature of sport is competition where ability tells, the reality is that race restricts. Just as in other social realms, we find in sport that the ascribed status of race gives advantage to some and disadvantage to others. Let's look at racism in sport, focusing on African Americans since they are the dominant racial minority in American sport.

At first glance, its seems impossible that Blacks are victims of discrimination in sport since some of them make huge fortunes from their athletic prowess, such as LaBron James who signed a seven-year deal with Nike for $90 million before he graduated from high school, and Tiger Woods who makes about $100 million annually. Moreover, it is argued that Blacks in sport are not victims of discrimination because, while only constituting 12 percent of the general population, they comprise 65 percent of the players in professional football, 80 percent of professional basketball players, and 10 percent of the players in major league baseball (and where Latinos constitute another 24 percent). Also about 60 percent of the football and basketball players in big-time college programs are African Americans.

Despite these empirical facts that seem to contradict racism in sport, it is prevalent in several forms. Let me cite some examples. First, Blacks are rarely found in those sports that require the facilities, coaching, and competition usually provided only in private—and typically racially segregated—clubs; sports such as swimming, golf, skiing, and tennis. Black athletes also are rarely found where it takes extraordinary up-front money, usually from corporate sponsors, to participate such as in automobile racing.

But even in the team sports where African American dominate numerically, there is evidence of discrimination. Sociologists have long noted that Blacks tend to be relegated to those team positions where the physical attributes of strength, size, speed, aggressiveness, and "instinct" are important but that they are underrepresented at those playing positions that require thinking and leadership and are the most crucial for outcome control. This phenomenon, known as stacking, continues today, at both the college and professional levels in football and baseball. Using professional football as the example, African Americans are underrepresented on offense and if on offense they tend to be at wide receiver and running back—the whitest positions are center, offensive guard, quarterback, punter, placekicker, and placekick holder. Blacks are overrepresented at all positions on defense, except middle linebacker. The existence of stacking reinforces negative stereotypes about racial minorities, as Whites appear, by the positions they play, to be superior to Blacks in cognitive ability and leadership qualities but behind them in physical prowess.

African Americans are also underrepresented in nonplaying leadership positions. At the professional level team ownership is an exclusively all-White club. In the league offices of the NCAA, major league baseball, the NBA, and the NFL, the employees are disproportionately White. The same is true, of course, for head coaches in big-time college and professional sports.

African Americans are also underrepresented in ancillary sports positions such as sports information director, ticket manager, trainer, equipment manager, scout, accountant, sportswriting, and sports broadcasting, especially play-by-play announcing.

Another consistent finding by sociologists is a form of discrimination known as "unequal opportunity for equal ability." This means that the entrance requirements for Blacks to obtain college scholarships or to play in the professional leagues are more rigorous than they are for Whites. In essence, Black players must be better than White players to succeed in the sports world. In baseball, for example, Blacks consistently have higher statistics (batting average, home runs, stolen bases, earned run average) than Whites. What's happening here is that superb Black athletes are not discriminated against but the substars do experience discrimination. The findings clearly indicate that the undistinguished Black player is less likely to play regularly than the equally undistinguished White player. As sociologist Jonathan Bower has said, "In sport mediocrity is a white luxury."

Paradox: Schools emphasize sports because of the personal and social benefits for participants, yet these same schools have generally resisted efforts by girls and women for participation and resources equal to that of boys and men. Research shows many benefits from sports for girls and women. When female athletes are compared to their non-athlete peers, they are found to have higher self-esteem and better body image. For high school girls, athletes are less likely than nonathletes to use illicit drugs; they are more likely to be virgins; if sexually active they are more likely to begin intercourse at a later age; and they are much less likely to get pregnant. These advantages are in addition to the standard benefits of learning to work with teammates for a common goal, striving for excellence, and the lessons of what it takes to win and how to cope with defeat. Yet, historically, women have been denied these benefits. And, even today, the powerful male establishment in sport continues to drag its collective feet on gender equity.

Title IX, passed in 1972, mandated gender equity in school sports programs. While this affected schools at all levels, I'll focus on the college level because this is where women have met the most resistance. Since 1972 women's intercollegiate programs have made tremendous strides, with participation quadrupling from 30,000 women in 1971 to 116,272 in 1996. Athletic scholarships for women were virtually unknown in 1972, now women athletes receive 35 percent of the athletic scholarship money that is distributed. These increases in a generation represent the good news concerning gender equity in collegiate sport. The bad news, however, is quite significant. Looking at the data for big-time schools for the 1995–96 school year, we find the following disparities by gender:

1. Head coaches of women's teams were paid 63 cents for every dollar earned by coaches of men's teams (and this inequity does not include many of the extras the coaches of men's teams are more likely than the coaches of women's teams to receive—lucrative radio and television deals, endorsements, cars, country club memberships, sweetheart business deals, and housing allowances).
2. Only seven schools met the proportionality test for equity—i.e., the number of women athletes should be within 5 percent of the proportion of women undergraduates enrolled. The average negative gap was 16 percent.
3. The average gender composition of an athletic department was 292 male athletes and 163 female athletes (65 percent male and 35 percent female), with a similar disproportionate distribution of scholarships.
4. The recruiting budget was skewed in favor of males with a 76 percent/24 percent ratio.
5. Operational expenditures were distributed even more unevenly at 78 percent/22 percent. And, most telling, it was not uncommon for a school with a big-time football program to spend twice as much on its football team as it spent on all its women's sports combined.
6. In a most ironic twist, in 1972, when Tide IX was enacted, more than 90 percent of women's teams were coached by women. But now that participation for women has quadrupled, the percentage of women's teams coached by women has dropped to 48 percent.
7. At the administrative level, women hold 36 percent of all administrative jobs in women's programs and only 19 percent of all women's programs are actually headed by a female administrator.

Clearly, as these data show, gender equity is not part of big-time college sports programs. In my view, universities must address the question: Is it appropriate for a college or university to deny women the same opportunities that it provides men? Shouldn't our daughters have the same possibilities as our sons in all aspects of higher education? Women are slightly more than half of the undergraduates in U.S. higher education. They receive half of all the master's degrees. Should they be second-class in any aspect of the university's activities? The present unequal state of affairs in sport is not inevitable. Choices have been made in the past that have given men advantage in university sports. They continue to do so, to the detriment of not only women's sports but also to the so-called minor sports for men.

These are a few paradoxes concerning contemporary sport in the United States. There are more but I'll let my colleagues and the other contributors speak directly or indirectly to them. Let me conclude my remarks with this statement and a plea. We celebrate sport for many good reasons. It excites and it inspires. We savor the great moments of sport when an athlete does the seemingly impossible or when the truly gifted athlete makes the impossible routine. We exult when a team or an athlete overcomes great odds to succeed. We are touched by genuine camaraderie among teammates and between competitors. We are uplifted by the biographies of athletes who have used sport to get an education that they would have been denied because of economic circumstance or who have used sport to overcome delinquency and drugs. But for all of our love and fascination with sport and our extensive knowledge of it, do we truly understand it? Can we separate the hype from the reality and the myths from the facts? Do we accept the way sport is organized without questioning? Unfortunately for many fans and participants alike there is a superficial, uncritical, and taken-for-granted attitude concerning sport. Sportswriter Rick Reilly of *Sports Illustrated* has written that "sport deserves a more critical examination. We need to ask more probing questions about sport." That has always been my goal; it continues to be my goal; and I hope that it is yours as well.

2

Sport as Secular Sacrament

Varda Burstyn

People who are indifferent to the magic of sport are often at a loss to explain the draw it has on its fans and practitioners. To such people it is not clear why the physical enactment of struggle by "champions," captured in the technical abstraction of records, resonates so powerfully, so emotionally with its fans. Yet clearly, these struggles provoke an intense and meaningful set of associations for their initiates: memories, fantasies, and identifications. Moreover, there is little understanding of why men in particular seem to need such apparently tribal genealogies that provide paternal, heroic, and protodivine ancestors.[1]

Yet these dimensions of feeling and identification approximate the experience of religion more than any other form of human cultural practice. This has long been acknowledged by commentators close to sport. Baron Pierre de Coubertin, founder of the modern Olympic Games, "insisted repeatedly on the religious character of the Games," according to Olympic historian John MacAloon. De Coubertin wrote in 1929 that "the central idea" of the Olympic revival was that "modern athletics is a religion, a cult, an impassioned soaring."[2] Today, thoughtful journalists remark on the same qualities. Réjean Tremblay, for example, a senior sports writer in Montreal (where post–Stanley Cup parties have sometimes turned into destructive riots) observed in the middle of the 1994 Stanley Cup playoffs that "many years ago people here were Catholics. Now they are Canadiens' fans. This is something unnatural. It goes much too far."[3] Kirk Makin of the *Globe and Mail* reported sport psychologist

Source: Excerpted from Varda Burstyn, *The Rites of Men: Manhood, Politics, and the Culture of Sport,* pp. 18–27. Copyright 1999 by University of Toronto Press, Inc. Reprinted with permission of the publisher.

Saul Miller's "revelation" one day at a Denver Broncos football game "while 75,000 fans roared and the team romped under its 40 foot Bronco mascot." Miller was on the field and "looked up at this huge horse up there, painted orange. I swear it looked like the great god Ba'al or something. It was their tribe, and they chanted and sang."[4]

Such "religious" fervour captures collectivities much larger than cities. Brazil's football culture is a form of national religion in itself. For example, in 1994, Isabel Vincent reported from Rio de Janeiro that "a much-needed economic plan to combat inflation—running at more than 40 per cent a month—will be put on hold, and the presidential election campaign, which was in full swing until a few days ago, will be suspended as Brazilians turn their attention to a much more urgent issue: Just how will the national soccer team do in the Copa, the World CUP?"[5]

In June 1997, after the Detroit Red Wings won the Stanley Cup, an estimated one million people turned up for the city's celebration. The players were paraded to the ceremony in thirty identical red Ford Mustang convertibles. After a star player was critically injured in an automobile accident, prayer vigils spontaneously appeared on the street outside his hospital. Red ribbons were hung on trees and street signs. Red flags and bumper stickers appeared on city streets. In the United States, ESPN (the cable sports network) has advertised football with the following offer: "Join our congregation this Sunday for an inspirational experience." The words accompanied a photo of a player kneeling with bowed head in front of a huge stadium audience. U.S. coffin manufacturers even produce "caskets in the colours of Alabama, Auburn and Georgia, as well as Tennessee" for that final touchdown.[6]

More than any church, sport and its associations have become the great cultural unifiers of the nineteenth and twentieth centuries, first in Anglo North American culture, then throughout Europe and the rest of the world. Sport's success lay in the development of a physical and mathematical language of meanings and loyalties, based on the gendered body, that superseded divisions of culture and religion. This language presented in clear physical and symbolic terms a great gendered master narrative of the imperial age.[7] The athletic champion came to represent individuals, working groups, and communities; the quantified athletic record communicated his strength to other communities. As the French theoretician of sport Jean-Marie Brohm expresses it: "Sport has powerfully contributed to a *cosmopolitan consciousness*;—a consciousness of a sporting humanity, in which the referential criteria are the records and the champion. In a sporting world the record and champions constitute a kind of *symbol of universality*."[8]

I want from the beginning of this study to assert what I see as the effectivity, indeed the agency, of symbols and myths—particularly as they are mobilized by specific economic interests—as a guiding principle in understanding the place and power of the dominant sport forms in our society. The embodied athlete has become, on a social scale, the living mythic symbol-bearer, and the idea of the athlete-hero is fundamental to the nature and success of sport. The sport nexus, with its vast bureaucracies and enterprises, depends on him and the symbolic and mythological services he performs through the ceremonies and rituals of sport. These combine competition, physical skill, strength, and display.[9] This ritual practice generates and sustains a *mythology*—a set of story-beliefs about society and the cosmos—that is ideologically laden. The rituals and mythologies of sport are the account sport gives of the world and the base on which its vast contemporary economies rise. [10]

Rituals are repetitive, sequenced actions that form the basis of ceremonies. In *Gender Advertisements,* Erving Goffman writes that

> The function of ceremony reaches in two directions: . . . the affirmation of basic social arrangements and the presentation of ultimate doctrines about man and the world. Typically, these celebrations are performed either by persons acting to one another or acting in concert before a congregation . . . in brief, the individual is given an opportunity to face directly a representation . . . of what he is supposed to hold dear, a presentation of the supposed ordering of his existence. [11]

Rituals encode and transmit information about basic, ideal social arrangements. They are, as anthropologist Lucia Nixon has pointed out, "an essential part of human culture." Nixon offers the following definition of rituals.

> When people in a particular group engage in ritual behaviour, they transmit information to themselves and to each other about their current state of being. . . . The information that people communicate in rituals is often a symbolic duplication and restatement of beliefs and social relationships within the group. Rituals are powerful, then, because they legitimate and validate the way people in a given society interact—whether those people realize it or not. [12]

As a ceremonial ritual that actively involves unconscious as well as conscious participation, sport is a social text of information with the power of communication. While its more popular forms can communicate many different messages, its elite and professional forms communicate the dominant world view or "mentality" of its age.

As a widespread ceremonial ritual of the industrial age, sport is remarkable for its ability to express two apparently contradictory sets of qualities: on the one hand, modernity, abstraction, efficiency, science, concept, and mind; on the other, the past, archaism, worship, emotionality, sex, and the body. Speaking of the growth of the Olympic movement and of spectacle as a performative genre, John MacAloon comments that "the forging of a new genre of cultural performance out of diffuse cultural themes and anxieties is nothing else than an attempt to gain control over them." [13] Reconciled in sport, these qualities are transmitted by it as the "ultimate doctrine" about "man and the world" both to its participants and to those around them. In the electronic age, sport does this in phenomenally powerful and far-reaching ways. Thus sport may include only a small part of society as active participants—largely, but not exclusively young males—yet still affect the whole.

The information of sport—the "ultimate doctrine" about the world contained in its ceremonies and rituals—is the particular mythology it perpetuates and celebrates. Mythologies are collections of myths organized along a recognizable set of central themes. They condense a number of explanatory ideas and exemplary ideals. In the existing culture of sport these are structured around ritual physical actions of territorial appropriation and physical strength. As organizing principles within human culture, myths and mythologies shape the perception of reality by those who believe in them. Some schools of thought conceive of myths primarily as ideological delusions that carry and support the views of historically and culturally specific dominant social groups: in effect, value-laden lies or fabrications. Those who believe them are thought to suffer from "false consciousness." Other approaches—Carl Jung and Joseph Campbell, for example, as well as promoters of the male mythopoetic movement—claim that myths encode and communicate transhistorical and universal truths and need to be attended to for this reason. As Joseph Campbell writes:

> The symbols of mythology are not manufactured; they cannot be ordered, invented, or permanently suppressed. They are spontaneous productions of the psyche, and each bears within it, undamaged, the germ power of its source. . . . It has always been the prime function of mythology and rite to supply the symbols that carry the human spirit forward, in counteraction to those other constant human fantasies that tend to tie it back. In fact it may well be that the very high incidence of neuroticism among ourselves follows from the decline among its of such effective spiritual aid. [14]

In my own view, myths are complex sets of ideas that combine both these dimensions. All cultures must face and give answers to similar—that is, transhistorical—questions: What is the origin and meaning of life and death? What roles should the sexes play? How can humans control the apparently uncontrollable course of existence? As a result, mythologies have similar elements from one culture to another. On the other hand, human cultures give very different answers to these questions, reflected in their differing mythologies. Mythologies combine elements of the continuity of such interrogation and the diversity of possible answers. They derive their power in no small measure from their special ability to address the contradictions between the two.

For the purposes of this particular study of sport and its broad relationships to specifically political ideology in the industrial epoch, the approach to myth taken by sport sociologist Jim McKay in his discussion of sport and the gender order is perhaps most useful. [15] McKay does not accept that contemporary myths purely embody fundamental, transhistorical truths; nor does he see myths as "total delusions or absolute falsehoods." Instead, "myths are partial truths that emphasize specific versions of reality and conceal or overlook others. In all cultures myths are crucial in defining what is natural, normal and legitimate. They are inextricably involved in relations of power, because they ensure that some accounts of reality count more than others." [16] It is in this sense—a partial account that emphasizes and privileges one version of reality over another—that myths and mythologies are ideological and political. If one account of reality—one mythology—predominates over all other existing but minoritarian accounts, it is the dominant ideology.

The core men's sports condition and inform the constitution of the gendered social order and its dominant ideology. The rites of men condition the rights of men, and hence the culture of sport influences broader political consciousness and capabilities. The rites of sport create value-bearing mythologies around particular kinds of heroic figures: large, strong, often violent, record-setting champions. The sport culture related to these rites shares with them a supralinguistic but clearly coded symbolic system that embodies a template of values—"manly" values—as social values. These values can often cut across differences in social station and conscious political ideology. Capitalists and communists, Whites and Blacks, men and women of every nation, all enjoy sport and the heroic narratives with which it is bound up. The ways in which the elemental physical content of sport has been gendered are central to its appeal. The actions that the dominant sport forms practice and celebrate are "higher, faster, stronger," in the succinct words of the Olympic motto. This is at once an industrial and a masculinist motto, for it condenses within its ideal bodies and activities the technomorphism of industrial capitalism (the ideal of the machine) and the biomorphism of maleness (the muscular superiority of males). It is, in this sense, a hypermasculinist slogan.[17]

The linkage of the modern ideal of the machine to the archaic ideal of the physically powerful male took place in the late nineteenth century. This fusion produced a sort of "maleness squared." In his 1978 study of gender and capitalism, political scientist Gad Horowitz coined the term "surplus masculinity" (an equivalent term to hypermasculinity) to define the hegemonic masculine and capitalist ideal of manhood. He noted that our gender arrangements, based on a template of compulsory heterosexuality, produce this surplus masculinity as a result of the denigration of femininity they require. A key product of this surplus masculinity, in Horowitz's view, is the "surplus aggressivity" of men as a gender, and of a social order that values domination more generally. Horowitz defined "surplus aggressivity" as more than the necessary aggressivity required to maintain relations of personal and social viability. In a gender arrangement of compulsory heterosexuality such as the one that has prevailed in capitalist societies, surplus aggressivity is produced through the creation of a feminine-phobic, overcompensating masculinity that tends to domination and violence.[18]

Many of the specific forms and actions of sport, and the idealizations of sport culture, are characterized by hypermasculinity and surplus aggressivity. They exhibit an excess of the qualities associated with "the most extreme potentialities of the male body" (to borrow Michael Messner's eloquent phrase) and the competitive and violently instrumental masculine "role," and a relative deficiency of those associated with the possibilities of the female body and the cooperative, supporting feminine "role."[19] In this sense, sport is a religion of domination and aggression constructed around a male godhead. At the political level, it tends to gender political consciousness and thus the frame of political evaluation for ideas of collectivity and stratification and the role of the state. As I trace in my discussion of sport and the neoconservative state, health, education, and welfare are seen as "feminine" and "soft" apparatus of government, wasteful and of dubious value in this hypermasculine ideological frame. Police, prisons, and the military, on the other hand, perceived as masculine, "hard" apparatus, are valued as disciplined and essential.[20]

The religious dimensions of sport and sport culture involve the interaction between two distinct yet interrelated levels of experience.[21] The first is the *personal-existential* experience of athletes—the way people who participate in sport feel about their own activities and the contexts in which they live them. The second is the *symbolic-ideological* experience—the dimension in which sport has shared meaning for broader numbers of people beyond its actual practitioners. This is the level at which sport is most influentially ideological for nonparticipants and participants alike. In many important ways these levels are clearly different. For the athlete, *achievement* (or "failure") in the agonistic competitive act is the primary experience. The pleasure or pain of the audience, on the other hand, is based entirely on their *identification* with the athletes for, in, and through whom they feel vicarious pleasure or disappointment. Nevertheless, both athletes and participants respond to, in Roone Arledge's words, "the joy of victory, the agony of defeat." In this respect, the athlete's and the audience's experiences overlap and interpenetrate in the mythological dimension, creating a shared realm of belief and feeling in which the athlete and the spectator are united in many of their hopes, fears, and interpretations of the outcome of any event or contest. In this overlapping space, the meanings of sport are kept alive and regenerated by the complicit relationship of athletes and spectators, each playing their respective roles and reaping their respective rewards.

When moments of primal physical intensity are socially shared through the performance of physical ritual, the athlete's intrinsic pleasure of bodily performance and his sacrificial pain, if pain has been involved, are crowned and embellished by a sense of belonging. The crowd feels a similar pleasure and pain and, if victory is achieved, a feeling of representation and affirmation. At that moment, athletes and spectators are transcendentally united in the celebration of their champions—symbolic figures who represent the strength, well-being, and fate of their communities. Listen to how Stanley Chikosa, a Zambian living in Canada at the time, explained the effect of the tragic airplane crash that destroyed that country's national soccer team in 1993.

> The country was in a state of total grief. People were weeping openly in the streets. . . . Flags were at half mast. A week of national mourning had been declared. Zambia is a country without a lot of heroes and in one blow we had lost many of our national heroes. . . . It will take years for Zambia to recover from something like this. It's more than the realization that Zambia's chances for qualifying for next year's World Cup are now gone. Soccer is the most popular game in Zambia, and the game is part of our national psyche.[22]

These feelings about soccer are shared by fans in the developed as well as developing world. They could equally be found in Italy, Germany, and Russia, as well as in England, where the game was first codified. In Canada, hockey plays the most important role in identifying the national population with a set of player-heroes who represent the country and are demigods of the "national psyche." In the fall of 1996, the Canadian national team lost the World Cup in hockey. Signs of depression, loss, and anger were evident across Canadian communities. When the team captured the Cup in 1997, there was jubilation.

The identification supporters have with their team—or, for that matter, with an individual athlete—can be very intense among boys and adult men. "It's not a club, it's mine," is how one supporter expressed it. "It's one of the most important things in my life."[23] Rick Parry, chief executive officer of England's Premier Football

League, expressed the identification of supporters with sports teams this way: "You can change your job, you can change your wife, but you can't change your football team. . . . You can move from one end of the country to another, but you never, ever lose your allegiance to your first team. That's what English soccer is all about. It's about fierce loyalty, about dedication."[24] And—unspoken but so absolute as to be taken for granted—it is about those qualities in the masculine mode. For, even as this book is written, the ties that have bound athletes to their communities—whether in working-class England or postcolonial Africa—are being unravelled by commercialization and free trade in athletic labor. And as the ties of locality, ethnicity, and nation come more and more undone, the ties of gender, of masculinity, become increasingly important.

Sport locates its practitioners—including its active supporters—in a male-defined and male-populated universe that is dynamic, like the constantly changing circumstances created by capitalist industrial growth. But, at the same time, it provides a constant—perhaps the one constant—in an ever-changing world where the requirements of manhood and masculinity are so hard to fulfill. In England, when teams lose, their supporters often follow them out of the stadium singing "You'll Never Walk Alone." In this sense, too, sport is like the church used to be—an alternative family, a support system as well as a system of meaning. When this dearly held illusion of a stable patriarchal genealogy is disrupted, economic and emotional repercussions can follow. During the major league players' strikes and lockouts in baseball and hockey in 1994 and 1995, when owners and players abandoned their fans in order to haggle greedily among themselves, reactions among loyalists ranged from disgust to rage at the violation of the sacred trust the athletes supposedly shared with them."[25] Attendance dropped at major league games and increased at minor league events. And there is evidence to support the view that baseball has never fully recovered. In fact, in industrial society, sport has overtaken many of the previous functions of an established patriarchal church and organized religion: the moral instruction of children, the ritual differentiation of men and women, the worship by both of a common divinity forged in the masculine mode, and the national and international experience of collective bonding around that divinity. Our domed stadiums are cathedrals of men's culture. Like the Catholic Church at the height of its influence, organized sport is both an international masculinist network of community-based associations and an extended, elite power apparatus of enormous influence.

One compelling explication of the religious nature and functions of sport comes from French sport sociologist Jean-Marie Brohm in his two major works *Sport: A Prison of Measured Time* and *The Political Sociology of Sport.*[26] Brohm is a Freudian Marxist who sees in sport the contemporary "opiate of the people"—a term Karl Marx used to describe organized religion. Sport acts as an opiate, in Brohm's view, in a number of ways. It mounts spectacles of physical mortification that model authoritarianism. It provides an integrative mechanism for the physical maintenance of the labor force. It teaches hierarchical social relations. And it displaces and shapes erotic energy in sadomasochistic ways. While Brohm's treatment of sport does not take masculinism sufficiently into account—much work of cultural theory inspired by traditional psychoanalysis and

Marxism deserves the same critic:sm—his key ideas have great merit and are powerfully presented. Another explanation of the sport-as-religion thesis comes from Donald Mrozek in his more historical *Sport and American Mentality 1880–1920*. Where some scholars emphasize the ability of sport to deliver very personal and concrete identity anchors (such as those of neighbourhood, community, and class), Mrozek emphasizes the protoreligious functions that American sport played in the coherence of a gendered *national* culture and consciousness in the late nineteenth and early twentieth centuries. Like Brohm, Mrozek addresses sport in wider terms of cosmological placement and the ability of sport to represent and animate more abstract ideologies. He focuses particularly on what he calls sport's ability to provide a number of "strategies of regeneration"— mythologies and social practices—that energized American society in the years covered by his study. Mrozek sees such strategies as binding together all human societies.[27] He also details . . . how sport was able to answer the new needs for such strategies required by the evolution of American society in the era of industrial expansion and national formation. Essential to this role was sport's ability to renew and strengthen ideals and institutions of masculinity and masculinism, as modernization shifted and destroyed old modalities of gender.

Employing the sacred code of records and the mythology of hypermasculine champions, sport and sport culture convey masculinism itself and the rightness of it. The largest "community"—a self-organizing collectivity with group identity, group agency, group differentiation, and group interests and rights—that sport constructs is the community of men and the dominant position of that community within mixed society. Insofar as sport is our way of preparing young males to act as physical enforcers of a vigorously defended economic and gender order grounded in inequality and domination, it is not fun and games. Instead, it should be understood as an established (state-supported) religion with a protomilitary ritual practice that serves to undemocratically demarcate the ownership of physical coercion, a territory that is still almost exclusively men's, and that spreads the values of domination within the larger social sphere.

NOTES

1. I am indebted to psychologist Adrienne Harris, and her excellent article on the tribal patriarchal elements of baseball. Adrienne Harris, "Women, baseball, and words," in Gary F. Waller, Kathleen McCormick, and Lois Fowlder, eds., *Lexington Introduction to Literature: Reading and Responding to Texts* (Lexington, MA, 1987).

2. John MacAloon, "Olympic Games and the theory of spectacle in modern societies," in John MacAloon, ed., *Rite, Drama, Festival, Spectacle* (Philadelphia 1984), 251.

3. Kirk Makin, "The peanuts and beer on Canada's spectator sport," *Globe and Mail* (May 21, 1994).

4. Ibid. See also Jim McKay, "Sport and the social construction of gender," in G. Lupton, T. Short, and P. Whip, *Society and Gender: An Introduction to Sociology* (Sydney 1992); on football hooliganism as a form of sacrificial violence within a sacred framework, see Michel Mafessoli, "Hooligans," *Quel Corps? Anthropophagie du sport*, no. 41 (April 1991) 66–69.

5. Isabel Vincent, "Every four years 'Copa' fever paralyzes a nation," *Globe and Mail* (May 30, 1994). In historian Donald Mrozek's words sport has become "the religious ritual of the machine age" in which he sees "sacrifice without purpose, performance without magic, obsoles-

cence without compensation, and values without meaning," *Sport and American Mentality, 1880–1910* (Knoxville: 1983), 11.

6. John Walters, "School spirit," Scorecard, *Sports Illustrated* (September 30, 1991).

7. Postmodern accounts of contemporary culture speak of a disintegration of the master narratives of modernism. In my view some of the master narratives they have identified are in various states of crisis and flux. But to speak of a disintegration of master gender narratives is to miss the historical and actual role that sport has played in modern and "postmodern" definitions of masculinity.

8. Jean-Marie Brohm, *Sociologie politique du sport* (Nancy: 1992), 126. For a contemporary paenization of the record and the significance of its hold, see Jack McCallum, "The record company," *Sports Illustrated* (January 8, 1990).

9. John MacAloon identifies spectacle, festival, ritual, and game as key in "the roster of performance types found in an Olympic Games." All these fit within the broader phenomenon of religion. J. MacAloon, "Olympic Games."

10. This formulation may appear to turn the Marxist dialectic on its head—myth (culture) as the base for economy, rather than vice versa. In effect these are two moments of a perpetual process of interaction between physical existence and our ideas of it. It is however crucial to assert the effectivity, indeed agency of myth, and particularly as it is mobilized by specific economic interests. For the human need for paradigmatic stories and ideas is the basis of all the cultural industries, where myth becomes commodified. For an interesting discussion of group and individual ritual by spectators and fans, see Susan Tyler Eastman and Karen E. Riggs, "Televised sports and ritual: Fan Experiences," *Sociology of Sport Journal* 11 (1994), 249–74.

11. Erving Goffman, *Gender Advertisements* (New York 1979), 1.

12. Lucia Nixon, "Rituals and power: The anthropology of homecoming at Queen's," *Queen's Quarterly* 2 (Summer 1987), 312–13. This essay examines the anthropology of male rituals—centrally but not exclusively football—at an elite Canadian university. Nixon takes as significant and meaningful the fact that the terms of play and entitlement to participation are gender-determined. "Bluntly put, Homecoming says that men define the world at Queen's, that they therefore have more power and prestige than women, that this is how things should be. It is a powerful ritual because it reinforces the asymmetrical female/male relationships described above for students, faculty and staff"; ibid., 326.

13. J. MacAloon, "Olympic Games," 273.

14. Joseph Campbell, *The Hero with a Thousand Faces* (Princeton 1973), 4, 11.

15. McKay, "Sport and the social construction of gender." A similar approach to the "veracity" of myths is taken by Sarah B. Pomeroy in her study of women in Greek and Roman civilizations. *Goddesses, Whores, Wives and Slaves: Women in Classical Antiquity* (New York 1975), 1.

16. McKay, "Sport and the social construction of gender," 247.

17. Jean-Marie Brohm's discussion of the physical and psychological conditioning of the athletic body into gestures and routines that support the social order is unparalleled. In *Sociologie politique du sport* and in his landmark *Sport: A Prison of Measured Time,* Brohm analyses how the repetitive and pain-related activities of sport act on the athlete's body and how these spectacles affect their audiences. He argues that the treatment of the human body as a machine should be considered constitutive of modern sport. *Sociologie politique du sport,* 80.

18. Gad Horowitz, *Repression,* 53–123 and 182–214.

19. Michael A. Messner, "Sports and male domination: The female athlete as contested ideological terrain," *Sociology of Sport Journal* 5 (1988), 206.

20. See Maria-Antonietta Macciocchi's treatment of fascist political mobilization of women's sexuality around patriarchal imagery and ideals in the 1920s and 1930s, and Jane Caplan's discussion of this topic. Maria-Antonietta Macciochi, ed., *Éléments pour une analyse du fascisme,* 2 vols (Paris 1976) and "Sexualité feminine dans l'idéologie fasciste," *Tel Quel* 66 (Paris: 1976). Jane Caplan, "Introduction to female sexuality in fascist ideology," *Feminist Review* 1 (1979), 56–68.

21. Michael Messner, "Boyhood, organized sports, and the construction of masculinities," *Journal of Contemporary Ethnography* 18 (4) (January 1990), 416–44.

22. *Sunday Morning,* Centrepoint, CBC Radio transcript, (May 30, 1993) 1.

23. Ibid.

24. Ibid.

25. See discussion of fan anger in relation to the baseball strike in Tom Verducci, "Anybody home?" *Sports Illustrated* (May 8, 1995), 20–3; Steve Wulf, "An unwhole new ball game," *Time,* (April 17, 1995), 48, and "Hands of stone, hearts of gold," *Time* (April 10, 1995), 94.

26. Brohm, *Sociologie politique du sport,* 26–8.

27. "Every culture has its own strategies of regeneration—beliefs, rituals and mechanisms for personal and social renewal. . . . The rationality and logic of regenerative behaviour depends essentially on the correspondence between a society's intent and the actual social result of the behaviour the society uses to attain it. . . . The constituent groups which favoured sport did so out of need. In different ways, each found in sport a strategy for regeneration and renewal." Mrozek, *Sport and American Mentality,* 3–6.

3

Sport in Society

An Inspiration or an Opiate?

Jay J. Coakley

People in American society generally see sport in a very positive way. Not only is sport assumed to provide a training ground for the development of desirable character traits and good citizens, but it is also believed to reaffirm a commitment to societal values emphasizing competition, success, and playing by the rules.

Does sport really do all these things? Is it as beneficial and healthy as people believe? These questions have generated considerable disagreement among sport sociologists. It seems that most of us in the sociology of sport are quick to agree that sport is a microcosm of society—that it mirrors the values, structure, and dynamics of the society in which it exists (Eitzen and Sage, 1978). However, we often disagree when it comes to explaining the consequences or the functions of sport in society. This disagreement grows out of the fact that sport sociologists have different theoretical conceptions of how society works. Therefore, they differ on their ideas about how sport functions within society. A description of the two major theoretical approaches used in sociology of sport will illustrate what I mean.

THE FUNCTIONALIST APPROACH

Sport Is an Inspiration

The majority of sport sociologists assume that society is most accurately conceptualized in terms of a *systems model.* They see society as an organized system of interre-

Source: "Sport in Society: An Inspiration or an Opiate?" by Jay J. Coakley. From *Sport in Society: Issues and Controversies,* 2nd ed., by Jay J. Coakley. Copyright © 1982 by C. V. Mosby. Reprinted by permission.

lated parts. The system is held together and operates because (1) its individual members generally endorse the same basic values and (2) the major parts in the system (such as the family, education, the economy, government, religion, and sport) all fit together in mutually supportive and constructive ways. In sociology, this theoretical approach is called *functionalism.*

When the functionalists describe and analyze how a society, community, school, or any other system works, they are primarily concerned with how the parts of that system are related to the operation of the system as a whole. For example, if American society is the system being studied, a person using a functionalist approach would be concerned with how the American family, the economy, government, education, religion, and sport are all related to the smooth operation of the society as a whole. The analysis would focus on the ways in which each of these subparts of society helps to keep the larger system going.

The functionalists also assume that a social system will continue to operate smoothly only if the four following things happen:

1. The members of the system must learn the values and the norms (i.e., the general rules or guidelines for behavior) that will lead them to want to do what has to be done to keep the system in operation. This process of shaping the feelings, thoughts, and actions of individuals usually creates some frustration and tension. Therefore, there must also be some channels through which people can let off steam in harmless ways.
2. The system must contain a variety of social mechanisms that bring people together and serve as catalysts for building the social relationships needed for coordinated action. Without a certain degree of cohesion, solidarity, and social integration, coordinated action would be impossible and the social system would stop functioning smoothly.
3. The members of the system must have the opportunity to learn what their goals should be within the system and the socially approved ways of achieving those goals.
4. The social system must be able to adjust to the demands and challenges of the external environment. It must have ways of handling and coping with changes in the social and physical environments so that it can continue to operate with a minimal amount of interference and disruption.

According to those using a functionalist approach, these four "system needs" are the basic minimum requirements for the smooth operation of any social system whether it be a society, community, club, large corporation, or neighborhood convenience store (Parsons and Smelser, 1965). These four basic system requirements are referred to as:

1. The need for pattern maintenance and tension management
2. The need for integration
3. The need for goal attainment
4. The need for adaptation

When you start with a functionalist conception of how society works, the answer to the question of what sport does for a society or community is likely to emphasize the ways in which sport satisfies the four basic needs of the social system. A brief review of how sport is related to each of these needs is a good way to summarize this approach.

Pattern Maintenance and Tension Management

The functionalists generally conclude that sport provides learning experiences that reinforce and extend the learning occurring in other settings. In other words, sport serves as a backup or a secondary institution for primary social institutions such as the family, school, and church. Through sport people learn the general ways of thinking, feeling, and acting that make them contributing members of society. They become socialized so that they fit into the mainstream of American life and therefore reaffirm the stability and continued operation of our society (Schafer, 1976).[1]

The pattern maintenance function of sport applies to spectators as well as those who are active participants. Sport is structured so that those who watch or play learn the importance of rules, hard work, efficient organization, and a well-defined authority structure. For example, sociologist Gunther Luschen (1967) shows how sport helps to generate the high levels of achievement motivation necessary to sustain the commitment to work required in industrialized countries. Along similar lines, Kleiber and Kelly (1980) have reviewed a number of studies concluding that participation in competitive games helps children learn how to handle adult roles in general and competitive relationships in particular. In fact, some recent discussions of sex roles have suggested that women may be at a disadvantage in business settings partly because they have not been involved in competitive sports to the same degree as their male counterparts (Hennig and Jardim, 1977; Lever, 1978).

Sport has also been thought to serve tension management functions in society by providing both spectators and participants with an outlet for aggressive energy (Vanderzwaag, 1972; Proctor and Eckard, 1976; Marsh, 1978). This idea prompted two widely respected sociologists, Hans Gerth and C. Wright Mills (1953), to suggest the following: "Many mass audience situations, with their 'vicarious' enjoyments, serve psychologically the unintended function of channeling and releasing otherwise unplacable emotions. Thus, great volumes of aggression are 'cathartically' released by crowds of spectators cheering their favorite stars of sport—and jeering the umpire." The idea that sport may serve tension management functions is complex and controversial.

Integration

A functionalist approach also emphasizes how sport serves to bring people together and provide them with feelings of group unity, a sense of social identification, and a source of personal identity. In short, a functionalist explains how sport creates and reaffirms the linkages between people so that cooperative action is possible. Luschen (1967) outlines how this occurs in the following: "Since sport is also structured along such societal subsystems as different classes, males, urban areas, schools, and communities, it functions for integration. This is obvious also in spectator sport, where the whole country or community identifies with its representatives in a contest. Thus, sport functions as a means of integration, not only for the actual participants, but also for the represented members of such a system."

Sport has been seen to serve integration functions in countries other than the United States also. For example, others have discussed how sport contributes to unity and solidarity in Switzerland (Albonico, 1967); France (Bouet, 1969); Germany (Brockmann, 1969); China (Chu and Segrave, 1979); the Soviet Union (Riordan, 1977); and Brazil (Lever, 1980).

Andrzej Wohl (1970), a sport sociologist from Poland, has argued that competitive sport could not exist if it recognized "local, nation or racial barriers or differences of world outlook." He points out that sport is so widely used to serve integration functions that it "is no secret for anybody any more."

Goal Attainment

Someone using a functionalist approach is likely to see sport as legitimizing and reinforcing the primary goals of the system as well as the means to be used to achieve those goals. In the United States, for example, sport is organized so that successful outcomes are heavily emphasized, and success is generally defined in terms of scores and win-loss records. Just as in the rest of society, the proper way to achieve success in sport is through a combination of competition, hard work, planning, and good organization. Therefore, the sport experience not only serves to legitimize the way things are done in other sectors of society but also it prepares people for participation in those sectors.

In other countries, different aspects of the sport experience are emphasized so that it serves as a supportive model for their goal priorities and the proper means to achieve goals. Capitalist countries are more likely to emphasize output and competition in sport while socialist countries will be more likely to emphasize cooperation and the development of a spirit of collectivism (Morton, 1963). Sport seems to be amazingly flexible in this respect; it has been shaped and defined in a variety of ways to serve goal attainment functions in many different social systems. This point has been developed and explained by Edwards (1973): "Most sports have few, if any, intrinsic and invariably social or political qualities . . . and those qualities which such activities do possess are sufficiently 'liquid' to fit comfortably within many diverse and even conflicting value and cultural traditions."

Adaptation

In preindustrial societies it is easy to see how sport serves a system's need for adaptation. Since survival in such societies depends on the development and use of physical skills, participation in games and sport activities is directly related to coping with the surrounding environment (Luschen, 1967). Dunlap (1951) makes this case in her study of the Samoans. Additionally, she found that the "factors of physical strength and endurance which were essential for success in their games were also essential for success in their wars."

In industrial societies, it is more difficult to see how sport satisfies the adaptation needs of the social system. However, in two articles on the functions of sport, Wohl (1970, 1979) has suggested that it is in this area that sport makes its most important contributions. He points out that in any society with technologically advanced transportation and communications systems, sport becomes the only sphere of activities in which physical skills are developed and perfected. Through sport it is possible to measure and extend the range of human motor skills and to adapt them to the environments we have created. Without sport it would be difficult to maintain a population's physical well-being at the levels necessary to keep an industrial society operating efficiently. Sport is so crucial in this regard that Wohl (1979) calls for the use of all the sport sciences to plan and control its development. In this way the contributions of sport to satisfying adaptation needs could be maximized.

In concluding our review of the functionalist approach to sport it should be pointed out that social scientists are not the only ones who use such an approach in explaining the relationship between sport and society. Most people view society and the role of sport in terms very similar to those used by the functionalists. They look for the ways in which sport contributes to the communities in which they live. They see sport providing valuable lessons for their children and opportunities for themselves to release the tensions generated by a job or other life events. Sport gives them something to talk about with strangers as well as friends and it provides occasions for outings and get-togethers. Many people believe that sport can serve as a model of the goals we should strive for and the means we should use in trying to achieve those goals. Finally, sport is viewed as a healthy activity for individuals as well as the entire country; it can extend life and keep us physically prepared to defend our country in case of war.

These beliefs about sport have lead to policy decisions on Little League programs, the funding of high school and college athletics, the support of professional teams and the Olympic movement, the development of physical education programs in schools, and the use of sport activities in military academies to prepare young men and women to be "combat ready." The widespread acceptance and the pervasive influence of the functionalist approach make it necessary for us to be aware of its weaknesses.

Limitations of the Functionalist Approach

Using a functionalist approach to answer the question of how sport is related to society can provide us with valuable insights, but it is not without its problems. Such an approach tends to emphasize the positive aspects of sport. This is because those using it often assume that if some part or component of a social system has existed for a long time, it is likely to be contributing to the system in a favorable way; if it were not, it would have been eliminated or gradually faded out of existence on its own. Since sport has been around for some time and is an increasingly significant component of our social system, most functionalists conclude that it *does* make positive contributions to society. This conclusion leads them to ignore or underemphasize the negative aspects of sport. After all, it is also possible that sport could distort values and behavioral guidelines (norms). Sport could destroy motivation, create frustration and tensions, and disrupt social integration. It could impede goal attainment and interfere with methods of coming to terms with the external social and physical environment by diverting a group's attention away from crucial personal and social issues.

Another problem with the functionalist approach is that it is based on the assumption that the needs of the individual parts of a social system overlap with the needs of the system as a whole. The possibility of internal differences or basic conflicts of interests within a social system is inconsistent with the assumption that any system is held together by a combination of common values and an interrelated, mutually supportive set of parts. If the needs of the total system were in serious conflict with the needs of the individual parts, the validity of the functionalist approach would be called into question.

This is one of the major weaknesses of functionalism. Although we may agree that many people in our society hold similar values, can we also argue that the structure of American society serves the needs of everyone equally? It would be naive to assume that is does. In fact, it may even frustrate the needs of certain groups and individuals and generate conflict. To conclude that sport exists because it satisfies the needs of the total system overlooks the possibility that sport may benefit some segments of the population more than others. Furthermore, if the interests of some groups within the system are met at the expense of others, the consequences of sport could be described as positive only if you were viewing them from the perspective of those privileged groups. Unfortunately, a functionalist approach often leads to underemphasizing differences of interests as well as the possibility of exploitation and coercion within the social system. It also leads to ignoring the role of sport in generating conflict and maintaining a structure in which at least some relationships are based on exploitation and coercion.

In sociology the theoretical approach that calls attention to these unpleasant characteristics of social systems and how sport is related to them is called conflict theory.

CONFLICT THEORY

Sport Is an Opiate

Conflict theory is not as popular as functionalism. It does fit with what most people think about how society is organized and how it operates. Instead of viewing society as a relatively stable system of interrelated parts held together by common values and consensus, conflict theorists view it as an ever-changing set of relationships characterized by inherent differences of interests and held together by force, coercion, and subtle manipulation. They are concerned with the distribution and use of power rather than with common values and integration. Their analysis of society focuses on processes of change rather than on what is required for a social system to continue operating smoothly.

Most beginning students in the sociology of sport are not very receptive to the use of conflict theory in explaining the relationship between sport and society. They say that it is too negativistic and critical of our way of life and the institution of sport. They prefer the functionalist approach because it fits closely with what they have always believed and because it has implications that do not threaten the structure of either society or sport. My response is that although functionalism is useful, it can often lead us to look at the world unrealistically and ignore a dimension of the relationship between sport and society that should be considered. Neither American society nor sport is without problems. Awareness and understanding of these problems require critical thought, and conflict theory is a valuable stimulus for such thought.

Conflict theory is based primarily on an updated revision of the ideas of Karl Marx. Those who use it generally focus their attention on capitalist countries such as the United States, but it has also been used to describe and understand any social system in which individuals arc perceived as not having significant control over their own lives. According to many conflict theorists this includes capitalist systems along with fascist or military/police regimes and socialist systems controlled by centralized, bureaucratic governments (Brohm, 1978).

In order to understand how conflict theorists view the role of sport in society, we will start with a simplified description of capitalism and how contemporary organized sport fits into its structure. Any capitalist system requires the development of a highly efficient work process through which an increasing number of consumer goods can be mass produced. Industrial bureaucracies have been created to meet this need. This means that in the interest of efficiency and financial profit, workers end up performing highly specialized and alienating jobs. These jobs are generally in the production, marketing and sales, or service departments of large organizations where the workers themselves have little control over what they do and experience little or no excitement or satisfaction in their day-to-day work lives. This situation creates a need for escape and for tension-excitement in their nonwork lives. Within capitalist systems, people are subtly manipulated to seek the satisfaction they need through consumerism and mass entertainment spectacles. Sport in such societies has emerged as a major form of entertainment spectacle as well as a primary context for the consumption of material goods. Additionally, the structure of sport is so much like the structure of work organizations and capitalist society as a whole that it serves to stabilize the system and promote the interests of people who are in positions of power.

Conflict theorists see sport as a distorted form of physical exercise that has been shaped by the needs of a capitalist system of production. A specific example of how sport has developed in this manner has been outlined by Goodman (1979) in an analysis of the history of playground and street life in one of New York City's working-class neighborhoods. Goodman shows how the spontaneous, free-flowing play activities of children in New York were literally banned from the streets in order to force participation in organized playground programs. The original goals of the playgrounds are best described through the words of one of the influential playground supervisors early in this century (Chase, 1909); "We want a play factory; we want it to run at top speed on schedule time, with the best machinery and skilled operatives. We want to turn out the maximum product of happiness." Thus the organized activities and sport programs became a means for training the children of immigrants to fit into a world of work founded on time schedules, the stopwatch, and production-conscious supervisors.

For the parents of these children the playground and recreation center programs had a different goal. It was clearly explained in the following section of a 1910 New York City Department of Education report (cited in Goodman, 1979): "The great problem confronting the recreation center principal and teachers is the filling of the leisure time of the working men and women with a combination of recreation and athletic activities which will help make their lives more tolerable." As Goodman points out, the purpose of the centers was to provide controlled leisure activities to take the people's minds off the exploitation and poor working conditions experienced in their jobs. The supervised activities were meant to pacify the workers so that they could tolerate those conditions and continue contributing to the growth of the economy. When they needed to be replaced, the organized playground activities would have prepared their children to take their roles.

Other conflict theorists have not limited their focus to a local community setting. They have talked in more general terms about the relationship between sport and society. Their discussions emphasize four major aspects of the role of sport. These include:

1. How sport generates and intensifies alienation
2. How sport is used by the state and the economically powerful as a tool for coercion and social control
3. How sport promotes commercialism and materialism
4. How sport encourages nationalism, militarism, and sexism

The following sections summarize the discussions of the conflict theorists on each of these four topics.

Alienation

According to the conflict theorists, sport serves to alienate people from their own bodies. Sport focuses attention on time and output rather than on the individual. Standardized rules and rigid structure destroy the spontaneity, freedom, and inventiveness characteristic in play. Jean-Marie Brohm (1978), a French sport sociologist, explains how sport affects the connection between athletes and their bodies: "[In sport the body is] experienced as an object, an instrument, a technical means to an end, a reified factor of output and productivity, in short, as a machine with the job of producing maximum work and energy." In other words, sport creates a setting in which the body is no longer experienced as a source of self-fulfillment and pleasure in itself. Pleasure and fulfillment depend on *what is done* with the body. Satisfaction is experienced only if the contest is won, if a record is set or a personal goal achieved, and if the body performs the way it has been trained to perform. When this happens sport becomes a "prison of measured time" and alienates athletes from their own bodies (Brohm, 1978).

Mumford (1934) extends the idea of alienation even further. In a classic analysis of contemporary civilization he describes the sport stadium as an "industrial establishment producing running, jumping or football playing machines." Building on this notion conflict theorists argue that commercialized sport (any sport in which profits are sought) reduces athletes to material commodities (Hoch, 1972). Thus the body becomes a tool not only for the setting of records but also for generating financial profits for nonparticipants—from team owners and tournament sponsors to concession operators and parking lot owners. The athletes may also benefit, but their rewards require them to forfeit the control of their bodies and become "gladiators" performing for the benefit of others.

Conflict theorists have pointed to the use of drugs and computer technology in sport as support for their analysis of how sport affects the definition of an athlete's body (Brohm, 1978). When the body is seen as an instrument for setting records and the improvement of times is defined as the measure of human progress, then the use of drugs, even harmful drugs, will be seen as a valuable aid in the quest for achievement. Computer technology used to analyze and improve the body's productive capacity further separates the physical act of sport participation from the subjective experience of the athlete. Just as on the assembly line, efficiency comes to be the major concern in sport and the worker (athlete) loses control over the means of production (the body).

Coercion and Social Control

Goodman's (1979) study of the working-class neighborhood in New York City led him to conclude that sport in that city was used as a means of making the lives of shop workers more tolerable. Other conflict theorists expand this notion and describe sport as an opiate interfering with an awareness of social problems and subverting collective attempts to solve those problems. According to Hoch (1972), sport perpetuates problems by providing people with either "(1) a temporary high . . . which takes their minds off problem[s] for a while but does nothing to deal with [them]; or (2) a distorted frame of reference or identification which encourages them to look for salvation through patently false channels."

Hoch's description of the personal and social impact of sport is similar to Marx's description of religion in society. To Marx, religion focuses attention on the supernatural, provides people with a psychological lift, and emphasizes improvement through changing the self rather than changing the social order. Religion destroys awareness of material reality and promotes the maintenance of the status quo by giving priority to the goal of spiritual salvation. Marx further concluded that organized religion can be exploited by people in positions of power in society. If the majority of individuals in a society believe that enduring pain, denying pleasure, and accepting their status in this life gains them spiritual salvation, those in power can be reasonably sure that those under their control will be hardworking and docile. If those in power go so far as to manifest their own commitment to religion, their hold over the people can be strengthened even further. Such a manifestation would, after all, show that they had something in common with the masses.

Conflict theorists make the case that in an advanced capitalist society where people are not likely to look to the supernatural for answers and explanations, religion may be supplemented by other activities with similar narcotic effects. Hoch points out that these contemporary "opiates" include "sport spectacles, whiskey, and repressively sublimated sex." These combined with other opiates such as nationalism, racism, and sexism distort people's perspectives and encourage self-defeating behavior. Among these, sport stands out as an especially powerful opiate. Unlike the others, sport spectatorship is often accompanied by an extremely intense identification with players, teams, and the values perceived to be the basis for success in athletics. According to Hoch, this identification brings sport further into the lives of the spectators and captures their attention on a long-term basis. When the game ends, fan involvement does not cease, but carries on between games and into the off-season. This means that workers think about and discuss the fate of their teams rather than the futility of their own lives. Thus they are less likely to become actively involved in political or revolutionary organizations. Petryszak (1978), in a historical analysis of sport, makes the case that the "ultimate consequence of . . . spectator sports in society is the reduction of the population to a position of complete passivity."

Beyond occupying people's time and distracting their attention and energy, sport helps maintain the position of those in power in other ways. Conflict theorists note that the major contact sports, such as football, hockey, and boxing, promote a justification for the use of "official" violence by those in authority positions. In other words, sport shapes our values in ways that lock us into a social system based on coercion and the exploitive use of power. The more we witness violent sports, the more we are apt to condone the use of official violence in other settings—even when it is directed against us.

Sport also serves the interests of those in power by generating the belief that success can be achieved only through hard work and that hard work always leads to success. Such a belief encourages people to look up to those who are successful as being paragons of virtue and to look down on the failures as being lazy and no good. For example, when teams win consistently, their success is attributed to hard work and discipline; when they lose consistently, losing often is blamed on a lack of hustle and poor attitude. Losses lead the fans to call for new players and coaches—not a restructuring of the game or its rules. Hoch (1972) points out that this way of looking at things blinds people to a consideration of the problems inherent in the social and economic structure and engenders the notion that success depends only on attitude and personal effort. It also leads to the belief that failure is to be blamed on the individual alone and is to be accepted as an indication of personal inadequacies and of a need to work harder in the future.

Conflict theories see sport as a tool for controlling people and maintaining the status quo. It is structured to promote specific political ideas and to regiment and organize the lives of young people so that they will become productive workers. For adults, the role of spectator reinforces a passive orientation toward life so that they will remain observers rather than the shapers of their own experience (Aronowitz, 1973).

Commercialism and Materialism

The conflict theorists emphasize that sport is promoted as a product to be consumed and that it creates a basis for capitalist expansion. For example, increasing numbers of individuals and families are joining athletic clubs where they pay to participate and pay for the lessons teaching them how to participate correctly and efficiently. Creating and satisfying these expanding interests have given rise to an entire new industry. Summer sport resorts, winter sport resorts, and local athletic clubs are all part of this profit-generating industry.

Furthermore, sporting goods manufacturers have found that effective advertising can lead more and more equipment to be defined as absolutely necessary for successful and healthy involvement. Potential consumers have been convinced that if they want to impress other people with their knowledge about the sport experience, they have to buy and show off only top-of-the-line equipment. It has come to the point where participants can prove themselves in sport through their ability to consume as well as their ability to master physical skills. Thus sport has been used to lead people to deal with one another in terms of material images rather than in terms of the human quality of experience.

Sport not only creates direct profits but also is used as an advertising medium (Brohm, 1978). Sport spectacles serve as important settings for selling cars, tires, beer, soft drinks, and insurance. The tendency for people to personally identify with athletes is also used to sell other products. The role of athlete, unlike most adult occupational roles, is highly visible, prestigious, and relatively easy to emulate. Therefore, the attachment to sport heroes serves as the basis for the creation of an interest in sport along with a general "need" for consumer goods.

This process affects young people as well as adults. Children are lured into the spectator role and the role of consumer by trading cards, Dallas Cowboy pajamas, Yankee baseball caps, NBA basketball shoes, and a multitude of other products that ultimately create adulthood desires to become season ticket purchasers. Participation in highly specialized sport programs leads children to conclude that the proper equipment is always necessary for a good time and that being a good runner, tennis player, and soccer player depends on owning three different pairs of the best shoes on the market.

Nationalism, Militarism, and Sexism

Conflict theorists point out that sport is used by most countries as the showplace for displaying their national symbols and military strength. In many developing countries, national sport programs are administered by the defense department; in industrialized countries sport is symbolically linked with warfare and strong militaristic orientations. The conflict theorists claim that the collective excitement generated by sport participation and mass spectator events can be converted into unquestioning allegiance to political beliefs and an irrational willingness to defend those beliefs. Nationalistic feelings are fed by an emphasis on demonstrating superiority over other countries and other political systems. Furthermore, sport provides a model of confrontation, which polarizes groups of people and stresses the necessity of being militarily prepared.

Finally, the conflict theorists argue that sport divides the sexes and perpetuates distorted definitions of masculinity and femininity. The organization of contemporary sport not only relegates women to a secondary, supportive role, but also leads people to define masculinity in terms of physical strength and emotional insensitivity. In fact, the model of the successful male is epitomized by the brute strength and the controlled emotions of the athlete. Sport further reinforces sexism by focusing attention on performance differences in selected physical activities. People then use those differences to argue that male superiority is grounded in nature and that the sexes should continue to be separated. This separation obscures the characteristics men and women have in common and locks members of both sexes into restrictive roles.

Conflict theorists see much of contemporary sport as a source of alienation and a tool of exploitation and control serving the needs of economic and political systems rather than the needs of human beings. They generally argue that it is impossible for sport to provide humanizing experiences when the society in which it exists is not humane and creative (Hoch, 1972).

Limitations of the Conflict Theory Approach

Like the functionalist approach, conflict theory has some weaknesses. The conflict theorists make good use of history, but they tend to overemphasize the role of capitalism in shaping all aspects, of social reality since the Industrial Revolution. Capitalism has been a significant force, but other factors must be taken into account in explaining what has happened during the last two centuries.

The emergence and growth of modern sport is a good case in point. Sport has been strongly influenced by capitalism, but the emergence of contemporary sport can be explained in terms of factors that existed prior to the Industrial Revolution. Guttmann (1978) has argued that modern sport is a product of a scientific approach to the world rather than of the needs of capitalist economic systems. This scientific approach to the world grew out of seventeenth-century discoveries in mathematics and is characterized by a commitment to quantification, measurement, and experimentation. According to Guttmann this scientific worldview has given rise to contemporary sport. This is the reason why sport is also popular in noncapitalist countries including China, Cuba, The Czech Republic, and the Soviet Union.

In their analysis of sport, many conflict theorists are too quick to conclude that sport inevitably creates alienation and serves as an "opiate of the masses." They tend to ignore the testimonials of athletes who claim that sport participation, even in a capitalist society, can be a personally creative, expressive, and liberating experience (Slusher, 1967; Spino, 1971; Bannister, 1980; Csikszentmihalyi, 1975; Sadler, 1977). This possibility, of course, is inconsistent with the idea that the athlete's body automatically becomes a tool of production controlled and used for the sake of political and economic goals.

The argument that sport is an opiate also has some weaknesses. It is probably true that athletes and fans are more likely than other people to have attitudes supportive of the status quo. However, it is not known if their involvement in sport caused these attitudes or if the attitudes existed prior to their involvement and caused them to be attracted to sport. It may be that sport attracts people who are already committed to the status quo. If this is the case, it is difficult to argue that sport provides an escape from reality for those who might otherwise be critical of the social order. Research suggests that the most alienated and the most dissatisfied people in society are the least likely to show an interest in sport. In fact, interest and involvement are greatest among those who are the most economically successful (Sillitoe, 1969; Edwards, 1973; Anderson and Stone, 1979).

Another weakness of conflict theory is that it often overemphasizes the extent to which sport is controlled by those in positions of power in society. The people who control the media, sport facilities, and sport teams do have much to say about the conditions under which top-level sport events are experienced and viewed by players and spectators alike. However, it is difficult to argue that all sport involvement is a result of the promotional efforts of capitalists or government bureaucrats. This is especially true when attention is shifted from professional level sport to sport at the local recreational level. Active sport participation generally occurs at levels where the interests of the participants themselves can be used as the basis for creating and developing programs.

Furthermore, certain sports have characteristics making them difficult to control by those who are not participants. Surfing is a good case in point; it does not lend itself to scheduling or television coverage, equipment needs are not extensive, and it does not generate much long-term spectator interest among those who have never been surfers. Therefore, the development of surfing and other similar sports has not been subject to heavy influence from outsiders whose main concerns are generating profits and creating sport spectacles.

SUMMARY AND CONCLUSION: WHO IS RIGHT?

Now that we have looked at the relationship between sport and society (see Table 3-1 for a review) from two different perspectives, which explanation is most correct? Is sport an inspiration or an opiate? I have found that the way people answer this question depends on what they think about the society in which sport exists. For example, those who are generally uncritical of American society will tend to agree with the functionalist approach

Table 3-1 Functionalism and Conflict Theory: A Summary of Their Assumptions about the Social Order and Their Explanations of the Relationship between Sport and Society

Functionalist Approach	*Conflict Theory*
Assumptions about the Social Order	
Social order based on consensus, common values, and interrelated subsystems	Social order based on coercion, exploitation, and subtle manipulation of individuals
Major Concerns in the Study of Society	
What are the essential parts in structure of social system?	How is power distributed and used in society?
How do social systems continue to operate smoothly?	How do societies change and what can be done to promote change?
Major Concerns in the Study of Sport	
How does sport contribute to basic social system needs such as pattern maintenance and tension management, integration, goal attainment, and adaptation?	How does sport create personal alienation? How is sport used to control thoughts and behavior of people, and maintain economic and political systems serving interests of those in power?
Major Conclusions about the Sport-Society Relationship	
Sport is valuable secondary social institution benefitting society as well as individual members of society	Sport is distorted form of physical exercise shaped by needs of autocratic or production-conscious societies
Sport is basically a *source of inspiration* on personal and social level	Sport lacks creative and expressive elements of play; *it is an opiate*
Goals of Sport Sociology	
To discover ways in which sport's contribution to stability and maintenance of social order can be maximized at all levels	To promote development of humane and creative social order so that sport can be source of expression, creative experiences, and physical well-being
Major Weaknesses	
Assumes that existence and popularity of sport prove that it is serving positive functions	Assumes that structures and consequences of sport are totally determined by needs of political and economic order
Ignores possibility of internal differences and basic conflicts of interest within social systems and therefore assumes that sport serves needs, of all system parts and individuals equally	Ignores factors other than capitalism in analyzing emergence and development of contemporary sport. Focuses too much attention on top-level spectator sport and overemphasizes extent to which all sport involvement is controlled and structured by power elite

when they look at sport in the United States. Those who are critical of American society will side with the conflict theorists. However, when the country in question is East Germany or China rather than the United States, some people may shift perspective. Those who do not agree with the way of life in East Germany or China will quickly become conflict theorists in their discussions of sport in these countries; those supportive of socialist systems will tend to become functionalists. It can be confusing to say that sport is an inspiration in one country and an opiate in another.

In order to eliminate some of the confusion on this issue, we need detailed research on how the structure of physical activities is related to the subjective experiences of participants (players and spectators). We also need to know how those experiences are related to attitudes and behavior patterns. We can assume that under certain circumstances, the consequences of sport will be constructive, and under other circumstances they will be destructive. Our task is to be able to clearly describe the circumstances under which these different consequences occur and to explain why they occur the way they do. This means that studies cannot be limited to specific countries or to specific groups of people. We need cross-cultural and comparative research focusing on all dimensions of the phenomenon of sport.

In developing research and exploring these issues we need to be aware of the ideas of both the functionalists and the conflict theorists. Each of their explanations of the relationship between sport and society alerts us to questions that must be asked and hypotheses that must be tested. Unless these and other theoretical perspectives are used, our understanding of sport will be needlessly restricted.

Unfortunately, research will never be able to show us what the relationship between sport and society *should* be. It only alerts us to the possibilities and provides us with a starting point for shaping what it will be in the future.

NOTE

1. Although the focus in this [selection] is the United States, the pattern maintenance function of sport has been described in other countries, including the Soviet Union (Morton, 1963; Riordan, 1977); East Germany (Santomier and Ewees, 1979); China (Johnson, 1973; Chu and Segrave, 1979); Finland (Olin, 1979); Australia (Murray, 1979); and Samoa (Dunlap, 1951).

REFERENCES

Albonico, R. 1967. Modern University Sport as a Contribution to Social Integration. *International Review of Sport Sociology* 2:155–162.

Anderson, D., and G. P. Stone. 1979. A Fifteen-Year Analysis of Socio-Economic Strata Differences in the Meaning Given to Sport by Metropolitans. In M. L. Krotee, ed. *The Dimensions of Sport Sociology.* Leisure Press, West Point, N.Y.

Aronowitz, S. 1973. *False Promises.* McGraw-Hill, New York.

Bannister, F. T. 1980. Search for "White Hopes" Threatens Black Athletes. *Ebony* 34(4):130–134.

Bouet, M. 1969. Integrational Functions of Sport in the Light of Research Based on Questionnaires. *International Review of Sport Sociology* 4:129–134.

Brockmann, D. 1969. Sport as an Integrating Factor in the Countryside. *International Review of Sport Sociology* 4:151–170.

Brohm, J-M. 1978. *Sport: A Prison of Measured Time.* Ink Links, London.

Chase, J. H. 1909. How a Director Feels. *Playground* 3 (4):13.

Chu, D. B., and J. O. Segrave. 1979. Physical Culture in the People's Republic of China. *Journal of Sport Behavior* 2 (3):119–135.

Csikszentmihalyi, M. 1975. *Beyond Boredom and Anxiety.* Jossey-Bass, San Francisco.

Dunlap, H. L. 1951. Games, Sports, Dancing, and Other Vigorous Recreational Activities and Their Function in Samoan Culture. *Research Quarterly* 22(3):298–311.

Edwards, H. 1973. *Sociology of Sport.* Dorsey Press, Homewood, IL.

Eitzen, D. S., and G. H. Sage. 1978. *Sociology of American Sport.* Wm. C. Brown, Dubuque, IA.

Gerth, H., and C. W. Mills. 1953. *Character and Social Structure.* Harcourt Brace Jovanovich, New York.

Goodman, C. 1979. *Choosing Sides.* Schocken, New York.

Guttmann, A. 1978. *From Ritual to Record: The Nature of Modern Sports.* Columbia University Press, New York.

Hennig, M., and A. Jardim. 1977. *The Managerial Woman.* Anchor, New York.

Hoch, P. 1972. *Rip Off the Big Game.* Doubleday, New York.

Johnson, W. O. 1973. Faces on a New China Scroll. *Sports Illustrated* 39 (14):42–67.

Kleiber, D. A., and J. R. Kelly. 1980. Leisure, Socialization and the Life Cycle. In S. Iso-Aloha, ed., *Social Psychological Perspectives on Leisure and Recreation.* Charles C. Thomas, Springfield, IL.

Lever, J. 1978. Sex Differences in the Complexity of Children's Play. *American Sociological Review* 43(4):471–483.

Lever, J. 1980. Multiple Methods of Data Collection: A Note on Divergence. Unpublished manuscript.

Luschen, G. 1967. The Interdependence of Sport and Culture. *International Review of Sport Sociology* 2:127–139.

Marsh, P. 1978. Aggro: *The Illusion of Violence.* J. M. Dent, London.

Morton, H. W. 1963. *Soviet Sport.* Collier, New York.

Mumford, L. 1934. *Technics and Civilization.* Harcourt Brace Jovanovich, New York.

Murray, L. 1979. Some Ideological Qualities of Australian Sport. *Australian Journal of Health, Physical Education and Recreation* 73:7–10.

Olin, K. 1979. Sport, Social Development and Community Decision-Making. *International Review of Sport Sociology* 14(3–4):117–132.

Parsons, T., and N.J. Smelser. 1965. *Economy and Society.* The Free Press, New York.

Petryszak, N. 1978. Spectator Sports as an Aspect of Popular Culture—An Historical View. *Journal of Sport Behavior* 1 (1):14–27.

Proctor, R. C., and W. M. Echard. 1976. "Toot-Toot" or Spectator Sports: Psychological and Therapeutic Implications. *American Journal of Sports Medicine* 4 (2):78–83.

Riordan, J. 1977. *Sport in Soviet Society.* Cambridge University Press, New York.

Sadler, W. A. 1977. Alienated Youth and Creative Sports Experience. *Journal of the Philosophy of Sport* 4 (Fall): 83–95.

Santomier, J., and K. Ewees. 1979. Sport, Political Socialization and the German Democratic Republic. In M. L. Krotee, ed, *The Dimensions of Sport Sociology.* Leisure Press, West Point, NY.

Schafer, W. E. 1976. Sport and Youth Counterculture: Contrasting Socialization Themes. In D. M. Landers, ed., *Social Problems in Athletics*. University of Illinois Press, Urbana.

Sillitoe, K. 1969. *Planning for Leisure*. University of Keele, London.

Slusher, H. S. 1967. *Man, Sport and Existence*. Lea & Febiger, Philadelphia.

Spino, M. 1971. *Running as a Spiritual Experience*. In J. Scott, *The Athletic Revolution*. The Free Press, New York.

Vanderzwaag, H. J. 1972. *Toward a Philosophy of Sport*. Addison-Wesley, Reading, MA.

Wohl, A. 1970. Competitive Sport and Its Social Functions. *International Review of Sport Sociology* 5:117–124.

Wohl, A. 1979. Sport and Social Development. *International Review of Sport Sociology* 14(3–4):5–18.

✳ FOR FURTHER STUDY ✳

Andrews, David L. 1996. "Rethinking Sports in America: Teaching Across Race, Class and Gender," *Center News* 14 (Center for Research on Women, University of Memphis), (Spring):3, 8.

Andrews, David L. 1996. "Deconstructing Michael Jordan: Reconstructing Postindustrial America," Sociology *of Sport Journal* 13(4):315–318.

Coakley, Jay. 2004. *Sport in Society: Issues and Controversies, 8th ed.* (New York: McGraw Hill).

Coakley, Jay, and Eric Dunning (eds.). 2000. *Handbook of Sport Studies* (London: Sage).

Crapeau, Dick. 1991–2001. A collection of "Sport and Society" essays over twenty years to commemorate the twentieth anniversary of *Aethlon: The Journal of Sport Literature* 20 (Fall): entire issue.

Eitzen, D. Stanley. 2003. *Fair and Foul: Beyond the Myths and Paradoxes of Sport,* 2nd ed. (Lanham, MD: Rowman and Littlefield).

Eitzen, D. Stanley, and George H. Sage. 2003. *Sociology of North American Sport,* 7th ed. (New York: McGraw-Hill).

Gerdy, John R. 2002. *Sports: The All-American Addiction* (Jackson: University of Mississippi Press).

Giulianotti, Richard. 2002. "Supporters, Followers, Fans, and Flaneurs," *Journal of Sport & Social Issues* 26 (February): 25–46.

Kee, Lorraine. 1998. "Lions and Christians: Football Has Been Called 'America's Religion,' Never Before Has It Seemed So True," *The Nation* (August 10/17):37–38.

Lever, Janet. 1983. *Soccer Madness* (Chicago: University of Chicago Press).

Miller, Toby. 1997. "Sport and Violence: Glue, Seed, State, or Psyche?" *Journal of Sport and Social Issues* 21 (August): 235–238.

Nixon, Howard L., II. 1991. "Sport Sociology That Matters: Imperatives and Challenges for the 1990s," *Sociology of Sport Journal* (September): 281–294.

Nixon, Howard L., II, and James H. Frey. 1996. A *Sociology of Sport* (Belmont, CA: Wadsworth).

Sage, George H. 1997. "Physical Education, Sociology, and Sociology of Sport: Points of Intersection," *Sociology of Sport Journal* 14(4):317–339.

Sage, George H. 1998. *Power and Ideology in American Sport: A Critical Perspective,* 2nd ed. (Champaign, IL: Human Kinetics).

PART TWO

Sport and Socialization: Organized Sports

The involvement of young people in adult-supervised sport is characteristic of contemporary American society. Today, millions of boys and girls are involved in organized baseball, football, hockey, basketball, and soccer leagues. Others are involved in swimming, skating, golf, tennis, and gymnastics at a highly competitive level. School-sponsored sports begin about the seventh grade and are highly organized, win-oriented activities.

Why do so many parents in so many communities strongly support organized sports programs for youth? Primarily because most people believe that sports participation has positive benefits for those involved. The following quotation from *Time* summarizes this assumption.

> Sport has always been one of the primary means of civilizing the human animal, of inculcating the character traits a society desires. Wellington in his famous aphorism insisted that the Battle of Waterloo had been won on the playing fields of Eton. The lessons learned on the playing field are among the most basic: the setting of goals and joining with others to achieve them; an understanding of and respect for rules; the persistence to hone ability into skill, prowess into perfection. In games, children learn that success is possible and that failure can be overcome. Championships may be won; when lost, wait until next year. In practicing such skills as fielding a grounder and hitting a tennis ball, young athletes develop work patterns and attitudes that carry over into college, the marketplace and all of life.[1]

However, parents often ignore the negative side of sports participation, a position that is summarized by Charles Banham:

> It [the conventional argument that sport builds character] is not sound because it assumes that everyone will benefit from sport in the complacently prescribed man-

ner. A minority do so benefit. A few have the temperament that responds healthily to all the demands. These are the only ones able to develop an attractively active character. Sport can put fresh air in the mind, if it's the right mind; it can give muscle to the personality, if it's the right personality. But for the rest, it encourages selfishness, envy, conceit, hostility, and bad temper. Far from ventilating the mind, it stifles it. Good sportsmanship may be a product of sport, but so is bad sportsmanship.[2]

The problem is that sports produce positive and negative outcomes. This dualistic quality of sport is summarized by Terry Orlick:

> For every positive psychological or social outcome in sports, there are possible negative outcomes. For example, sports can offer a child group membership or group exclusion, acceptance or rejection, positive feedback or negative feedback, a sense of accomplishment or a sense of failure, evidence of self-worth or a lack of evidence of self-worth. Likewise, sports can develop cooperation and a concern for others, but they can also develop intense rivalry and a complete lack of concern for others.[3]

The first selection in this part, by sociologist Jay J. Coakley, describes the organized youth sports of today and compares them with the spontaneous games more characteristic of youth in previous generations. The second selection is the introductory essay to a three-part series in *Sports Illustrated* on high school sports by Alexander Wolff. He raises issues such as win-at-all-costs coaches, year-round specialization by athletes, unethical behaviors, and the competition of travel teams. He concludes this essay with:

> If it's true that by our children you shall know us, high school sports implicate us as a dedicated, focused, proudly self-reliant people, or an obsessed, blinkered, hopelessly atomized society—take your pick.

The final selection, by sociologist Timothy Jon Curry, reports the findings from an ethnographic study of the men's locker room. What do young men learn in the locker room? What is promoted? What is denigrated? Curry found that the locker room is a place where young men "do gender." Heterosexuality, bravado, physical aggression, and affirmation of the traditional male role are valued and enhanced through the male bonding in locker rooms. Commonly, conversations in locker rooms involve sexual boasting, talk about women as sex objects, homophobic talk, and aggressive and hostile talk toward women. Thus, the peer culture of the locker room tends to channel behaviors and attitudes in ways that destroy human relationships and promote aggression toward "others." Curry concludes: "It is my view that sexist locker room talk is likely to have a cumulative negative effect on young men because it reinforces the notions of masculine privilege and hegemony, making that world view seem normal and typical. Moreover, it does so in a particularly pernicious fashion."

NOTES

1. "Comes the Revolution: Joining the Game at Last, Women Are Transforming American Athletics," *Time* (June 26, 1978):55.

2. Charles Banham, "Man at Play," *Contemporary Review* 207 (August 1965):62.

3. T. D. Orlick, "The Sports Environment: A Capacity to Enhance—A Capacity to Destroy," paper presented at the Canadian Symposium of Psycho-Motor Learning and Sports Psychology (1974), p. 2.

4

Play Group versus Organized Competitive Team

A Comparison

Jay J. Coakley

One way to begin to grasp the nature and extent of the impact of participation in sport is to try to understand the sport group as a context for the behavior and the relationships of youngsters. In a 1968 symposium on the sociology of sport, Gunther Luschen from the University of Illinois delivered a paper entitled "Small Group Research and the Group in Sport." While discussing the variety of different group contexts in which sport activities occur, he contrasted the spontaneously formed casual play group with the organized competitive team. He was primarily interested in the social organization and the amount of structural differentiation existing in sport groups in general, but some of his ideas give us a basis for comparing the characteristics of the spontaneous play group and the organized competitive Little League team in terms of their implications for youngsters. In general, any group engaging in competitive physical activity can be described in terms of the extent and complexity of its formal organization. Simply put, we can employ a continuum along which such groups could be located depending on how formally organized they are. Figure 4-1 illustrates this idea.

The spontaneous play group is an example of a context for competitive physical activities in which formal organization is absent. Its polar opposite is the sponsored competitive team in an organized league. It follows that the amount of formal organization has implications for the actions of group members, for their relationships

Source: "Play Group versus Organized Competitive Team: A Comparison" by Jay J. Coakley. From *Sport in Society: Issues and Controversies* by Jay J. Coakley. Copyright © 1978 by C. V. Mosby. Reprinted by permission.

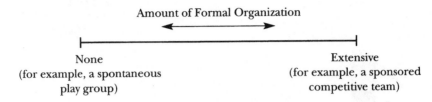

Amount of Formal Organization

None
(for example, a spontaneous
play group)

Extensive
(for example, a sponsored
competitive team)

Figure 4–1 A Formal Organization Continuum for Groups in Competitive Physical Activities

Table 4-1 Comparison of Two Groups

The Spontaneous Play Group: *No Formal Organization*	*The Sponsored Competitive Team:* *High Formal Organization*
Action is an outgrowth of the interpersonal relationships and of the decision-making processes of participating members.	Action is an outgrowth of a predesignated system of role relationships and of the role-learning abilities of group members.
Rewards are primarily intrinsic and are a function of the experience and the extent of the interpersonal skills of the group members.	Rewards are primarily extrinsic and are a function of the combined technical skills of group members.
Meanings attached to actions and situations are emergent and are subject to changes over time.	Meanings are predominantly predefined and are relatively static from one situation to the next.
Group integration is based on the process of exchange between group members.	Group integration is based on an awareness of and conformity to a formalized set of norms.
Norms governing action are emergent, and interpretation is variable.	Norms are highly formalized and specific, with variability resulting from official judgments.
Social control is internally generated among members and is dependent on commitment.	Social control is administered by an external agent and is dependent on obedience.
Sanctions are informal and are directly related to the maintenance of action in the situation.	Sanctions are formal and are related to the preservation of values as well as order.
Individual freedom is high, with variability a function of the group's status structure.	Individual freedom is limited to the flexibility tolerated within role expectations.
Group is generally characterized by structural instability.	Group is generally characterized by structural stability.

with one another, and for the nature of their experiences. Table 4-1 outlines the characteristics of the two groups that would most closely approximate the polar extremes on the continuum.

Before going any further, I should point out that the two descriptions in Table 4-1 represent "ideal type" groups. In other words, the respective sets of characteristics represent hypothetical concepts that emphasize each group's most identifiable and important elements. Ideal types are necessarily extreme or exaggerated examples of the phenomenon under investigation and as such are to be used for purposes of comparison rather than as depictions of reality. Our concern here is to look at an actual group in which youngsters participate and to compare the actual group with the ideal types in order to make an assessment of what the real group might be like as a context for experience. Of course, the real group will not be an exact replica of either of the ideal types, but will more or less resemble one or the other.

GETTING THE GAME STARTED

The characteristics of each group suggest that the differences between the spontaneous play group and the organized competitive team would be quite apparent as soon as initial contact between the participants occurs. In the spontaneous play group, we might expect that the majority of time would be spent on dealing with organizational problems, such as establishing goals, defining means to those goals, and developing expectations of both a general and a specific nature for each of the participants. Being a member of a *completely* spontaneous play group would probably be similar to being involved in the initial organizational meeting of a group of unacquainted college freshmen who are supposed to come up with a class project. Both would involve a combination of some fun, a good deal of confusion, much talking, and little action. For the context of the organized competitive team, we might imagine a supervisor (coach) blowing a whistle that brings a group of preselected youngsters of similar ages and abilities running to fall into a routine formation to await an already known command. This would resemble a "brave new world" of sport where there would be some action, a good deal of listening to instructions, much routinization, and little fun. Fortunately, most group contexts for youngsters' sport participation fall somewhere between these two extremes. The trick is, of course, to find which points on the continuum would have a maximization of both fun and action along with the other characteristics seen as most beneficial to the young participants' development.

From my observations of youngsters in backyards, gyms, parks, and playgrounds, I have concluded that, for the most part, they are quite efficient in organizing their sport activities. The primary organizational details are often partially worked out by physical setting, available equipment, and time of the year, all of which influence the choice of activity and the form the activity will take. To the extent that the participants know one another and have played with each other before, there will be a minimum amount of time devoted to formation of norms—rules from previous games can be used. But despite the ability of most youngsters to get a competitive physical activity going, there seems to be a tendency for adults to become impatient with some of the "childish" disagreements of the young participants. Adults often become impatient because they do not understand the youngsters' "distortions" of the games—games the adults know are supposed to be played another way. Adults who want to teach youngsters to play the game the *right way* and to help young players avoid disagreements and discussions in order to build up more action time seem to be everywhere. These adults see a very clear need for organization, that is, establishing regular practice times, scheduling contests, and giving positive rewards and encouragement to those whose performances are seen as deserving. Although their motives may be commendable, these adults usually fail to consider all of the differences between the informally organized group and the formally organized team.

Most importantly, the game in the park is in the control of the youngsters themselves, whereas the organized competitive team is supervised and controlled by adults. In the play group, getting the game under way depends on the group members being able to communicate well enough to make organizational decisions and to evoke enough cooperation so that a sufficient amount of the group's behavior is conducive to the achievement of the goals of the game, however they have been defined. In this situation, interpersonal skills are crucial, and youngsters will probably be quick to realize that playing the game depends on being able to develop and maintain positive relationships or, at least, learning to cope with interpersonal problems in a way that will permit cooperative action. This constitutes a valuable set of experiences that become less available to participants as the amount of the group's formal organization increases. It is a rare adult coach who allows youngsters to make many decisions on how the game should be organized and played. In fact, most decisions have been made for the coach; the availability of the practice field has been decided, the roles defined, the rules made, the sanctions outlined, the team colors picked, the games scheduled, etc. Occasionally the players are allowed to vote on their team name, but that happens only if the team is new and does not already have one. In all, *the emphasis in the organized setting is on the development of sport skills, not on the development of interpersonal skills.*

PLAY OF THE GAME

Differences between the two groups do not disappear once the game begins. For the spontaneous play group, the game experience is likely to be defined as an end in itself, whereas for the organized team, the game is a means to an end. In the play group, the game is unlikely to have implications beyond the setting in which it occurs, and the participants are primarily concerned with managing the situation so that action can be preserved for as long as possible. To this end, it is quite common for the participating youngsters to develop sets of norms accompanied by rather complex sets of qualifications and to establish handicaps for certain participants. These tactics serve to compensate for skill differences and to ensure that the game proceeds with scores close enough so that excitement and satisfaction can be maximized for as many of the players as possible. For example, if one of the pitchers in an informal baseball game were bigger or stronger than the rest of the youngsters, he/she would be required to pitch the ball with "an arch on it" to minimize the ball's speed and to allow all the batters a chance to hit it. Exceptionally good batters might be required to bat left-handed (if they were right-handed) to minimize the chances of hitting a home run every time they came to bat. A youngster having a hard time hitting the ball might be given more than three strikes, and the pitcher might make a special effort to "put the ball over the plate" so that the batter would have a good chance of hitting the ball rather than striking out. Since a strikeout is a relatively unexciting event in a game where the primary goal is the involvement of all players, one of the most frequently made comments directed to the pitcher by his/her team-mates in the field is "C'mon, let 'em hit it!"

Similar examples of norm qualifications and handicap systems can be found in other sport groups characterized by a low degree of formal organization. Sometimes these little adaptations can be very clever, and, of course, some participants have to be warned if they seem to be taking unfair advantage of them. This may occur in cases where a young player tends to call time-outs whenever the opposition has his team at a disadvantage or when someone begins to overuse an interference or a "do-over" call to nullify a mistake or a failure to make a play. Although the system of qualifications and handicaps may serve to allow the participants to have another chance when they make mistakes and to avoid the embarrassment associated with a relative lack of skills, the major function of such systems seems to be to equalize not only the players, but also the teams competing against one another. Through such techniques, scores will remain close enough that neither team will give up and destroy the game by quitting. In a sense, the players make an attempt to control the competition so that the fun of all will be safeguarded. Adults do the same thing when given the chance. None of us enjoys being overwhelmed by an opponent or over-coming an opponent so weak that we never had to make an effort.

For the formally organized competitive team, however, the play of the game may be considerably different. The goal of victory or the promotion of the team's place in the league standings replaces the goal of maximizing individual participant satisfaction. The meanings and rewards attached to the game are largely a function of how the experience is related to a desired outcome—either victory or "a good show." Players may even be told that a good personal performance is almost always nullified by a team defeat and that to feel satisfied with yourself without a team victory is selfish (as they say in the locker room, "There is no 'u' in team" or "Defeat is worse than death because you have to live with defeat").

Since victories are a consequence of the combined skills of the team members, such skills are to be practiced and improved and then utilized in ways that maximize the chances for team success. Granting the other team a handicap is quite rare unless any chance for victory is out of their grasp. If this is the case, the weaker players may be substituted in the lineup of the stronger team *unless,* of course, a one-sided score will serve the purpose of increasing the team's prestige or intimidating future opponents.

Also, if one player's skill level far exceeds that of the other participants, that player will often be used where he can be most effective. In the Little League game, it is frequently the bigger youngster with the strongest arm who is made the pitcher. This may help to ensure a team's chances for victory, but it also serves to nearly eliminate the rest of the team's chances for making fielding plays and for being involved in the defensive play of the game. In a 6-inning game, the fact that a large number of the 18 total outs for the opponents come as strikeouts means that a number of fielders may never have a chance to even touch the ball while they are out in the field. A similar thing happens in football. The youth-league team often puts its biggest and strongest players in the backfield rather than in the line. The game then consists of giving those youngsters the ball on nearly every play. For the smaller players on the defensive team, the primary task may be getting out of the way of the runner to avoid being stepped on. Thus on the organized team, intimidation may become a part of playing strategy. Unfortunately, intimidation increases apprehension and inhibits some of the action in the game as well as the involvement of some of the players. Generally, it seems that on the organized team the tendency to employ the skills of the players to win games takes precedence over devising handicaps to ensure fun and widespread participation.

One way to become aware of some of the differences between the informal play group and the formally organized competitive team is to ask the participants in each group the scores of their games. In the formally organized setting, the scores are often one-sided with members of the winning team even boasting about how they won their last football game 77 to 6, their last baseball games 23 to 1, or their last soccer game 14 to 0. Such scores lead me to question the amount of fun had by the players. In the case of the losers it would be rare to find players who would be able to maintain an interest in a game when they are so completely beaten. If the winners say they enjoyed themselves, the lesson they may be learning through such an experience should be seriously questioned. It may be that the major lesson is if your opponents happen to be weak, take advantage of that weakness so totally that they will never be able to make a comeback. Such experiences, instead of instilling positive relationships and a sincere interest in sport activities, are apt to encourage distorted assessments of self-worth and to turn youngsters off to activities that, in modified forms, could provide them with years of enjoyment.

In addition to the differences in how the game is organized and how the action is initiated, there are also differences in how action for the two groups is maintained. In the informally organized group, the members are held together through the operation of some elementary processes of exchange that, in a sense, serve as the basis for the participants obtaining what they think they deserve out of the experience (Polgar, 1976). When the range of abilities is great, the older, bigger, more talented participants have to compromise some of their abilities so that the younger, smaller, and less talented will have a chance to gain the rewards necessary to continue playing. The play of the game depends on maintaining a necessary level of commitment among all participants. This commitment then serves as a basis for social control during the action. Although there are some exceptions, those in the groups with the highest combined skill and social prestige levels act as leaders and serve as models of normal behavior. For these individuals to deviate from the norms in any consistent manner would most likely earn them the reputation of being cheaters or bad sports. In fact, consistent deviation from the group norms by any of the participants is likely to be defined by the others as disruptive, and the violator will be reminded of his/her infraction through some type of warning or through a threat of future exclusion from group activities. When sanctions are employed in the informal play group, they usually serve an instrumental function—they bring behavior in line so that the game can continue. Sanctions are usually not intended to reinforce status distinctions, to preserve an established social structure, or to safeguard values and principles. Interestingly, self-enforcement of norms in the play group is usually quite effective. Deviation is not totally eliminated, but it is kept within the limits necessary to preserve action in the game. The emphasis is not so much on keeping norms sacred, but on making sure that the norms serve to maintain the goal of action. In fact, norms may change or be reinterpreted for specific individuals or in specific situations so that the level of action in the play activities can be maximized. The importance of maintaining a certain level of action is demonstrated by the informal sanctions directed at a participant who might always be insisting on too rigid an enforcement of norms. This is the person who continually cries "foul" or who always spots a penalty. To be persistent in such a hard-nosed approach to norm enforcement will probably earn the player the nonendearing reputation of being a baby, a crier, or a complainer.

In the informally organized play group, the most disruptive kind of deviant is the one who does not care about the game. It is interesting that the group will usually tolerate any number of different performance styles, forms, and individual innovations as long as they do not destroy action. Batting left-handed when one is right-handed is okay if the batter is at least likely to hit the ball, thus keeping the action going. Throwing behind-the-back passes and trying a crazy shot in basketball or running an unplanned pass pattern in football are all considered part of the game in the play group *if action is not destroyed.* Joking around will frequently be tolerated and sometimes even encouraged *if action can continue.* But if such behavior moves beyond the level of seriousness required to maintain satisfying action for all the participants, commitment decreases, and the group is likely to dissolve. In line with this, usually those participants with the highest amount of skill are allowed the greatest amount of freedom to play "as the spirit moves them." Although such behavior may seem to indicate a lack of seriousness to the outsider, the skill of the player is developed enough to avoid a "disruptive" amount of mistakes. At the same time, such freedom gives high-ability participants a means through which their interest level can be maintained. Similar free-wheeling behavior by a low-ability participant would be viewed with disfavor, since the behavior would frequently bring the action level below what would be defined as acceptable by the rest of the group.

In contrast to the play group, the maintenance of action on the formally organized team depends on an initial commitment to playing as a part of the team. This commitment then serves as a basis for learning and conforming to a preestablished set of norms.[1] The norms apply equally to everyone, and control is administered through the coach-supervisor. Regardless of how priorities are set with respect to goals, goal achievement rests primarily on obedience to the coach's directives rather than on the generation of personal interests based on mutually satisfying social exchange processes. Within the structure of the organized competitive team, deviation from the norms is defined as serious not only when it disrupts action, but also when it could have been disruptive or when it somehow challenges the organized structure through which action occurs. Thus sanctions take on a value-supportive function as well as an instrumental function. This is demonstrated by the coaches who constantly worry about their own authority, that is, whether they command the respect of their players.

In the interest of developing technical skills, the norms for the formally organized competitive team restrict not only the range of a player's action, but also the form of such actions. Unique batting, throwing, running, shooting, or kicking styles must be abandoned in the face of what the coach considers to be correct form. Joking around on the part of any team member is usually not tolerated regardless of the player's abilities, and the demonstration of skills is usually limited to the fundamentals of the game.

If commitment cannot be maintained under these circumstances, players are often not allowed to quit. They may be told by the coach that "We all have to take our bumps to be part of the team" or "Quitters never win and winners never quit." Parents may also point out that "Once you join a team, it is your duty to stick it out for the whole season" or "We paid our money for you to play the whole season; don't waste what we've given you." With this kind of feedback, even a total absence of personal commitment to the sport activity may not lead to withdrawal from participation. What keeps youngsters going is a commitment to personal honor and integrity or obedience to a few significant people in their lives.

WHEN THE GAME IS OVER: MEANING AND CONSEQUENCES

The implications of the game after completion are different for the members of the informal play group than they are for the members of the formally organized competitive team. For the latter, the game goes on record as a win or a loss. If the score was close, both winners and losers may initially qualify the outcome in terms of that closeness.[2] But, as other games are played, all losses and wins are grouped respectively regardless of the closeness of scores. In the informal play group, the score of a game may be discussed while walking home; however, it is usually forgotten quickly and considered insignificant in light of the actions of individual players. Any feelings of elation that accompany victory or of let-down that accompany defeat are short-lived in the play group—you always begin again on the next day, in the next game, or with the next activity. For the organized competitive team, such feelings are less transitory and are often renewed at some future date when there is a chance to avenge a previous loss or to show that a past victory was not just a fluke. Related to this is the fact that the organized team is usually geared to winning, with the coaches and players always reminding themselves, in the Norman Vincent Peale tradition, that "We can win . . . if we only play like we can." This may lead to defining victories as the expected outcomes of games and losses as those outcomes that occur when you do not perform as you are able. When this happens, the elation and satisfaction associated with winning can be buried by the determination to win the next one, the next one, and so on. Losses, however, are not so quickly put away. They tend to follow you as a reminder of past failures to accomplish what you could have if you had executed your collective skills properly. The element of fun in such a setting is of only minor importance and may be eliminated by the seriousness and determination associated with the activity.

The final difference between the two groups is related to the stability of each. The informal play group is characteristically unstable, whereas the opposite is true of the organized team. If minimal levels of commitment cannot be maintained among some members of the play group, the group may simply dissolve. Dissolution may also result from outside forces. For example, since parents are not involved in the organization of the play group, they may not go out of their way to plan for their youngster's participation by delaying or arranging family activities around the time of the group's existence. When a parent calls a youngster home, the entire group may be in serious jeopardy. Other problems that contribute to instability are being told that you cannot play in the street, that someone's yard is off limits, that park space is inaccessible, or that necessary equipment is broken or unavailable. These problems usually do not exist for the organized team. Consent by parents almost guarantees the presence of a player at a scheduled practice or game, space and equipment are reserved in advance, and substitute players are available when something happens to a regular team member. Because the team is built around a structure of roles rather than a series of interacting persons, players can be replaced without serious disruption, and the action can continue.

NOTES

1. In some cases, "commitment" may not be totally voluntary on the part of the player. Parents may sign up a son or daughter without the youngster's full consent or may, along with peers, subtly coerce the youngster to play.

2. Such qualifications are, of course, used for different effects. Winners use them to show that their challengers were able or that victory came under pressure. Losers use them to show how close they came to victory.

5

High School Sports

Alexander Wolff

Valley Falls gave the Big Reds a real send-off, lining the sidewalks from one end of
Main Street to the other to cheer the red-and-white bus on its way. The school
band, one hundred strong, led the way. "Bring it back, gang," Petey shouted,
"We'll be waiting up Saturday night!" Then they were on their way, singing and
cheering.

From Pitcher's Duel, A Chip Hilton Sports Story, by Clair Bee

The numbers—and what do sports train us to trust more than numbers?—tell us
that high school athletics have never been healthier. Roughly four million boys and
three million girls, more than every before, participate in one or more of some 50
athletic endeavors before kiting off to the rest of their lives. If we believe that nothing
is worth doing unless it's done well, sports justify a place in our secondary schools
many times over, for kids today seem to have at their disposal every resource, from
weight rooms to legions of assistant coaches to a full calendar of competition, to help
them become as good as they desire.

But we're not, alas, in Valley Falls anymore. The win-at-all costs coaches and
preprofessional priorities commonplace in college sports have seeped into grades 12,
11, 10, and below. So-called travel teams have toppled Chip Hilton as an adolescent
icon, replacing him with Conrad Hilton. As coaches demand year-round proof of
dedication, kids spend a greater and greater proportion of time practicing rather
than playing, and many state high school federations, which once enforced strict

Source: Alexander Wolff, "High School Sports," *Sports Illustrated* (November 18, 2002), pp. 76, 78.

rules on summer activity, throw up their hands, sometimes eliminating those rules altogether.

If there's a common element to what's happening in high school sports, it's a disconnection from community, a nationwide trend in various aspects of American life that Harvard professor Robert Putnam laid out in his 2000 book about social isolation, *Bowling Alone*. It's no longer enough to play for the greater glory of Valley Falls, as your older siblings and parents did. Nor is it enough to drift leisurely from sport to in-season sport. The National Federation of State High School Associations doesn't track how many high schoolers play a single sport as opposed to two or three, but no one involved in youth sports disputes that there's a marked trend toward specialization. Dr. Lyle Micheli, executive director of the Sports Medicine Clinic at Boston Children's Hospital, says he sees many more instances of overuse injuries, such as tendinitis and stress factors, than of acute traumatic injuries like ankle sprains, where even 10 years ago the reverse was true. "Overuse injuries are common in individual sports like gymnastics and figure skating and tennis," Micheli says. "But they're becoming more of a factor in team sports because the sports organizations and coaches are saying, 'If you're really serious about soccer, you shouldn't be playing lacrosse in the spring.'"

In some towns cheerleading squads have vanished because so many girls have left the sidelines to get in the game. And while that's hardly something to lament, another gift of Title IX, the college scholarship, has led girls to become as susceptible as boys to year-round specialization, even as pioneers like soccer's Kristine Lilly and softball's Dot Richardson advise girls to play the field as long as they can.

Coaches recruit across district lines, often mocking the spirit, if not the letter, of rules banning the practice. California law explicitly prohibits transfers for athletic purposes, yet since 1994 that state has also permitted open enrollment—and so the 529 schools in the California Interscholastic Federation's Southern Section report that, between September '99 and December 2001, nearly 3,800 kids pulled on the uniform of a different school without changing their address of record. Sometimes teams even reach across national borders for their ringers: Tucson's Amphitheater High did so to get nine Mexican baseball players in '98; Modesto (Calif.) Christian High did the same to land two English basketball players, who led the school to a 2001 state title game.

Nothing flouts traditional standards of community more than travel teams, which rarely have any formal connection to a local high school. With names that sound like escort services (Gold, Elite, Premier), they serve as catch basins for the most driven athletes from a region, not a town or neighborhood, and go off to play rivals far beyond the crosstown high school. Kids who are forced to choose between a high school team and travel team often go with the travel team, because that's where the college recruiters look. Small wonder high school coaches, fearful of losing their best players, cave in to kids who want to play on travel teams, even during the high school season. Chicago's Catholic League has long offered ice hockey, but participation has plunged as travel teams have proliferated.

While extensive travel is still largely a summertime phenomenon, secondary schools that can do so are putting together national schedules for their basketball teams, like the one Akron St. Vincent–St. Mary High will play this season with its NBA-ready forward, LeBron James. "It's all about the kids," a St. Vincent–St. Mary official said, straight-faced, after the school announced the Fighting Irish's plan to play arenas in Philadelphia; Chapel Hill, N.C.; and Dayton and Columbus, Ohio. The promoter booking the dates is billing it as the Scholastic Fantastic LeBron James Tour.

As he watches talented classmates pursue sports with a more and more mercenary purpose, it's harder for the typical high school kid to muster the school spirit that marked the Clair Bee era. Mount Carmel, a private school in a misbegotten neighborhood on Chicago's lakefront, would probably no longer exist if not for sports. But because the school has produced such professionals as Chris Chelios of the Detroit Red Wings, Donovan McNabb of the Philadelphia Eagles, and Antoine Walker of the Boston Celtics, wannabes make the one- or two-hour round-trip commute from the suburbs.

Indeed, it's often parents who urge kids to cast aside a second or third sport, in hopes of the financial windfall of a scholarship. While this isn't a betrayal of community per se, it's a centrifugal urge that entails setting one's sights on some distant cynosure of celebrity and wealth, and leaving the humble old neighborhood behind. Wisconsin athletic director Pat Richter, a three-year, three-sport letterman with the Badgers (1960, 1961, and 1962) who played nine seasons in the NFL, calls this the brass-ring theory. According to the NCAA not even one in 330 high school athletes will land a college grant-in-aid.

These changes are taking their greatest toll on baseball, that languid American pastime we still associate with community. When Cincinnati Moeller High baseball coach Mike Cameron was developing such major leaguers as Buddy Bell, Barry Larkin, and Ken Griffey Jr., he usually had 90 kids try out for the team. In recent seasons he's gotten half that many, and those who do make the team rarely spend their summers playing sandlot ball. The decline in baseball coincides with the boom in soccer, whose coaches expect kids to begin travel-team play just as ballplayers report.

"The temptation of a scholarship drives a lot of families," says one father, whose twin boys each play three sports at a small high school in Vermont. "My sons enjoy the renaissance sports experience I cherished as a kid, but it could cost them the opportunity to play a varsity college sport. I guess that's the price of our competitive 'evolution of the species.'" Even nonscholarship Ivy League and Division III schools— which once celebrated well-roundedness as a virtue—are encouraging the trend toward specialization. "Despite support for the notion of the three-sport athlete, many colleges aren't looking for the well-rounded student anymore, but the well-rounded class," says Dan Doyle, author of the forthcoming *Encyclopedia of Sports Parenting.* "That means X number of male soccer players, X number of female softball players, etc."

So travel-team coaches thrust contracts in front of nine-year-old girls, asking them to pledge to put soccer ahead of every other sporting pursuit. The girls sign them, with an approving nod from mom and dad. "You see these parents who want their kids to be champions but want it to be a stress-free, enjoyable process," says Caroline Silby, a sports psychologist based in Washington, D.C. "That's not possible. Emotionally, what a child needs and a child champion needs is the same."

During the months he spent following the football team at Odessa (Texas) Permian High for his 1990 book *Friday Night Lights,* author H. G. Bissinger heard cautionary words that haunted him throughout his season there. They came from a father who saw, Bissinger writes, "the irresistible allure of high school sports, but he also saw the inevitable danger of adults' living vicariously through their young. And he knew of no candle that burned out more quickly than that of the high school athlete."

The brief transit of the schoolboy idol is a bittersweet archetype of American culture, the stuff of Springsteen songs and Updike novels. Yet we ask these athletes to come alight sooner, and burn brighter, than ever. Over the next month *Sports Illustrated* will feature four snapshots of where high school sports stand today, for better or worse. This week you'll meet two boys from Louisville, both with the chops to excel at three sports and the will to ignore the siren song of specialization. Next week we'll take you to Bradenton, Fla., to the campus of a private academy for serious jocks, set up by International Management Group, much like the New York City high school that trains singers and dancers and was the inspiration for the movie *Fame.* Then we'll visit Indiana, once home to Hoosier Hysteria, but where high school basketball is no longer packing gyms or knitting together the state's far-flung counties. Finally we'll drop in on a 96-year-old Thanksgiving football rivalry in greater St. Louis, where high school teams still play for school and community.

If Chip Hilton's Valley Falls is our Eden, places like Modesto Christian and Akron St. Vincent–St. Mary are outside the gates. But even at schools untouched by scandal or sellout, there's singing and cheering, fewer bands and "real send-offs." Classmates no longer wait up for the Big Reds boys' varsity to return on Saturday night, if only because so many have practices of their own on Sunday morning, that brass ring in their sights. To answer the question of whether we believe high school to be a precious interval in a young life or some Scholastic Fantastic stopover on the way to the Show is to learn a lot about who we are.

If it's true that by our children you shall know us, high school sports implicate us as a dedicated, focused, proudly self-reliant people, or an obsessed, blinkered, hopelessly atomized society—take your pick. But one thing is certain. In spite of all the trappings of tradition, notwithstanding the dads in the stands with three-letter sweaters in their closets, we are not who we once were.

6

Fraternal Bonding in the Locker Room

Timothy Jon Curry

The men's locker room is enshrined in sports mythology as a bastion of privilege and a center of fraternal bonding. The stereotyped view of the locker room is that it is a retreat from the outside world where athletes quietly prepare themselves for competition, noisily celebrate an important victory, or silently suffer a defeat. Given the symbolic importance of this sports shrine, it is surprising that there have been so few actual studies of the dynamics of male bonding in locker rooms. The purpose of this study was to explore a new approach to this aspect of fraternal bonding by collecting locker room talk fragments and interpreting them from a profeminist perspective. Profeminism in this context meant adapting a feminist perspective to men's experience in sport, giving special attention to sexist and homophobic remarks that reveal important assumptions about masculinity, male dominance, and fraternal bonding.

Although seldom defined explicitly, the fraternal bond is usually considered to be a force, link, or affectionate tie that unites men. It is characterized in the literature by low levels of disclosure and intimacy. Sherrod (1987), for example, suggests that men associate different meanings with friendships than women do, and that men tend to derive friendships from doing things together while women are able to maintain friendships through disclosures. This view implies that men need a reason to become close to one another and are uncomfortable about sharing their feelings.

Source: Reprinted by permission from T. J. Curry, 1991, "Fraternal Bonding in the Locket Room: A Profeminist Analysis of Talk about Competition and Women," *Sociology of Sport Journal* 8(2), pp. 119–135.

Some of the activities around which men bond are negative toward women and others who are perceived as outsiders to the fraternal group. For example, Lyman (1987) describes how members of a fraternity bond through sexist joking relationships, and Fine (1987) notes the development of sexist, racist, and homophobic attitudes and jokes even among preadolescent Little Leaguers. Sanday (1990) examines gang rape as a by-product of male bonding in fraternities, and she argues that the homophobic and homosocial environments of such all-male groups make for a conducive environment for aggression toward women.

Sport is an arena well suited for the enactment and perpetuation of the male bond (Messner, 1987). It affords separation and identity building as individual athletes seek status through making the team and winning games (Dunning, 1986), and it also provides group activity essential for male bonding (Sherrod, 1987) while not requiring much in the way of intimate disclosures (Sabo & Panepinto, 1990). Feminist scholars have pointed out that the status enhancement available to men through sports is not as available to women, and thus sport serves to legitimate men's domination of women and their control of public life (Bryson, 1987; Farr, 1988). In addition, since most sports are rule bound either by tradition or by explicit formal codes, involvement in sports is part of the typical right-and-rules orientation of boys' socialization in the United States (Gilligan, 1982).

For young men, sport is also an ideal place to "do gender"—display masculinity in a socially approved fashion (West & Zimmerman, 1987). In fact the male bond is apparently strengthened by an effective display of traditional masculinity and threatened by what is not considered part of standard hegemonic masculinity. For example, as Messner (1989, p. 192) relates, a gay football player who was aggressive and hostile on the field felt "compelled to go along with a lot of locker room garbage because I wanted that image [of attachment to more traditional male traits]— and I know a lot of others who did too. . . . I know a lot of football players who very quietly and secretly like to paint, or play piano. And they do it quietly, because this to them is threatening if it's known by others." Since men's bonding is based on shared activity rather than on the self-disclosures (Sherrod, 1987), it is unlikely that teammates will probe deeply beneath these surface presentations.

Deconstructing such performances, however, is one way of understanding the "interactional scaffolding of social structure and the social control process that sustains it" in displays of masculinity central to fraternal bonding (West & Zimmerman, 1987, p. 147). Pronger (1990, pp. 192–213) has provided one such deconstruction of doing gender in the locker room from the perspective of a homosexual. He notes the irony involved in maintaining the public facade of heterosexuality while privately experiencing a different reality.

Two other studies of locker rooms emphasized the cohesive side of male bonding through sports, but neither of these studies was concerned specifically with gender displays or with what male athletes say about women (Snyder, 1972; Zurcher, 1982). The recent uproar over the sexual harassment of a woman reporter in the locker room of the NFL's New England Patriots, described by Heymann (1990), suggests that this work is a timely and important undertaking.

PROCEDURES

This study of locker room talk follows Snyder (1972), who collected samples of written messages and slogans affixed to locker room walls. However, since the messages gathered by Snyder were originally selected by coaches and were meant to serve as normative prescriptions that would contribute to winning games, they mostly revealed an idealistic, public side of locker room culture. From reading these slogans one would get the impression that men's sports teams are characterized by harmony, consensus, and "esoteric in-group traditions" (Snyder, 1972, p. 99).

The approach taken here focuses on the spoken aspects of locker room culture—the jokes and put-downs typically involved in fraternal bonding (Fine, 1987; Lyman, 1987). Although this side of locker room culture is ephemeral, situational, and generally not meant for display outside of the all-male peer groups, it is important in understanding how sport contributes to male bonding, status attainment, and hegemonic displays of masculinity.

The Talk Fragments

The talk fragments were gathered in locker rooms from athletes on two teams participating in contact sports at a large midwestern university with a "big-time" sports program. The first team was approached at the beginning of its season for permission to do a field study. Permission was granted and assurances were made that anonymity would be maintained for athletes and coaches. I observed the team as a nonparticipant sport sociologist, both at practices and during competition, for well over a month before the first talk fragments were collected. The talk fragments were gathered over a 2-month period and the locker room was visited frequently to gather field notes. Note gathering in the locker room was terminated upon saturation; however, the team's progress was followed and field observations continued until the end of the season.

Intensive interviews were conducted with some of the athletes and coaches during all 9 months of the research. These interviews concerned not only locker room interaction but also the sport background and life histories of the respondents. Additionally, after the talk fragments were gathered, five of the athletes enrolled in my class on sport sociology and wrote term papers on their experiences in sport. These written documents, along with the interviews and observations made outside the locker room, provided a rich variety of materials for the contextual analysis and interpretation of the conversations held inside the locker room. They also lent insight into how the athletes themselves defined locker room talk.

The talk fragments were collected in plain view of the athletes, who had become accustomed to the presence of a researcher taking notes. Fragments of talk were written down as they occurred and were reconstructed later. Such obvious note taking may have influenced what was said, or more likely what was not said. To minimize the obtrusiveness of the research, eye contact was avoided while taking notes. A comparison between the types of conversations that occurred during note taking versus when note taking was not done yielded few differences. Even so, more talk fragments were gathered from a second locker room as a way of both increasing the validity of the study and protecting the anonymity of the athletes and coaches from the first locker room.

The Second Locker Room

Field notes concerning talk from a second locker room were gathered by a senior who had enjoyed a successful career as a letterman. His presence in the locker room as a participant observer was not obtrusive, and the other student-athletes reacted to him as a peer. He gathered talk fragments over a 3-month period while his team was undergoing conditioning and selection procedures similar in intensity to that of the original team. He met with me every week and described his perceptions of interaction in the locker room. His collection of talk fragments was included as part of a written autobiographical account of his experience in sport while at college. These research procedures were modeled after Zurcher's (1983) study of hashers in a sorority house and Shaw's (1972) autobiographical account of his experience in sport.

One additional point needs to be stressed here: Unlike anecdotal accounts of locker room behavior or studies based on the recollections of former athletes, these conversations were systematically gathered live and in context over a relatively brief period of time. Consequently the stories and jokes may not be as extreme as those remembered by athletes who reflect upon their entire career in sport (e.g., Messner, 1987; Pronger, 1990), or as dramatic as the episode of sexual harassment that took place in the locker room of the New England Patriots (Heymann, 1990).

The strength of this study lies in situating the conversations within the context of the competitive environment of elite collegiate sport rather than capturing the drama of a single moment or the recollections of particularly memorable occasions. In other words, no one study, including this one, can hope to cover the entire gambit of locker room culture and various distinctive idiocultures of different teams (Fine, 1987). A variety of studies that use different methods and incorporate different perspectives are needed for that endeavor.

Profeminist Perspective

Messner (1990) has recently argued that a profeminist perspective is needed to overcome male bias in research in the sociology of sport. For decades, Messner claims, male researchers have been prone to writing about sports from a masculine standpoint and have neglected gender issues. He further states that since men have exclusive access to much of the social world of sport, they also have the primary responsibility of providing a more balanced interpretation of that world by paying special attention to gender oppression. He maintains that such balance is best achieved at this point by adopting a value-centered feminist perspective rather than a supposedly value-free but androcentric perspective.

Adopting a feminist standpoint requires assuming that "feminist visions of an egalitarian society are desirable" (Messner, 1990, p. 149). Ultimately, research guided by such an assumption will contribute to a deeper understanding of the costs and the privileges of masculinity and may help build a more just and egalitarian world. Messner does not offer explicit guidelines as to how an androcentric researcher might begin to undertake such a shift in perspectives, however, although he does refer to a number of exemplary studies.

As a method of consciously adopting a profeminist perspective in this research, a review of feminist literature on sports and socialization was undertaken, feminist colleagues were consulted on early drafts of the manuscript, and a research assistant trained in feminist theory was employed to help with the interpretation of talk fragments. She shared her ideas and observations regarding the talk fragments, written documents, and field notes with me and suggested some additional references and sources that proved useful.

The talk fragments were selected and arranged to provide a sense of the different themes, ideas, and attitudes encountered. In focusing on the talk fragments themselves, two categories emerged (through a grounded theory approach) as especially important for situating and interpreting locker room behavior from a profeminist perspective: (a) the dynamics of competition, status attainment, and bonding among male athletes, and (b) the dynamics of defending one's masculinity through homophobic talk and talk about women as objects. A numbering system for each talk fragment (Athlete 1, 2, Sam, etc.) is used below to keep track of the different speakers. Names have been changed and the numbering system starts over for each talk fragment.

COMPETITION, STATUS ATTAINMENT, AND BONDING

Locker room talk is mostly about the common interests that derive from the shared identity of male student-athlete. Underlying these interactions is an ever-present sense of competition, both for status and position on the team itself and between the team and its opponents. While sport provides an activity to bond around, one's position on the team is never totally secure. An injury or poor performance may raise doubts about one's ability and lead to one's replacement. Such basic insecurities do not promote positive social relationships in the locker room, and they help explain some of the harshness of the talk that the athletes directed toward each other and toward women.

For example, competition can have a subtle influence on the relationships athletes have with others on the team and cause them to be quite tentative, as illustrated by the following statements obtained from two interviews:

> One of the smaller guys on the team was my best friend . . . maybe I just like having a little power over [him]. . . . It doesn't matter if the guy is your best friend, you've got to beat him, or else you are sitting there watching. Nobody wants to watch.

That's one of my favorite things about the sport, I enjoy the camaraderie. [Who are your friends?] Usually it's just the starters. . . . You unite behind each other a lot. The other guys don't share the competition with you like the starters do.

The competition can extend beyond sport itself into other domains. It is not unusual for athletes to have as their closest friends men who are not on the team, which helps them maintain some defensive ego boundaries between themselves and the team. It also provides a relief from the constant competition, as one athlete indicates:

[My] better friends aren't on the team. Probably because we are not always competing. With my [athlete] friends, we are always competing . . . like who gets the best girls, who gets the best grades. . . . Seems like [we] are competitive about everything, and it's nice to have some friends that don't care . . . you can just relax.

Competition, Emotional Control, and Bonding

A variety of studies have indicated that male athletes are likely to incorporate competitive motivation as part of their sport identity (e.g., Curry & Weiss, 1989). As competition and status attainment become important for the male athlete in establishing his identity, noninstrumental emotion becomes less useful, perhaps even harmful to his presentation of a conventionally gendered self (Sherrod, 1987). In addition, by defining themselves in terms of what is not feminine, men may come to view emotional displays with disdain or even fear (Herek, 1987). However, control over emotions in sport is made difficult by the passions created by an intense desire to win. One athlete described his feelings of being consumed by competition while in high school and his need to control the emotions:

My junior year, I had become so obsessed with winning the district. . . . I was so overcome that I lost control a week before the tournament. I was kicking and screaming and crying on the sofa . . . since then I have never been the same. True, now I work harder than that year but now when I start to get consumed [with something] I get fearful and reevaluate its importance.

As part of learning to control emotions, the athletes have learned to avoid public expressions of emotional caring or concern for one another even as they bond, because such remarks are defined as weak or feminine. For example, the remarks of the following athlete illustrate how this type of socialization can occur through sport. This athlete's father was very determined that his son would do well in sports, so much so that he forced the boy to practice daily and became very angry with the boy's mistakes. To understand his father's behavior, the boy went to his mother:

I would come up from the cellar and be upset with myself, and I would talk to my mother and say, "Why does he yell so much?" and she would say, "He only does it because he loves you."

While the father emphasized adherence to rules and discipline, the boy had to depend on his mother to connect him to his father's love. Distancing from each other emotionally is of course dysfunctional for the relationships among male athletes and leads to an impoverishment of relationships (Messner, 1987).

Maintaining a "safe" distance from one another also influences what is said and what is not said in front of others about topics of mutual concern, such as grades and women. Failure to address such common problems openly means that they must be dealt with indirectly or by denial. For example, the deriding of academic work by male athletes has been noted by other investigators (Adler & Adler, 1991) and is not typical of female athletes (Meyer, 1990). The reason may be that when athletes make comments that might be construed as asking for help or encouragement, their behavior is considered nonmasculine. They are thus subject to ridicule, as illustrated in the following two talk fragments:

Fragment 1
Athlete 1: [spoken to the athlete who has a locker near him, but loud enough to be heard by others] What did you get on your test?
Athlete 2: 13 [pause], that's two D+'s this week. That's a student-athlete for you. [sighs, then laughs quietly]
Athlete 1: That's nothing to laugh about.
Athlete 2: [contritely] I mean an athlete-student, but things are looking up for me. I'm going to do better this week. How did you do on that test?
Athlete 1: Got a 92.
Athlete 3: Yeah, who did you cheat off of? [group laughter]

Fragment 2
Athlete 1: [to coach, shouted across room] I'm doing real bad in class.
Coach: Congratulations!
Athlete 1: [serious tone, but joking] Will you call the professor up and tell him to give me an A?
Coach: [obviously sarcastically] Sure thing, would tonight at 9 be all right?

Competition and a Sense of Self

Considering the time-consuming nature of big-time college sports, it is not surprising that they become the central focus of athletes' lives. Approximately 30 hours a week were spent in practice, and often the athletes were too tired after a hard practice to do much else than sleep.

Fragment 3
Athlete 1: [collapses on bench] Shit, I'm going to bed right now, and maybe I'll make my 9 o'clock class tomorrow.
Athlete 2: 40 minutes straight! I thought he'd never stop the drills.
Athlete 1: Left you gasping for air at the end, didn't it?
Athlete 2: You mean gasping for energy.

Sports and competition become the greater part of the athlete's world. Through his strivings to excel, to be a part of the team and yet stand out on his own, he develops a conception of who he is. Thus the athlete's sense of self can be seen as being grounded in competition, with few alternative sources of self-gratification (Adler & Adler, 1991). The rewards for such diligence are a heightened sense of self-esteem. When one athlete was asked what he would miss most if he were to leave sports, he declared, "the competition . . . the attitude I feel about being [on the team]. It makes me feel special. You're doing something that a lot of people can't do, and wish they could do." In other words, his knowledge of his "self" includes status-enhancing presumptions about character building through sport.

This attitude is not atypical. For example, another man claimed, "I can always tell a [refers to athletes in same sport he plays]. They give off cues, good attitude, they are sure of themselves, bold, not insecure." This sense of specialness and status presumption cements the male bond and may temporarily cut across social class and racial differences. Later in life the experiences and good memories associated with fellowship obtained through sport may further sociability and dominance bonding (Farr, 1988). For the elite college athlete, however, this heightened self-esteem is obtained at some costs to other activities. Often academic studies and social or romantic involvements get defined as peripheral to the self and are referred to with contempt in the locker room, as illustrated in the fourth fragment.

Most everyone has vacated the locker room for the showers. Sam and a few of his friends are left behind. Sam is red-shirting (saving a year's eligibility by not participating on the team except for practices) and will not be traveling with the team. What he is going to do instead is the subject of several jokes once all the coaches have left the locker room:

Fragment 4
Athlete 1: What are you going to do, Sam, go to the game?
Sam: I can't, I sold my ticket. [laughs] I'm going to the library so I can study. [cynically] Maybe I'll take my radio so I can listen to the game. [pause] I hate my classes.
Athlete 1: Oh, come on, that's not the right attitude.
Sam: And I hope to get laid a few times too.
Athlete 1: Hey come on, that's not a nice way to talk.
Sam: How else are you supposed to talk in a locker room?

Sam's comment also leads us directly to the question of peer group influence on presentation of a gendered self. A general rule of male peer groups is that you can say and do some things with your peers that would be inappropriate almost anywhere else. For male athletes this rule translates into an injunction to be insulting and antisocial on occasion (Fine, 1987; Lyman, 1987). You are almost expected to speak sarcastically and offensively in the locker room, as Sam indicates above. Thus, hostile talk about women is blended with jokes and put-downs about classes and each other. In short, while sport leads to self-enhancement, the peer culture of male athletics also fosters antisocial talk, much of which is directed toward the athletes themselves.

Rigidities of the Bond

Competition in sports, then, links men together in a status-enhancing activity in which aggression is valued (Dunning, 1986). The bond between male athletes I usually felt to be a strong one, yet it is set aside rather easily. The reason for this is that the bond is rigid, with sharply defined boundaries. For example, when speaking about what it is that bonds athletes to their sport and other athletes, a coach remarks,

> They know they are staying in shape, they are part of something. Some of them stay with it because they don't want to be known as quitters. There's no in between. You're a [team member or not a team member]. The worst guy on the team is still well thought of if he's out there every day going through it. There's no sympathy in that room. No sympathy if you quit. You might die but you're not going to quit.

This rigid definition of who is or is not a team member reflects Gilligan's (1982) concept of a rights/rules moral system for males, which emphasizes individuality, instrumental relations, achievement, and control. In short the male athlete is either on the team or not. There is no gray area: It is clearly a black or white situation. If one follows the "rules," then he has the "right" to participate in bonding. If one does not follow the rules (i.e., quits), he ceases to exist in a bonding capacity. However, as Coakley (1990) has observed, following the rules to their extremes can lead to "positive" deviance, including a refusal to quit in spite of injury. Athlete 1 below endured a number of small and severe injuries, but throughout his ordeal refused to consider leaving the team.

Fragment 5
Athlete 1: My shin still hurts, can't get it to stop.
Athlete 2: Well, that's it then—time to quit.
Athlete 1: Not me, I'm not a quitter.
Athlete 2: Oh, come on, I can see through that. You'll quit if you have to.
Athlete 1: No way.

Even though injured, an athlete is still a member of the team if he attends practice, even if only to watch the others work out. However, his bond with the others suffers if he cannot participate fully in the sport. Sympathy is felt for such athletes, in that their fate is recognized and understood. As one athlete empathized during an interview, "I feel for the guys who are hurt who are usually starters. . . . [They] feel lonely about it, feel like they want to be back out there, feel like they want to prove something."

Perhaps what these athletes need to prove is that they are still a part of the activity around which the bonds are centered. As Sherrod (1987) suggests, the meanings associated with friendship for men are grounded in activities, giving them a reason to bond. Past success or status as a team member is not enough to fully sustain the bond; bonding requires constant maintenance. With boundaries so rigid, the athletes must constantly establish and reestablish their status as members involved in the bond by the only way they know how: through competition.

Rigid definitions of performance requirements in sport combine to form an either/or situation for the athlete and his ability to bond with teammates. If he stays within these boundaries, he is accepted and the bond remains intact. If he fails, he is rejected and the bond is severed. One athlete sums up this position with the following comments: "You lose a lot of respect for guys like that. Seems like anybody who's quit, they just get pushed aside. Like [name deleted], when he used to be [on the team] he hung around with us, and now that he's not, he ain't around anymore." Thus an athlete may find his relations severed with someone he has known for half his life, through participation in sport in junior high and high school, simply because the other person has left the team.

TALK ABOUT WOMEN

Competitive pressures and insecurities surrounding the male bond influence talk about women. As discussed above, competition provides an activity bond to other men that is rewarding, even though the atmosphere of competition surrounding big-time sports generates anxiety and other strong emotions that the athletes seek to control or channel. Competition for positions or status on the team also curtails or conditions friendships, and peer group culture is compatible with antisocial talk and behavior, some of which is directed at the athletes themselves.

The fraternal bond is threatened by inadequate role performance, quitting the team, or not living up to the demands of masculinity. Consequently, fear of weakening the fraternal bond greatly affects how athletes "do gender" in the locker room and influences the comments they make about women. In this regard, locker room talk may again be characterized both by what is said and what is not said. Conversations that affirm a traditional masculine identity dominate, and these include talk about women as objects, homophobic talk, and talk that is very aggressive and hostile toward women—essentially talk that promotes rape culture.

Woman as Person, Woman as Object

Two additional distinctions now need to be made in categorizing locker room talk about women. One category concerns women as real people, persons with whom the athletes have ongoing social relationships. This category of locker room talk is seldom about sexual acquisition; most often it is about personal concerns athletes might wish to share with their best friend on the team. Because the athletes do not want their comments to be overheard by others who might react with ridicule, this type of talk usually occurs in hushed tones, as described in the following fragment. Talk about women as objects, on the other hand, often refers to sexual conquests. This type of talk is not hushed. Its purpose seems mainly to enhance the athletes' image of themselves to others as practicing heterosexuals.

Fragment 6
Athlete 1 to 2: I've got to talk to you about [whispers name. They go over to an empty corner of the locker room and whisper. They continue to whisper until the coaches arrive. The athletes at the other end of the locker room make comments.]
Athlete 3: Yeah, tell us what she's got.
Athlete 4: Boy, you're in trouble now.
Assistant Coach: You'll have to leave our part of the room. This is where the real men are.

The peer culture of the locker room generally does not support much talk about women as persons. Norms of masculinity discourage talking seriously about social relations, so these types of conversations are infrequent (Fine, 1987; Sabo & Panepinto, 1990). Inevitably, personal revelations will quickly be followed by male athletic posturing, jokes, and put-downs, as in the talk fragment above. While the jokes may be amusing, they do little to enhance personal growth and instead make a real sharing of intimacies quite difficult. The ridicule that follows these interactions also serves to establish the boundaries of gender-appropriate behavior. This ridicule tells the athlete that he is getting too close to femaleness, because he is taking related-ness seriously. "Real men" do not do that. Perhaps just taking the view of women as persons is enough to evoke suspicion in the locker room.

To avoid this suspicion, the athlete may choose to present his attitude toward women in a different way, one that enhances his identity as a "real man." The result-ing women-as-objects stories are told with braggadocio or in a teasing manner; they are stage performances usually requiring an audience of more than one, and may be told to no one in particular:

Fragment 7
I was taking a shower with my girlfriend when her parents came home. I never got dressed so fast in my life.

These types of stories elicit knowing smiles or guffaws from the audience, and it is difficult to tell whether or not they are true. In any event the actual truth of such a story is probably less important than the function it serves in buttressing the athlete's claim as a practicing heterosexual.

Fragment 8
Athlete 1: How was your Thanksgiving?
Athlete 2: Fine, went home.
Athlete 1: I bet you spent the time hitting high schools!
Athlete 2: Naw, only had to go back to [one place] to find out who was available.

Women's identities as people are of no consequence in these displays. The fact that women are viewed as objects is also evident in the tendency of men to dissect woman's bodies into parts, which are then discussed separately from the whole person. Athlete 1 in Fragment 9 below is describing a part of a woman's body as if it existed separately from the woman, as if it was in the training room and the woman was not:

Fragment 9
Athlete 1: I just saw the biggest set of Ta-Tas in the training room!
Athlete 2: How big were they?
Athlete 1: Bigger than my mouth.

This perspective toward women highlights the fact that the use of women's bodies is more important than knowing them as people. Perhaps this attitude is also based in the athlete's focus on maintaining control, whether physically through athletic performance or mentally through strict adherence to rules and discipline. Since the male athlete's ideas about control center around physical strength and mental discipline, they stand in sharp contrast to ideas about females, who are generally thought of as physically weak and emotional. Following the implications of these ideas a bit further, women as persons are emotional and cannot be easily controlled; women as objects, however, have no volition and can be more easily controlled.

Doing Gender through Homophobic Talk

From Herek's (1987) notion that through socialization boys learn to be masculine by avoiding that which is feminine or homosexual, it follows that in the locker room an athlete may be singled out if his demeanor is identified as unmasculine in any way. The reasoning may be seen as follows: (a) "real men" are defined by what they are *not* (women and homosexuals); (b) it is useful to maintain a separation from femaleness or gayness so as not to be identified as such; (c) expression of dislike for femaleness or homosexuality demonstrates to oneself and others that one is separate from it and therefore must be masculine. For example, when an athlete's purple designer underwear is discovered, a teammate asks, "and did you get earrings for Christmas?" When he protests, this reply, directed to all of the athletes in the room is offered: "Guess I hit a . . . nerve. I won't begin on the footsies today, maybe tomorrow."

This example illustrates that every aspect of the athlete's appearance runs the risk of gender assessment. That which is under suspicion of being at odds with traditional definitions of masculinity threatens the bond and will be questioned. Connell (1990, pp. 88–89) provides further graphic example of gender assessment among athletes. He describes the life a determinedly heterosexual Australian Iron-Man competitor, whose first coital experience at 17 was both arranged and witnessed by his surf-club friends, and who felt he had to "put on a good show for the boys." Presumably, his performance allowed him and his friends to reaffirm to themselves and others that their sexual preferences remained within the boundaries of the bond.

Not only is being homosexual forbidden, but tolerance of homosexuality is theoretically off limits as well. The sanctions associated with this type of boundary maintenance manifest themselves in jokes and story telling about homosexuals.

Fragment 10
Athlete 1: When I was at [high school] we all lined up to watch the other guys come in. Fred pretended to be interested in one of them and said "I like that one" [he gestures with a limp wrist]. . . . We were all so fucking embarrassed, nobody would give him a ride home. It was the funniest thing!
Athlete 2: Yeah, once we all stopped in at [a local bar] and Tom got up to dance with one of the fags, actually took his hand and started to dance! Boy was the fag surprised. [group laughter]

Making fun of homosexuals by mimicking stereotyped gay gender displays brings laughter in the locker room partly because it helps distance the athletes from being categorized as gay themselves. Such hegemonic gender displays also take more aggressive forms. Perhaps male athletes are especially defensive because of the physical closeness and nudity in the locker room and the contact between males in sport itself. This latter idea is evident in the following remarks of a coach:

We do so much touching that some people think we're queer. In 37 years I've never for sure met a queer [athlete]. At [a certain college] we had a [teammate] that some of the fellows though was queer. I said "pound on him, beat on him, see what happens." He quit after 3 days. He never approached anyone anyway.

Locker Room Talk Promotes Rape Culture

Maintaining the appearance of a conventional heterosexual male identity, then, is of the utmost importance to the athlete who wants to remain bonded to his teammates. Also, as discussed previously, the perception of women as objects instead of persons encourages expressions of disdain or even hatred toward them on the part of the male athletes. Thus, the striving to do gender appropriately within the constraints of the fraternal bond involves talk that manages to put down women while also ridiculing or teasing each other, as the following fragments indicate:

Fragment 11
Assistant Coach 1: [announcement] Shame to miss the big [football] game, but you have to travel this week to keep you out of trouble. Keep you from getting laid too many times this weekend. Here are the itineraries for the trip. They include a picture of Frank's girlfriend. [Picture is of an obese woman surrounded by children. Frank is one of the best athletes on the team.]
Assistant Coach 2: Yeah, when she sits around the house, she really sits around the house.
Assistant Coach 3: She's so ugly that her mother took her everywhere so she wouldn't have to kiss her good-bye. [group laughter]

Jibes and put-downs about one's girlfriend or lack of sexual success are typified by this exchange. Part of the idealized heterosexual male identity consists of "success" with women, and to challenge that success by poking fun at the athlete's girlfriend is an obvious way to insult him. These jibes were directed at one of the best athletes on the team, whose girlfriend was not in town. It is important to note that these insults were delivered by the assistant coaches, who are making use of their masculine identity as a common bond they share with the student-athletes. By ridiculing one of the better athletes, they are not threatening any of the more vulnerable team members and at the same time they are removing some of the social distance between themselves and the students. After receiving such an insult, the athlete has to think of a comeback to top it or lose this round of insulting. Fine (1987) also noted such escalation of insults in his study of the Little League. This attitude is recognized and understood by other athletes:

Fragment 12
You guys harass around here real good. If you knew my mother's name, you would bring her into it too.

Thus a negative view of women prevails in the locker room and serves to facilitate the bond between athletes and their coaches. At times the competition involved with these exchanges does not involve insults directed at one another. The athletes compete instead to see who can express the most negative attitudes toward women, as illustrated by the final comments from a discussion of different types of women:

Fragment 13
Let me tell you about those [names an ethnic minority] women. They look good until they are 20, then they start pushing out the pups. By the time they're 40, they weigh 400 pounds.

This negative orientation is fed by other, related attitudes about women, such as those that concern women's sports, as indicated by the following remarks made by a coach: "[Our sport] has been taking a beating in lots of colleges. It's because of the emphasis on women's sports. Too bad, because [our sport] is cheaper. Could make money . . ." (he continues with comments about women's sports not paying their way).

At their extreme, these attitudes promote aggression toward women and create an environment supportive for rape culture (Beneke, 1982; Sanday, 1990). A fairly mild form of this aggression is suggested in the following talk fragment, in which two athletes are talking about Jerry, an athlete who is a frequent butt of their jokes. Jerry has just left the locker room and this conversation occurs when he is out of hearing distance:

Fragment 14
Athlete 1: Hey Pete, did you know Jerry is a sexual dynamo?

Pete: Why do you say that?
Athlete 1: He said he was with two different girls in the same day and both girls were begging, and I emphasize begging, for him to stop. He said he banged each of them so hard that they begged for him to stop.
Pete: I think he's becoming retarded.
Athlete 1: Do you believe he said this to me?
Pete: Well, what did you do?
Athlete 1: I laughed in his face.
Pete: What did he do?
Athlete 1: Nothing, he just kept telling me about this; it was hilarious.

The preceding fragment can be seen as describing rape in that the women involved with the athlete "begged for him to stop," and in this case the athletes choose to use the story to put down Jerry and thus negate his claim to sexual dynamism. The rape reference is more obvious in the following fragment. To set the scene, the team was visited by high school athletes and their parents; the athletes were being recruited by the coaches. The mother of one recruit drew attention from a group of athletes because she was extremely attractive. This conversation occurs in the locker room just after she left with her son:

Fragment 15
Athlete 1: She's too young to be his mother!
Athlete 2: Man, I'd hurt her if I got ahold of her.
Athlete 3: I'd tear her up.
Athlete 4: I'd break her hips. [all laugh]
Athlete 3: Yeah, she was hot!

Thus locker room talk about women, though serving a function for the bonding of men, also promoted harmful attitudes and creates an environment supportive of sexual assault and rape. Competition among teammates, the emphasis upon women as objects, sexual conquest as enviable achievement, peer group encouragement of antisocial comments and behavior, and anxiety about proving one's heterosexuality—all of these ideas are combined in the preceding fragment to promote a selfish, hostile, and aggressive approach to sexual encounters with women.

CONCLUSIONS

Sex and aggression are familiar themes in men's talk, and it is no surprise to find them of paramount importance in the locker room. Fine's (1987) work with preadolescent Little League baseball players indicated that the conversations of 9- to 12-year-old boys reflected similar concerns. What comes through less clearly in the conversation is the fulfillment that men find in such talk. It is an affirmation of one's masculine identity to be able to hold one's own in conversations about women, to top someone else's joke, or to share a story that one's peers find interesting. In this way the athlete's identity as a man worthy of bonding with is maintained.

College athletes often speak of the rewards of team membership as being an important reason for participating in a sport, and one of the rewards is the give and take of the peer culture is the locker room. The combination of revelation and braggadocio requires a shifting interpretation between fantasy and reality, and the ready willingness to insult means that a false interpretation may subject one to ridicule.

There are no definitive studies that document the effects of participating in locker room culture. On the one hand, behavior in locker rooms is both ephemeral and situational and probably does not reflect the actual values of all the participants. From this perspective, the locker room is just a place to change clothing and to shower, and one should not make too much of what goes on there. In discussing locker room interaction with some of the athletes involved, I found that most distanced themselves from it and denied its importance to them, particularly with respect to devaluing academic work. In some cases locker room talk even served as a negative reference for athletes, who quietly went about their business and avoided involvement. However, it is important to note that no one ever publicly challenged the dominant sexism and homophobia of the locker room. Whatever oppositional thoughts there may have been were muttered quietly or remained private.

On the other hand, there is evidence that years of participating in such a culture desensitizes athletes to women's and gay rights and supports male supremacy rather than egalitarian relationships with women. For instance, Connell's (1990) life history of an Iron Man indicated that this incredibly fit young man was unable to tolerate a "girl" who stood up for her own interests, and so had a series of girlfriends who were compliant with his needs and schedule. Moreover, Connell observes that this attitude is typical among the other male supremacists who constitute the Australian surfing subculture.

Another illustration is provided by the recent harassment of Lisa Olson in the locker room of the New England Patriots. This episode also supports the idea that locker room talk promotes aggressive antifemale behavior. The details of this case involved grown men parading nude around the seated reporter as she was conducting an interview. Some of the men "modeled themselves" before her, one "adjusted" his genitals and shook his hips in an exaggerated fashion, and one naked player stood arm's length from her and said "Here's what you want. Do you want to take a bit out of this?"—all to the accompaniment of bantering and derisive laughter (Heymann, 1990, p. 9A). No one tried to stop the humiliating activity, nor did management intervene or sincerely apologize until forced to by the NFL commissioner. In fact, the initial reaction of the team's owner was to support the players. The owner, Victor ("I liked it so much, I bought the company"—Remington) Kiam, was heard to say, "What a classic bitch. No wonder none of the players like her." However, his concern for the sales of his women's shaving products resulted in the following damage control campaign:

> He took out full-page ads in three major U.S. newspapers to protest his innocence, offered testimonials from three people who denied he said anything derogatory

about Olson, and blamed the Patriots front office personnel for not telling him of the Olson locker room incident sooner. (Norris, 1991, p. 23)

Finally, Sanday (1990, p. 193) concludes her study of gang rape by fraternity members by indicating that "Sexism is an unavoidable byproduct of a cultural fascination with the virile, sexually powerful hero who dominates everyone, male and female alike." If this is true, then sexism in locker rooms is best understood as part of a larger cultural pattern that supports male supremacy.

It is my view that sexist locker room talk is likely to have a cumulative negative effect on young men because it reinforces the notions of masculine privilege and hegemony, making that worldview seem normal and typical. Moreover, it does so in a particularly pernicious fashion. By linking ideas about masculinity with negative attitudes toward women, locker room culture creates a no-win situation for the athlete who wishes to be masculine and who wants to have successful, loving, nurturing relationships with women: "real men" are not nurturant. Similarly, locker room talk provides no encouragement for the "real man" who seeks egalitarian relationships. As Pronger (1990) notes, the myth of masculinity prevalent in the locker room cannot be maintained in the face of equitable relations between men and women or in the acceptance of homosexuality.

Finally, by linking ideas about status attainment with male bonding and masculinity, locker room culture makes it more difficult for young men to realize that women also desire success and status attainment through hard work and self-discipline. In other words, through participating in sport young men are taught that discipline and effort are needed for success and that one's acceptance depends on successful performance. But since these lessons are usually learned in all-male groups, they do not generalize easily to women and may create barriers to men's acceptance of women in the workplace.

REFERENCES

Adler, P.A., & Adler, P. (1991). *Buckboards & blackboards: College athletes and role engulfment.* New York: Columbia University Press.

Beneke, T. (1982). *Men on rape.* New York: St. Martin's Press.

Bryson, L. (1987). Sport and the maintenance of masculine hegemony. *Women's Studies International Forum, 10,* 349–360.

Coakley, J.J. (1990). *Sport in society: Issues and controversies.* St. Louis: Mosby.

Connell, R.W. (1990). An Iron Man: The body and some contradictions of hegemonic masculinity. In M.A. Messner & D.F. Sabo (Eds.), *Sport, men, and the gender order* (pp. 83–95). Champaign, IL: Human Kinetics.

Curry, T.J., & Weiss, O. (1989). Sport identity and motivation for sport participation: A comparison between American college athletes and Austrian student sport club members. *Sociology of Sport Journal, 6,* 257–268.

Dunning, E. (1986). Social bonding and violence in sport. In N. Elias & E. Dunning (Eds.), *Quest for excitement: Sport and leisure in the civilizing process* (pp. 224–244). Oxford: Basil Blackwell.

Farr, K.A. (1988). Dominance bonding through the good old boys sociability group. *Sex Roles, 18,* 259–277.

Fine, G.A. (1987). *With the boys: Little League baseball and preadolescent culture.* Chicago: University of Chicago Press.

Gilligan, C. (1982). *In a different voice: Psychological theory and woman's development.* Cambridge, MA: Harvard University Press.

Herek, G.M. (1987). On heterosexual masculinity: Some psychical consequences of the social construction of gender and sexuality. In M. S. Kimmel (Ed.), *Changing men: New directions in research on men and masculinity* (pp. 68–82). Beverly Hills: Sage.

Heymann, P.B. (1990, Nov. 28). Report describes what happened in locker room. *USA Today,* pp. 9A, 7C.

Lyman, P. (1987). The fraternal bond as a joking relationship: A case study of the role of sexist jokes in male group bonding. In M. S. Kimmel (Ed.), *Changing men: New directions in research on men and masculinity* (pp. 148–163). Beverly Hills: Sage.

Messner, M.A. (1987). The meaning of success: The athletic experience and the development of male identity. In H. Brod (Ed.), *The making of masculinities: The new men's studies* (pp. 193–209). Boston: Allen & Unwin.

Messner, M.A. (1989). Gay athletes and the gay games: An interview with Tom Waddell. In M.S. Kimmel & M.A. Messner (Eds.), *Men's lives* (pp. 190–193). New York: Macmillan.

Messner, M.A. (1990). Men studying masculinity: Some epistemological issues in sport sociology. *Sociology of Sport Journal, 7,* 136–153.

Meyer, B.B. (1990). From idealism to actualization: The academic performance of female college athletes. *Sociology of Sport Journal, 7,* 44–57.

Norris, M. (1991, Feb. 2). Mr. Nice Guy. *TV Guide,* pp. 22–29.

Pronger, B. (1990). *The arena of masculinity: Sport, homosexuality, and the meaning of sex.* New York: St. Martin's Press.

Sabo, D.F., & Panepinto, J. (1990). Football ritual and the social reproduction of masculinity. In M.A. Messner & D.F. Sabo (Eds.), *Sport, men, and the gender order* (pp. 115–126). Champaign, IL: Human Kinetics.

Sanday, P.R. (1990). *Fraternity gang rapes: Sex, brotherhood, and privilege on campus.* New York: New York University Press.

Shaw, G. (1972). *Meat on the hoof.* New York: St. Martin's Press.

Sherrod, D. (1987). The bonds of men: Problems and possibilities in close male relationships. In H. Brod (Ed.), *The making of masculinities: The new men's studies* (pp. 213–239). Boston: Allen & Unwin.

Snyder, E.E. (1972). Athletic dressing room slogans as folklore: A means of socialization. *International Review of Sport Sociology, 7,* 89–100.

West, C., & Zimmerman, D.H. (1987). Doing gender. *Gender & Society 1,* 125–149.

Zurcher, L.A. (1982). The staging of emotion: A dramaturgical analysis. *Symbolic Interaction, 5,* 1–19.

Zurcher, L.A. (1983). Dealing with an unacceptable role: Hashers in a sorority house. In L.A. Zurcher (Ed.), *Social roles: Conformity, conflict, and creativity* (pp. 77–89). Beverly Hills: Sage.

✻ FOR FURTHER STUDY ✻

Bissenger, H. G. 1990. *Friday Night Lights: A Town, A Team, and a Dream* (New York: Perseus Books.

Cavanaugh, Ed. 2003. "Basketball Lifts Cairo's Gloom," *Chicago Tribune* (March 14):1, 28.

Curry, Timothy Jon. 1998. "Beyond the Locker Room: Campus Bars and College Athletes," *Sociology of Sport Journal* 15 (3):205–215.

Curry, Timothy Jon. 2001. "Reply to 'A Conversation (Re)Analysis of Fraternal Bonding in the Locker Room,'" *Sociology of Sport Journal* 18 (3):339–344.

Curtis, James, William McTeer, and Philip White. 2003. "Do High School Athletes Earn More Pay? Youth Sports Participation and Earnings as an Adult." *Sociology of Sport Journal* 20 (1):60–76.

Eitle, Tamela McNulty, and David J. Eitle. 2002. "Just Don't Do It: High School Sports Participation and Young Female Adult Sexual Behavior," *Sociology of Sport Journal* 19 (4):403–418.

Fejgin, Naomi. 1994. "Participation in High School Competitive Sports: A Subversion of School Mission or Contribution to Academic Goals?" *Sociology of Sport Journal* 11 (September):211–220.

Ferguson, Andrew. 1999. "Inside the Crazy Culture of Kids Sports," *Time* (July 12):52–60.

Fine, Gary Alan. 1987. *With the Boys: Little League Baseball and Preadolescent Culture* (Chicago: University of Chicago Press).

Foley, Douglas E. 1990. *Learning Capitalist Culture: Deep in the Heart of Tejas* (Philadelphia: University of Pennsylvania Press).

Frey, Darcy. 1991. *The Last Shot: City Streets, Basketball Dreams* (Boston: Houghton Mifflin).

Goldsmith, Pat Antonio. 2003. "Race Relations and Racial Patterns in School Sports Participation," *Sociology of Sport Journal* 20 (2):147–171.

Haworth, Karla. 1998. "The Pressure and Profits of Top Basketball Camps," *The Chronicle of Higher Education* (August 7):A41–A42.

Hyman, Mark. 2001. "Reading, Writing—and Winning," *Business Week* (April 2):58–60.

Jimerson, Jason B. 2001. "A Conversation (Re)Analysis of Fraternal Bonding in the Locker Room," *Sociology of Sport Journal* 18(3), (Spring): 317–338.

Latimer, Clay. 2003. "Pulling Strings: For Better or Worse, Parents' Role in Prep Sports Evolving into More Agent than Cheerleader," *Rocky Mountain News* (March 8): 1B, 11B, 13B.

May, Reuben A. Buford. 2001. "The Sticky Situation of Sportsmanship: Contexts and Contradictions in Sportsmanship Among High School Boys Basketball Players," *Journal of Sport & Social Issues* 25 (November): 372–389.

Miracle, Andrew, and C. Roger Rees. 1994. *Lessons of the Locker Room: The Myth of School Sports* (Amherst, NY: Prometheus Books).

Parker, Rosemary. 1993. "Learning by Intimidation?" *Newsweek* (November 8):14.

Rees, C. Roger, and Andrew W. Miracle. 2001. "Education and Sport." Pp. 277–290 in *Handbook of Sports Studies,* Jay Coakley and Eric Dunning (eds.), (London: Sage).

Watts, Jay. 2002. "Perspectives on Sport Specialization," *JOPERD* 73 (October):33–37, 50.

Wolff, Alexander. 2002. "The High School Athlete," *Sports Illustrated,* three-part series (November 18, 25, and December 2).

PART THREE

Sport and Socialization: The Mass Media

The mass media have a tremendous impact on sports. First, the popularity of sport is due in large measure to the enormous attention it receives from the mass media. Second, television has infused huge sums of money into sport, affecting franchise moves and salaries. Third, television (and the money it offers) has changed the way sports are played (for example, the scheduling of games, the interruption of the flow of games for commercial breaks, the shift from match play to medal play in tournament golf, and rule changes such as liberalizing offensive holding in football to increase scoring and, therefore, viewer interest). Fourth, television has affected college sports by making recruiting more national than regional and by focusing the nation's attention (and heaping television's money) on the games by a relatively few schools. Thus, television has exacerbated the gap between the "haves" and the "have nots." Moreover, since television money goes to the successful, it has heightened the pressure to win, and for some, the necessity to cheat in order to win.

Another consequence of the media—the effect on perceptions—is the focus of this section. The media direct attention toward certain acts and away from others. While the media appear to simply report what is happening, or what has just happened, during a sporting event, they actually provide a constructed view by what they choose to cover, their focus, and the narrative themes they pursue.[1] As Alan and John Clarke have said:

> It selects *between* sports for those which make "good television," and it selects *within* a particular event, it highlights particular aspects for the viewers. This selective highlighting is not "natural" or inevitable—it is based on certain criteria, certain media assumptions about what is "good televison." But the media do not only select, they also provide us with definitions of what has been selected. They interpret events for us, provide us with frameworks of meaning in which to make sense

of the event. To put it simply, television does not merely consist of pictures, but also involves a commentary on the pictures—a commentary which explains to us what we are seeing. . . . These selections are socially constructed—they involve decisions about what to reveal to the viewers. The presentation of sport through the media involves an active process of re-presentation: what we see is not the event, but the event transformed into something else—a media event.[2]

The first selection in this section, by Dan C. Hilliard, shows that sport itself and the media portrayal of sport are ideological—that is, supportive of conservative values. Moreover, television is antisociological because it focuses on the personal rather than the social and it avoids serious analysis of social problems or political issues.

The second selection, by sociologist Michael A. Messner, provides data from three studies that show that the media consistently throughout the 1990s gave relatively little attention to women's sports, thus leaving largely intact "the masculinist cultural center of the sport-media-commercial complex."

The last selection, by Michael A. Messner, Michele Dunbar, and Darnell Hunt, complements the previous Messner selection. It explores themes in televised sports that combine to construct a masculinity formula consistent with the entrenched interests of the sports/media/commercial complex.

NOTES

1. D. Stanley Eitzen and George H. Sage, *Sociology of North American Sport,* 6th ed. (Madison, WI: Brown & Benchmark, 1997), chap. 9.

2. Alan Clarke and John Clarke, "Highlights and Action Replays—Ideology, Sport and the Media," in *Sport, Culture, and Ideology,* Jennifer Hargreaves (Ed.), (Boston: Routledge & Kegan Paul, 1982), pp. 69, 71.

7

Televised Sport and the (Anti)Sociological Imagination

Dan C. Hilliard

I recently began my undergraduate course in sociology of sport by outlining the cultural studies paradigm and showing how I thought it could be used to understand sport as a prime purveyor of ideology. After class a student came forward to ask me to clarify some points I had made in the lecture. After I answered her questions, she said, "I've been involved in sports all my life, but I've never looked at sport that way before." Her experience is, I think, typical. Sage (1990) states,

> Although sport practices embody specific and identifiable purposes, values, and mean- ings, they are typically viewed by both participants and spectators as ahistorical and apolitical in nature. This is true largely because most of our written and broadcast information does not confront people with questions about the larger social issues and political and economic consequences of modern sport and physical activity. Instead, we are fed a diet of traditional slogans, cliches, and ritualized trivia about sport. These may all be very comforting but they do not come to grips with reality. (p. 11)

In his 1959 landmark essay, C. Wright Mills urged the adoption of a "socio- logical imagination," which articulated the connection between "personal troubles" and "public issues." If Mills's pleading is the basis for a critical sociology, then the "sport-media complex" (Jhally, 1989) is profoundly antisociological.

Source: "Televised Sport and (Anti)Sociological Imagination" by Dan C. Hilliard. From *Journal of Sport and Social Issues* 18, pp. 88–99. Copyright © 1994 by Sage Publications. Reprinted by permission of Sage Publications, Inc.

In the past decade, a great deal of attention has been paid to the ideological work of sport in general and mediated sport in particular. Commercialized, professionalized, rationalized, mediated sport has been found to reproduce all sorts of hegemonic values. What may have been overlooked is that this fundamentally antisociological perspective provides a foundation for the ideological work of mediated sport by foreclosing the possibility of any significant criticism of the status quo.

Clearly, the powerful of the "SportsWorld" (Lipsyte, 1975) benefit from an uncritical rendering of sport by the mass media. Without invoking conspiracy theories or notions of a monolithic cultural elite, Gruneau (1989) has noted an "elective affinity" between the interests of athletes, sports promoters, sponsors, and television sports production personnel that leads producers of television sports programming to frame their coverage in conventional ways. In addition to preexisting values, sports television work routines are also likely to be involved. In a related context, Theberge and Cronk (1986) have demonstrated that the work routines of newspaper sportswriters affect the coverage given to women athletes.

My purpose here is to explore more fully the sources of the antisociological bias in television programming in general and televised sport in particular. I intend to do so by looking at three aspects of the literature on television: television's "media logic," televised sport as news, and televised sport as entertainment. I shall then apply points gleaned from this literature to NBC's coverage of the 1992 Summer Olympic Games.

TELEVISION'S MEDIA LOGIC

Duncan and Brummett (1987) identify four dimensions of television's "media logic": narrative, intimacy, commodification, and rigid time segmentation. They claim that each is present in the various sports television programs they analyzed. I would argue that the presence of each encourages a focus on "personal troubles" rather than "public issues" within the world of sport.

By *narrative* Duncan and Brummet (1987) mean that television tells a story, usually in a predictable fashion using stock plots and characters. Gruneau (1989), in his observational study of a Canadian television sports production, discovered how directors and reports constructed a story line for the telecast. Of course, the athletic contest itself provides a basis for narrative, but if the drama is insufficient, television commentators move the story along by "the deliberate invention of moments" (Sorkin, 1986, pp. 180–181). Duncan and Brummett (1987) indicate that conflict or opposition is often a part of the narrative, and of course, in televised sport, conflict between opposing teams is the basis for drama. But conflict does not necessarily reveal social issues. Hallin (1986) notes, "A great deal of television's conflict is good-against-evil conflict, evil being located outside the mainstream of society" (p. 33). Fiske (1987) argues that narrative is essentially conservative in positing a disruption, solution, and restoration of equilibrium, and that it does its ideological work by identifying the sources of disruption and restoration. This would seem particularly true of the world of sport, where the disruption is ordinarily the "artificial" conflict between competing teams which is resolved by the "best team winning."

Intimacy refers both to the visual closeness of the television viewer to the subject matter and to the development of an emotional attachment between actor and viewer. The former is certainly present in televised sport, but it is the latter that is critical in producing an antisociological frame for televised sport. The development of audience identification with characters is a principal means by which viewers' attention to the narrative is maintained. As Gitlin (1985) says, "Whether in sports, entertainment, documentaries, or news, the networks believe that what glues the audience to the tube is this personal feeling for the characters" (p. 187). Sports telecasts create audience identification with athletes through human interest features, which become the basis for the story line of the telecast, and by on-the-sport interviews with winners. Gruneau (1989) found that Canadian sport television producers did background research on the athletes they were to cover; this research resulted in "hero notes" that were integrated into the telecast. This focus on the individual athlete diverts attention away from any social or collective issues. Fiske (1987) states, "Individualism diverts attention away from any questioning of the social system, for individual 'solutions' to social problems are always possible" (p. 153).

Commodification refers both to the close tie between programming and commercial time and to the use of the language of commodification in the description of sports events (Duncan & Brummett, 1987). In sports telecasts, as in all of television, there is an attempt to produce a seamless relation of programming to commercials, so that viewers will not be tempted to "zap" the commercials with their remote controls. Miller (1986) argues that this is accomplished by a process of "mutual approximation" in which programs and commercials become more and more alike. Certainly, the concerns of advertisers loom large in television programming. Gitlin (1985) quotes the advertising executive's adage "Television programs are the meat in a commercial sandwich" (p. 92). More analytically, Miller (1988) argues that the purpose of television programming is not only to attract an audience that can be sold to advertisers but also to put that audience in a buying mood. It seems obvious that programming that raises serious questions about social justice or that dwells on patterns of exploitation or inequality in society would risk taking the audience out of the buying mood.

Rigid time segmentation refers to the way in which program segments, commercials, and entire programs are organized into short, rigid blocks of time (Duncan & Brummett, 1987). Although sports programming may be somewhat more flexible than other types of programming in this regard, it is still rigidly segmented, as the failure of constant action sports like soccer and the necessity of "television timeouts" in football and basketball attest. Rigid time segmentation contributes to a focus on events and people rather than conditions and analysis by virtue of limiting the time that may be devoted to any particular topic. A typical "sound bite" is about 10 seconds, in which time one may convey an emotion or an attitude but not an argument. Most news segments are about 1.5 minutes; the longest are rarely longer than 3 minutes. In my experience with NBC's telecast of the 1992 Summer Olympics, event coverage segments rarely lasted more than 8 minutes, features rarely more than 3 minutes, and on-the-spot interviews rarely 1 minute. Such short segments militate against more than a mention of underlying social conditions or issues.

TELEVISED SPORT AS NEWS AND ENTERTAINMENT

Televised sport contains elements of both the news and entertainment genres (Critcher, 1987). Perhaps the distinction is irrelevant; as Hallin (1986) points out, television news has taken on many of the features of entertainment. However, the point is that, whether one thinks of televised sport as being similar to news or similar to entertainment programming, there are tendencies that work against any significant analysis of social issues.

To the extent that televised sport attempts to present real events in real time, it follows some of the conventions of television news programs. Although this may be more true of the NFL Game of the Week, which is broadcast live, than of the 1992 Summer Olympics, which was broadcast to North American audiences taped and heavily edited, all sports programming relies on an aura of realism to keep its audience. Gitlin (1980) summarizes the assumptions of television news personnel about their work as follows:

> Several assumptions about news value serve, for the most part, to secure (the hegemonic) boundary: that news involves the novel event, not the underlying, enduring condition; the person, not the group; the visible conflict, not the deep consensus; the fact that "advances the story," not the one that explains or enlarges it. (p. 263)

Thus the canons of television news work to focus the viewer's attention on personal troubles rather than public issues. Hargreaves (1986) identifies a similar set of "media sport news values" that guides production work and tends to support dominant ideology.

Several of the major characteristics of television entertainment programming have been discussed above in reference to narrative and intimacy. However, two additional characteristics of television programming emerge from the literature that seem to apply directly to sports programming. The first has to do with the protagonists represented in television drama (and sport is surely represented as drama on television). Protagonists are heroic figures, fighting against stiff odds and ultimately prevailing over the various obstacles they encounter. Gitlin (1987) notes that throughout television "the major characters are winners" (p. 255). Gitlin (1986) sharpens this notion about protagonists as winners by referring to such action series as the *A-Team* and *Miami Vice*. In shows such as these, the protagonists are individuals or teams of rugged individualists waging war against faceless evil and the interference of meddling bureaucrats. Televised sport frequently develops the story of an athlete on the quest for excellence, overcoming seemingly insurmountable obstacles along the way. This is a story line that television viewers are well prepared to accept.

The second characteristic of television as entertainment is more a matter of style. Television is discussed as the postmodern medium *par excellence* (Miller, 1986), "the ultimate recombinant form" (Gitlin, 1985, p. 80) juxtaposing discordant images in a collage of visuals that levels images and their attendant meanings. This style becomes evident in sports coverage such as the Olympics telecasts, with coverage jumping from venue to venue, from studio to event, from event coverage to commercial to studio interview. Such a style discourages the viewer from making any meaningful connections among the stream of images; each is simply to be enjoyed for its own sake.

In summary, the literature on television as a medium suggests a number of ways in which television programming—whether entertainment, news, or sport—discourages the development of a "sociological imagination." Television deals with controversy and conflict by focusing on the personal and anecdotal rather than on social patterns. Thus television can, for example, be highly critical of individual business persons without being critical of capitalism (Gitlin, 1980). Television discourages its audience from critical social analysis.

REFLECTIONS ON NBC'S COVERAGE
OF THE 1992 SUMMER OLYMPICS

Without attempting any systematic empirical analysis, I wish to illustrate the previous discussion of the antisociological bias of television by reference to NBC's coverage of the 1992 Summer Olympics from Barcelona. I have organized my remarks into two categories: the first dealing with the structure of the two weeks of coverage and the second dealing with the handling of controversy as part of that coverage.

The structure of the telecast is interesting in that the two weeks of coverage, consisting of over 150 hours of air time, is much more extensive than the typical sports telecast. Coverage was divided into several segments each day. Weekday coverage consisted of a morning show, a prime-time show, and a late night show. Weekend coverage featured extended coverage during the middle of the day, usually from 11 a.m. until 5 p.m., followed by a 1-hour news break and then prime-time evening coverage.

It became clear to me that the different portions of sports coverage mimicked their nonsport counterparts; that is, the morning coverage mimicked *Today*, prime-time coverage attempted to emulate nighttime drama, and the late night coverage tried to adopt many of the features of late night television more generally. The morning show was hosted by veteran sportscaster Dick Enberg and *Today* host Katie Couric; it incorporated many studio interviews, inserted brief reports on world news, and took regular breaks for local news and weather to provide a format with which regular morning viewers would be familiar. Prime-time coverage developed major athletic story lines that might be expected to draw a general audience as well as committed sports fans, such as the women's gymnastics competition between the U.S. and Unified teams and men's basketball featuring Michael Jordan, Charles Barkley, and other members of the "Dream Team." These story lines were developed with ample use of human interest features. The late night coverage was billed as "Club Barcelona" and integrated celebrity interviews, features on Barcelona nightlife, and music videos into its sports coverage to create a program that fans of Jay Leno, David Letterman, and Arsenio Hall would be comfortable with.

It is also clear to me that the narrative and intimacy themes discussed by Duncan and Brummett (1987), and more particularly the disruption, solution, restoration type of narrative discussed by Fiske (1987), were the principal organizing features of the coverage. Time after time, the audience was presented with stories of athletes overcoming difficulty in their pursuit of Olympic gold. Pablo Morales's swimming comeback was called the most compelling story of the games so far. Canadian rower Silken Laumann's return to competition only 6 weeks after a devastating injury was an incredible story of courage and fortitude. Mike Barrowman set a swimming world record after he dedicated these Olympics to his father's memory. Boxer Oscar de la Hoya was moved to tears in the studio when he saw for the first time the feature detailing his dedication of his quest for gold to his deceased mother. Trent Dimas's gold medal on the high bar, after injuries and financial difficulties almost forced him out of gymnastics, was called "the single biggest gold medal surprise of these Olympic games." Distance runner Mirsada Buric from Bosnia-Hercegovina trained amid sniper fire and was held captive by Serbian troops for 13 days; Katie Couric dubbed her "a true Olympian" for reaching the competition in Barcelona. Even the region of Cataluna and the city of Barcelona were fit into this overarching story line, overcoming the oppression of Franco's regime in order to modernize and play host to the Olympics.

Given the almost limitless amount of material that would fit this story line, it is not surprising that analytical or investigative pieces were rare during the two weeks of coverage. Indeed, controversy hardly raised its ugly head in Barcelona. During the entire two weeks of coverage, only four stories involving controversy emerged. Three of these had to do with scoring, judging, and administration of events. These were the U.S. men's volleyball team's loss to Japan as a result of an official protest, the judging of the boxing competition, and the results of the men's 10-kilometer run. In each case, coverage carried over several days and focused on "the fact that advances the story" (Gitlin, 1980) rather than on analysis or explanation.

The volleyball controversy developed when match officials gave U.S. player Bob Samuelson a second yellow card with Japan leading 15–14 in the fifth game of the match. This should have resulted in an automatic point being awarded to the Japanese team, which would also have given them the game and the match. Officials failed to award the penalty point, Japan protested after the match, their protest was upheld, and an apparent American victory was negated. Early coverage focused on the competence of the officials and asked how the officials could have overlooked the fact that a second yellow card had been awarded and whether it was proper to award a yellow card at such a critical juncture in the match. Later, it was reported that one of the match officials has been dismissed. After all members of the U.S. team shaved their heads in support of the bald Samuelson, NBC turned the shaving into a story in its own right; indeed, the new story line became "U.S., men undefeated since shaving their heads." The coverage was superficial and repetitive and focused attention on the competence and judgment of individuals rather than on the rules themselves.

The scoring of the boxing competition developed as a story after U.S. team captain Eric Griffin, an overwhelming favorite for the gold medal in his weight class, lost a close decision in a pre-medal round. Following the bout, detailed explanations of the computerized judging system, which required three ringside judges to register a blow within 3 seconds of one another for the blow to "score," were given. Commentators went over slow-motion tapes of the bout and pointed out blows that should have "scored" but did not. Later, the scorecards of the individual judges were analyzed, and all three scored the fight in favor of Griffin. An official protest was filed, but the original scoring was upheld. Griffin's "surrogate father" was interviewed and declared the international amateur boxing administrators "a bunch of gutless old men." Thereafter, the scoring of boxing became the story line of the boxing coverage. Virtually every bout was discussed in terms of the scoring system. Some remarks seemed to implicate the system as a whole (for example, Dick Enberg remarked that Eric Griffin had been defeated by a computer), whereas the boxing analysts consistently argued that it was the incompetence of individual judges and referees that was at fault. Expert commentator Al Bernstein stated, "The refereeing in this tournament has been worse than atrocious," and later added, "Forget the system. It's the judges."

The third controversial ruling involved the men's 10,000-meter run, where Moroccan Khalid Skah pulled away from a Kenyan runner late in the race. The Kenyan delegation protested on the basis that another Moroccan runner who had been lapped interfered in the race. The Kenyan protest was initially upheld but was later overturned by the IAAF, the governing body of track and field. Skah received his gold medal to the jeers of the crowd. Because no U.S. athlete was involved, coverage of this controversy was less extensive. Expert distance running commentator Craig Masbach argued that the IAAF ruling was just, as Skah would have won without the interference of his countryman.

Another controversy involved U.S. sprinter Gwen Torrence's allegation that several finalists in the women's 100-meter sprint had used illegal performance-enhancing drugs. Torrence was interviewed on several occasions and explained that her statement was based on "personal suspicions" rather than specific knowledge. In interviews with other track and field stars, such as Florence Griffith Joyner and Carl Lewis, the issue of drugs was raised, but the athletes argued that better drug testing had reduced levels of illegal drug use in the sport. In the absence of hard evidence or specific allegations, the reporting centered more on the judgment Torrence used in making her remarks than on the substance of her "suspicions."

In summary, the controversies covered were either explained away as being noncontroversial after all, as in the Khalid Skah case, or as being the result of individual misjudgment or incompetence. Coverage of controversy does not result in a focus on social or political issues.

Equally revealing of the antisociological bias of television coverage is a look at the potentially controversial stories that were not covered in depth. There were frequent references to serious injury of competitors in the coverage of gymnastics but always in the form of background information on athletes. These remarks were made in passing and were never the basis for serious discussion. Whereas a public issues approach would have treated the rate of injuries as an issue, the personal troubles approach fit within existing narrative forms by treating injury as just another obstacle to be overcome. Similarly, coverage of the 3-day equestrian cross-country even included visuals of horses hung up on immovable rock walls, exhausted at the end of competition, and even being hauled away in ambulances. The course was so difficult that it was criticized by both animal rights activists and many experienced equestrians. But rather than raise serious questions about the safety of the event, the television commentators reassured their audience that every precaution was being taken to care for the horses.

Yet another issue that might have resulted in more systematic investigation was that of drug use. A Chinese woman volleyball player, a woman marathoner representing the Unified team, and U.S. hammer thrower Jud Logan were disqualified after they failed postevent drug tests. These events were briefly reported, but no details were ever provided. When U.S. shotputters Mike Stulce and Jim Doehring won gold and silver medals, respectively, no mention was made of the fact that each had previously been suspended by the IAAF for steroid use. Other than Gwen Torrence's stated "suspicions," the only attention given to drug use involved rumors concerning steroid use by the Chinese women swimmers. Bob Costas referred to the Chinese women as "uncommonly masculine" and reported in a studio segment that rumors were rife during the swim competition about their use of drugs; however, no U.S. coaches or athletes were willing to make allegations on camera. Costas's studio discussion pointed out that former East German coaches were now involved with the Chinese swim program and were suspected of having introduced illegal drugs into their training program. Late night cohost Jim Lampley later picked up this same theme, making remarks that made the distinction between individual athletes who chose to use drugs versus athletic training systems, such as those of the Chinese and East Germans, who exploited unknowing young girls for the purposes of national glory.

This last example illustrates a major exception to the television rule of emphasizing the personal over the public: Communist states are represented in stereotypical fashion as monolithic systems exploiting their citizens. Eitzen (1992) has recently demonstrated the "framing of cultural values," which stereotypically juxtaposes negative traits of the Soviet system with positive ones of our own. By July 1992, the Soviet Union was no more, and Soviet hegemony was no longer newsworthy. Whereas CBS's coverage of the 1992 Winter Olympics had focused considerable attention on the demise of the Soviet Union, NBC's coverage of the summer games treated it as ancient history. However, the remaining communist states of China and Cuba were the focus of attention, as was the East German sports program of the earlier era.

A feature on the Chinese diving program used negative wording and implied exploitation as it discussed the process whereby the Chinese identify and develop talent. A feature on Cuban boxer Felix Savon referred to Cuba as "archaic" and as "the land time forgot." Savon was portrayed as "the last great soldier of the revolution"; at one point, he was pictured in front of a billboard that read "Marxismo, Leninismo, o Muerte." Savon was portrayed to American audiences as the fool who would devote himself to a system doomed to failure. Another feature dealt with Cuban boxing coaches who have left Cuba to coach around the world. After the feature ended, Jim Lampley in the studio editorialized, "Better they should send coaches to Ireland than guns and soldiers to Mozambique." The point is that a double standard is in operation. Television uncovers the sport-ideology connection in its coverage of the communist states, just as it obscures the same connection in coverage of American athletes.

A final example illustrates several of the points made here. By far the most extensive feature of the entire two weeks of coverage was a retrospective on the terrorist actions at the 1972 Munich Olympics in which 12 Israeli athletes were murdered. Some 45 minutes of taped narrative, interrupted by a commercial break, recounted the events that unfolded in Munich. A studio introduction asserted that part of the reason for the decision to air the feature was that "new information" had recently become available. Once coverage began, the only "new" information was that "recently released secret German documents indicate that the [Black September commandos] picked up weapons from the East Germans" after they entered the Olympic compound. Using 1972 footage as well as interviews with German authorities and the surviving Israeli athletes, the events of the tragic day were recounted. It was described as "a tragedy of errors," and Israelis criticized the decisions made by German authorities. The next day, Anouk Spitzer, the daughter of one of the Israeli athletes killed in the attack, was interviewed in the studio and stated, "The Germans made so many mistakes." The reading of the events offered by this coverage was that individuals in positions of authority in West Germany made questionable decisions that cost the lives of the Israeli athletes. The audience was left to ask not "What social forces contributed to such an extreme act?" but "What could have been done differently to save innocent lives?" At the same time, the communist bogeyman was implicated.

CONCLUSION

The literature on television as a medium suggests that television, whether news or entertainment, has reason to focus on the personal rather than on the social and to avoid serious analysis of social problems or political issues. My review of NBC's coverage of the 1992 Summer Olympics shows this to be the case for sports coverage as well. This should not be surprising. Newspaper and magazine sports coverage rarely delves too deeply into the real workings of the "SportsWorld" (Lipsyte, 1975), and the print medium is much more disposed to in-depth analysis than is television (Postman, 1985). Because television is so much a part of the way most people experience sport, recognition of the antisociological bias in televised sport may be a first step in developing greater public awareness of the ideological work embedded in sports programming.

REFERENCES

Critcher, C. (1987). Media spectacles: Sport and mass communication. In A. Cashadan (Ed.), *Studies in communication.* Oxford: Blackwell.

Duncan, M. C., & Brummett, B. (1987). The mediation of spectator sport. *Research Quarterly, 58,* 168–177.

Eitzen, D.S. (1992). Sports and ideological contradictions: Learning from the cultural framing of Soviet values. *Journal of Sport & Social Issues,* 16 (2), 144–149.

Fiske, J. (1987). *Television culture.* New York: Methuen.

Gitlin, T. (1980). *The whole world is watching. Berkeley:* University of California Press.

Gitlin, T. (1985). *Inside prime time.* New York: Pantheon.

Gitlin, T. (1986). We build excitement. In T. Gitlin (Ed.), *Watching television* (pp. 136–161). New York: Pantheon.

Gitlin, T. (1987). Television's screens: Hegemony in transition. In D. Lazare (Ed.), *American media and mass culture* (pp. 240–265). Berkeley: University of California Press.

Gruneau, R. (1989). Making spectacle: A case study in television sports production. In L. Wenner (Ed.), *Media, sports & society* (pp. 134–154). Newbury Park, CA: Sage.

Hallin, D. (1986). We keep America on top of the world. In T. Gitlin (Ed.), *Watching television* (pp. 9–41). New York: Pantheon.

Hargreaves, J. (1986). *Sport, power and culture.* New York: St. Martin's.

Jhally, S. (1989). Cultural studies and the sports/media complex. In L. Wenner (Ed.), *Media, sports & society* (pp. 70–93). Newbury Park, CA: Sage.

Lipsyte, R. (1975). *SportsWorld.* New York: Quadrangle.

Miller, M. C. (1986). Deride and conquer. In T. Gitlin (Ed.), *Watching television* (pp. 183–228). New York: Pantheon.

Miller, M. C. (1988). *Boxed in: The culture of TV.* Evanston, IL: Northwestern University Press.

Postman, N. (1985). *Amusing ourselves to death.* New York: Viking.

Sage, G. (1990). *Power and ideology in American sport.* Champaign, IL: Human Kinetics.

Sorkin, M. (1986). Faking it. In T. Gitlin (Ed.), *Watching television* (pp. 162–182). New York: Pantheon.

Theberge, N., & Cronk, A. (1986). Work routines in newspaper sports departments and the coverage of women's sports. *Sociology of Sport Journal, 3,* 195–203.

8

Center of Attention

The Gender of Sports Media

Michael A. Messner

More than ninety thousand fans at the Rose Bowl, in Pasadena, California, were on their feet cheering. Millions more were enjoying the dramatic moment in front of their television sets. It was July 10, 1999, and soccer star Brandi Chastain had just blasted the game-winning kick past the Chinese goalie. The U.S. team had won the World Cup, culminating several weeks of intense excitement that included print and electronic media saturation, the extent of which was unprecedented in the history of U.S. women's sports. The day after the championship match, a newspaper reporter called me and asked, "Do you think that the tremendous attention that these women are getting will spill over into greater media coverage of women's sports in general?" My answer was simple: "Well, that depends on you, doesn't it?"

In fact, during that exciting moment for women's sports in the United States, my colleagues Margaret Carlisle Duncan and Cheryl Cooky and I were collecting data for a study on gender in televised sports that, among other things, compared the quantity and quality of televised news coverage of women's and men's sports. We had conducted this study previously, first in 1989 and then again in 1993, so we had baseline data with which to compare our 1999 data.[1] What we found—that over the course of the decade of the 1990s very little had changed in the ways televised sports news covered women's and men's sports—ran counter to the common belief that there has been a recent explosion of media attention given to women's sports. After

Source: Michael A. Messner, *Taking the Field: Women, Men, and Sports* (Minneapolis: University of Minnesota Press, 2002), excerpt from pp. 91–106.

all, wasn't the news coverage of the women's soccer team's World Cup victory amazing? And didn't it seem during the weeks leading up to the 2000 Olympic Games in Sydney that everywhere one turned, one saw magazine covers, commercial advertisements, television images, and commentary that trumpeted the arrival of U.S. women athletes such as track star Marion Jones, soccer teammates Mia Hamm and Brandi Chastain, and swimming champion Jenny Thompson? Where women athletes used to be simply ignored (what George Gerbner in 1978 referred to more generally as the "symbolic annihilation" of women in the media), weren't we now witnessing an exploding array of images and celebratory commentary about women athletes?[2]

We have indeed entered a new era in media coverage and cultural imagery of women's sports. Women athletes are no longer simply "symbolically annihilated." There is, in fact, a larger and more varied array of images and commentary of athletic women than ever before. Electronic entertainment, in particular, has grown dramatically. However the proliferation of cable television, the Internet, specialized sports magazines and sports radio talk shows has not launched a feminist revolution in sport. To the contrary, it has set the stage for the creation and exploitation of new, ever more precisely defined marketing niches. What this means is that respectful coverage of women's sports can easily be relegated to small, marginal cable channels, web sites, or specialized magazines.[3] While this may be good for a few fans of women's sports, it leaves largely intact the masculinist cultural center of the sport-media-commercial complex. To begin with but one example, in its December 2000 issue, *Sports Illustrated for Women,* a magazine that began publishing in 1997, featured a triumphant cover photo of tennis player Venus Williams, with the caption "Venus! Sportswoman of the Year," along with "We Salute the Women Who Ruled in 2000." The existence of this magazine and its celebration of Williams and other women athletes surely can be viewed as a sign of progress for women's sports and as a new source of positive imagery for girls and women. However, and ironically, the very existence of *Sports Illustrated for Women* (which issues bimonthly to 400,000 readers) may leave the parent (father?) magazine, *Sports Illustrated* (a weekly with 3.15 million readers), off the hook in terms of any obligation its publishers and editors might otherwise have felt to incorporate more and better women's sports reporting. With Venus and the other "women who ruled in 2000" safely in the ghetto of *SI for Women,* the magazine that represents the cultural center for print sports media can present itself as standing above gender (notice, it's not called *Sports Illustrated for Men*),[4] representing all of sports and naming Tiger Woods as sportsman of the year.

Much of the emergent cultural imagery of women's sports is relegated to the margins of the mass media, thus leaving the masculinist center mostly intact. But still, the enthusiasm for women's sports is expanding too quickly for the imagery of women athletes to be totally and continually ghettoized. The proliferation of images of women athletes is (increasingly, I think) making sports media a contested ideological terrain, where meanings of sexuality, gender, and race are being contested and reconstructed.[5] In this chapter, I will look at how the cultural center, what I refer to as the sport-media-commercial complex, has responded to the explosion of women's sports participation. Next, I will describe the dominant images that come out of the masculinist cultural center of sport. After discussing the ways that the media deal with the common problems and contradictions that are generated at the institutional center of sports, I will end the chapter by raising questions about audiences and consumers of sports media.

SILENCE, SPORTS BRAS, AND WRESTLING PORN

Girls' and women's increased sports participation rates and the rapid closing of the muscle and performance gaps between women and men are far too dramatic to be entirely ignored by the mass media.[6] How has the sport-media-commercial complex responded to the explosion of female athleticism? There are four patterned ways that the dominant sports media deal with women's sports: silence, humorous sexualization, backlash, and selective incorporation of standout women athletes.

Silence

When my colleagues and I looked at the coverage of women's sports in three network affiliates' televised news broadcasts, the most striking finding of our analysis was the lack of change over the past decade. In the 1990 and 1994 studies, we noted that female athletes rarely received coverage on the televised sports news. As Table 8-1 shows, the latest study revealed only a slight increase in the proportion of sports news devoted to coverage of women's sports and women athletes over the ten-year time period.

Even worse was ESPN's popular sports highlights show *SportsCenter,* which earned its name as "sport's *center*" by devoting only 2.2 percent of its coverage to women's sports.[7] *SportsCenter's* ironic, often snidely humorous style, described by sport scholar Grant Farred as "cool as the other side of the pillow,"[8] has successfully set the tone for the growth of other sports highlights shows that also appear to offer up a standard staple of men's baseball, men's basketball, men's football, with occasional smidgens of men's ice hockey, auto racing, and some golf and tennis.

Table 8-1. Percentage distribution of network sports news, by sex

	1989	1993	1999
Men	92.0	93.8	88.2
Women	5.0	5.1	8.7
Neutral or both			
Men and women	3.0	1.1	3.1

Humorous Sexualization

To simply point out that the network affiliates devoted 8.2 percent and *SportsCenter* 2.2 percent of their air time to women's sports actually *overstates* the extent to which women's sports were given fair and respectful coverage on these shows. A qualitative analysis of the ways that women and men are presented on the sports news reveals further gender asymmetries. Two themes that persisted from the previous studies were (1) the choice to devote a considerable proportion of the already-thin coverage of women's sports to humorous feature stories on nonserious women's sports, and (2) the (often humorous) sexualization of athlete women and nonathlete women.

As in the earlier studies, we found in 1999 that while most of the few reports on serious women's sports (such as basketball, tennis, golf, and soccer) were fairly brief, the occasional, more in-depth women's sports story was often a gag feature or a story on a marginal, but visually entertaining, pseudosport. For instance, two stations did long features on a "nude bungee jumping" story, including a film clip of the nude woman, strategically painted with St. Patrick's Day green shamrocks, leaping from a bridge while the commentator asked, "Do we have to slow that down?" When interviewed, the bungee jumper said, "That was amazing. I will remember it forever," to which the commentator replied, "And so will we," as co-anchors laughed along with him. Similarly, two stations offered up lengthy feature stories on the wrestler-model Sable. Sable was aiming to promote World Wrestling Federation (WWF) wrestling, but reporters emphasized her scanty, dominatrix-style attire and her appearance in *Playboy* magazine. One station devoted twenty-seven seconds at 6:00 p.m. and twenty-one seconds at 11:00 p.m. to Sable and reported on no other women's sports during those shows. Sable was shown at a photo shoot (not wrestling), with a commentator noting, "As you can see, Sable doesn't keep much behind the scenes herself." Another station's coverage of Sable was even more in-depth: at two minutes and forty-eight seconds, this was the longest single news story on women's sports in our 1999 sample. The news commentator invited viewers into this story by stating, "We're your source for wrestling porn." He then described Sable as a "sexy villainess" and insulted her in an interview by asking if she could count to ten. When, with a disgusted look on her face, she did so, the commentator countered, "Ah, yes: beauty and brains." He went on to joke approvingly about Sable's appearance in *Playboy,* and after a film clip of her wrestling (in slow motion in a bikini), he concluded by saluting and saying, "Sable, a champion of women's rights. We salute her." This station then managed to squeeze a ten-second report on women's tennis into its 11:00 p.m. show, but the Sable story otherwise represented all the coverage of "women's sports" that day.

The wrestling porn comment about Sable seems to express an unstated policy among many sports news commentators: part of the entertainment of sports news shows is the opportunity they present for viewers to engage in sexual voyeurism. The producers supply the images, and the commentators supply the locker-room humor. For instance, a commentator discussed the NFL's decision to allow referees once again to use an instant replay to review on-field decisions: "The problem," he dead-panned as viewers were shown a clip of referees huddled around a monitor, "[is] what will the referees actually be looking at: the play, or as we found out, something else?" Next, viewers got a peek at what the referees were supposedly watching on the moni-tor: a Victoria's Secret fashion show and a clip of the movie *Eyes Wide Shut,* with Tom Cruise kissing Nicole Kidman while both appear naked.

If women athletes in sexy pseudosports fail to supply television news commen-tators with enough material for sexual titillation, there is a supporting cast of nonathlete women who are available for humorous voyeurism. Two of the three network affili-ates continually offered viewers visual shots of young bikini-clad women in the sun-drenched stands of baseball games, often adding their own tongue-in-cheek com-ments about the women's attractiveness. For instance, a commentator enthusiastically said, "Helloooooo Pittsburgh!" while viewers were treated to a shot of a woman in the stands. The next day, when viewers were presented an image of a blond woman in a crop-top, the same commentator said, "Speaking of perfect, it was a perfect day today in Anaheim." Sexually humorous stories and references to other women in supportive nonathlete roles were sprinkled throughout the news reports. One station took up nearly three minutes of combined broadcast time on its two July 25, 1999, broadcasts reporting on "Laker Girl" (cheerleader) tryouts: among other things, viewers learned that it was the job of these "sizzling beauties" to "sex it up" on TV.

The sports news' humorous focus on scantily clad women spectators, cheer-leaders, and nude or nearly nude women in pseudosports makes a conventionally conservative statement about women's "place"—on the sidelines, in support roles, and as objects of sexualized humor—in a cultural realm that is still defined, at least in these TV programs, as a man's world. But it is the humorous sexualization of actual women athletes that brings into sharpest focus some of the current paradoxes of gender and sexuality swirling around women's sports. In the aftermath of the World Cup championship by the U.S. soccer team, two television stations focused little on the accomplishments of the team and instead continued to reintroduce the story about soccer star Brandi Chastain's having, at the moment of victory, stripped off her jersey, revealing her sports bra. One commentator seemed unable to resist the Chastain sports bra story. Three days in a row, he made joking references to this story. First, he reported, "Today, the ponytail express stopped in midtown Manhattan, where it was announced that Nike will exploit Brandi Chastain's striptease by fashioning her to a line of sports bras." The next day, he noted that the women soccer players' "ponytail express" appeared in a golf tournament and that Chastain managed to keep her shirt on but "took off her sweater during warm-ups." And then on the next day, in a humorous spoof on the film *Eyes Wide Shut,* the sports news included a clip of Chastain in her sports bra as part of a collage of half-clothed people. Said the commentator, "It seems like Hollywood is really influencing the sports world. Everybody's getting na-ked. I'm not complaining. That's just the way it is."[9]

Sports news commentators' penchant for sexual humor about women athletes has not been confined to soccer players. A story on a tennis match between Mary

Pierce and Anna Kournikova focused typically on Kournikova's image as a sexually attractive young woman. Noting her boyfriend in the crowd, the commentator said, "That's what it takes to date Anna Kournikova: you have to be willing to go watch her play in the afternoon and then fly across the country and play yourself at night. . . . And it's well worth it, I think most would agree." He and the anchorperson then shared a knowing laugh. As I write this, Kournikova has still never won a major tournament. Nevertheless, she garners about ten million dollars a year in corporate endorsements (fifty-eighth on the *Forbes* worldwide celebrity power list), has appeared on the covers of *Esquire, Forbes, Vogue,* and *Cosmopolitan,* [10] and has scores of official and unofficial web sites devoted to her.[11] Simply put, Anna Kournikova is a major icon in popular culture, and her quick rise to such prominence, at least as much for her physical appearance as for her on-court tennis accomplishments, has made her a lightning rod for debates about media sexualization of women athletes. In its June 5, 2000, issue, *Sports Illustrated (SI)* ran a cover story on Kournikova that made no pretenses that it was focusing not on her tennis abilities but on her sexual attractiveness.[12] In response, the Women's Sports Foundation slammed *SI:*

> We see a 19-year-old, #15 ranked tennis player primarily illustrated by photographs of her in short skirts, slit skirts, off-the-shoulder gypsy blouses or with eligible men with only two tennis action shots out of 11 photos. *This is not about journalistic integrity. This is about selling magazines.* When circulation declines, put sex on the cover. . . . Female athletes should be portrayed as athletes in athletic uniforms displaying their sports skills. When have we ever seen major sports periodicals depicting Michael Jordan or other male athletes stuffed into tight-fitting uniforms that display their genitalia as a way of getting more women to buy magazines?[13]

This sort of response to *SI*'s (and other media's) unabashed celebratory sexploitation of the image of Kournikova has been criticized by sport historian Allen Guttmann as typical of feminists' tendency to deny the obviously erotic nature of sports:

> Many feminist sport sociologists continue, however, to deny the erotic attraction of the female athlete and to blame the mass media for what they—the feminists— call "sexualization," a term that implicitly denies the sexuality inherent in the athletic performance and the athletic body upon which that performance is inscribed.[14]

Guttmann is correct to be wary of the antisex neo-Victorianism present in a strand of Western feminism, and he is certainly correct in asserting that many people find erotic pleasure in sports spectating. However, his argument that "the athletic body" is inherently "erotic" ignores the *profoundly social* dynamic that underlies not only what is defined as "sexual" but also how mass media displays of sexuality are *contextualized* in cultural discourses that are defined by, and in turn help to define, group power relations. Former tennis star and feminist activist Billie Jean King understands this context. In her response to the Kournikova *SI* issue, King underlined that pro tennis is a sexualized commercial enterprise that is characterized by an asymmetrical gender dynamic:

> It doesn't bother me at all if some of the guys come out to watch women's tennis because they want to see a beautiful woman. Who could hold that against Anna? Still, it's unfortunate when others with a high skill factor don't win the endorsements. Sure, the good-looking guys get more endorsements, but the difference in men's sports is that the ugly ones get their share, too.[15]

King, of course, knows from her own experience that on the women's tour, "others" fail to win the big endorsement money not always because they are "ugly" but because they are not (or are suspected of not being) heterosexual.[16] Heterosexually attractive women athletes are actively used by professional women's leagues like the LPGA and the WNBA to promote their sport with consumers.[17] In the words of sports media scholar Pamela Creedon, promoters know that "little girls and sweethearts sell. . . . Homosexuality doesn't sell."[18] And media people who are friendly to women's sports will often play along with this strategy, thinking that they are helping to promote women's sports by dispelling the myth that all women athletes must be masculine dykes. But even when it is a well-meaning strategy to promote sports for girls and women, the practice of foregrounding the heterosexually attractive women in order to promote a sport tends symbolically to erase lesbian, bisexual, queer, and unfeminine-appearing women. It also costs these "other" women thousands, sometimes millions, of dollars in lost endorsement money. And it contributes to a restabilization of narrow cultural codes of heterosexual femininity that have been restrictive for girls and women.

The racial context of Kournikova's meteoric rise to (hetero)sex-goddess celebrity status is equally important. The blond, tanned, long-limbed, and lightly muscled Kournikova clearly conforms to dominant cultural standards of white feminine beauty. Her form of beauty stands in stark contrast to the highly muscular and very black bodies of ascendant young stars Serena and Venus Williams. The Williams sisters appear to be challenging dominant cultural definitions of feminine beauty and expanding these definitions to include both muscularity and blackness; by contrast, the elevation of Kournikova to celebrity status can be read as a market-driven reassertion of conventional and culturally dominant white definitions of feminine beauty.[19]

Surely, as a *Sports Illustrated* marketing ploy, the Kournikova issue was a smashing success, following in the footsteps of the magazine's highly lucrative swimwear issue, which has become a huge, multimedia, annual cultural event.[20] But the cultural significance of these sexploitation issues of a popular national sports magazine must be read against the backdrop of what the magazine normally does, which is to cover the central *men's* sports, week after week, year after year. In the 123 issues of the magazine from 1998 until the Kournikova issue came out, *Sports Illustrated* published only five covers featuring women athletes: basketball coach Pat Summit, figure skater Michelle Kwan, tennis player Serena Williams, soccer player Brandi Chastain (in her sports bra), and the U.S. women's World Cup team—that's 4 percent of the covers devoted to women's sports. It is against the backdrop of the near absence of respectful stories of women athletes in mainstream magazines such as *Sports Illustrated* that the cultural meanings of sexualized features like the Kournikova issue or the annual swimmer issue must be read and interpreted. The mass media, it seems, are much more likely to pull women athletes to the center of cultural discourse when they are athletes who can be appreciated and exploited for their sexual appeal. Otherwise, they are relegated to the margins of the cultural radar screen.

However, this notion of the culture industry pulling certain women to the center while pushing others out to the margins of cultural discourse is still less than adequate to explain the "sexualization" of some women athletes. After all, many will argue that nobody "forces" Anna Kournikova, swimmer Jenny Thompson, or high jumper Amy Acuff to pose nearly nude or in sexy clothes that suggest heterosexual access for national magazines or calendars. It's a mistake simply to view these athletes as disempowered dupes who have allowed themselves to be "objectified" by a powerful cultural system. We must also take into account the agency of the women doing the posing. These are strong and talented young women who believe that they are making choices about their lives and their bodies. What's more, they often see no contradiction between projecting an aesthetic of desirable heterosexual femininity *and* an athletic habitus of physical strength, power, and competence. This thinking, scholars like Susan Bordo argue, is explained by an emergent breakdown in the cultural codings of masculinity and femininity as bipolar dominant-subordinate opposites.[21] And this change is especially evident among younger women, many of whom are forging new conceptions of feminine attractiveness that include muscular power. For example, when *Sports Illustrated* ran a pre-Olympics photo of swimmer Jenny Thompson, standing in a powerful pose, wearing only red boots and Wonder Woman shorts, with her fists covering her bare breasts, debate raged over the photo's meanings. Donna Lopiano of the Women's Sports Foundation told *Sports Illustrated for Women*, "It's incongruous to take that body you've worked so hard for and use it for sex."

But to Jenny Thompson, there was nothing incongruous in her pose. She disagreed vehemently with the contention that *Sports Illustrated* had turned her into a disempowered sexualized object:

> My stance in the picture was one of strength and power and *girls rule!* It's nothing sexual. I wasn't pouting or giving a sexual look. I was like, here I am. I'm strong. The body is something to be celebrated, and Olympians have amazing bodies. So I think its a work of art. . . . Someone called this—this idea of being proud of who you are and willing to show it off—a new feminism. I think that's pretty cool: I've started a new feminism.[22]

Indeed, cultural studies scholar Leslie Heywood argues that it is a mistake to employ second-wave feminist concepts of sexual objectification to interpret the meanings of some women athletes' willingness to pose nearly naked. Heywood observes that the Thompson photo in *SI* "expresses neither seductiveness nor vulnerability" and is thus not so easily seen as business-as-usual passive feminine objectification:

> Contemporary gender codes cannot be so easily polarized as they once were, though images like the Kournikova spread seek to reinforce them. . . . Female athletes in the generations post–Title IX have come to redeem the erasure of individual women that the old *Playboy* model sexualization performs, rewriting the symbology of the female body from empty signifiers of ready access, blank canvases or holes on which to write one's desires, to the active, self-present sexuality of a body that signifies achievement and power. The athletic body, when coded as athletic, redeems female sexuality and makes it visible as an assertion of female presence.[23]

This assertion that female athletes are active agents whose actions and images are rewriting the cultural symbology of women's bodies in ways that incorporate sexuality as part of the project of empowerment accurately reflects an emergent sensibility that Heywood and others have called "third wave feminism."[24] However, Heywood's optimistic conclusion that we are now witnessing a "new iconography that redeems sexuality from objectification and women from codes of easy access and vulnerability" needs to be considered cautiously, within a broad, institutional analysis. If the powerful-sexy shots of women continue mostly to be relegated to the sports ghettos of *ESPN2* or *Sports Illustrated for Women*, this leaves the larger, more central institutions like *Sports Illustrated* and *SportsCenter* off the hook, still at the center, and able to continue to spew out an almost unabated stream of reporting and imagery that largely erases women or sexualizes them in trivial ways. Given this institutional pattern, we must temper our optimism concerning the growing gender fluidity and sexual symmetries in popular imagery of males and females. These images exist, but they are mostly out there in market niches that are peripheral with respect to the cultural center of sport imagery, where a male-as-subject, female-as-object asymmetry still largely prevails.

NOTES

1. The three studies were based on 1989, 1993, and 1999 data and were published in 1990, 1994, and 2000, respectively. See: Amateur Athletic Foundation of Los Angeles, *Gender Stereotyping in Televised Sports*; Amateur Athletic Foundation of Los Angeles, *Gender Stereotyping in Televised Sports: A Followup to the 1989 Study*; Amateur Athletic Foundation of Los Angeles, *Gender in Televised Sports: 1989, 1993, and 1999*.

2. Gerbner, "The Dynamics of Cultural Resistance."

3. It is of course debatable whether new media sources should simply be looked at as "marginal" to the traditional center of sports media or whether or perhaps new developments will involve the growth

of multiple "centers." This question is perhaps most applicable to the development of what Stephen McDaniel and Christopher Sullivan call "cybersport." See McDaniel and Sullivan, "Extending the Sports Experience."

4. A key part of the symbolic marginalization of women's sports and women athletes is asymmetrical gender marking. Men's events, leagues, and records are symbolically represented as the universal norm (e.g., "the national championship game," "the National Basketball Association," and "the most points ever scored in a game"), while women's events, leagues, and records are always gender marked (e.g., "the women's national championship game," "the ?Women's National Basketball Association," and "the most points ever scored in a women's game"). This asymmetrical gender marking tends to position women's sports and women athletes symbolically as secondary and derivative to men's sports. My colleagues and I have tracked this asymmetrical gender marking in our studies of women's and men's televised sports. See Messner, Duncan, and Jensen, "Separating the Men from the Girls"; Amateur Athletic Foundation of Los Angeles, *Gender in Televised Sports: 1989, 1993, and 1999.*.

5. I first made the argument that women athletes represent a "contested ideological terrain" in the late 1980s. With participation rates of girls and women continuing to rise and with the expansion of electronic media and commercialization of women's sports beginning to grow, this ideological contest has continued but shifted. Messner, "Sports and Male Domination." There is also a rich foundation of research on ways that the mass media have covered women athletes. Key texts and overviews of the research include Duncan and Hasbrook., "Denial of Power in Televised Women's Sports"; Cohen, "Media Portrayals of the Female Athlete"; and Kane, "Media Coverage of the Post-Title IX Female Athlete."

6. Parts of this section of the chapter were previously published in Messner, Duncan, and Cooky, "Silence, Sports Bras, and Wrestling Porn."

7. The finding in our study that *SportsCenter* devoted only 2.2 percent of its airtime to covering women athletes and women's sports was consistent with findings in other recent studies. Eastman and Billings, "Sportscasting and Sports Reporting." Billings also observed that ESPN's highly promoted series of shows on their "top one hundred athletes of the century" included eighty-nine men, eight women, and three horses. As such, the list echoes cultural biases against women athletes in the past and reinforces them today. Billings, "In Search of Women Athletes."

8. Farred, "Cool as the Other Side of the Pillow."

9. Amateur Athletic Foundation of Los Angeles, *Gender in Televised Sports.*

10. As noted in Deford, "Advantage, Kournikova," 97, 100.

11. On the basis of a Lykos.com count of hits on sports celebrities' web sites, Kournikova ranked number one in early 2001. Sable was two, followed by fellow wrestlers Trish Stratus and the Rock. Basketball players Michael Jordan and Vince Carter ranked numbers five and six, respectively, followed by golfer Tiger Woods (seven), basketball player Allen Iverson (eight), tennis player Martina Hingis (nine), and skateboarder Tony Hawk (ten). This sort of list is most likely a good indicator of the celebrity tastes of young sports fans who have internet access. "Now You Know."

12. Deford, "Advantage, Kournikova."

13. As quoted in Amateur Athletic Foundation of Los Angeles, *Sports-letter,* 1.

14. Guttmann, "Nature, Nurture, and the Athletic Body." Guttmann develops these ideas more fully in his book *The Erotic in Sport.*

15. As quoted in Amateur Athletic Foundation of Los Angeles, *Sports-letter,* 1.

16. In 1970, King led a boycott in protest of pay inequities between women and men on the pro tennis tour and within three years launched the separate women's Virginia Slims pro tour.

17. Sport studies scholar Pat Griffin notes that the existence of lesbians in sports has been met with various kinds of homophobic response that she categorizes as silence, denial, apology, promotion of a heterosexy image, attacks on lesbians, and preference for male coaches. See Griffin, "Changing the Game." See also Griffin, *Strong Women, Deep Closets*; Lenskyj, "Sexuality and Femininity in Sport Contexts"; and Kane and Lenskyj, "Media Treatment of Female Athletes."

18. Creedon, "Women, Sport, and Media Institutions." This trend has been noted by sport scholars in Australia as well. See Lenskyj, "'Inside Sport' or 'On the Margins'?"; and Mikosza and Phillips, "Gender, Sport and the Body Politic."

19. For informative discussions of race and gender in cultural definitions of feminine beauty, see Banet-Weiser, *The Most Beautiful Girl in the World*; Chancer, *Reconcilable Differences*; Collins, *Black Feminist Thought*; and Zones, "Beauty Myths and Realities and Their Impact on Women's Health."

20. Davis, *The Swimsuit Issue and Sport.*

21. Bordo, *The Male Body.*

22. Anderson, "The Other Side of Jenny," 120–21.

23. Heywood, "Bodies, Babes, and the WNBA, or, Where's Tiger Naked in a Cape When You Really Need Him?"

24. Heywood and Drake, eds., *Third Wave Agenda.*

9

The Televised Sports Manhood Formula

Michael A. Messner, Michele Dunbar
Darnell Hunt

A recent national survey found 8- to 17-year-old children to be avid consumers of sports media, with television most often named as the preferred medium (Amateur Athletic Foundation of Los Angeles, 1999). Although girls watch sports in great numbers, boys are markedly more likely to report that they are regular consumers of televised sports. The most popular televised sports with boys, in order, are pro football, men's pro basketball, pro baseball, pro wrestling, men's college basketball, college football, and Extreme sports.[1] Although counted separately in the Amateur Athletic Foundation (AAF) study, televised sports highlights shows also were revealed to be tremendously popular with boys.

What are boys seeing and hearing when they watch these programs? What kinds of values concerning gender, race, aggression, violence, and consumerism are boys exposed to when they watch their favorite televised sports programs, with their accompanying commercials? This chapter, based on a textual analysis, presents the argument that televised sports, and their accompanying commercials, consistently present boys with a narrow portrait of masculinity, which we call the Televised Sports Manhood Formula.

SAMPLE AND METHOD

We analyzed a range of televised sports that were identified by the AAF study as those programs most often watched by boys. Most of the programs in our sample aired during a single week, May 23–29, 1999, with one exception. Because pro football is

Source: Michael A. Messner, Michele Dunbar, and Darnell Hunt, "The Televised Sports Manhood Formula," *Journal of Sport & Social Issues* 24 (November 2000), pp. 380–394.

not in season in May, we acquired tapes of two randomly chosen National Football League (NFL) *Monday Night Football* games from the previous season to include in our sample. We analyzed televised coverage, including commercials and pregame, halftime, and postgame shows (when appropriate), for the following programs:

1. two broadcasts of *SportsCenter* on ESPN (2 hours of programming);
2. two broadcasts of Extreme sports, one on ESPN and one on Fox Sports West (approximately 90 minutes of programming);
3. two broadcasts of professional wrestling, including *Monday Night Nitro* on TNT and *WWF Superstars* on USA (approximately 2 hours of programming);
4. two broadcasts of National Basketball Association (NBA) play-off games, one on TNT and the other on NBC (approximately 7 hours of programming);
5. two broadcasts of NFL *Monday Night Football* on ABC (approximately 7 hours of programming); and
6. one broadcast of Major League Baseball (MLB) on TBS (approximately 3 hours of programming).

We conducted a textual analysis of the sports programming and the commercials. In all, we examined about 23 hours of sports programming, nearly one quarter of which was time taken up by commercials. We examined a total of 722 commercials, which spanned a large range of products and services. We collected both quantitative and qualitative data. Although we began with some sensitizing concepts that we knew we wanted to explore (e.g., themes of violence, images of gender and race, etc.), rather than starting with preset categories we used an inductive method that allowed the dominant themes to emerge from our reading of the tapes.

Each taped show was given a first reading by one of the investigators, who then constructed a preliminary analysis of the data. The tape was then given a second reading by another of the investigators. This second independent reading was then used to modify and sharpen the first reading. Data analysis proceeded along the lines of the categories that emerged in the data collection. The analyses of each separate sport were then put into play with each other and common themes and patterns were identified. In one case, the dramatic pseudosport of professional wrestling, we determined that much of the programming was different enough that it made little sense to directly compare it with the other sports shows; therefore, we only included data on wrestling in our comparisons when it seemed to make sense to do so.

DOMINANT THEMES IN TELEVISED SPORTS

Our analysis revealed that sports programming presents boys with narrow and stereotypical messages about race, gender, and violence. We identified 10 distinct themes that, together, make up the Televised Sports Manhood Formula.

Table 9-1 Race and Sex of Announcers

White Men	White Women	Black Men	Black Women
24	3	3	1

WHITE MALES ARE THE VOICES OF AUTHORITY

Although one of the two *SportsCenter* segments in the sample did feature a White woman coanchor, the play-by-play and ongoing color commentary in NFL, wrestling, NBA, Extreme sports, and MLB broadcasts were conducted exclusively by White, male play-by play commentators.

With the exception of *SportsCenter,* women and Blacks never appeared as the main voices of authority in the booth conducting play-by-play or ongoing color commentary. The NFL broadcasts occasionally cut to field-level color commentary by a White woman, but her commentary was very brief (about 3½ minutes of the nearly 3 hours of actual game and pregame commentary). Similarly, one of the NBA broadcasts used a Black man for occasional on-court analysis and a Black man for pregame and halftime analysis, whereas the other NBA game used a White woman as host in the pregame show and a Black woman for occasional on-court analysis. Although viewers commonly see Black male athletes—especially on televised NBA games—they rarely hear or see Black men or women as voices of authority in the broadcast booth (Sabo & Jansen, 1994). In fact, the only Black commentators that appeared on the NBA shows that we examined were former star basketball players (Cheryl Miller, Doc Rivers, and Isaiah Thomas). A Black male briefly appeared to welcome the audience to open one of the Extreme sports shows but he did not do any play-by-play; in fact, he was used only to open the show with a stylish, street, hip-hop style for what turned out to be an almost totally White show.

SPORTS IS A MAN'S WORLD

Images or discussion of women athletes is almost entirely absent in the sports programs that boys watch most. *SportsCenter*'s mere 2.9% of news time devoted to women's sports is slightly lower than the 5% to 6% of women's sports coverage commonly found in other sports news studies (Duncan & Messner, 1998). In addition, *SportsCenter*'s rare discussion of a women's sport seemed to follow men's in newsworthiness (e.g., a report on a Professional Golfers' Association [PGA] tournament was followed by a more brief report on a Ladies Professional Golf Association [LPGA] tournament). The baseball, basketball, wrestling, and football programs we watched were men's contests so they could not perhaps have been expected to cover or mention women athletes. However, Extreme sports are commonly viewed as "alternative" or "emerging" sports in which women are challenging masculine hegemony (Wheaton & Tomlinson, 1998). Despite this, the Extreme sports shows we

Table 9-2 Sex Composition of 722 Commercials

Men Only	Women Only	Women and Men	No People
279 (38.6%)	28 (3.9%)	324 (44.9%)	91 (12.6%)

watched devoted only a single 50-second interview segment to a woman athlete. This segment constituted about 1% of the total Extreme sports programming and, significantly, did not show this woman athlete in action. Perhaps this limited coverage of women athletes on the Extreme sports shows we examined is evidence of what Rinehart (1998) calls a "pecking order" in alternative sports, which develops when new sports are appropriated and commodified by the media.

MEN ARE FOREGROUNDED IN COMMERCIALS

The idea that sports is a man's world is reinforced by the gender composition and imagery in commercials. Women almost never appear in commercials unless they are in the company of men, as Table 9-2 shows.

That 38.6% of all commercials portray only men actually understates the extent to which men dominate these commercials for two reasons. First, nearly every one of the 91 commercials that portrayed no visual portrayals of people included a male voice-over. When we include this number, we see that more than 50% of commercials provide men-only images and/or voiceovers, whereas only 3.9% portray only women. Moreover, when we combine men-only and women and men categories, we see that men are visible in 83.5% of all commercials and men are present (when we add in the commercials with male voice-overs) in 96.1% of all commercials. Second, in the commercials that portray both women and men, women are often (although not exclusively) portrayed in stereotypical, and often very minor, background roles.

WOMEN ARE SEXY PROPS OR PRIZES FOR MEN'S SUCCESSFUL SPORT PERFORMANCES OR CONSUMPTION CHOICES

Although women were mostly absent from sports commentary, when they did appear it was most often in stereotypical roles as sexy, masculinity-validating props, often cheering the men on. For instance, "X-sports" on Fox Sports West used a bikini-clad blonde woman as a hostess to welcome viewers back after each commercial break as the camera moved provocatively over her body Although she mentioned the show's sponsors, she did not narrate the actual sporting event. The wrestling shows generously used scantily clad women (e.g., in pink miniskirts or tight Spandex and high heels) who overtly displayed the dominant cultural signs of heterosexy attractiveness[2] to escort the male wrestlers

Table 9-3 Instances of Women Being Depicted as Sexy Props or Prizes for Men

	SportsCenter	Extreme	Wrestling	NBA	MLB	NFL
Commercials	5	5	3	10	4	6
Sport programs	0	5	13	3	0	4
Total	5	10	16	13	4	10

Note: NBA = National Basketball Association, MLB = Major League Baseball, and NFL = National Football League.

to the ring, often with announcers discussing the women's provocative physical appearance. Women also appeared in the wrestling shows as sexually provocative dancers (e.g., the "Gorgeous Nitro Girls" on TNT).

In commercials, women are numerically more evident, and generally depicted in more varied roles, than in the sports programming. Still, women are underrepresented and rarely appear in commercials unless they are in the company of men. Moreover, as Table 9-3 illustrates, the commercials' common depiction of women as sexual objects and as "prizes" for men's successful consumption choices articulates with the sports programs' presentation of women primarily as sexualized, supportive props for men's athletic performances. For instance, a commercial for Keystone Light Beer that ran on *SportsCenter* depicted two White men at a baseball game. When one of the men appeared on the stadium big screen and made an ugly face after drinking an apparently bitter beer, women appeared to be grossed out by him. But then he drank a Keystone Light and reappeared on the big screen looking good with two young, conventionally beautiful (fashion-model-like) women adoring him. He says, "I hope my wife's not watching!" as the two women flirt with the camera.

As Table 9-3 shows, in 23 hours of sports programming, viewers were exposed to 58 incidents of women being portrayed as sexy props and/or sexual prizes for men's successful athletic performances or correct consumption choices. Put another way, a televised sports viewer is exposed to this message, either in commercials or in the sports program itself, on an average of twice an hour. The significance of this narrow image of women as heterosexualized commodities should be considered especially in light of the overall absence of a wider range of images of women, especially as athletes (Duncan & Messner, 1998; Kane & Lenskyj, 1998).

WHITES ARE FOREGOUNDED IN COMMERICALS

The racial composition of the commercials is, if anything, more narrow and limited than the gender composition. As Table 9-4 shows, Black, Latino, or Asian American people almost never appear in commercials unless the commercial also has White people in it (the multiracial category in the table).

To say that 52.2% of the commercials portrayed only Whites actually understates the extent to which images of White people dominated the commercials for

Table 9-4 Racial Composition of 722 Commercials

White Only	Black Only	Latino/a Only	Asian Only	Multiracial	Undetermined	No People
377 (52.2%)	28 (3.9%)	3 (0.4%)	2 (0.3%)	203 (28.1%)	18 (2.5%)	91 (12.6%)

two reasons. First, if we subtract the 91 commercials that showed no actual people, then we see that the proportion of commercials that actually showed people was 59.7% White only. Second, when we examine the quality of the portrayals of Blacks, Latinos, and Asian Americans in the multiracial commercials, we see that people of color are far more often than not relegated to minor roles, literally in the background of scenes that feature Whites, and/or they are relegated to stereotypical or negative roles. For instance, a Wendy's commercial that appeared on several of the sports programs in our sample showed White customers enjoying a sandwich with the White owner while a barely perceptible Black male walked by in the background.

AGGRESSIVE PLAYERS GET THE PRIZE; NICE GUYS FINISH LAST

As Table 9-5 illustrates, viewers are continually immersed in images and commentary about the positive rewards that come to the most aggressive competitors and of the negative consequences of playing "soft" and lacking aggression.

Commentators consistently lauded athletes who most successfully employed physical and aggressive play and toughness. For instance, after having his toughness called into question, NBA player Brian Grant was awarded redemption by *SportsCenter* because he showed that he is "not afraid to take it to Karl Malone." *SportsCenter* also informed viewers that "the aggressor usually gets the calls [from the officials] and the Spurs were the ones getting them." In pro wrestling commentary, this is a constant theme (and was therefore not included in our tallies for Table 9-5 because the theme permeated the commentary, overtly and covertly). The World Wrestling Federation (WWF) announcers praised the "raw power" of wrestler "Shamrock" and approvingly dubbed "Hardcore Holly" as "the world's most dangerous man." NBA commentators suggested that it is okay to be a good guy off the court but one must be tough and aggressive on the court: Brian Grant and Jeff Hornacek are "true gentlemen

Table 9-5 Statements Lauding Aggression or Criticizing Lack of Aggression

SportsCenter	Extreme	NBA	MLB	NFL
3	4	40	4	15

Note: NBA = National Basketball Association, MLB = Major League Baseball, and NFL = National Football League.

Table 9-6 Humorous or Sarcastic Discussion of Fights or Near-Fights

SportsCenter	Extreme	NBA	MLB	NFL
10	1	2	2	7

Note: NBA = National Basketball Association, MLB = Major League Baseball, and NFL = National Football League.

of the NBA . . . as long as you don't have to play against them. You know they're great off the court; on the court, every single guy out there *should* be a killer."

When players were not doing well, they were often described as "hesitant" and lacking aggression, emotion, and desire (e.g., for a loose ball or rebound). For instance, commentators lamented that "the Jazz aren't going to the hoop, they're being pushed and shoved around," that Utah was responding to the Blazers' aggression "passively, in a reactive mode," and that "Utah's got to get Karl Malone toughened up." *SportsCenter* echoed this theme, opening one show with a depiction of Horace Grant elbowing Karl Malone and asking of Malone, "Is he feeble?" Similarly, NFL broadcasters waxed on about the virtues of aggression and domination. Big "hits"; ball carriers who got "buried," "stuffed," or "walloped" by the defense; and players who get "cleaned out" or "wiped out" by a blocker were often shown on replays, with announcers enthusiastically describing the plays. By contrast, they clearly declared that it is a very bad thing to be passive and to let yourself get pushed around and dominated at the line of scrimmage. Announcers also approvingly noted that going after an opposing player's injured body part is just smart strategy: In one NFL game, the Miami strategy to blitz the opposing quarterback was lauded as "brilliant"— "When you know your opposing quarterback is a bit nicked and something is wrong, Boomer, you got to come after him."

Previous research has pointed to this heroic framing of the male body-as-weapon as a key element in sports' role in the social construction of narrow conceptions of masculinity (Messner, 1992; Trujillo, 1995).

This injunction for boys and men to be aggressive, not passive, is reinforced in commercials, where a common formula is to play on the insecurities of young males (e.g., that they are not strong enough, tough enough, smart enough, rich enough, attractive enough, decisive enough, etc.) and then attempt to convince them to avoid, overcome, or mask their fears, embarrassments, and apparent shortcomings by buying a particular product. These commercials often portray men as potential or actual geeks, nerds, or passive schmucks who can overcome their geekiness (or avoid being a geek like the guy in the commercial) by becoming decisive and purchasing a particular product.

BOYS WILL BE (VIOLENT) BOYS

Announcers often took a humorous "boys will be boys" attitude in discussing fights or near-fights during contests, and they also commonly used a recent fight, altercation, or disagreement between two players as a "teaser" to build audience excitement.

Fights, near-fights, threats of fights, or other violent actions were overemphasized in sports coverage and often verbally framed in sarcastic language that suggested that this kind of action, although reprehensible, is to be expected. For instance, as *SportsCenter* showed NBA centers Robinson and O'Neill exchanging forearm shoves, the commentators said, simply, "much love." Similarly, in an NFL game, a brief scuffle between players is met with a sarcastic comment by the broadcaster that the players are simply "making their acquaintance." This is, of course, a constant theme in pro wrestling (which, again, we found impossible and less than meaningful to count because this theme permeates the show). We found it noteworthy that the supposedly spontaneous fights outside the wrestling ring (what we call unofficial fights) were given more coverage time and focus than the supposedly official fights inside the ring. We speculate that wrestling producers know that viewers already watch fights inside the ring with some skepticism as to their authenticity so they stage the unofficial fights outside the ring to bring a feeling of spontaneity and authenticity to the show and to build excitement and a sense of anticipation for the fight that will later occur inside the ring.

GIVE UP YOUR BODY FOR THE TEAM

Athletes who are "playing with pain," "giving up their body for the team," or engaging in obviously highly dangerous plays or maneuvers were consistently framed as heroes; conversely, those who removed themselves from games due to injuries had questions raised about their character, their manhood.

This theme cut across all sports programming. For instance, *SportsCenter* asked, "Could the dominator be soft?" when a National Hockey League (NHL) star goalie decided to sit out a game due to a groin injury. Heroically taking risks while already hurt was a constant theme in Extreme sports commentary. For instance, one bike competitor was lauded for "overcoming his fear" and competing "with a busted up ankle" and another was applauded when he "popped his collarbone out in the street finals in Louisville but he's back on his bike here in Richmond, just 2 weeks later!" Athletes appear especially heroic when they go against doctors' wishes not to compete. For instance, an X Games interviewer adoringly told a competitor, "Doctors said don't ride but you went ahead and did it anyway and escaped serious injury" Similarly, NBA player Isaiah Rider was lauded for having "heart" for "playing with that knee injury." Injury discussions in NFL games often include speculation about whether the player will be able to return to this or future games. A focus on a star player in a pregame or halftime show, such as the feature on 49ers' Garrison Hearst, often contain commentary about heroic overcoming of serious injuries (in this case, a knee blowout, reconstructive surgery, and rehabilitation). As one game began, commentators noted that 37-year-old "Steve Young has remained a rock . . . not bad for a guy who a lotta people figured was, what, one big hit from ending his career." It's especially impressive when an injured player is able and willing to continue to play with aggressiveness and reckless abandon: "Kurt Scrafford at right guard-bad neck and all—is just out there wiping out guys." And announcers love the team leader who plays hurt:

Table 9-7 Comments on the Heroic Nature of Playing Hurt

SportsCenter	Extreme	NBA	MLB	NFL
9	12	6	4	15

Note: NBA = National Basketball Association, MLB = Major League Baseball, and NFL = National Football League.

Drew Bledso gamely tried to play in loss to Rams yesterday; really admirable to try to play with that pin that was surgically implanted in his finger during the week; I don't know how a Q.B. could do that. You know, he broke his finger the time we had him on Monday night and he led his team to two come-from-behind victories, really gutted it out and I think he took that team on his shoulders and showed he could play and really elevated himself in my eyes, he really did.

SPORTS IS WAR

Commentators consistently (an average of nearly five times during each hour of sports commentary) used martial metaphors and language Of war and weaponry to describe sports action (e.g., battle, kill, ammunition, weapons, professional sniper, depth charges, taking aim, fighting, shot in his arsenal, reloading, detonate, squeezes the trigger, attack mode, firing blanks, blast, explosion, blitz, point of attack, a lance through the heart, etc.).

Some shows went beyond commentators' use of war terminology and actually framed the contests as wars. For instance, one of the wrestling shows offered a continual flow of images and commentary that reminded the viewers that "RAW is WAR!" Similarly, both NFL *Monday Night Football* broadcasts were introduced with explosive graphics and an opening song that included lyrics "Like a rocket burning through time and space, the NFL's best will rock this place . . . the battle lines are drawn." This sort of use of sport/war metaphors has been a common practice in televised sports commentary for many years, serving to fuse (and confuse) the distinctions between values of nationalism with team identity and athletic aggression with military destruction (Jansen & Sabo, 1994). In the shows examined for this study, war themes also were reinforced in many commercials, including commercials for movies, other sports programs, and in the occasional commercial for the US. military.

SHOW SOME GUTS!

Commentators continually depicted and replayed exciting incidents of athletes engaging in reckless acts of speed, showing guts in the face of danger, big hits, and violent crashes.

This theme was evident across all of the sports programs but was especially predominant in Extreme sports that continually depicted crashing vehicles or bikers in an exciting manner. For instance, when one race ended with a crash, it was showed again in slow-motion replay, with commentators approvingly dubbing it "unbeliev-

Table 9-8 Martial Metaphors and Language of War and Weaponry

SportsCenter	Extreme	Wrestling	NBA	MLB	NFL
9	3	15	27	6	23

Note: NBA = National Basketball Association, MLB = Major League Baseball, and NFL = National Football League.

Table 9-9 Depictions of Guts in Face of Danger, Speed, Hits, Crashes

SportsCenter	Extreme	NBA	MLB	NFL
4	21	5	2	8

Note: NBA = National Basketball Association, MLB = Major League Baseball, and NFL = National Football League.

able" and "original." Extreme sports commentators; commonly raised excitement levels by saying "he's on fire" or "he's going huge!" when a competitor was obviously taking greater risks. An athlete's ability to deal with the fear of a possible crash, in fact, is the mark of an "outstanding run": "Watch out, Richmond," an X-games announcer shouted to the crowd, "He's gonna wreck this place!" A winning competitor laughingly said, "I do what I can to smash into [my opponents] as much as I can." Another competitor said, "If I crash, no big deal; I'm just gonna go for it." NFL commentators introduced the games with images of reckless collisions and during the game a "fearless" player was likely to be applauded: "There's no chance that Barry Sanders won't take when he's running the football." In another game, the announcer noted that receiver "Tony Simmons plays big. And for those of you not in the NFL, playing big means you're not afraid to go across the middle and catch the ball and make a play out of it after you catch the ball." Men showing guts in the face of speed and danger was also a major theme in 40 of the commercials that we analyzed.

THE TELEVISED SPORTS MANHOOD FORMULA

Tens of millions of U.S. boys watch televised sports programs with their accompanying commercial advertisements. This study sheds light on what these boys are seeing when they watch their favorite sports programs. What values and ideas about gender, race, aggression, and violence are being promoted? Although there are certainly differences across different kinds of sports, as well as across different commercials, when we looked at all of the programming together, we identified 10 recurrent themes, which we have outlined above. Taken together, these themes codify a consistent and (mostly) coherent message about what it means to be a man. We call this message the Televised Sports Manhood Formula:

> What is a Real Man? A Real Man is strong, tough, aggressive, and above all, a winner in what is still a Man's World. To be a winner he has to do what needs to be done. He must be willing to compromise his own long-term health by showing guts in the face of danger, by fighting other men when necessary, and by "playing hurt" when he's injured. He must avoid being soft; he must be the aggressor, both

on the "battle fields" of sports and in his consumption choices. Whether he is playing sports or making choices about which snack food or auto products to purchase, his aggressiveness will net him the ultimate prize: the adoring attention of conventionally beautiful women. He will know if and when he has arrived as a Real Man when the Voices of Authority—White Males—*say* he is a Real Man. But even when he has finally managed to win the big one, has the good car and the right beer, and is surrounded by beautiful women, he will be reminded by these very same Voices of Authority just how fragile this Real Manhood really is: After all, he has to come out and prove himself all over again tomorrow. You're only as good as your last game (or your last purchase).

The major elements of the Televised Sports Manhood Formula are evident, in varying degrees, in the football, basketball, baseball, Extreme sports, and *SportsCenter* programs and in their accompanying commercials. But it is in the dramatic spectacle of professional wrestling that the Televised Sports Manhood Formula is most clearly codified and presented to audiences as an almost seamless package. Boys and young men are drawn to televised professional wrestling in great numbers. Consistently each week, from four to six pro wrestling shows rank among the top 10 rated shows on cable television. Professional wrestling is not a real sport in the way that baseball, basketball, football, or even Extreme sports are. In fact, it is a highly stylized and choreographed "sport as theatre" form of entertainment. Its producers have condensed—and then amplified—all of the themes that make up the Televised Sports Manhood Formula. For instance, where violence represents a thread in the football or basketball commentary, violence makes up the entire fabric of the theatrical narrative of televised pro wrestling. In short, professional wrestling presents viewers with a steady stream of images and commentary that represents a constant fusion of all of the themes that make up the Televised Sports Manhood Formula: This is a choreographed sport where all men (except losers) are Real Men, where women are present as sexy support objects for the men's violent, monumental "wars" against each other. Winners bravely display muscular strength, speed, power, and guts. Bodily harm is (supposedly) intentionally inflicted on opponents. The most ruthlessly aggressive men win, whereas the passive or weaker men lose, often shamefully. Heroically wrestling while injured, rehabilitating oneself from former injuries, and inflicting pain and injury on one's opponent are constant and central themes in the narrative.

GENDER AND THE SPORTS/MEDIA/COMMERCIAL COMPLEX

In 1984, media scholar Sut Jhally pointed to the commercial and ideological symbiosis between the institutions of sport and the mass media and called it the sports/media complex. Our examination of the ways that the Televised Sports Manhood Formula reflects and promotes hegemonic ideologies concerning race, gender, sexuality, aggression, violence, and consumerism suggests adding a third dimension to Jhally's analysis: the huge network of multi-billion-dollar automobile, snack food, alcohol, entertainment, and other corporate entities that sponsor sports events and broadcasts. In fact, examining the ways that the Televised Sports Manhood Formula cuts across sports programming and its accompanying commercials may provide important clues as to the ways that ideologies of hegemonic masculinity are both promoted by—and in turn serve to support and stabilize—this collection of interrelated institutions that make up the sports/media/commercial complex. The Televised Sports Manhood Formula is a master discourse that is produced at the nexus of the institutions of sport, mass media, and corporations who produce and hope to sell products and services to boys and men. As such, the Televised Sports Manhood Formula appears well suited to discipline boys' bodies, minds, and consumption choices within an ideological field that is conducive to the reproduction of the entrenched interests that profit from the sports/media/commercial complex. The perpetuation of the entrenched commercial interests of the sports/media/commercial complex appears to be predicated on boys accepting—indeed glorifying and celebrating—a set of bodily and relational practices that resist and oppose a view of women as fully human and place boys' and men's long-term health prospects in jeopardy.

At a historical moment when hegemonic masculinity has been destabilized by socioeconomic change, and by women's and gay liberation movements, the Televised Sports Manhood Formula provides a remarkably stable and concrete view of masculinity as grounded in bravery, risk taking, violence, bodily strength, and heterosexuality. And this view of masculinity is given coherence against views of women as sexual support objects or as invisible and thus irrelevant to men's public struggles for glory. Yet, perhaps to be successful in selling products, the commercials sometimes provide a less than seamless view of masculinity. The insecurities of masculinity in crisis are often tweaked in the commercials, as we see weak men, dumb men, and indecisive men being eclipsed by strong, smart, and decisive men and sometimes being humiliated by smarter and more decisive women. In short, this commercialized version of hegemonic masculinity is constructed partly in relation to images of men who don't measure up.

This analysis gives us hints at an answer to the commonly asked question of why so many boys and men continue to take seemingly irrational risks, submit to pain and injury, and risk long-term debility or even death by playing hurt. A critical examination of the Televised Sports Manhood Formula tells us why: The costs of masculinity (especially pain and injury), according to this formula, appear to be well worth the price; the boys and men who are willing to pay the price always seem to get the glory, the championships, the best consumer products, and the beautiful women. Those who don't—or can't—pay the price are humiliated or ignored by women and left in the dust by other men. In short, the Televised Sports Manhood Formula is a pedagogy through which boys are taught that paying the price, be it one's bodily health or one's money, gives one access to the privileges that have been historically linked to hegemonic masculinity—money, power, glory, and women. And the barrage of images of femininity as model-like beauty displayed for and in the service of successful men suggests that heterosexuality is a major lynchpin of the Televised Sports Manhood Formula, and on a larger scale serves as one of the major linking factors in the conservative gender regime of the sports/media/commercial complex.

On the other hand, we must be cautious in coming to definitive conclusions as to how the promotion of the values embedded in the Televised Sports Manhood

Formula might fit into the worlds of young men. It is not possible, based merely on our textual analysis of sports programs, to explicate precisely what kind of impact these shows, and the Televised Sports Manhood Formula, have on their young male audiences. That sort of question is best approached through direct research with audiences. Most such research finds that audiences interpret, use, and draw meanings from media variously, based on factors such as social class, race/ethnicity, and gender (Hunt, 1999; Whannel, 1998). Research with various subgroups of boys that explores their interpretations of the sports programs that they watch would enhance and broaden this study.

Moreover, it is important to go beyond the preferred reading presented here that emphasizes the persistent themes in televised sports that appear to reinforce the hegemony of current race, gender, and commercial relations (Sabo & Jansen, 1992). In addition to these continuities, there are some identifiable discontinuities within and between the various sports programs and within and among the accompanying commercials. For instance, commercials are far more varied in the ways they present gender imagery than are sports programs themselves. Although the dominant tendency in commercials is either to erase women or to present them as stereotypical support or sex objects, a significant minority of commercials present themes that set up boys and men as insecure and/or obnoxious schmucks and women as secure, knowledgeable, and authoritative. Audience research with boys who watch sports would shed fascinating light on how they decode and interpret these more complex, mixed, and paradoxical gender images against the dominant, hegemonic image of the Televised Sports Manhood Formula.

NOTES

1. There are some differences, and some similarities, in what boys and girls prefer to watch. The top seven televised sports reported by girls are, in order, gymnastics, men's pro basketball, pro football, pro baseball, swimming/diving, men's college basketball, and women's pro or college basketball.

2. Although images of feminine beauty shift, change, and are contested throughout history, female beauty is presented in sports programming and commercials in narrow ways. Attractive women look like fashion models (Banet-Weiser, 1999): They are tall, thin, young, usually (although not always) White, with signs of heterosexual femininity encoded and overtly displayed through hair, makeup, sexually provocative facial and bodily gestures, large (often partially exposed) breasts, long (often exposed) legs, and so forth.

REFERENCES

Amateur Athletic Foundation of Los Angeles. (1999). *Children and sports media.* Los Angeles: Author.

Banet-Weiser, S. (1999). *The most beautiful girl in the world: Beauty pageants and national identity.* Berkeley: University of California Press.

Duncan, M. C., & Messner, M. A. (1998). The media image of sport and gender. In L. A. Wenner (Ed.), *MediaSport* (pp. 170–195). New York: Routledge.

Hunt, D. (1999). *O.J. Simpson facts and fictions,* New York: Cambridge University Press.

Jansen, S. C., & Sabo, D. (1994). The sport/war metaphor: Hegemonic masculinity, the Persian Gulf war, and the new world order. *Sociology of Sport Journal, 11,* 1–17.

Jhally, S. (1984). The spectacle of accumulation: Material and cultural factors in the evolution of the sports/media complex. *Insurgent Sociologist,* 12(3), 41–52.

Kane, M. J., & Lenskyj, H. J. (1998). Media treatment of female athletes: Issues of gender and sexualities. In L. A. Wenner (Ed.), *MediaSport* (pp. 186–201). New York: Routledge.

Messner, M. A. (1992). *Power at play: Sports and the problem of masculinity.* Boston: Beacon.

Rinehart, R. (1998). Inside of the outside: Pecking orders within alternative sport at ESPN's 1995 "The eXtreme Games." *Journal of Sport and Social Issues, 22,* 398–415.

Sabo, D., & Jansen, S. C. (1992). Images of men in sport media: The social reproduction of masculinity. In S. Craig (Ed.), *Men, masculinity, and the media* (pp. 169–184). Newbury Park, CA: Sage.

Sabo, D., & Jansen, S. C. (1994). Seen but not heard: Images of Black men in sports media. In M. A. Messner & D. F. Sabo (Eds.), *Sex, violence and power in sports: Rethinking masculinity* (pp. 150–160). Freedom, CA: Crossing Press.

Trujillo, N. (1995). Machines, missiles, and men: Images of the male body on ABC's *Monday Night Football. Sociology of Sport Journal, 12,* 403–423.

Whannel, G. (1998). Reading the sports media audience. In L. A. Wenner (Ed.), *MediaSport* (pp. 221–232). New York: Routledge.

Wheaton, B., & Tomlinson, A. (1998). The changing gender order in sport? The case of windsurfing subcultures. *Journal of Sport and Social Issues, 22,* 252–274.

* FOR FURTHER STUDY *

Armstrong, Ketra L. 1999. "Nike's Communication with Black Audiences: A Sociological Analysis of Advertising Effectiveness via Symbolic Interactionism," *Journal of Sport and Social Issues* 23 (August):266–286.

Bishop, Ronald. 2003. "Missing in Action: Feature Coverage of Women's Sports in *Sports Illustrated*," *Journal of Sport & Social Issues 27* (May):184–194.

Brookes, R. 2002. *Representing Sport* (London: Arnold).

Denham, Bryan E., Andrew C. Billings, and Kelby K. Halone. 2002. "Differential Accounts of Race in Broadcast Commentary of the 2000 NCAA Men's and Women's Final Four Basketball Tournaments," *Sociology of Sport Journal* 19 (3):315–332.

Duncan, Margaret Carlisle. 1994. "The Politics of Women's Body Images and Practices: Foucalt, the Panopticon, and *Shape* Magazine," *Journal of Sport and Social Issues* 18 (February):48–65.

Dworkin, Shari Lee, and Faye Linda Wachs. 1998. "'Disciplining the Body': HIV Positive Male Athletes, Media Surveillance and the Policing of Sexuality," *Sociology of Sport Journal* 15 (1):1–20.

Higgs, Catriona T., and Karen H. Weiller, "Gender Bias and the 1992 Summer Olympic Games: An Analysis of Television Coverage," *Journal of Sport and Social Issues* 18 (August):234–246.

Juffer, Jane. 2002. "Who's the Man? Sammy Sosa, Latinos, and Televisual Redefinitions of the 'American' Pastime," *Journal of Sport & Social Issues* 26 (November): 381–402.

Messner, Michael A., Margaret Carlisle Duncan, and Cheryl Cooky. 2003. "Silence, Sports Bras, and Wrestling Porn," *Journal of Sport & Social Issues* 27 (February): 38–51.

Messner, Michael A., Margaret Carlisle Duncan, and Kerry Jensen, "Separating the Men from the Girls: The Gendered Language of Televised Sports," *Gender and Society* 7 (1992):121–137.

Urquhart, Jim, and Jane Crossman. 1999. "The *Globe and Mail* Coverage of the Winter Olympic Games: A Cold Place for Women Athletes," *Journal of Sport and Social Issues* 23 (May): 193–202.

Wachs, Faye Linda, and Shari L. Dworkin. 1997. "Sexual Identity and Media Framing of HIV-Positive Athletes," *Journal of Sport and Social Issues* 21 (November):327–347.

Wannel, G. 2000. "Sports and the Media." Pp. 291–308 in *Handbook of Sport Studies,* Jay Coakley and Eric Dunning (eds.),. (London: Sage).

PART FOUR

Sport and Socialization: Symbols

A symbol is anything that carries a particular meaning recognized by members of a culture. A wink, a raised finger (which one is important), a green light, a double stripe on the highway, and a handshake are all symbols with meaning for people in the United States. Part of the socialization process for children or other newcomers to a culture is the learning of symbols. While some symbols are relatively unimportant, others—such as the Constitution, the U.S. flag, or a cross—have great importance to certain segments of the population. Some of the symbols found in sport are very important.

The three selections in this section consider three symbols. The first, by Douglas Lederman, describes the use of the Confederate flag and the singing of the Southern anthem, "Dixie," in conjunction with sports at the University of Mississippi. These symbols represent pride by whites in their heritage. For others, especially African Americans, these are symbols of centuries of racial oppression. Should these symbols be used by a school that is supposed to represent all of the citizens of Mississippi?

The second selection, by Laurel R. Davis, highlights another battle over symbols. Here the issue is the use of Native American names, mascots, and ceremonial acts by athletic teams. There are teams such as the Scalpers and the Savages, as well as the Indians with mascots dressed in warpaint and fans doing the "tomahawk chop." Many Native Americans object to these common practices because they demean Native American heritage and encourage negative stereotypes.

The third chapter, by D. Stanley Eitzen and Maxine Baca Zinn, looks at sexist naming of women's athletic teams. They found in a study of all four-year colleges and universities in the United States that over half had sexist names, logos, or mascots. This use of demeaning symbols for women's teams has several negative functions for women: through their use women are trivialized, made invisible, and de-athleticized.

10

Old Times Not Forgotten

A Battle over Symbols

Douglas Lederman

As the ball carrier sprints across the goal line for a touchdown, thousands of University of Mississippi students erupt in cheers.

They thrust their arms to the sky, many holding flags aloft, as the band breaks into a stirring song. Backs are slapped, high fives exchanged. It is one of those magical moments that bring classmates together and unify a community.

But not one of the university's 700 black undergraduates is seated among the thousands in the students' section. Most blacks say they don't feel at home there, in part because the flags the students are waving are those of the Confederacy, and the song is the Southern anthem, "Dixie."

Much has changed here since 1962, when the university and the state gained national notoriety for resisting James Meredith's attempts to enroll as the institution's first black student. Blacks are now integrated into most aspects of daily life on the campus.

But the progress is obscured, and even undermined, by an enduring battle over the university's continued use of its Old South symbols, official and informal. The debate ignited again last spring when three black members of the band refused to play "Dixie," saying the song should not be performed at university-sponsored events because it offends black students.

Most white students and alumni insist—no, more than that, they practically swear—that there is nothing racist in their use of the symbols. Whatever link the flag and song might once have had with slavery and the South's segregationist past, they

Source: "Old Times Not Forgotten: A Battle over Symbols Obscures U. of Mississippi's Racial Changes" by Douglas Lederman. From *The Chronicle of Higher Education.* Copyright 1993. Reprinted with permission.

argue, has been supplanted in their hearts and minds by an association with the university they love. Waving the flag and cheering the playing of "Dixie" evince Southern heritage, they say, not bigotry.

"THEY'RE OUR FRIENDS"

They just represent Ole Miss to us," says Lettye Williams, a retired schoolteacher who picnicked with her husband and fellow alumni before a football game last month. "We do not see these as racist symbols. Just because you're proud to be a Southerner doesn't mean you don't like blacks. They're our friends. We work with them. We live with them."

Black students don't believe that everyone who waves the Confederate battle flag or claps along to "Dixie" is racist. But history, most of them agree, has forever tainted the flag and the song, making them inappropriate symbols for an institution that is supposed to represent all of Mississippi's citizens. The flag and "Dixie" were adopted by the university only in the late 1940s, embraced defiantly by students opposed to integration. Mississippians who violently protested Mr. Meredith's admission also rallied around the flag and "Dixie," a fact not easily forgotten by many blacks here.

They, along with many faculty members, believe Mississippi must cast off the vestiges of its Old South past if it is to thrive in the New South. Symbols, they argue, should unite, not divide, especially at a public institution in a state with a black population of 35 percent.

"No matter how much things have changed, African Americans will always remember why all of this was brought here—to keep us out," says Jesse Holland, a black senior who edits the *Daily Mississippian,* the student newspaper.

Many critics of "Dixie" want the university's chancellor, R. Gerald Turner, to stop or at least discourage the band from playing the song, just as the university officially dissociated itself from the Confederate flag a decade ago.

Many white alumni and students vow to fight such a move, and some alums say they will halt their financial support if Mississippi abandons "Dixie." Some professors also complain that banning the song by fiat would be a form of censorship.

Mr. Turner has been grappling with this issue on and off since he got here in 1983, and he has won praise from many quarters for his efforts to improve race relations. The chancellor is under pressure from all sides, but he is asking for patience. Mississippi, he believes, must at some point formally review the appropriateness of all its symbols, but he says the time is not yet right for such a study.

When that discussion does take place, Mr. Turner and others say, it will focus on a broader question raised by the dispute over "Dixie": Is it possible for an institution to shed its Confederate roots, yet remain fervently, profoundly Southern?

The university is not alone in facing that dilemma. Georgia, for instance, is bitterly divided over whether to strip the Confederate battle flag from its state banner. And just this month, the University of Alabama stirred protests when it adopted an Old South theme for its football homecoming. But few institutions have been identified so closely with the Old South legacy, good and bad, as this one.

"If this university isn't Southern," Mr. Turner says, "it's not anything."

CULTIVATING AN IMAGE

That's true partly because of its location and history. The main administration building was a hospital for Civil War soldiers, over 700 of whom are buried in a graveyard here. And the university and Oxford have been home to Southern writers who have shaped the country's perceptions of the region, from William Faulkner to Eudora Welty.

The university has also cultivated that image, carving out a niche among other public universities in the region as a bastion of the Old South. It has done that largely through its use of symbols, which extend well beyond the flag and "Dixie," which is neither fight song nor alma mater, but a popular, unofficial theme song.

The sports teams are called the Rebels, and the mascot is Colonel Reb, a caricature of an Old South plantation owner. Even the university's nickname, Ole Miss, has antebellum origins. It isn't short for Old Mississippi, as most people think, but rather is what some slaves called the wives of their owners.

The institution's image attracts students who yearn as much for its conservative, traditional nature as for the beauty of its campus and the quality of its education. But Mississippi has had trouble distancing itself from the negative aspects of what the Old South stood for, despite its advances.

"THERE IS A NEW ORDER HERE"

Signs of those advances are plentiful. This summer Mr. Turner hired the university's first black vice-chancellor; its basketball coach is also black. This year's group of 701 black undergraduates (8 percent of the 10,369 total) is its largest in history, and two white fraternities became integrated last year for the first time.

"You see white and black students together here today in ways that never before were possible," says William Ferris, director of the university's Center for the Study of Southern Culture. "That gives you hope. There is a new order here."

That's not so obvious on Saturdays during football season.

Ten hours before an evening home game, alumni and students begin filling the tree-lined expanse known as "the Grove" with picnic tables and tents. For the rest of the day, they eat, reminisce, and get fired up for the game. The people are friendly, the atmosphere inviting.

THE OLD OLE MISS

But Confederate flags hang from trees and serve as centerpieces amid the fried chicken and iced tea on many a picnic table. And just as at the game, blacks are virtually invisible in the Grove—except when the football squad, half of whose players are black, parades through the crowd en route to the stadium.

This is the *old* Ole Miss, the one that was in its prime when the university first embraced its Confederate trappings.

The university's teams became known as "the Rebels" in 1936, but Confederate flags and "Dixie" did not become an exalted part of the football ritual until 1948, when dozens of Mississippi students took part in the "Dixiecrat" political convention, which was dedicated to the fight against desegregation.

"The song and the Confederate battle flag were adopted by the all-white university specifically as a gesture of white supremacy," says Warren Steel, a music professor whose arguments helped persuade the Faculty Senate last spring to discourage the playing of "Dixie" at campus events. "People can honestly say, 'I don't think about bigotry,' but the history is there."

Tim Jones didn't know that history when he joined Mississippi's band. But after learning the origins of the university's affiliation with "Dixie" and its other symbols, he decided he could no longer play the song in good conscience.

TIME FOR PROTEST

So at a basketball game last spring, as the band took up "Dixie," Mr. Jones put down his drum, got to his feet, and crossed his arms in front of his chest.

"There's a line in the song that says, 'Old times there are not forgotten,'" says Mr. Jones, a senior. "When you talk about old times in the South, the only thing my people think about is slavery."

Mr. Jones's protest, which was backed by the Black Student Union, came 10 years after the last major flare-up over the symbols. In 1983, a black cheerleader refused to carry the Rebel flag and the alumni association discouraged its use. Saying the flag's meaning had changed because it had been appropriated by groups like the Ku Klux Klan, the university abandoned it as an official symbol.

Mississippi stopped distributing flags before games and selling them in the bookstore, and dropped the symbol from all its T-shirts and other items. The university also introduced the "Battle M" flag, a blue M with white stars on a red background, hoping it would replace the Confederate flag in its fans' hearts.

That hasn't happened. Although use of the Confederate banner waned in the mid-1980s, Rebel flags now vastly outnumber the "Battle M" at football games. If anything, the dispute over the university's symbols seems to make many whites more, not less, inclined to cling to the past.

"If it wasn't so controversial, we probably wouldn't want to wave them," says John Kennedy, a junior. "I can understand how they feel, but we feel kind of abused. If they take 'Dixie' away, I think race relations will get worse."

"AN ESCAPE" FROM DISCUSSION

The widening gap between the two sides is evidenced by T-shirts. On the front of one is the "X" popularized by the movie *Malcom X,* under the words "you wear yours. . . ." On the back is the Confederate flag, framed by the words "We'll wear ours."

"The controversy tends to polarize people and worsen race relations, and it is an escape from discussing real issues in race relations," says Mr. Steel, the music professor. "That's why I wish we would just resolve this now."

Mr. Turner says the issue will be decided not by the advocates on either side but by the "middle ground," which he says has not yet formed a consensus. The chancellor admits that people may be uneasy about the continuing debate, but he says it is necessary. Meanwhile, Mr. Turner is formulating what he calls a "framework" for the coming debate about how the university should present itself in the future.

"It is difficult to communicate how much things have changed here when you have symbols that are Confederate, not Southern," says Mr. Turner. "Somehow we need to ferret out things that are Southern from those that are Confederate."

UPDATING TRADITION

Charles Reagan Wilson, a professor of history and Southern studies, argues that for Southern tradition to survive, it must be "extended," or updated, to take recent history into account. The trick for the university, he argues, is to remain relevant to all Mississippians, black and white, without losing its distinctive character.

One alternative, he says, is to mix symbols of the confederacy with those of the civil-rights movement, reflecting Mississippi's "complex, tortured history by focusing on the two events that most shaped the South."

Another option, he says, is to give new meaning to traditional symbols. Keep using the Confederate flag, Mr. Wilson says, but redefine it: "Make a new flag that shows a white and a black hand grasping the Confederate flag," for instance. As for "Dixie," he and others say, the band's repertoire already includes a compromise: "From Dixie with Love," which meshes "Dixie" with "The Battle Hymn of the Republic," and "All My Trials," an old spiritual, reflecting all of the factors at work in the Civil War.

A third possibility, Mr. Wilson says, is to focus on Southern cultural symbols that are "anchored in the past but are not Confederate." A flag featuring a magnolia tree, for example, could be a "good common symbol of the South and of Mississippi."

Whether any of those solutions would appease either side of the debate is another question.

The problem, says Charles W. Eagles, a history professor who specializes in race relations and the civil-rights movement, is that the campus houses two very different institutions: the University of Mississippi and Ole Miss.

Every time Mr. Eagles walks through the student union, he is irked by a quotation from an alumnus that adorns a wall. It says: "The University is respected, but Ole Miss is loved. The University gives a diploma and regretfully terminates tenure, but one never graduates from Ole Miss."

CAPTURING THE PLACE

"That captures this place. For some of us—those who believe in the University of Mississippi—the symbols prevent the university from being everything it can be. Others—those that are faithful to Ole Miss—think that if you took the symbols away, there wouldn't be anything there.

"The symbols are seen as a real burden for the University of Mississippi. But they're the backbone of Ole Miss."

11

The Problems with Native American Mascots

Laurel R. Davis

INTRODUCTION

Sport has not been widely discussed in the field of multicultural education. Yet, sport is central to the lives of many students. It is critical that multicultural educators attend to the field of sport, because it plays a significant role in the socialization of youth. There are many sport-related topics that multicultural educators could address. This chapter focuses on the existence of Native American mascots in school-sponsored sport.

Because of the prevalence of stereotypes of Native Americans in United States popular culture, many have difficulty understanding the problems with Native American mascots. Even those who oppose these mascots often have trouble clearly articulating the reasons for their opposition. The purpose of this chapter is to lay out the main arguments against the use of Native American mascots. All of the arguments mentioned in this chapter are used by activists who are working to eliminate these mascots.

THE MASCOTS ARE RACIST STEREOTYPES

The most common argument against Native American mascots is that they represent racist stereotypes of Native Americans. Stereotypes of Native Americans appear throughout United States popular culture, such as in movies; government seals; advertisements and symbols for products like butter, beer, and paper; and statues and

Source: Laurel R. Davis, "The Problems with Native American Mascots," *Multicultural Education* 9 (Summer 2002): 11–15.

paintings that non-Natives have in their homes. Scholars have observed two main stereotypes: the "bloodthirsty savage," which conveys the notions that Native Americans are wild, aggressive, violent, and brave; and the "noble savage," which conveys the notions that Native Americans are primitive, childlike, silent, and part of the natural world (Bataille & Silet, 1980; Hilger, 1986; Lyman, 1982; Williams, 1980).

It is the stereotype of Native Americans as bloodthirsty savage that led non-Natives to choose Native American mascots for sport. Traits associated with this stereotype, such as having a fighting spirit, and being aggressive, brave, stoic, dedicated, and proud, are associated with sport, and thus selecting a Native American mascot links sport teams with such traits. The appeal of this stereotype to many in sport is illustrated by the following quotations from supporters of Native American mascots: "I can think of no greater tribute to the American Indian than to name a team's warriors after courageous, cunning and feared warriors of the Indian nations, the braves" (Shepard, 1991, p. 14A); and "I look at that mascot, that Indian head, and it stirs me up. I think of getting real aggressive, and it brings out the aggressiveness in me. And it makes me go out there and really wrestle hard and fight hard, you know, because that's what those Indians were" (cited in Davis, 1993, p. 15).

When all the mascots representing Native Americans are considered (e.g., Indians, Redskins, Braves, Chiefs), it turns out that Native Americans are the most common mascot in United States sport. The other mascots that are most common are animals, most of which are also associated with aggression and fighting (e.g., tigers). Of course it is offensive that Native Americans are perceived, and used as symbols, in the same way as animals.

Stereotypes are misleading generalizations about a category of people. When people believe stereotypes they tend to think that all, or almost all, people who belong to a particular category behave in the same way, and they tend to ignore the wide diversity of behavior exhibited by people within the category. So, regarding the stereotype associated with the mascots, not all Native Americans in the past were aggressive, brave, dedicated fighters. And today, most Native Americans do not occupy their time fighting. And many non-Natives are aggressive, brave, dedicated fighters. Of course, many Native Americans take pride in their ethnic/racial background and are dedicated people. But, do they have more pride and dedication than other groups? And, since Native Americans have extremely high rates of suicide, health problems, and poverty, asserting that this racial group has more pride than other groups is shallow.

The stereotype of Native Americans as aggressive is particularly offensive because it distorts the historical reality of European and European-American aggression (i.e., white invasion of Native American lands and conquering of people on these lands). Belief in this stereotype works to obscure the oppression, violence, and genocide initiated by European Americans against Native Americans, and serves as justification for these acts. This stereotype is part of a mythological history of the Western United States, according to which cowboys and so-called pioneers led a glorious and adventurous life fighting Native Americans. One reason the resistance to elimination of Native American mascots is so vigorous and emotionally charged is because when the activists critique the mascots they are also criticizing a form of American identity that is linked to myths about the Western United States (Davis, 1993).

Native American mascots, and most other images of Native Americans in popular culture, are stereotypes that focus on the past, and thus these stereotypes reinforce the problematic view that associates Native Americans only with the past. Thus, this stereotyping works to obscure the lives of contemporary Native Americans. As one interview subject said, "Respect the living Indian, you know. Don't memorialize us . . . [The mascots are] almost like a monument to the vanished American Indian" (Davis, 1993, p. 13). Of course, recognizing and understanding the lives of contemporary Native Americans challenges this stereotype.

Native American mascots misrepresent, distort, and trivialize many aspects of Native American cultures, such as drumming, dancing, singing, and some aspects of religion. As an interview subject stated, "I compose memorial songs, I compose burial songs for my grandmothers and my grandfathers, my family. And, when people [imitate that at an athletic event, like at a baseball game, it hurts me, to see that people are making a mockery of me. We don't do that, what they're doing, this chanting" (Davis, 1993, p. 13). Most of those who support the mascots do not understand the meanings or realities of Native American lives and cultures. Thus, it is particularly ironic that many who want to retain Native American mascots think they are honoring Native Americans. As an interview subject asserted, "How can you honor me, when you don't know the first damn thing about me?" (Davis, 1993, p. 14).

Another irony related to the belief that Native Americans are being honored by the mascots is that "positive" views of Native Americans, and the practice of using symbols of Native Americans to represent sport teams and the like, began soon after the last of the Native American nations were conquered or subdued (Davis, 1993). Thus, one has to ask, who is being "honored" by Native American mascots, Native Americans or those who subdued Native Americans?

The mascots, and most other images of Native Americans in popular culture, lump all nations (i.e., "tribes") of Native Americans together, incorrectly conveying that there is a single Native American culture and rendering the diversity of Native American cultures invisible. For example, only some Native American nations have political structures that are dominated by a male chief, and headdresses are worn by members of only some nations.

Ethnic/racial groups other than Native Americans have occasionally been used as mascots. There are several reasons why these mascots are not as problematic as Native American mascots. First, these other mascots tend to either represent a people that lived in the past and are not alive today (e.g., Spartans), or they were selected by people from this ethnic group (e.g., Scots). Second, most of the mascots that represent other ethnic groups do not have the same association with aggression (e.g., Irish). And, third, Native Americans should not have to condition their responses to be the same as other ethnic/racial groups.

One of the reasons many do not see Native American mascots, and other images of Native Americans in popular culture, as stereotypes and as racist is that the majority of these images seem to be positive. Most stereotypes of racial/ethnic groups are obviously negative, such as African Americans as criminals and Mexican Americans as lazy. It is easier to understand that overtly negative stereotypes are stereotypes and are racist. On the other hand, some stereotypes appear to be positive, such as Asians as intelligent, Jews as good at business, and Native Americans as brave. Yet, despite their positive tone, these are problematic stereotypes, in that many people from these groups do not fit the stereotype, and underneath the positive facade lie some problematic beliefs and consequences. For example, the stereotype that all Asians are intelligent contributes to the extra pressure and discrimination many Asian Americans face, and this stereotype is often used to disparage other Persons of Color. The stereotype that all Jews are good in business serves as a foundation for another stereotype—that Jews are taking over the world economy, a stereotype which has been used to legitimate anti-Semitic actions such as the Holocaust. There are problematic beliefs and consequences that stem from the so-called positive stereotypes of Native Americans as well.

Some people argue that they should be able to retain their Native American mascots if they portray the mascots in a culturally authentic and nonstereotypical manner. There are three problems with this idea. One is that a school/team cannot control how others, such as the media and other schools/teams, use their mascot. For example, the media might print a headline announcing an "attack" by the school/ team with the Native American mascot. The second problem with this idea is that the schools/teams with the Native American mascots will not be able to avoid stereo-types. Native Americans are a category of people that live in many different societies, each with a different culture, and within each Native American society there is much diversity. Thus, how does one portray what Native Americans are "really like"? Imag-ine creating a mascot that represented African Americans, Jewish Americans, Puerto Ricans, or European Americans. Because of the wide diversity of people within these categories, any mascot one could imagine would be a stereotype. Third, it is inappro-priate for non-Natives to imitate Native Americans, even if they do so in a culturally accurate way. We would find it offensive to see a Christian portray her/himself as Jewish or an European American portray her/himself as African American, even if the portrayal is culturally accurate (e.g., using an authentic dialect and clothing). Imitating another's culture, even if we do it accurately, seems like we are mimicking and mocking the other, especially if the imitation is done for entertainment, like it is at a sporting event.

The mascot stereotypes, and other images of Native Americans in popular cul-ture, influence the way non-Natives both perceive and treat Native Americans.

The mascot stereotypes, and other similar images, limit the abilities of the public to understand Native American realities. As the late Michael Dorris (1992) put it, "War-bonnetted apparitions pasted to football helmets or baseball caps act as opaque, impermeable curtains, solid walls of white noise that for many citizens block or distort all vision of the nearly 2 million native Americans today" (p. 19A).

A second argument against the mascots, and many other images of Native Americans in popular culture, is that they have a negative impact on Native Ameri-can lives. Many people argue that symbols, such as images and language, are trivial issues that do not matter. Yet, reams of scholarship demonstrate that symbols exert a significant influence on both our perceptions and behaviors.

Native American mascots create a hostile climate for many Native Americans, and sensitive non-Natives, in the schools and communities with these mascots. It is hard to feel comfortable in and committed to a school/community, and perform to the best of one's ability in school or work, when constantly surrounded by stereotypes that offend.

The mascots, and many other images of Native Americans in popular culture, negatively influence the self-image and self-esteem of Native Americans, especially children. One activist tells the story of how she instilled pride in her children regarding their Native American heritage and how she thought her children were secure. Yet, when she took them to a game with a Native American mascot she witnessed a major "blow to their self-esteem" as they "sank in their seats," not wanting to be identified as Native American (Davis, 1993). Another activist called the mascot issue a "mental health" issue (Ode, 1992, p. 2E).

Mascot stereotypes (and other images of Native Americans in popular culture) affect more than mental health and comfort within a school/community. Other problems Native Americans commonly face, such as poverty, cultural destruction, poor health, and inadequate education, are intertwined with public images of Native Americans. These images played a role in creating such problems, and now these images constrain Native American efforts to effectively address such problems.

Because of the current power structure in the United States, the quality of lives Native Americans will lead in the future depends on whether the general public has an accurate understanding of past and present Native American lives. If the public cannot understand the problem with Native American mascots, and other images of Native Americans in popular culture, they certainly will not understand sovereignty or other issues that affect the quality of Native American lives.

NATIVE AMERICANS SHOULD CONTROL IMAGES OF THEMSELVES

A third argument against the mascots is that Native Americans should have control over societal definitions of who they are. Currently, Native Americans have little power to shape public images of themselves, and the voices of Native Americans are rarely heard. Non-Natives continually assert that the mascots are honoring Native Americans, despite the fact that most pan-ethnic Native American organizations (i.e., organizations consisting of Native American nations from throughout the United States) have stated otherwise (Rosenstein, 1996). One Native American writer said: "I'll decide what honors me and what doesn't. . . . Minority groups have had enough of whites telling them what to think" (MacPhie, 1991, p. 19A). It is plain arrogance, and lack of respect, for non-Natives to think that they know more about Native Americans, and what honors them, than Native Americans themselves.

Of course, one can find some people from every racial/ethnic group to agree with any opinion, as people from one racial/ethnic group never all have the same opinion, so supporters of Native American mascots have been able to find Native Americans (and other People of Color) to defend their use of these mascots. Many Native Americans have learned stereotypes of Native Americans from the same sources that non-Natives have. Some Native Americans have even profited from selling images of these stereotypes to non-Natives. It is important not to blame these Native Americans, but to recognize the social forces that affect them, such as the media, extreme poverty, and inadequate education, In light of the fact that most pan-ethnic Native American organizations have issued statements against the mascots, it is offensive for non-Natives to use Native Americans, or other People of Color, to justify the position that the mascots should be retained.

OTHER ISSUES ASSOCIATED WITH THE MASCOTS

Finally, there are several other issues associated with the Native American mascot controversy that need to be addressed. The first issues are tradition and intent. Supporters of Native American mascots regularly point out that they do not intend to offend anyone, they intend to honor Native Americans, and they are just having fun and affirming tradition. It is worth pointing out that not all traditions are good ones. Some examples of bad traditions are racially segregated facilities and the exclusion of women from schools. Many people have benefitted from the elimination of such traditions.

It is also crucial to note that intent is not the most important issue here. If a belief or action has problematic consequences (i.e., if it has negative societal effects), then we should eliminate it, regardless of intent. For example, drunk drivers or men who continually comment on the sexual attractiveness of women they work with, usually do not intend to harm anyone, and yet the consequences of such actions are often problematic and thus we should work to eliminate these behaviors. Many times, despite our best intentions, when we lack the necessary knowledge, our behavior can be quite harmful to others. Although most people who support Native American mascots do not intend to harm Native Americans, the consequences of the mascots are problematic and therefore the mascots should be eliminated.

The final issue is the small percentage of people who object to Native American mascots. Many supporters of Native American mascots argue that the mascots must not be problematic because only a small number of people object to them. Polls do indicate that if this issue were put to voters, the majority of people in most parts of the United States would vote to retain the mascots (Sigelman, 1998). Yet, there are two reasons that the focus on numbers and majority rule is problematic.

First, it is important to note that the majority of people in the United States are uncritical of stereotypes of Native Americans, including the mascots, because of lack of education about Native American issues. Most Americans have had little to no substantial contact with Native Americans and thus have distorted perspectives that come from television, movies (especially "Westerns"), and "tourist traps" that feature stereotypes of Native Americans. We have been inundated with stereotypes of Native Americans in United States popular culture from birth, so we have come to believe these stereotypes (Green, 1988). So, it is not surprising that large numbers of people do not understand this issue.

It seems that in areas of the United States where the Native American population is larger and politically active, the non-Native population has a greater understanding of Native American issues because they have been educated by local Native Americans and media coverage of these Native Americans (Davis, 1993). The task of educating the United States public or regional populations about Native American stereotypes and lives is a difficult one.

Second, Native Americans represent only about one percent of the United States population, so issues they care about, and most others do not, will not likely win public approval. People who are Jewish, and people who travel in wheelchairs, also represent a small percentage of the United States population, yet this does not mean that others should ignore their feelings and concerns. Even if the percentage of people who are offended is small, others should still try to be sensitive. Part of being a good citizen is trying to empathize with other people, especially those who are different from ourselves. Of course, we should attempt to understand why other people are offended by something, but even if we cannot achieve this understanding, the considerate thing to do is to respond to others' concerns.

Those who support the use of Native American mascots often claim that they want to retain the mascots because they "respect" Native Americans. Respect is a meaningless word when the positions of most pan-ethnic Native American organizations are ignored. Real respect is carefully listening to, attempting to understand, and addressing Native American concerns about this issue. On a related note, it is not accurate to say that every possible symbol or mascot will be objectionable to someone. There are many symbols, including most other sport mascots, that are not offensive to any groups of people.

CONCLUSION

In conclusion, equality and justice in society depend on our abilities to empathize with those who are different from us. If we listen carefully to the Native American individuals and organizations that call for an elimination of Native American mascots, it will be clear that there are valid reasons why we should work to eliminate these mascots, and other problematic images of Native Americans, in society. The state of Minnesota has made a coordinated effort to eliminate Native American mascots in its public schools and has been quite successful. The rest of the country needs to follow its lead.

REFERENCES

Bataille, G., & Silet, C. L. P. (Eds.) (1980). *The Pretend Indians: Images of Native Americans in the Movies.* Ames, IA: Iowa State University.

Davis, L. R. (1993). Protest Against the Use of Native American Mascots: A Challenge to Traditional American Identity. *Journal of Sport and Social Issues,* 17(1): 9–22.

Dorris, M. (1992, April 24). Crazy Horse Isn't a Good Name for a Malt Liquor. *Star Tribune,* p. 19A.

Green, R. (1988). The Tribe Called Wannabee: Playing Indian in America and Europe. *Folklore,* 99: 30–55.

Hilger, M. (1986). *The American Indian in Film.* Methuen, NJ: Scarecrow.

Lyman, C. M. (1982). *The Vanishing Race and Other Illusions.* Washington, DC: Smithsonian Institute.

MacPhie, R. P. (1991, October 25). This "Real Live Indian" Offended by Chop. *Star Tribune,* p. 19A.

Ode, K (1992, January 23). Bellecourt's New AIM. *Star Tribune,* pp. 1E–2E.

Rosenstein, J. (1996). *In Whose Honor? American Indian Mascots in Sports.* Video produced and directed by Jay Rosenstein. Champaign, IL: Jay Rosenstein.

Shepard, B. (1991, October 26). [Letter to the Editor.] *Star Tribune,* p. 14A.

Sigelman, L. (1998). Hail to the Redskins? Public Reactions to a Racially Insensitive Team Name. Sociology of *Sport Journal,* 15(4): 317–325.

Williams, L. E. (1980). Foreword. In J. E. O'Conner, *The Hollywood Indian: Stereotypes of Native Americans in Films* (pp. ix–xvi). Trenton, NJ: New Jersey State Museum.

12

The De-Athleticization of Women

The Naming and Gender Marking of Collegiate Sport Teams

D. Stanley Eitzen and Maxine Baca Zinn

Sport is an institution with enormous symbolic significance that contributes to and perpetuates male dominance in society (Hall, 1984, 1985). This occurs through processes that exclude women completely, or if they do manage to participate, processes that effectively minimize their achievements. Bryson (1987) has argued that sport reproduces patriarchal relations through four minimalizing processes: definition, direct control, ignoring, and trivialization. This chapter examines several of these processes but focuses especially on how the trivialization of women occurs through the sexist naming practices of athletic teams.

THE PROBLEM

American colleges and universities typically have adopted nicknames, songs, colors, emblems, and mascots as identifying and unifying symbols. This practice of using symbols to achieve solidarity and community is a common group practice, as Durkheim showed in his analysis of primitive religions (Durkheim, 1947). Durkheim

Source: Reprinted by permission from D. S. Eitzen and M. B. Zinn, 1989, "The De-Athleticization of Women: The Naming and Gender Marking of Collegiate Sport Teams," *Sociology of Sport Journal* 65 (4), pp. 362–370.

noted that people in a locality believed they were related to some totem, which was usually an animal but was occasionally a natural object as well. All members of a common group were identified by their shared symbol, which they displayed by the emblem of their totem. This identification with an animal, bird, or other object is common in institutions of higher learning where students, former students, faculty members, and others who identify with the local academic community display similar colors, wave banners, wear special clothing and jewelry, and chant or sing together. These behaviors usually center around athletic contests. Janet Lever (1983, p. 12) connects these activities with totemism:

> Team, worship, like animal worship, makes all participants intensely aware of their own group membership. By accepting that a particular team represents them symbolically, people enjoy ritual kinship based on a common bond. Their emblem, be it an insignia or a lapel pin or a scarf with team colors, distinguishes fellow fans from both strangers and enemies.

A school nickname is much more than a tag or a label. It conveys, symbolically as Durkheim posits, the characteristics and attributes that define the institution. In an important way, the school's symbols represent the institution's self-concept. Schools may have names that signify the school's ethnic heritage (e.g., the Bethany College Swedes), state history (University of Oklahoma Sooners), mission (U.S. Military Academy at West Point Cadets), religion (Oklahoma Baptist College Prophets), or founder (Whittier College Poets). Most schools, though, use symbols of aggression and ferocity (e.g., birds such as hawks, animals such as bulldogs, human categories such as pirates, and even the otherworldly such as devils) (see Fuller & Manning, 1987).

While school names tend to evoke strong emotions of solidarity among followers, there is also a potential dark side. The names chosen by some schools are demeaning or derogatory to some groups. In the past two decades or so, Native American activists have raised serious objections to the use of Indians as school names or mascots because their use typically distorts Native American traditions and reinforces negative stereotypes about them by depicting them as savages, scalpers, and the like. A few colleges (e.g., Stanford and Dartmouth) have taken these objections seriously and deleted Indian names and mascots. Most schools using some form of reference to Indians, however, have chosen to continue that practice despite the objections of Native Americans. In fact, Indian or some derivative is a popular name for athletic teams. Of the 1,251 four-year schools reported by Franks (1982), some 21 used Indian, 13 were Warriors, 7 were Chiefs, 6 were Redmen, 5 were Braves, 2 were Redskins, and individual schools were Nanooks, Chippewas, Hurons, Seminoles, Choctaws, Mohawks, Sioux, Utes, Aztecs, Savages, Tribe, and Raiders. Ironically though, Native Americans is the only racial/ethnic category used by schools where they are not a significant part of the student body or heritage of the school. Yet the members of schools and their constituencies insist on retaining their Native American names because these are part of their collective identities. This allegiance to their school symbol is more important, apparently, than an insensitivity to the negative consequences evoked from the appropriation and depiction of Native Americans.

The purpose of this chapter is to explore another area of potential concern by an oppressed group—women—over the names given their teams. The naming of women's teams raises parallel questions to the issues raised by Native Americans. Are the names given to university and college women's sport teams fair to women in general and women athletes in particular, or do they belittle them, diminish them, and reinforce negative images of women and their secondary status?

THEORETICAL BACKGROUND: LANGUAGE AND GENDER

Gender differentiation in language has been extensively documented and analyzed. An expanding body of literature reveals that language reflects and helps maintain the secondary status of women by defining them and their place (Henley, 1987, p. 3). This is because "every language reflects the prejudices of the society in which it evolved" (Miller & Swift, 1980, p. 3). Language places women and men within a system of differentiation and stratification. Language suggests how women and men are to be evaluated. Language embodies negative and positive value stances and valuations related to how certain groups within society are apprised (Van Den Bergh, 1987, p. 132). Language in general is filled with biases about women and men. Specific linguistic conventions are sexist when they isolate or stereotype some aspect of an individual's nature or the nature of a group of individuals based on their sex.

Many studies have pointed to the varied ways in which language acts in the defining, deprecation, and exclusion of women in areas of the social structure (Thorne, Kramarae, & Henley, 1985, p, 3). Our intent is to add to the literature by showing how the linguistic marking systems adopted by many college and university teams promote male supremacy and female subordination.

Names are symbols of identity as well as being essential for the construction of reality. Objects, events, and feelings must be named in order to make sense of the world. But naming is not a neutral process. Naming is an application of principles already in use, an extension of existing rules (Spender, 1980, p. 163). Patriarchy has shaped words, names, and labels for women and men, their personality traits, expressions of emotion, behaviors, and occupations. Names are badges of femininity and masculinity, hence of inferiority and superiority. Richardson (1981, p. 46) has summarized the subconscious rules governing the name preference in middle-class America:

> Male names tend to be short, hard-hitting, and explosive (e.g., Bret, Lance, Mark, Craig, Bruce, etc.). Even when the given name is multisyllabic (e.g., Benjamin, Joshua, William, Thomas), the nickname tends to imply hardness and energy (e.g., Ben, Josh, Bill, Tom, etc.). Female names, on the other hand, are longer, more melodic, and softer (e.g., Deborah, Caroline, Jessica, Christina) and easily succumb to the diminutive "ie" ending form (e.g., Debbie, Carrie, Jessie, Christie). And although feminization of male names (e.g., Fredricka, Roberta, Alexandra) is not uncommon, the inverse rarely occurs.

While naming is an important manifestation of gender differentiation, little research exists on naming conventions other than those associated with gender and given names. Only one study (Fuller & Manning, 1987) examines the naming practices of college sport teams, but it focuses narrowly on the sexism emanating from the violence commonly attributed to these symbols. Because of their emphasis Fuller and Manning considered only three sexist naming practices. The study presented here builds on the insights of Fuller and Manning by looking at eight sexist naming categories. The goal is to show that the naming traditions of sports teams can unwittingly promote the ideology of male superiority and sexual difference.

Our argument is that the names of many women's and men's athletic teams reinforce a basic element of social structure—that of gender division. Team names reflect this division as well as the asymmetry that is associated with it. Even after women's advances in sport since the implementation of Title IX, widespread naming practices continue to mark female athletes as unusual, aberrant, or invisible.

DATA AND METHODS

The data source on the names and mascots of sports teams at 4-year colleges and universities was Franks (1982). This book provides the required information plus a history of how the names were selected for 1,251 schools. Since our research focused on comparing the names for men's and women's teams, those schools limited to one sex were not considered. Also, schools now defunct were omitted from the present analysis. This was determined by eliminating those schools not listed in the latest edition of *American Universities and Colleges* (American Council of Education, 1987). Thus the number of schools in the present study was 1,185.

The decision on whether a school had sexist names for its teams was based on whether the team names violated the rules of gender neutrality. A review of the literature on language and gender revealed a number of gender-linked practices that diminish and trivialize women (Henley, 1987; Lakoff, 1975; Miller & Swift, 1980; Schulz, 1975; Spender, 1980).

1. Physical markers: One common naming practice emphasizes the physical appearance of women ("belle"). As Miller and Swift (1980, p. 87) argue, this practice is sexist because the "emphasis on the physical characteristics of women is offensive in contexts where men are described in terms of achievement."
2. Girl or gal: The use of "girl" or "gal" stresses the presumed immaturity and irresponsibility of women. "Just as *boy* can be blatantly offensive to minority men, so *girl* can have comparable patronizing and demeaning implications for women" (Miller & Swift, 1980, p. 71).
3. Feminine suffixes: This is a popular form of gender differentiation found in the names of athletic, social, and women's groups. The practice not only marks women but it denotes a feminine derivative by establishing a "female negative trivial category" (Miller & Swift, 1977, p. 58). The devaluation is accomplished by tagging words with feminine suffixes such as "ette" or "esse."

4. Lady: This label has several meanings that demean women athletes. Often "lady" is used to indicate women in roles thought to be unusual, if not unfortunate (Baron, 1986, p. 114). Lady is used to "evoke a standard of propriety, correct behavior, and elegance" (Miller & Swift, 1977, p. 72), characteristics decidedly unathletic. Similarly, lady carries overtones recalling the age of chivalry. "This makes the term seem polite at first, but we must also remember that these implications are perilous: they suggest that a 'lady' is helpless, and cannot do things for herself" (Lakoff, 1975, p. 25).

5. Male as a false generic: This practice assumes that the masculine in language, word, or name choice is the norm while the feminine is ignored altogether. Miller and Swift (1980, p. 9) define this procedure as, "Terms used of a class or group that are not applicable to all members." The use of "mankind" to encompass both sexes has its parallel among athletic teams where both men's and women's teams are the Rams, Stags, or Steers. Dale Spender (1980, p. 3) has called this treatment of the masculine as the norm as "one of the most pervasive and pernicious rules that has been encoded."

6. Male name with a female modifier: This practice applies the feminine to a name that usually denotes a male. This gives females lower status because it indicates inferior quality (Baron, 1986, p. 112). Examples among sports teams are the Lady Friars, Lady Rams, and Lady Gamecocks. Using such oxymorons "reflects role conflict and contributes to the lack of acceptance of women's sport" (Fuller & Manning, 1987, p. 64).

7. Double gender marking: This occurs when the name for the women's team is a diminutive of the men's team name and adding "belle" or "lady" or other feminine modifier. For example, the men's teams at Mississippi College are known as the Choctaws, while the women's teams are designated as the Lady Chocs. At the University of Kentucky the men's teams are the Wildcats and the women's teams are the Lady Kats. By compounding the feminine, the practice intensifies women's secondary status. Double gender marking occurs "perhaps to underline the inappropriateness or rarity of the feminine noun or to emphasize its negativity" (Baron, 1986, p. 115).

8. Male-female-paired polarity: Women's and men's teams can be assigned names that represent a female/male opposition. When this occurs, the names for the men's teams always are positive in that they embody competitive and other traits associated with sport while the names for women's teams are lighthearted or cute. The essence of sports is competition in which physical skills largely determine outcomes. Successful athletes are believed to embody such traits as courage, bravura, boldness, self-confidence, and aggression. When the names given men's teams imply these traits but the names for women's teams suggest that women are playful and cuddly, then women are trivialized and de-athleticized. Some egregious examples of this practice are: Fighting Scots/Scotties, Blue Hawks/Blue Chicks, Bears/Teddy Bears, and Wildcats/Wildkittens.

Although these eight categories make meaningful distinctions, they are not mutually exclusive. The problem arises with teams using the term lady. They might be coded under "lady" (Lady Threshers), or "male name with a female modifier" (Lady Rams), or "double gender marking" (Lady Kats). Since team names of all three types could be subsumed under the "lady" category, we opted to separate those with lady that could be included in another category. In other words, the category "lady" includes only those teams that could not be placed in either of the other two categories.

FINDINGS

The extent and type of symbolic derogation of women's teams were examined in several ways. We found, first, that of the 1,185 four-year schools in the sample, 451 (38.1%) had sexist names for their athletic teams. Examining only team logos (903 schools, or 76% of the sample, provided these data), 45.1% were sexist. For those schools with complete information on both names and logos, 493 of the 903 (54.6%) were sexist on one or both. We found that many schools have contradictory symbols, perhaps having a gender-neutral name for both male and female teams (Bears, Tigers) but then having a logo for both teams that was clearly having stereotypical and therefore unathletic characteristics. The important finding here is that when team names and logos are considered, more than half of the colleges and universities trivialize women's teams and women athletes.

The data on names were analyzed by the mode of discrimination, using the naming practices elaborated in the previous section (see Table 12-1). This analysis

Table 12-1 Naming Practices That De-Athleticize Women's Teams

Naming Practices	N	%	Examples
Physical markers	2	0.4	Belles, Rambelles
Girl or Gal[a]	1	0.2	Green Gals
Feminine suffix	29	6.4	Tigerettes, Duchesses
Lady[b]	114	25.3	Lady Jets, Lady Eagles
Male as false generic	248	55.0	Cowboys, Hokies, Tomcats
Male name with female modifier	21	4.7	Lady Rams, Lady Centaurs, Lady Dons
Double gender marking	10	2.2	Choctaws/Lady Chocs, Jaguars/Lady Jags
Male-Female-paired polarity	26	5.8	Panthers/Pink Panthers, Bears/Teddy Bears
Totals	451	100.0	

[a]Several female teams were designated as Cowgirls but they were not included if the male teams were Cowboys. We assumed this difference to be nonsexist.

[b]Actually 139 of the 451 schools (30.8%) used Lady, but we placed 25 of them in other, more meaningful categories.

reveals, first, that over half the cases (55.0%) fall into the category of using a male name as a false generic. This usage contributes to the invisibility of women's teams. The next popular type of sexism in naming is the use of "lady" (25.3%) in Table 12-1, but actually 30.8% since some of the teams using lady are classified in what we considered more meaningful categories (see second footnote under Table 12-1). This popular usage clearly de-athleticizes women by implying their fragility, elegance, and propriety. This is also the consequence of the use of the feminine suffix (6.4%). Another 5.8% of the schools with sexist naming patterns use the male/female paired polarity where male teams have names with clear referents to stereotypically masculine traits while the names for women's teams denote presumed feminine traits that are clearly unathletic. The other important category was the use of a male name with a female modifier (4.7%). This naming practice clearly implies that men are more important than women; men are represented by nouns whereas women are represented by adjectives. Few schools use the other linguistic categories (physical markers, girl or gal, and double gender marking).

The next question addressed was whether the institutions that diminished women through team naming were clustered among certain types of schools or in a particular geographical region. We thought perhaps that religious schools might be more likely to employ traditional notions about women than public schools or private secular schools (see Table 12-2). The data show that while religious colleges and universities are slightly more likely to have sexist naming practices than public or independent schools, the differences were not statistically significant.

We also controlled for region of the country, assuming that southern schools might be less likely than schools in other regions of the United States to be progressive about gender matters (see Table 12-3). The data show that the differences between schools in the South and the non-South are indeed statistically different, with Southern schools more likely to use sexist names for their athletic teams. Table 12-4 analyzes these data by type of discrimination. Three interesting and statistically significant differences are found. Southern schools are much more likely than non-Southern schools to incorporate feminine suffixes and use lady in their naming of female teams. Both of these naming practices emphasize traditional notions of femininity. The other difference in this table is in the opposite direction—non-Southern

Table 12-2 Prevalence of Sexist Team Names by Type of School

Naming Practice	PUBLIC[a]		INDEPENDENT		RELIGIOUS	
	N	*%*	*N*	*%*	*N*	*%*
Nonsexist	289	64.7	135	63.4	310	59.0
Sexist	158	35.3	78	36.6	215	41.0
Totals	447	100.0	213	100.0	525	100.0

$\chi^2 = 3.45$, *df* = 2, not significant.

[a]The determination of public, independent, or religious was provided in the description of each school in American Council of Education *(1987)*.

Table 12-3 Prevalence of Sexist Team Names by Region

Naming Practice	NON-SOUTH		SOUTH[a]	
	N	%	N	%
Nonsexist	500	65.4	264	34.6
Sexist	264	34.6	187	44.4
Totals	764	100.0	451	100.0

$\chi^2 = 10.79$, corrected for continuity $df = 1$, p < .001.

[a]Included in the South are schools from Missouri, Arkansas, Virginia, West Virginia, Mississippi, Maryland, Texas, Oklahoma, Louisiana, Alabama, Georgia, Kentucky, Tennessee, North Carolina, South Carolina, Florida, and the District of Columbia.

Table 12-4 Naming Practices That De-Athleticize Women's Teams by Region

Naming Practices	NON-SOUTH		SOUTH		Level of Significance
	N	%	N	%	
Physical markers	0	0.0	2	100.0	n.s.
Girl or Gal	0	0.0	1	100.0	n.s.
Feminine suffix	10	34.4	19	65.6	p < .025
Lady	47	41.2	67	58.8	p < .001
Male as false generic	173	70.0	75	30.0	p < .001
Male name with female modifier	14	66.7	7	33.3	n.s.
Double gender marking	5	50.0	5	50.0	n.s.
Male-/Female-paired polarity	15	58.0	11	42.0	n.s.
Totals	264	58.5	187	41.0	

schools are more likely to use male names as a false generic than are Southern schools. This naming practice ignores women's teams. Southern schools on the other hand, with their disproportionate use of feminine suffixes and lady, call attention to their women's teams but emphasize their femininity rather than their athleticism.

DISCUSSION

This research has shown that approximately three-eighths of American colleges and universities employ sexist names and over half have sexist names and/or logos for their athletic teams. This means that the identity symbols for athletic teams contribute to the maintenance of male dominance within college athletics. As Polk (1974) has noted in an article on the sources of male power, since men have shaped society's institutions they tend to fit the value structure of such institutions. Nowhere is this more apparent than in sport. Since the traditional masculine gender role matches most athletic qualities better than the traditional feminine gender role, the images and symbols are male. Women do not fit in this scheme. They are "others" even when they do participate. Their team names and logos tend to perpetuate and strengthen the image of female inferiority by making them either invisible or trivial or consistently nonathletic.

Institutional sexism is deeply entrenched in college sports. The mere changing of sexist names and logos to nonsexist ones will not alter this structural inequality, but it is nevertheless important. As institutional barriers to women's participation in athletics are removed, negative linguistic and symbolic imagery must be replaced with names and images that reflect the new visions of women and men in their expanding and changing roles.

In the past decade the right of women to rename or relabel themselves and their experiences has become a tool of empowerment. For feminists, changing labels to reflect the collective redefinition of what it means to be female has been one way to gain power. As Van Den Bergh (1987) explains, renaming can create changes for the powerless group as well as promoting change in social organization. Renaming gives women a sense of control of their own identity and raises consciousness within their group and that of those in power. Because language is intimately intertwined with the distribution of power in society, the principle of renaming can be an important way of changing reality.

Since language has a large impact on people's values and their conceptions of women's and men's rightful place in the social order, the pervasive acceptance of gender marking in the names of collegiate athletic teams is not a trivial matter. Athletes, whether women or men, need names that convey their self-confidence, their strength, their worth, and their power.

REFERENCES

American Council of Education. (1987). *American universities and colleges* (14th ed.). New York: Walter de Gruyter.

Baron, D. (1986). *Grammar and gender.* New Haven: Yale University Press.

Bryson, L. (1987). Sport and the maintenance of masculine hegemony. *Women's Studies International Forum, 10,* 349–360.

Durkheim, E. (1947). *The elementary forms of religious life* (J. W. Sivain Trans.). New York: Free Press.

Franks, R. (1982). *What's in a nickname? Exploring the jungle of college athletic mascots.* Amarillo, TX: Ray Franks Publ.

Fuller, J. R., & Manning, E. A. (1987). Violence and sexism in college mascots and symbols: A typology. *Free Inquiry in Creative Sociology, 15,* 61–64.

Hall, M. A. (1984). Feminist prospects for the sociology of sport. *Arena Review, 8,* 1–9.

Hall, M. A. (1985). Knowledge and gender: Epistemological questions in the social analysis of sport. *Sociology of Sport Journal,* 25–42.

Henley, N. M. (1987). This new species that seeks a new language: On sexism in language and language change. In J. Penfield (Ed.), *Women and language in transition* (pp. 3–27). Albany: State University of New York Press.

Lakoff, R. (1975). *Language and woman's place.* New York: Harper & Row.

Lever, J. (1983). *Soccer madness.* Chicago: University of Chicago Press.

Miller, C., & Swift, K. (1977). *Words and women: New language in new times.* Garden City, NY: Doubleday/Anchor.

Miller, C., & Swift, K. (1980). *The handbook of nonsexist writing.* New York: Lippincott & Crowell.

Polk, B. B. (1974). Male power and the women's movement. *Journal of Applied Behavioral Sciences,* 10(3), 415–431.

Richardson, L. W. (1981). *The dynamics of sex and gender* (2nd ed.). Boston: Houghton Mifflin.

Schulz, M. (1975). The semantic derogation of women. In B. Thorne & N. Henley (Eds.), *Language and sex: Difference and dominance* (pp. 64–75). Rowley, MA: Newbury House.

Spender, D. (1980). *Man made language.* London: Routledge & Kegan Paul.

Thorne, B., Kramarae, C., & Henley, N. (1985). Language, gender, and society: Opening a second decade of research. In B. Thorne & N. Henley (Eds.), *Language, gender, and society* (pp. 7–24). Rowley, MA: Newbury House.

Van Den Bergh, N. (1987). Renaming: Vehicle for empowerment. In J. Penfield (Ed.), *Women and language and transition* (pp. 130–136). Albany: State University of New York Press.

* FOR FURTHER STUDY *

Banks, Dennis J. 1993. "Tribal Names and Sports Mascots," *Journal of Sport and Social Issues* 17 (April):5–8.

Britt, Brian, 1996. "Neo-Confederate Culture," *Z Magazine* 9 (December):26–30.

Churchill, Ward. 1993. "Crimes Against Humanity," *Z Magazine* 6:43–47.

Davis, Laurel R. 1993. "Protest Against the Use of Native American Mascots: A Challenge to Traditional American Identity," *Journal of Sport and Social Issues* 17 (April):9–22.

Duncan, Margaret Carlisle. 1993. "Representation and the Gun That Points Backwards," *Journal of Sport and Social Issues* 17 (April):42–46.

Edelson, Paula, 1991. "Just Whislin' Dixie," *Z Magazine* 4 (November):72–73.

Eitzen, D. Stanley, and Maxine Baca Zinn. 1993. "The Sexist Naming of College Athletic Teams and Resistance to Change," *Journal of Sport and Social Issues* 17 (April):34–41.

Fuller, J. R., and E. A. Manning. 1987. "Violence and Sexism in College Mascots and Symbols: A Typology," *Free Inquiry in Creative Sociology* 15:54–61.

King, C. Richard, and C. F. Springwood (eds.). 2001. *Team Spirits: The Native American Mascots Controversy* (Lincoln, NB: Bison Books and the University of Nebraska Press).

King, C. Richard, Ellen J. Staurowsky, Lawrence Baca, Laurel R. Davis, and Cornel Pewewardy. 2002. "Of Polls and Race Prejudice: *Sports Illustrated*'s Errant 'Indian Wars,'" *Journal of Sport & Social Issues* 26 (November): 381–402.

Malec, Michael A. 1993. "Patriotic Symbols in Intercollegiate Sports During the Gulf War," *Sociology of Sport Journal* 10 (March):98–106.

Peweewardy, C. D. 1991. "Native American Mascots and Imagery: The Struggle of Unlearning Indian Stereotypes," *Journal of Navajo Education* 9:19–23.

Shea, Christopher. 1993. "A Cloud over Symbols," *The Chronicle of Higher Education* (November 10):A33, A35.

Sigelman, Lee. 1998. "Hail to the Redskins? Public Reactions to a Racially Insensitive Team Name" *Sociology of Sport Journal* 15 (4):317–325.

Staurowsky, Ellen J. 2000. "The Cleveland 'Indians': A Case Study in American Indian Cultural Dispossession," *Sociology of Sport Journal* 17 (4):307–330.

PART FIVE

Problems of Excess: Overzealous Athletes, Parents, and Coaches

This section examines some forms of deviance in sport. One manifestation of this—positive deviance—is by the athletes. We usually think of deviance as the rejection of commonly accepted norms and expectations for behavior. Positive deviance, however, results from the overacceptance of and overconformity to norms and expectations.[1] Athletes may pursue goals in sports with such zeal that it undermines family relationships and work responsibilities. Athletes may harm themselves as they use drugs to become bigger, faster, and stronger. They may starve themselves to meet weight requirements. They may injure themselves by overtraining. The first selection, by journalist Larry Tye, examines this type of deviance in youth sport.

The second selection, by journalist Joan Ryan, shows how positive deviance by the athletes combined with incredibly demanding coaches and ambitious parents results, sometimes, in damaged bodies and psyches of young female elite gymnasts and ice skaters.

The third selection, by *Los Angeles Times* writer Mike Bresnahan, describes the intrusion of the corporate world, in this case Nike, into high school sports.

NOTE

1. Jay J. Coakley, *Sport in Society: Issues and Controversies,* 6th ed. (New York: McGraw-Hill. 1998), chapter 6.

13

Kids and Sports

Injured at an Early Age

Larry Tye

One look at Roberta Hanson's legs tells you something is out of joint.

The right one is the color of mahogany, a striking contrast to her otherwise pale flesh. There's a 2-inch scar on the inside of the shin, and a bit higher are two quarter-inch blemishes that look as though they were made by a screwdriver. On the lower thigh, there's another 2-inch scar, and just above the kneecap a knob of flesh juts out.

The left knee is almost a mirror image of the right.

Hanson's knees were ravaged when she tore both anterior cruciate ligaments, one of which was made worse when the injury was misdiagnosed and the surgery botched. At different times, she also damaged the growth plate in her right ankle and tore ligaments in both ankles, fractured her right wrist, and had recurrent stress fractures in both shins.

Listening to her run through her wounds, you'd think she'd gone to war. In fact, she's been in a different sort of combat, the kind waged on basketball courts and football fields in today's world of do-or-die kids' sports. Growing numbers of children are getting into the game, and playing with the kind of passion Hanson showed as a soccer standout at Holliston High School and Fairfield University.

And like Hanson, more and more young athletes are damaging their still-growing muscles, joints, and bones, to the point where sports is now the leading cause of injury among adolescents.

Source: Larry Tye, "Injured at an Early Age," *The Boston Globe* (September 30, 1997), pp. A1, A18. Reprinted with permission.

Of greatest concern are the so-called overuse injuries, things such as stress fractures, tendinitis, and bursitis that often result from overdoing it during training or playing a single sport year-round—something that used to be rare for young people. Now, many sports-medicine specialists say there's an epidemic of youthful overuse injuries.

"Insofar as more and more kids are doing organized sports, I would say yes, there is an epidemic," explains Dr. Lyle Micheli, who runs the sports medicine program at Children's Hospital in Boston and was one of the first to sound the alarm about over-use injuries.

"An understanding of how those injuries come about is just starting to grow," adds Micheli. "We know about it at the college level and the Olympic level. But youth sports coaches are very hazy on it."

Hanson, who is now 22 and coaching youth soccer in Holliston, says part of the reason she got injured so much was "that the preventive stuff was lacking within my training until I reached college. I did flexibility work, strength training, and cross-training in college, but by the time I got there I already was beat up." She also attributes it to playing or practicing six days a week, three to four hours a day, year round, to the point where "I never gave my body time to recover."

But like so many young athletes passionate about their sports, she wouldn't do it differently if she could do it over: "It wouldn't be worth giving up the competitiveness and intensity of that high level of play in order not to risk the injuries."

INGREDIENTS FOR INJURY

The overuse injuries Micheli worries about are the same aching knees, ankles, and shoulders that orthopedic specialists have treated over the years in marathoners and other endurance athletes. Today, however, they're turning up in gymnasts and swimmers, along with baseball, football, hockey, soccer, and lacrosse players—many of whom are teenagers, preteens, or younger.

Young athletes with overuse injuries typically fit a profile: They're on a competitive team or play individual sports at a competitive level. They play a single sport most or all of the year, and go to summer camp to fine-tune their skills. They've recently increased the duration or intensity of training, pushing to the limit in preparation for a big event. And their injury started as an ache or pain, something they and their coach were sure they could play through, but it wouldn't go away.

Some have old wounds that never fully healed or anatomical anomalies, such as one leg being longer than the other, which can predispose them to injury. Others seem to start off perfectly healthy.

All of them, doctors say, use joints and muscles too much, and don't allow enough healing time for the stress-related injuries they develop.

Adults and children are both susceptible to injury when they put too much stress on their bones, tendons, and other body parts. But children have growth tissue that adults don't, leaving them even more vulnerable to overuse problems in cartilage that lines joint surfaces, in joints where tendons and ligaments attach, and in growth plates where young bodies transform cartilage into bone.

One of the earliest overuse injuries to be diagnosed and named was Little League Elbow, a condition in which young pitchers have problems flexing their arms and sometimes end up needing surgery. Swimmer's Shoulder is another, caused by a repetition of shoulder strokes that can reach 400,000 for a typical male over a 10-month season, and 660,000 for females.

Overuse injuries were first noticed in boys, but physicians say girls are even more susceptible, especially as they enter puberty. That's probably because of their increased body fat, their relative decrease in muscle strength, and the changing alignment of their lower body, says Dr. Sally Harris, a team doctor for Stanford University and USA Women's Basketball.

How widespread are overuse injuries?

That's tough to pinpoint, in part because they are difficult to diagnose, and because none of the traditional sports-medicine organizations has been tracking them.

But Harris, who chairs the American Academy of Pediatrics's Section on Sports Medicine and Fitness, writes that overuse injuries "now account for the majority of sports injuries seen in children." Others put the number closer to 40 percent.

Anecdotal evidence from doctors across America lends weight to those claims, although some say rising reports of overuse injuries are partly due to physicians becoming more attuned to such hazards as more kids play sports.

Whatever the doctors say, youthful athletes themselves know all about overuse injuries, and many now accept them as part of the price of competition.

The problems that required the surgical repair of her right knee were due to "some combination of growing really fast and overuse," says Bates Gregory, a 16-year-old from Duxbury who used to spend up to five hours a day practicing gymnastics and now devotes equal time to her new sport of diving. Her left knee fell victim to those forces even earlier, and was operated on two years before the right one.

"Overuse injuries are just part of the sport today," says Gregory. "In diving we all have our injuries to our shoulder and knee and what have you, and we all work through them."

Bates's mother, Elizabeth Burnham, isn't quite so philosophical: "It does disturb me, because I question what physical shape she'll be in when she's in her 30s or 40s."

But Burnham says she and her husband won't try to stop their daughter from diving, in part because "she loves it and I can't even imagine what she'd be like without it."

OVER 2 MILLION HURT

There's another huge class of injuries affecting kids—the breaks, tears, and other wounds that can be traced to a single blow, twist, or fall. Unlike overuse injuries, this group is so sudden and traumatic that it's tough to miss, and it's documented well enough that we have a good idea how many there are and in which sports they occur.

Athletes Hurting to Play

The statistics speak for themselves: For young athletes, injuries are a part of life.

Hospital visits

According to the U.S. Consumer Product Safety Commission's 1996 estimates, 753,255 kids up to age 14 visited hospitals for sports-related injuries. The most painful sport: basketball.

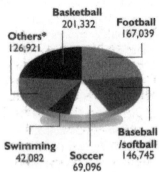

Basketball 201,332
Football 167,039
Others* 126,921
Swimming 42,082
Soccer 69,096
Baseball /softball 146,745

Hurt, but still playing

One hundred former Globe All-Scholastics were asked in a poll about their sports-related injuries:

Have you ever had a serious injury?

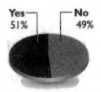

Yes 51%   No 49%

Have you ever played a sport while you were seriously hurt?

Yes 33%   No 67%

Types of injuries

Those athletes who have been hurt were asked what types of injuries they have experienced.

- At least one **broken bone:** 89 percent
- Some kind of serious **knee injury:** 33 percent
- Sprained or broken **ankles:** 22 percent
- Some kind of **stress fracture:** 17 percent
- **Shoulder separated** at least once: 15 percent
- At least one **concussion:** 13 percent

*Others include track and field, hockey, gymnastics, volleyball, wrestling, diving, and tennis.
Source: U.S. Consumer Product Safety Commission, based on extrapolations from its survey of about 100 hospitals.

Take basketball. The U.S. Consumer Product Safety Commission says that, in 1996, more than 201,000 Americans aged 14 or younger suffered basketball-related injuries serious enough to land them in a hospital. Football and baseball claimed slightly smaller tolls of 167,000 and 147,000, respectively, while soccer was responsible for 69,000 hospitalizations.

All told, the commission says major team sports resulted in more than 750,000 kids under 15 visiting hospitals last year. Add in the bruises and sprains that never make it to the hospital, and the number of youthful sports injuries is estimated to be well over 2 million.

Most of those injuries occur in practices rather than games, according to the Needham-based National Youth Sports Safety Foundation. One in six high school athletes is at least temporarily out of action each year because of injury. And while more injuries occur in team sports, those incurred in individual or recreational activities like bicycling generally are more severe.

Which sports are most dangerous? Researchers in Washington State spent 15 years tracking injuries among 60,000 high school students around Puget Sound, and they recently made public their surprising findings.

The highest injury rate was in girls' cross-country running, followed at some distance by football, wrestling, girls' soccer, boys' cross-country, girls' gymnastics, and boys' soccer. The highest rate of "major injuries"—those that make a player miss at least 15 practices or games—was in wrestling, with girls' cross-country and football tied for second.

"I was surprised to find cross-country for girls and boys right up there mixing it up with the big, bad guys in football and wrestling," said Dr. Stephen Rice, chief author of the study. "I also was really surprised that when girls and boys were doing exactly the same sport, girls had higher rates of injuries every time."

That's consistent with other studies showing that girls suffer more injuries to the ankles, knees, and other joints. The difference is especially apparent with tears of the anterior cruciate ligament, the most common knee injury among athletes. Girls suffer two to six times as many torn ACLs as boys, which could be a function of a more vulnerable anatomy or less conditioning.

Overall, however, young females playing organized sports are less likely to get hurt than young males, in part because they're less likely to play high-risk sports. For girls, the rate is 21 injuries per 100 participants per season, compared with 39 for boys, according to the Youth Sports Safety Foundation.

PLAYING IN PAIN

As troubling as the incidence of sports injuries is, equally disturbing is how many kids keep playing despite their wounds, making them worse. And how many reinjure themselves.

Both happened to Michelle Savoie. The first time she tore her ACL four years ago, it was misdiagnosed as an over-extension so she iced it, took aspirin, and rested briefly. She resumed playing soccer for Waltham High for three weeks before the pain became so bad it was clear that she needed to be operated on. The second time, a year or so later, she tore her other ACL; this time doctors operated immediately. Her third knee surgery, last spring, was to take out screws they'd put in during the first one. Last month surgeons went in again to that knee, cleaning the bone and trimming the ACL.

"I've played through injuries because I wanted to; I've played competitively for a long time because I love it," says Savoie, who now plays for the University of Vermont. "I've had these surgeries to prevent degenerative injuries later in life.

"I think I can definitely finish out my college career; after that I might not want to play anymore."

There is no national data on reinjuries and playing hurt, but a *Globe* survey this summer of former All-Scholastics suggests the magnitude of the situation: 51 percent of 90 respondents said they'd had at lest one serious injury. Of those, 89 percent broke at least one bone, 33 percent suffered a major knee injury, 22 percent sprained or broke an ankle, 17 percent had a stress fracture, 15 percent separated a shoulder, and 13 percent had at least one concussion.

One in three said they played with a serious injury.

"My trainer knew I had two broken fingers, but I was willing to play no matter what," recalls Stephen O'Hara, an All-Scholastic swimmer who also played football at Xaverian and now is a sophomore at St. Michael's College in Vermont. "I also was willing to play with minor concussions. . . . At the time we were short of players and I was willing to do whatever I could to help."

Gretchen Bell, who is just starting at Dartmouth, had similar experiences during her high school days playing soccer.

"The spring of my sophomore year, I hurt my lower back but it kind of went away," she recalls. "I finished both seasons and went to the doctor but it was misdiagnosed as muscular and I was sent to a physical therapist. I went to a chiropractor who read some X-rays and misdiagnosed it again. I played for five months and finally another doctor diagnosed it correctly as a stress fracture of the lower back. I was completely out for about two months.

"I played four games at the end of my junior year soccer season. I had to wear a brace 24 hours a day for six months."

Doctors say they're hearing more stories like Bell's and O'Hara's as youth sports become more competitive and coaches make it clear that being out with an injury can cost a player a hard-won spot in the lineup.

There's another injury that young athletes are turning up with more these days, one that doesn't show up on X-rays or MRIs but, doctors say, is every bit as disabling as a fracture or tear. The child reports more pain than can be explained by an injury and often says he or she can't play anymore.

"They're not hysterical, crazy kids where they're making up the pain," says Dr. Michael Goldberg, head of orthopedics at New England Medical Center and Tufts Medical School. "It's because, in addition to their physical injury, they're having a lot of psychological adjustment issues as a result of stress surrounding sports. We see it more in individual sports among gymnasts, ballet dancers, and figure skaters. The reason is the performance pressure in much greater in individual sports."

14

Female Gymnasts and Ice Skaters
The Dark Side

Joan Ryan

Unlike women's tennis, a sport in which teenage girls rise to the highest echelon year after year in highly televised championships, gymnastics and figure skating flutter across our screens as ephemerally as butterflies. We know about tennis burnout, about Tracy Austin, Andrea Jaeger, Mary Pierce, and, more recently, about Jennifer Capriati, who turned pro with $5 million in endorsement contracts at age thirteen and ended up four years later in a Florida motel room, blank-eyed and disheveled, sharing drugs with runaways. But we hear precious little about the young female gymnasts and figure skaters who perform magnificent feats of physical strength and agility, and even less about their casualties. How do the extraordinary demands of their training shape these young girls? What price do their bodies and psyches pay?

I set out to answer some of these questions during three months of research for an article that ran in the *San Francisco Examiner,* but when I finished I couldn't close my notebook. I took a year's leave to continue my research, focusing this time on the girls who never made it, not just on the champions.

What I found was a story about legal, even celebrated, child abuse. In the dark troughs along the road to the Olympics lay the bodies of the girls who stumbled on the way, broken by the work, pressure, and humiliation. I found a girl whose father left the family when she quit gymnastics at age thirteen, who scraped her arms and legs with razors to dull her emotional pain, and who needed a two-hour pass from a psychiatric hospital to attend her high school graduation. Girls who broke their necks

Source: Excerpted from *Little Girls in Pretty Boxes,* by Joan Ryan, pp. 3–15. Copyright © 1996 by Joan Ryan. Used by permission of Doubleday, a division of Random House, Inc.

149

and backs. One who so desperately sought the perfect, weightless gymnastics body that she starved herself to death. Others-many-who became so obsessive about controlling their weight that they lost control of themselves instead, falling into the potentially fatal cycle of bingeing on food, then purging by vomiting or taking laxatives. One who was sexually abused by her coach and one who was sodomized for four years by the father of a teammate. I found a girl who felt such shame at not making the Olympic team that she slit her wrists. A skater who underwent plastic surgery when a judge said her nose was distracting. A father who handed custody of his daughter over to her coach so she could keep skating. A coach who fed his gymnasts so little that federation officials had to smuggle food into their hotel rooms. A mother who hid her child's chicken pox with makeup so she could compete. Coaches who motivated their athletes by calling them imbeciles, idiots, pigs, cows.

I am not suggesting that gymnastics and figure skating in and of themselves are destructive. On the contrary, both sports are potentially wonderful and enriching, providing an arena of competition in which the average child can develop a sense of mastery, self-esteem, and healthy athleticism. But this chapter isn't about recreational sports or the average child. It's about the elite child athlete and the American obsession with winning that has produced a training environment wherein results are bought at any cost, no matter how devastating. It's about how our cultural fixation on beauty and weight and youth has shaped both sports and driven the athletes into a sphere beyond the quest for physical performance.

The well-known story of Tonya Harding and Nancy Kerrigan did not happen in a vacuum; it symbolizes perfectly the stakes now involved in elite competition—itself a reflection of our national character. We created Tonya and Nancy not only by our hunger for winning but by our criterion for winning, an exaggeration of the code that applies to ambitious young women everywhere: Talent counts, but so do beauty, class, weight, clothes, and politics. The anachronistic lack of ambivalence about femininity in both sports is part of their attraction, hearkening back to a simpler time when girls were girls, when women were girls for that matter: coquettish, malleable, eager to please. In figure skating especially, we want our athletes thin, graceful, deferential, and cover-girl pretty. We want eyeliner, lipstick, and hair ribbons. Makeup artists are fixtures backstage at figure-skating competitions, primping and polishing. In figure skating, costumes can actually affect a score. They are so important that skaters spend $1500 and up on one dress—more than they spend on their skates. Nancy Kerrigan's dresses by designer Vera Wang cost upward of $5000 each.

Indeed, the costumes fueled the national fairy tale of Tonya and Nancy. Nancy wore virginal white. She was the perfect heroine, a good girl with perfect white teeth, a 24-inch waist, and a smile that suggested both pluck and vulnerability. She remained safely within skating's pristine circle of grace and femininity. Tonya, on the other hand, crossed all the lines. She wore bordello red-and-gold. She was the perfect villainess, a bad girl with truckstop manners, a racy past, and chunky thighs. When she became convinced Nancy's grace would always win out over her own explosive strength, Tonya crossed the final line, helping to eliminate Nancy from competition. The media frenzy tapped into our own inner wranglings about the good-girl/bad-girl paradox, about how women should behave, about how they should look and what they should say. The story touched a cultural nerve about women crossing societal boundaries—of power, achievement, violence, taste, appearance—and being ensnared by them. In the end, both skaters were trapped, Tonya by her ambition and Nancy by the good-girl image she created for the ice—an image she couldn't live up to. The public turned on Nancy when foolish comments and graceless interviews made it clear she wasn't Snow White after all.

Both sports embody the contradiction of modern womenhood. Society has allowed women to aspire higher, but to do so a woman must often reject that which makes her female, including motherhood. Similarly, gymnastics and figure skating remove the limits of a girl's body, teaching it to soar beyond what seems possible. Yet they also imprison it, binding it like the tiny Victorian waist or the Chinese woman's foot. The girls aren't allowed passage into adulthood. To survive in the sports, they beat back puberty, desperate to stay small and thin, refusing to let their bodies grow up. In this way the sports pervert the very femininity they hold so dear. The physical skills have become so demanding that only a body shaped like a missile—in other words, a body shaped like a boy's—can excel. Breasts and hips slow the spins, lower the leaps, and disrupt the clean, lean body lines that judges reward. "Women's gymnastics" and "ladies' figure skating" are misnomers today. Once the athletes become women, their elite careers wither.

In the meantime, their childhoods are gone. But they trade more than their childhoods for a shot at glory. They risk serious physical and psychological problems that can linger long after the public has turned its attention to the next phenom in pigtails. The intensive training and pressure heaped on by coaches, parents, and federation officials—the very people who should be protecting the children—often result in eating disorders, weakened bones, stunted growth, debilitating injuries, and damaged psyches. In the last six years two U.S. Olympic hopefuls have died as a result of their participation in elite gymnastics.

Because they excel at such a young age, girls in these sports are unlike other elite athletes. They are world champions before they can drive. They are the Michael Jordans and Joe Montanas of their sports before they learn algebra. Unlike male athletes their age, who are playing quarterback in high school or running track for the local club, these girls are competing on a worldwide stage. If an elite gymnast or figure skater fails, she fails globally. She sees her mistake replayed in slow motion on TV and captured in bold headlines in the newspaper. Adult reporters crowd around, asking what she has to say to a country that had hung its hopes on her thin shoulders. Tiffany Chin was seventeen when she entered the 1985 U.S. Figure Skating Championships as the favorite. She was asked at the time how she would feel if she didn't win. She paused, as if trying not to consider the possibility. "Devastated," she said quietly. "I don't know. I'd probably die."

Chin recalled recently that when she did win, "I didn't feel happiness. I felt relief. Which was disappointing." Three months before the 1988 Olympics, Chin retired when her legs began to break down. Some, however, say she left because she could no longer tolerate the pressure and unrelenting drive of her stern mother. "I feel I'm lucky to have gotten through it," she said of skating. "I don't think many people are that lucky. There's a tremendous strain on people who don't make it. The money, the sacrifices, the time. I know people emotionally damaged by it. I've seen nervous breakdowns, psychological imbalances."

An elite gymnast or figure skater knows she takes more than her own ambitions into a competition. Her parents have invested tens of thousands of dollars in her training, sometimes hundreds of thousands. Her coach's reputation rides on her performance. And she knows she might have only one shot. By the next Olympics she might be too old. By the next year she might be too old. Girls in these sports are under pressure not only to win but to win quickly. They're running against a clock that eventually marks the lives of all women, warning them they'd better hurry up and get married and have children before it's too late. These girls hear the clock early. They're racing against puberty.

Boys, on the other hand, welcome the changes that puberty brings. They reach their athletic peak after puberty when their bodies grow and their muscles strengthen. In recent years Michael Chang and Boris Becker won the French Open and Wimbledon tennis titles, respectively, before age eighteen, but in virtually every male sport the top athletes are men, not boys. Male gymnastics and figure-skating champions are usually in their early to mid-twenties; female champions are usually fourteen to seventeen years old in gymnastics and sixteen to early twenties in figure skating.

In staving off puberty to maintain the "ideal" body shape, girls risk their health in ways their male counterparts never do. They starve themselves, for one, often in response to their coaches' belittling insults about their bodies. Starving shuts down the menstrual cycle—the starving body knows it cannot support a fetus—and thus blocks the onset of puberty. It's a dangerous strategy to save a career. If a girl isn't menstruating, she isn't producing estrogen. Without estrogen, her bones weaken. She risks stunting her growth. She risks premature osteoporosis. She risks fractures in all bones, including her vertebrae, and she risks curvature of the spine. In several studies over the last decade, young female athletes who didn't menstruate were found to have the bone densities of postmenopausal women in their fifties, sixties, and seventies. Most elite gymnasts don't begin to menstruate until they retire. Kathy Johnson, a medalist in the 1984 Olympics, didn't begin until she quit the sport at age twenty-five.

Our national obsession with weight, our glorification of thinness, has gone completely unchecked in gymnastics and figure skating. The cultural forces that have produced extravagantly bony fashion models have taken their toll on gymnasts and skaters already insecure about their bodies. Not surprisingly, eating disorders are common in both sports, and in gymnastics they're rampant. Studies of female college gymnasts show that most practice some kind of disordered eating. In a 1994 University of Utah study of elite gymnasts—those training for the Olympics—59 percent admitted to some form of disordered eating. And in interviewing elites for this book, I found only a handful who had not tried starving, throwing up, or taking laxatives or diuretics to control their weight. Several left the sport because of eating disorders. One died. Eating disorders among male athletes, as in the general male population, are virtually unknown.

"Everyone goes through it, but nobody talks about it, because they're embarrassed," gymnast Kristie Phillips told me. "But I don't put the fault on us. It's the pressures that are put on us to be so skinny. It's mental cruelty. It's not fair that all these pressures are put on us at such a young age and we don't realize it until we get older and we suffer from it."

Phillips took laxatives, thyroid pills, and diuretics to lose weight. She had been the hottest gymnast in the mid-1980s, the heir apparent to 1984 Olympic superstar Mary Lou Retton. But she not only didn't win a medal at the 1988 Summer Games, she didn't even make the U.S. team. She left the sport feeling like a failure. She gained weight, then became bulimic, caught in a cycle of bingeing and vomiting. Distraught, she took scissors to her wrists in a botched attempt to kill herself. "I weighed ninety-eight pounds and I was being called [by her coach] an overstuffed Christmas turkey," Phillips said in our interview. "I was told I was never going to make it in life because I was going to be fat. I mean, in *life*. Things I'll never forget."

Much of the direct blame for the young athletes' problems falls on the coaches and parents. Obviously, no parent wakes up in the morning and plots how to ruin his or her child's life. But the money, the fame, and the promise of great achievement can turn a parent's head. Ambition gets perverted. The boundaries of parents and coaches bloat and mutate, with the parent becoming the ruthless coach and coach becoming the controlling parent. One father put gymnastics equipment in his living room and for every mistake his daughter made at the gym she had to repeat the skill hundreds of times at home. He moved the girl to three gyms around the country, pushing her in the sport she came to loathe. He said he did it because he wanted the best for her.

Coaches push because they are paid to produce great gymnasts. They are relentless about weight because physically round gymnasts and skaters don't win. Coaches are intolerant of injuries because in the race against puberty, time off is death. Their job is not to turn out happy, well-adjusted young women; it is to turn out champions. If they scream, belittle, or ignore, if they prod an injured girl to forget her pain, if they push her to drop out of school, they are only doing what the parents have paid them to do. So sorting out the blame when a girl falls apart is a messy proposition; everyone claims he was just doing his job.

The sports' national governing bodies, for their part, are mostly impotent. They try to do well by the athletes, but they, too, often lose their way in a tangle of ambition and politics. They're like small-town governments: personal, despotic, paternalistic, and absolutely without teeth. The federations do not have the power that the commissioners' offices in professional baseball, football, and basketball do. They cannot revoke a coach's or an athlete's membership for anything less than criminal activity. (Tonya Harding was charged and sentenced by the courts before the United States Figure Skating Association expelled her.) They cannot fine or suspend a coach whose athletes regularly leave the sport on stretchers.

There simply is no safety net protecting these children. Not the parents, the coaches, or the federations.

Child labor laws prohibit a thirteen-year-old from punching a cash register for forty hours a week, but that same child can labor for forty hours or more inside a gym or an ice skating rink without drawing the slightest glance from the government. The U.S. government requires the licensing of plumbers. It demands that even the tiniest coffee shop adhere to a fastidious health code. It scrutinizes the advertising claims on packages of low-fat snack food. But it never asks a coach, who holds the lives of his young pupils in his hands, to pass a minimum safety and skills test. Coaches in this country need no license to train children, even in a high-injury sport like elite gymnastics. The government that forbids a child from buying a pack of cigarettes because of health concerns never checks on the child athlete who trains until her hands bleed or her knees buckle, who stops eating to achieve the perfect body, who takes eight Advils a day and offers herself up for another shot of cortisone to dull the pain, who drinks a bottle of Ex-Lax because her coach is going to weigh her in the morning. The government never takes a look inside the gym or the rink to make sure these children are not being exploited or abused or worked too hard. Even college athletes—virtually all of whom are adults—are restricted by the NCAA to just twenty hours per week of formal training. But no laws, no agencies, put limits on the number of hours a child can train or the methods a coach can use.

Some argue that extraordinary children should be allowed to follow extraordinary paths to realize their potential. They argue that a child's wants are no less important than an adult's and thus she should not be denied her dreams just because she is still a child. If pursuing her dream means training eight hours a day in a gym, withstanding abusive language, and tolerating great pain, and if the child wants to do it and the parents believe it will build character, why not let her? Who are we to tell a child what she can and cannot do with her life?

In fact, we tell children all the time what they can and cannot do with their lives. Restricting children from certain activities is hardly a revolutionary concept. Laws prohibit children from driving before sixteen and drinking before twenty-one. They prohibit children from dropping out of school before fifteen and working full-time before sixteen. In our society we put great value on protecting our children from physical harm and exploitation, and sometimes that means protecting them from their own poor judgment and their parents' poor judgment. No one questions the wisdom of the government in forbidding a child to work full-time, so why is it all right for her to train full-time with no rules to ensure her well-being? Child labor laws should address all labor, even that which is technically nonpaid, though top gymnasts and figure skaters *do* labor for money.

In recent years the federations have begun to pay their top athletes a stipend based on their competition results. The girls can earn bonuses by representing the United States in certain designated events. Skaters who compete in the World Figure Skating Championships and the Olympic Games, for example, receive $15,000. They earn lesser amounts for international competitions such as Skate America. They also earn money from corporate sponsors and exhibitions. The money might not cover much more than their training expenses, which can run $75,000 for a top skater and $20,000 to $30,000 per year for a top gymnast, but it's money—money that is paid specifically for the work the athletes do in the gym and the skating rink.

The real payoff for their hard work, however, waits at the end of the road. That's what the parents and athletes hope anyway. When Mary Lou Retton made millions on Madison Avenue after winning the gold medal at the 1984 Olympics, she changed gymnastics forever. "Kids have agents now before they even make it into their teens," Retton says. Now the dream is no longer just about medals but about Wheaties boxes and appearance fees, about paying off mom and dad's home equity loans, and trading in the Toyota for a Mercedes. It doesn't seem to matter that only six girls every four years reach the Olympics and that winning the gold once they get there is the longest of long shots. Even world champion Shannon Miller didn't win the all-around Olympic gold in 1992.

Figure skating, even more than gymnastics, blinds parents and athletes with the glittering possibilities, and for good reason. Peggy Fleming and Dorothy Hamill are still living off gold medals won decades ago. Nancy Kerrigan landed endorsements with Reebok, Evian, Seiko, and Campbell's soup with only a bronze medal in 1992. With glamorous and feminine stars like Kerrigan and Kristi Yamaguchi to lead the way, the United States Figure Skating Association has seen the influx of corporate sponsorship climb 2000 percent in just five years. Money that used to go to tennis is now being shifted to figure skating and gymnastics as their popularity grows. The payoff in money and fame now looms large enough to be seen from a distance, sparkling like the Emerald City, driving parents and children to extremes to reach its doors.

I'm not suggesting that all elite gymnasts and figure skaters emerge from their sports unhealthy and poorly adjusted. Many prove that they can thrive under intense pressure and physical demands and thus are stronger for the experience. But too many can't. There are no studies that establish what percentage of elite gymnasts and figure skaters are damaged by their sports and in what ways. So the evidence I've gathered for this book is anecdotal, the result of nearly a hundred interviews and more than a decade of covering both sports as a journalist.

The bottom line is clear. There have been enough suicide attempts, enough eating disorders, enough broken bodies, enough regretful parents, and enough bitter young women to warrant a serious reevaluation of what we're doing in this country to produce Olympic champions. Those who work in these sports know this. They know the tragedies all too well. If the federations and coaches truly care about the athletes and not simply about the fame and prestige that come from trotting tough little champions up to the medal stand, they know it is past time to lay the problems on the table, examine them, and figure out a way to keep their sports from damaging so many young lives. But since those charged with protecting young athletes so often fail in their responsibility, it is time the government drops the fantasy that certain sports are merely games and takes a hard look at legislation aimed at protecting elite child athletes.

It is also my hope that by dramatizing the particularly intense subculture of female gymnasts and figure skating, we can better understand something of our own nature as a country bent on adulating, and in some cases sacrificing, girls and young women in a quest to fit them into our pretty little boxes.

15

Swoosh Comes to Shove

Mike Bresnahan

Even before the start of the season, when Westchester High boys' basketball team was ranked no. 1 in the nation, opposing coaches were saying it.

Westchester, with its top eight players all likely to earn college scholarships, was so much better than the rest that it belonged in a league of its own.

Now that the season has ended with a state championship and a 32-2 record, many in the City basketball coaching ranks are still talking about the Comets.

They say Westchester has an edge—corporate sponsorship—that is ruining the competitive balance of the playing court.

"What you have is professional players in high school," said Ronald Quiette, the boys' basketball coach at Los Angeles Jordan. "Let them all play each other. Set up two leagues: The semi-professional league, and the rest of us."

Westchester and Santa Ana Mater Dei were among a select 15 teams in the nation that sports apparel giant Nike outfitted for free this season. For Westchester players, that meant an investment of more than $15,000. From headbands to high-tops, each Comet player received more than $1,300 in gear—including five pairs of the newest top-of-the-line shoes. And there is more.

The team had its expenses to a prestigious holiday tournament in Houston paid for by a Nike affiliate. The estimated cost of that trip: $7,000. Westchester also played in three other out-of-state events last season, trips worth about $20,000 that were paid for almost entirely by organizers seeking a prominent headliner for their tournaments.

Source: Mike Bresnahan, "Swoosh Comes to Shove," *Los Angeles Times* (April 10, 2002).

156

Special associations such as the one between Westchester and Nike concern high-ranking school sports administrators, who worry that the lines of fair play are being erased.

The California Interscholastic Federation, which governs athletic competition for the state's 1,292 high schools, doesn't have rules prohibiting such arrangements. But some might be coming in at least one of its 10 sections.

The director of the CIF's largest section said he is tired of endorsement deals such as the ones between Nike and Westchester that seem to allow continued success for "the privileged few."

James Staunton, commissioner of the 522-school Southern Section, said he thinks that restrictive legislation is a potential hot topic for an April 25 meeting of athletic representatives, where voting members from each of his section's 73 leagues will be in attendance.

"The only thing we can do would be to alter our bylaws to make it impossible to do this, even if a district would accept it through their policies," Staunton said. "If the time is right and the council can craft a rule that can at least put a damper on this, I think it would pass in a heartbeat."

Even though Westchester is a member of the Los Angeles City Section, any policy-making decision by the Southern Section is sure to be considered by the CIF's other regional governing bodies.

Staunton, a former high school principal, said Nike's "selectivity" is what disturbs him. "It's not the product; it's how they're doing it," he said. "It's run so contrary to what we're trying to do with the kids. Their business decision interferes with our attempts to try to provide a level playing field . . . and to get away from direct influence on kids."

While most high school teams do car washes and bake sales to raise funds for equipment, uniforms, and travel, Westchester, a public school, attracts all-star-caliber athletes from across the South Bay and parts of Los Angeles. The players admit they have been at least partially enticed by thousands of dollars in free apparel and paid trips to national tournaments that are attended by hundreds of college scouts.

"People who don't play [for Westchester], they're like, 'Damn you're lucky,'" said Scott Cutley, a starter for the Comets at forward. "They see our shoes. They see us traveling. They say things like, 'I'll sit on the end of the bench just to be a part of everything.'"

Some do. Jonathan Smith, a top player at Lawndale Leuzinger High, transferred to Westchester before this season only to become an end-of-the-bench reserve. But he doesn't regret his choice.

"There's a lot of exposure," he said. "At Leuzinger, we only traveled to tournaments in the South Bay. At Westchester, we travel everywhere. The shoes, they're nice too."

And, he added, "We win a lot."

WINNING TRADITION

In the five years they have been partners with Nike, the Comets have won four City Section championships and two state titles. Mater Dei, the other school with full sponsorship, has won Southern Section titles in 10 of the past 11 years.

Fairfax, Crenshaw, Compton Dominguez, Bellflower St. John Bosco, Santa Margarita, Santa Monica Crossroads, and Glendora, which received smaller Nike contributions—most often, shoes and equipment bags—also are perennial powerhouses.

Westchester opponents think this is not a coincidence, although at all of these schools it is hard to determine what arrived first—success or Nike.

"That's Nike's money and they can do whatever they want with it, but it creates parity problems," Reseda Coach Mike Wagner said. "No kid in his right mind is not going to want to go to Westchester, where they get their shoes and sweats and bags."

The result, Wagner said, was a season played to a nearly predetermined climax. It is why a meeting of City Section coaches in October was noticeably void of the usual preseason optimism.

"Every coach in the room knew there was Westchester, Fairfax, and then 58 other schools," Wagner said. "We all knew they'd play for the City championship."

They were right. Westchester defeated Fairfax for the City title and then swept its way to the state Division I championship.

Wagner isn't the only local coach who wishes Nike would share the wealth.

"Let them help all the schools, not just individual schools," said Dave Uyeshima, coach at Hamilton High, which lost two games to Westchester by a combined 109 points.

Almost as aggravating to local coaches as the Comets' tie to Nike is that Westchester's banner season came courtesy of 12 players all hailing from places outside the school's primary attendance area.

Critics say that loose transfer rules, along with Nike's sponsorship money, encouraged a collection of star athletes to converge at Westchester, which is located within window-rattling distance of Los Angeles International Airport.

Hassan Adams, the 6-foot-4 guard who was the Comets' best player, is attending his third high school. He is from Inglewood, as are starting point guard Ashanti Cook, sixth man Brandon Heath, and reserve Bobby Brown. The others come from Santa Monica, Hawthorne, Torrance, Lawndale, Carson, Hancock Park, and the Crenshaw district.

Only one month into the season, four of the Comets' five seniors had already signed letters of intent with major-college basketball programs—Adams to Arizona, Cook to New Mexico, Heath to San Diego State and Brandon Bowman to Georgetown. At least two others—juniors Cutley and Trevor Ariza—are considered certain major-college recruits for next season.

"An all-star team," Wagner said. "There are college teams they could beat."

PAST PENALTIES

Three times in the past two years Westchester has been formally accused of breaking City Section rules, and twice it has been penalized. The Comets were slapped with a year's probation when Adams played for the team in a 2000 summer tournament before his transfer to the school was official, and 6-7 center Ashton Thomas was declared ineligible for varsity competition this season because of an improper transfer from Leuzinger.

Westchester had two transfers in its title-winning starting lineup this season—Adams and Bowman, a senior forward who transferred in as a sophomore. Neither player says he was "recruited," although Adams acknowledges a long friendship with Westchester assistant Marlon Morton, whom he met 10 years ago while playing on the courts of St. Andrews Park in South Los Angeles.

Barbara Fiege, commissioner of athletics for the 62 high schools in the Los Angeles Unified School District, understands the frustration of coaches who struggle to compete with the Comets, but she stops well short of accusing Westchester of recruiting.

"When there are transfer students that go to a school, you can't jump to that first conclusion that they were recruited by people at the school," she said.

While critics say that a roster lacking a single player from the school's neighborhood is evidence enough of recruiting, other coaches defend Westchester's Ed Azzam and members of his staff by saying that top players are sophisticated enough to know which teams are equipped to offer them the most.

The winning equation isn't complicated: Free gear + free travel = talented players, and a team entices even more top players because of the exposure it gets and the college recruiters it attracts.

Azzam said coaches who complain about his team's partnership with Nike are expressing "sour grapes" and "maybe a little jealousy."

"I don't think the kids come to the school because we wear Nike or we get this or that," he said. "Some people think they're going to get exposure or free shoes. But I hope it's because we teach. I'd like to think they come here because they get better and because they want to go to a program where they have the opportunity to win."

Some of his coaching colleagues remain unconvinced.

"It's tough when people say we'll give you three pairs of Nikes and two sweatsuits and we'll go to Vegas or Houston or other places," said Travis Showalter, the recently resigned Leuzinger coach who lost Smith and Thomas to the Comets before last season. "That's tough to compete against. There's no way I [could] match up financially."

SONNY DAYS

Shoe companies such as Nike and competitors Adidas, AND 1, and Reebok, which also sponsor high school basketball teams, know they are in a position to be criticized for their ties to teenage athletes. It's a calculated risk. Forming a bond with a top high school player is potentially lucrative if that player one day signs an NBA contract and becomes a star.

Nike won't soon forget the image of Sonny Vaccaro, a former consultant who left the company to become a prominent member of Adidas, sitting with Kobe Bryant's family at the 1996 NBA draft. When Bryant was selected with the 13th pick, he popped out of his chair and embraced his family, then his friends, and then Vaccaro, with whom he had formed a bond during his years at Philadelphia's Lower Merion High.

Two NBA championships with the Lakers later, Bryant still has a contract with Adidas. His "Kobe Two" shoes hit stores in February. Retail price: $130.

Adidas, Nike's closest competitor, has a budget of about $250,000 to support partnerships with about 40 high schools nationwide, a company source said.

Nike won't divulge what it spends on its "grass roots basketball operation"—its sponsorship of high school and age-group youth teams—but industry experts estimate that in recent years it has grown to $3 million to $4 million annually.

Tony Dorado, the director of Nike's high school basketball operation, believes it is money well spent, especially with so many teenagers jumping directly to the NBA or into the starting lineups of major colleges. That exposure may easily be worth $3–4 million.

Most of the 150 high schools connected with Nike get free shoes, T-shirts, and balls or athletic bags for each player, donations that are tied for the company's sales and marketing strategy rather than charity.

"We're a for-profit company," Dorado said. "I was hired to make sound business decisions, and that's what I do."

Critics might howl, but one prominent sports marketing analyst said Nike and other shoe companies "are just following the tenets of capitalism. The strong survive and the good get better."

Rick Burton, executive director of the Warsaw Sports Marketing Center at the University of Oregon, said, "When we look at the commercialism of youth athletics, we can't speak about total purity, Corporations have been asked to fund and sponsor Little League teams for 40 years. We're OK with it when it was the local Albertsons or the barber shop."

Dorado said Nike's deal with Westchester fits the company's business philosophy of partnering with winners, "We're always going to be associated with the best," Dorado said, "whether it be Westchester or a gold-medal speedskater."

NOT ONLY SPORTS

Local administrators have been grappling for a solution almost as long as coaches have been grumbling about inequity.

Commissioner Fiege said Nike sponsored the City Section basketball championships a few years ago, but was turned down by district officials when it expressed interest in expanding its contribution. The reason: The television program *60 Minutes* had just broadcast its October 1996 investigative piece on Nike and child labor.

"It just didn't seem like the right fit at the time," Fiege said.

Fiege said the CIF, and its individual sections, have occasionally considered strictly regulating sports sponsorships, but decided against it for a variety of reasons.

"If you single out donations to athletic teams, what do you do about the $25,000 worth of computers IBM gives to such and such a school for their business department?" Fiege said, "Once you open those doors to discussion, it's not as easy as one would think to keep it to athletics. You're singling out athletes if you take a hard line and single out Adidas or Nike, but then it's OK to accept IBM or Coca-Cola. How can I sit here and say Coca-Cola is OK and Nike isn't? It's murky."

Marlene Canter, the LAUSD's board member from Westchester's area, District 4, said that while she was proud of the Comets' achievements, the team's Nike contract was an example of "overabundance."

"On the one hand, I'm happy to have attracted Nike's attention," she said. "On the other hand, I'd feel much more comfortable if Nike would be looking at Westchester as a school, saying, 'What can we do to help school [academic] achievement?' Academics is really the ball we need to keep our eye on."

Uyeshima, who recently completed his 18th season as Hamilton's coach, said local administrators need to start looking at teams like Westchester with a more critical eye.

"Downtown, they don't care," he said, referring to Fiege and other City Section officials. "They get a team that goes to the state championship every year. It's frustrating. It seems like they have so many schools and so many things going on, they can't look into it."

In addition to calling for Nike to more equally distribute its sponsorship riches, Uyeshima and others would like to see rules instituted on transfers.

LACK OF CONTROL?

From the local real-estate agent who advertises in the football program to the car dealership that has a banner on the outfield fence of the softball diamond, many high school sports programs have sponsors.

But Marie Ishida, the CIF's executive director, said many schools don't seem aware that there are established guidelines for accepting corporate gifts.

"We've tried to address in our constitution and bylaws that the school's district determines how to divvy up that stuff so that no one group of kids gets all of it," she said. "I'm not sure how many districts are doing that, however, or if they're necessarily aware they should be doing that." One CIF rule stipulates that teams are supposed to report single-source donations of $500 or more to an administrative source—most often, the school principal.

Westchester's basketball team easily surpassed that standard—per player—but Principal Dana Perryman said the team had "established a practice" with a previous principal and that she "didn't know that much" about the Comets' association with Nike.

"Other than tennis shoes, I don't know what else they gave them," she said. "I trust Mr. Azzam and I trust Mr. [Brian] Henderson [athletic director]. They care about the kids. I don't think they would do anything to jeopardize them."

Dave Goosen, whose Venice High teams never beat the Comets during his five years as coach, said the Westchester administration's lack of institutional control makes it culpable for what he says is illegal recruiting by the basketball staff.

"They're just willing to look the other way because when Westchester wins a state title it's publicity for the school," said Goosen, who resigned before the past season, in part because he was tired of being overrun by his Nike-powered foes in the Western League.

"I felt like we were going to war with sticks and stones, and Westchester and Fairfax had machine guns," Goosen said.

* FOR FURTHER STUDY *

Anderson, Sally. 2001. "Practicing Children: Consuming and Being Consumed by Sports," *Journal of Sport & Social Issues* 25 (August): 229–250.

Eitzen, D. Stanley. 1996. "The Paradox of Sport: The Contradictory Lessons Learned," *The World &I* 11 July):307–321.

Eitzen, D. Stanley. 2000. "Social Control." *Handbook of Sport and Society,* Eric Dunning and Jay J. Coakley (Eds.) (London: Sage, Ltd.).

Eitzen, D. Stanley. 2004. *Fair and Foul: Beyond the Myths and Paradoxes of Sport,* 2nd ed. (Lanham, MD: Rowman and Littlefield), chapter 5.

Feinstein, John. 1986. *A Season on the Brink: A Year with Bob Knight and the Indiana Hoosiers,* (New York: Macmillan).

Fejgin, Naomi, and Ronit Hanegby. 2001. "Gender and Cultural Bias in Perceptions of Sexual Harassment in Sport," *International Review for the Sociology of Sport* 36 (December): 459–478.

Franklin, Tim. 1997. "'General' Corrupts Essence of Leadership," *Chicago Tribune* (March 23), Section 3, p. 13.

Johns, David. 1998. "Fasting and Feasting: Paradoxes of the Sport Ethic," *Sociology of Sport Journal* 15 (1):41–63.

King, Kelley. 2002. "High School Sports: The Ultimate Jock School," *Sports Illustrated* (November 25):49–54.

Parker, Rosemary, 1993. "Learning by Intimidation?" *Newsweek* (November 8):14.

Shaw, Gary. 1972. *Meat on the Hoof: The Hidden World of Texas Football* (New York: St. Martin's Press).

Watts, Jay. 2002. "Perspectives on Sport Specialization," *Journal of Physical Education, Recreation, and Dance* 73 (October):33–37, 50.

PART SIX

Problems of Excess: Sport and Deviance

Sport and *deviance* would appear on the surface to be antithetical terms. After all, sports contests are bound by rules, school athletes must meet rigid grade and behavior standards in order to compete, and there is a constant monitoring of athletes' behavior because they are public figures. Moreover, sport is assumed by many to promote those character traits deemed desirable by most in society: fair play, sportsmanship, obedience to authority, hard work, and commitment to excellence.

The selections in this part show, to the contrary, that deviance is not only prevalent in sport but that the structure of sport in American society actually promotes deviance. Players and coaches sometimes cheat to gain an advantage over an opponent. Some players engage in criminal violence on and off the playing field. Some players use performance-enhancing drugs. Some players are sexually promiscuous.

The first selection, by D. Stanley Eitzen, provides an overview of deviance by looking at the dark side of competition in society as well as sport. This is an important consideration because the value Americans place on competition is at the heart of much deviance.

The next selection, by English professor Leslie Heywood, describes various forms of sexual harassment that female athletes experience: questioning of their femininity; lesbian baiting; the sexual advances of coaches; inappropriate comments about their bodies and sexuality; and the policing of their sexuality.

The third selection, by journalist Jill Neimark, summarizes what is known about the serious problem of gang rape by athletes. This essay is related to others in this volume, especially Curry's "Fraternal Bonding in the Locker Room."

The final selection, by Richard E. Lapchick, counters the implication by Jill Neimark in the preceding selection that athletes are prone toward sexual violence. He argues that male athletes are unfairly stereotyped as being more likely than others their age to be violent and, especially, gender violent. He concludes that "the distortions about our athletes and the crimes that a few of them commit need to be put in their real social context. The misleading perceptions need to be corrected so we can focus on the truth and what is really necessary."

16

Ethical Dilemmas in American Sport
The Dark Side of Competition

D. Stanley Eitzen

Although there are a number of prominent American values, I am going to focus on the consequences of the two that I consider the most central—achievement and competition. We Americans glorify individual achievement in competitive situations. A recent book, *The Winner-Take-All Society,* shows how we heap incredible rewards on winners and barely reward others in a number of markets including sport.

The values we promote throughout American society are believed to be good. They motivate. They promote excellence. They make individuals and society productive. They fit with capitalism. And, they make life interesting.

We believe that sports participation for children and youth prepares them for success in a competitive society. According to folk wisdom, these young people will take on a number of desirable character traits from sport. They will learn to persevere, to sacrifice, to work hard, to follow orders, to work together with others, and to be self-disciplined. Assuming that these traits are learned through sport, what else is learned through the sports experience? This is the central question I wish to discuss. I will focus on the dark side of competition, emphasizing ethical dilemmas.

Now I want you to know that while I am going to be critical of sport, much of the time I celebrate sport. I was an athlete in high school and college. I have coached youth sports and several high school sports. My children participated from youth

Source: D. Stanley Eitzen, "Ethical Dilemmas in American Sport: The Dark Side of Competition," *Vital Speeches of the Day* (January 1, 1996), pp. 182–185.

sports through college sport. The last 25 years I have been an active researcher and teacher in the sociology of sport. I am energized by sport. Going to sports events and watching them on television adds zest to my existence. I savor the great moments of sport, when my favorite team and athletes overcome great odds to defeat superior opponents. I am transfixed by the excellence of athletes. I am moved by the genuine camaraderie among teammates. Of course, I suffer when these same athletes make mistakes and fall short of expectations. The key is that I genuinely love sport. I want you to place my critical analysis of sport within the context of my great affection for sport. I love sport, and in criticizing it, I hope to improve it.

Sport has a dark side. It is plagued with problems. Big-time sport has corrupted academe. Coaches sometimes engage in outrageous behaviors, but if they win, they are rewarded handsomely. Gratuitous violence is glorified in the media. Some athletes take drugs. Some athletes are found guilty of gang rape and spouse abuse. Many athletes cheat to achieve a competitive edge. Sports organizations take advantage of athletes. In the view of many, these problems result from bad people. I believe that stems from a morally distorted sports world—a world where winning supersedes all other considerations, where moral values have become confused with the bottom line. And winning-at-any-price has become the prevailing code of conduct in much of sport.

This chapter is divided into three parts: (1) a brief examination of the high value placed on success in sport; (2) the ethical dilemmas in sport that can be traced to this emphasis on success; and (3) the consequences of unethical practices in sport.

SUCCESS: WINNING IS EVERYTHING

My thesis is that American values are responsible for many of the ethical problems found in sport. We glorify winners and forget losers. As Charles Schulz, the creator of the Peanuts comic strip, puts it: "Nobody remembers who came in second." Let me quote a few famous coaches on the importance of winning:

- "Winning isn't everything, it is the only thing." (Vince Lombardi)
- "Defeat is worse than death because you have to live with defeat." (Bill Musselman)
- "In our society, in my profession, there is only one measure of success, and that is winning. Not just any game, not just the big game, but the last one." (John Madden)
- "There are only two things in this league, winning and misery." (Pat Riley)
- "Our expectations are to play for and win the national championship every year . . . second, third, fourth, and fifth don't do you any good in this business." (Dennis Erickson, when he was head football coach at the University of Miami)

Americans want winners, whether winning is in school or in business or in politics or in sport. In sport, we demand winners. Coaches are fired if they are not successful; teams are booed if they play for ties. The team that does not win the Super Bowl in a given year is a loser. My team, the Denver Broncos, has made it to the Super Bowl three times and lost that big game each time. In the minds of the Bronco coaches, players, fans, as well as others across the United States, the Broncos were losers in each of those years even though they were second out of twenty-eight teams, which, if you think about it, is not too shabby an accomplishment.

One other example shows how we exalt first place and debase second place. A football team, composed of fifth graders were undefeated going into the Florida state championship game. They lost that game in a close contest. At a banquet for these boys following that season, each player was given a plaque on which was inscribed a quote from Vince Lombardi: "There is no room for second place. I have finished second twice at Green Bay and I never want to finish second again. There is a second place bowl game but it is a game for losers played by losers. It is and always has been an American zeal to be first in anything we do and to win and to win and to win."

In other words, the parents and coaches of these boys wanted them to not be satisfied with being second. Second is losing. The only acceptable placement is first.

If second is unacceptable and all the rewards go to the winners, then some will do whatever it takes to be first. It may require using steroids, or trying to injure a competitor, or altering the transcript of a recruit so that he or she can play illegally. These, of course, are unethical practices in sport, the topic of this chapter.

ETHICAL DILEMMAS

This section points to some questionable practices in sport that need to be examined more closely for their ethical meaning and consequences.

The Culture of Certain Sports

The essence of sport is competition. The goal is to win. But to be ethical this quest to win must be done in a spirit of fairness. Fairness tends to prevail in certain sports such as golf and tennis but in other sports the prevalent mood is to achieve an unfair advantage over an opponent. Getting such a competitive edge unfairly is viewed by many in these sports as "strategy" rather than cheating. In these sports some illegal acts are accepted as part of the game. Coaches encourage them or look the other way, as in the case of steroid use. Rule enforcers such as referees and league commissioners rarely discourage them, impose minimal penalties, or ignore them altogether.

The forms of normative cheating are interesting and important to consider because they are more widespread and they clearly violate ethical principles. Nevertheless, they are accepted by many. In basketball, for example, it is common for a player to pretend to be fouled in order to receive an undeserved free throw and give the opponent an undeserved foul. In football players are typically coached to use illegal techniques to hold or trip opponents without detection. The practice is common in baseball for the home team to "doctor" its field to suit its strengths and minimize the strengths of a particular opponent. A fast team can be neutralized, for example, by slowing down the base paths with water or sand.

Home teams have been known to gain an edge by increasing the heat by several degrees from normal in the visitors' dressing room to make the athletes sluggish. At my school the visiting football team's dressing room is painted pink. This upset the coach of Hawaii because the color pink, he argued, reduces strength and makes people less aggressive.

Let's look at sportspersonship in sport, using three examples. First, in a state championship basketball game in Colorado, Agate was playing Stratton. Agate because of a mixup over keys could not dress in time. The referees called a technical foul, allowing Stratton to begin the game with two free throws. The Stratton coach, however, told his player to miss the shots.

A second example involves a football game between Dartmouth and Cornell a number of years ago, with Dartmouth winning. Later, after reviewing the films, it was established that Dartmouth had received a fifth down on its winning drive. The Dartmouth president forfeited the win.

As a third example, consider the case of a basketball team in Alabama a few years ago that won the state championship—the first ever for the school. A month or so later, the coach found that he had unknowingly used an ineligible player. No one else knew of the problem. Moreover, the player in question was in the game only a minute or two and had not scored. The coach notified the state high school activities association and, as a result, the only state championship in the school's history was forfeited.

Each of these examples has an unusual resolution. They represent acts of true sportspersonship. Usually, we hear of the opposite situations, a team scoring with a fifth down as the University of Colorado did to defeat Missouri in the year Colorado won the national championship but refused to forfeit (not only did this school accept the victory, so, too, did its coach, the very religious Bill McCartney). Last year, Stanford and Northwestern played to a 41-41 tie. After reviewing the films, the referees admitted that they gave Stanford an undeserved touchdown, yet Stanford did not forfeit. What did the fans of these offending schools say? What did the media outlets say? What did the school administrations say? At my school, Colorado State, the football team upset LSU in 1992. On CSU's winning drive there was a fumble. A LSU player fell on the ball, but in the ensuing pile up, a CSU player ended up with the ball illegally. The player, Geoff Grenier, was quoted in the newspaper that he elbowed and kicked a player in the pile to get the ball. The referees did not see this action and awarded the ball to CSU. CSU's coach, Earle Bruce, said: "One player who should get credit for the victory is Geoff Grenier. If we had lost the ball, the game was over. Geoff found a way to get the ball." The point: the coaches, players, and fans of the "winning" teams accepted these ill-gotten gains as victories. Isn't this strange behavior in an activity that pretends to be built on a foundation of rules and sportspersonship. To the contrary. Such activities involved "normative cheating"—acts to achieve an unfair advantage that are accepted as part of the game. The culture of most sports is to get a competitive advantage over the opponent even if it means taking an unfair advantage. When this occurs, I argue, sport is sending a message—winning is more important than being fair. In this way, sport is a microcosm of society where the bottom line is more important than how you got there. That, my friends, is a consequence of the huge importance we put on success in our society.

Violence

Another area of ethical concern has to do with normative violence in sport. Many popular sports encourage player aggression. These sports demand body checking, blocking, and tackling. But the culture of these sports sometimes goes beyond what is needed. Players are taught to deliver a blow to the opponent, not just to block or tackle him. They are taught to gang tackle, to make the ball carrier "pay the price." The assumption is that physically punishing the other player will increase the probability of the opponent fumbling, losing his concentration, and executing poorly the next time, or having to be replaced by a less talented substitute. Coaches often reward athletes for extra hard hits. In this regard, let me cite several examples from a few years ago:

- At the University of Florida a football player received a "dead roach" decal for his helmet when he hit an opponent so hard that he lay prone with his legs and arms up in the air.
- Similarly, University of Miami football players were awarded a "slobber knocker" decal for their helmets if they hit an opposing player so hard that it knocked the slobber out of his mouth.
- The Denver Broncos coaching staff, similar to other NFL teams yet contrary to league rules, gave monetary awards each week to the players who hit their opponents the hardest.

To show the assumption of unethical violence by opponents in football, in a 1993 playoff game, a player from the Buffalo Bills put a splint on the outside of his good leg so that opponents would concentrate on that leg rather than on his bad leg.

This emphasis on intimidating violence is almost universally held among football and hockey coaches, their players, and their fans. The object is not to just hit, but to hit to punish, and even to injure. The unfortunate result is a much higher injury rate than necessary. Clearly, these behaviors are unethical. John Underwood, a writer for *Sports Illustrated*, has said this about these practices: "Brutality is its own fertilizer. From 'get by with what you can' it is a short hop to the deviations that poison sport. . . . But it is not just the acts that border on criminal that are intolerable, it is the permissive atmosphere they spring from. The 'lesser' evils that are given tacit approval as 'techniques' of the game, even within the rules."

Player Behavior

Players engage in a number of acts that are unethical but are considered part of their sport. These include: (a) use of intimidation (physical aggression, verbal aggression such as taunting and "trash talking," physical threats, and racial insults); (b) use of drugs to enhance performance (steroids, amphetamines, blood doping); (c) use of illegal equipment (changing a baseball with a "foreign" substance, or roughing one side, a "corked" bat, and a hockey stick curved beyond the legal limits); and (d) use of unethical tactics (e.g., a punter acting as if he had been hit by a defender).

The Behavior of Coaches

Coaches are rewarded handsomely if they win. In addition to generous salary raises, successful college coaches receive lucrative contracts from shoe companies and for other endorsements, media deals, summer camps, speaking engagements, country club memberships, insurance annuities, and the like. With potential income of college coaches approaching $1 million at the highest levels, the temptations are great to offer illegal inducements to prospective athletes or to find illicit ways to keep them eligible (phantom courses, surrogate test takers, altered transcripts). Because winning is so important, some coaches drive their athletes too hard, take them out of the classroom too much, and encourage them to use performance-enhancing drugs. They may also abuse their athletes physically. Verbal assaults by coaches are routine.

Coaches may encourage violence in their players. Vince Lombardi, the famous football coach, once said that "to play this game, you have to have that fire within you, and nothing stokes that fire like hate." Let me cite two examples of how coaches have tried to whip their players into a frenzy that could lead to violence: (1) you'll likely remember that Jackie Sherrill, the coach at Mississippi State, at the end of the last practice before they were to play the Texas Longhorns, had a bull castrated in front of his players. (2) In a less celebrated case, a high school coach in Iowa playing a team called the "Golden Eagles" spray-painted a chicken gold and had his players stomp it to death in the locker room before the contest.

Are these actions by coaches in educational settings appropriate? What lesson is being taught to athletes when their coaches blatantly ask the players to cheat? Consider, for example, the situation when a high school football coach in Portland sent a player into the game on a very foggy night. The player asked: "Who am I going in for?" "No one," the coach replied, "the fog is so thick the ref will never notice you."

Is it all right for coaches to crush the opposition? This is the case in college football this season, as it is imperative to be ranked in the top two at season's end, so your team can play in the Fiesta Bowl for the national championship (and, by the way, each team receives $12 million). But this happens at other levels as well. A Laramie, Wyoming, girls junior high school basketball team won a game by a score of 81-1, using a full-court press the entire game. Is that OK?

In general it appears coaches condone cheating, whether it be an offensive lineman holding his opponent or a pitcher loading a baseball so that it is more difficult to hit. For example, consider this statement by Sparky Anderson, the former manager of the Detroit Tigers: "I never teach cheating to any of my players but I admire the guys who get away with it. The object of the game is to win and if you can cheat and win, I give you all the credit in the world."

Spectator Behavior

Spectator behavior such as rioting and throwing objects at players and officials is excessive. The question is how are we to evaluate other common but unsportspersonlike practices? Spectators not only tolerate violence, they sometimes encourage it. They do so, when they cheer an opponent's injury, or with bloodlust cheers such as:

Kill, Kill!
Hate, Hate,
Murder, Murder!
Mutilate!

What about those unethical instances where fans try to distract opponents by yelling racial slurs, or as in the case of Arizona State fans several years ago chanting "P-L-O" to Arizona's Steve Kerr, whose father had been killed by terrorists in Beirut?

Athletic Directors and Other Administrators

The administrators of sport have the overall responsibility to see that the athletic programs abide by the spirit of the rules and that their coaches behave ethically. They must provide safe conditions for play, properly maintained equipment, and appropriate medical attention. Are they showing an adequate concern for their players, for example, when they choose artificial turf over grass, knowing that the rate and severity of injuries are higher with artificial turf?

There are several other areas where athletic directors and administrators may be involved in questionable ethics. They are not ethical when they "drag their feet" in providing equal facilities, equipment, and budgets for women's athletic programs. Clearly, athletic directors are not ethical when they schedule teams that are an obvious mismatch. The especially strong often schedule the especially weak to enhance their record and maintain a high ranking while the weak are enticed to schedule the strong for a good pay day, a practice, 1 suggest, that is akin to prostitution.

Finally, college administrators are not ethical when they make decisions regarding the hiring and firing of coaches strictly on the won-lost record. For the most part school administrators do not fire coaches guilty of shady transgressions if they win. As John Underwood has characterized it, "We've told them it doesn't matter how clean they keep their program. It doesn't matter what percentage of their athletes graduate or take a useful place in society. It doesn't even matter how well the coaches teach the sport. All that matters are the flashing scoreboard lights."

The Behavior of Parents

Parents may push their children too far, too fast. Is it appropriate to involve children as young as five in triathalons, marathons, and tackle football? Should one-year-olds be trying to set records as was the case in 1972 when the national record for the mile run for a one-year-old was set by Steve Parsons of Normal, Illinois, at 24:16.6 (one day short of his second birthday). Is such a practice appropriate or is it a form of child abuse? Is it all right to send ten-year-old children away from home to work out eight hours a day with a gymnastics coach in Houston, a swimming coach in Mission Viejo, California, or a tennis coach in Florida?

Parents may encourage their child to use drugs (diuretics for weight control, drugs to retard puberty, growth hormones, or steroids).

Parents sometimes are too critical of their children's play, other players, coaches, and referees. Some parents are never satisfied. They may have unrealistic expectations for their children and in doing so may rob them of their childhood and their self-esteem.

The Behaviors of Team Doctors and Trainers

There are essentially two ethical issues facing those involved in sports medicine, especially those employed by schools or professional teams. Most fundamentally these team doctors and trainers often face a dilemma resulting from their ultimate allegiance—is it to their employer or to the injured athlete? The employer wants athletes on the field not in the training room. Thus, the ethical question—should pain-killing drugs be administered to an injured player so that he or she can return to action sooner than is prudent for the long-term health of the athlete?

A second ethical issue for those in sports medicine is whether they should dispense performance-enhancing drugs and the related issue of whether or not they should help drug-using athletes pass a drug test.

Organizational Behavior

Immorality is not just a matter of rule breaking or bending the rules—the rules themselves may be immoral. Powerful organizations such as universities, leagues, Little League baseball, and the U.S. Olympic Committee have had sexist rules and they exploit athletes. The rules of the NCAA are consistently unfair to college athletes. For example, the NCAA rules require that athletes commit to a four-year agreement with a school, yet schools only have to abide by a year by year commitment to the athlete. Moreover, the compensation of athletes is severely limited while the schools and the NCAA make millions.

This listing of areas of ethical concern for various aspects of sport is not meant to be exhaustive but rather to highlight the many ethical dimensions present in the sports world. I now turn to the consequences of unethical practices.

THE ETHICAL CONSEQUENCES
OF UNETHICAL PRACTICES IN SPORT

A widely held assumption of parents, educators, banquet speakers, and editorial writers is that sport is a primary vehicle by which youth are socialized to adopt the values and morals of society. The ultimate irony is, however, that sport as it is presently conducted in youth leagues, schools, and at the professional level does not enhance positive character traits. As philosopher Charles Banham has said, many do benefit from the sports experience but for many others sport "encourages selfishness, envy, conceit, hostility, and bad temper. Far from ventilating the mind, it stifles it. Good sportsmanship may be a product of sport, but so is bad sportsmanship."

The "winning-at-all-costs" philosophy pervades sport at every level and this leads to cheating by coaches and athletes. It leads to the dehumanization of athletes and to their alienation from themselves and from their competitors. Under these conditions, it is not surprising that research reveals consistently that sport stifles moral reasoning and moral development. For example, from 1987 to the present physical educators Sharon Stoll and Jennifer Beller have studied over 10,000 athletes from the ninth grade through college. Among their findings:

1. Athletes score lower than their non-athlete peers on moral development.
2. Male athletes score lower than female athletes in moral development.
3. Moral reasoning scores for athletic populations steadily decline from the ninth grade through university age, whereas scores for non-athletes tend to increase.

This last point is very significant: the longer an individual participates in sport, the less able they are to reason morally. Stoll and Beller say: "While sport does build character if defined as loyalty, dedication, sacrifice, and teamwork, it does not build moral character in the sense of honesty, responsibility, and justice." Thus, I believe the unethical practices so common in sport have negative consequences for the participants. Gresham's law would seem to apply to sport—bad morality tends to defeat good morality; unfairness tends to encourage unfairness. Sociologist Melvin Tumin's principle of "least significant morality" also makes this point: "In any social group, the moral behavior of the group as an average will tend to sink to that of the least moral participant, and the least moral participant will, in that sense, control the group unless he is otherwise restrained and/or expelled. . . . Bad money may not always drive out good money, though it almost always does. But 'bad' conduct surely drives out 'good' conduct with predictable vigor and speed."

The irony, as sport psychologists Brenda Jo Bredemeir and David Shields have pointed out, is that often "to be good in sports, you have to be bad." You must, as we have seen, take unfair advantage and be overly aggressive if you want to win. The implications of this are significant. Moral development theorists agree that the fundamental structure of moral reasoning remains relatively stable from situation to situation. Thus, when coaches and athletes in their zeal to succeed corrupt the ideals of sportspersonship and fair play, they are likely to employ or condone similar tactics outside sport. They might accept the necessity of dirty tricks in politics, the manipulation of foreign governments for our benefit, and business practices that include using misleading advertising and selling shoddy and/or harmful products. The ultimate goal in politics, business, and sport, after all, is to win. And winning may require moving outside the established rules. Unfortunately, this lesson is learned all too often in sport.

Sport has the potential to ennoble its participants and society. Athletes strain, strive, and sacrifice to excel. But if sport is to exalt the human spirit, it must be practiced within a context guided by fairness and humane considerations. Competition is great but it can go too far. Personally, I know that my competitive drive has gone too far when:

a. The activity is no longer enjoyable—i.e., there is too much emphasis on the outcome and not enough on the process.
b. I treat my opponents with disrespect.
c. I am tempted to gain an unfair advantage.
d. I cannot accept being less than the best even when I have done my best.

I believe that many times those intimately involved in sport have stepped over these lines. When they make those choices, when the goal of winning supersedes other goals, they and sport are diminished. Sport, then, rather than achieving its ennobling potential has the contrary effect. Rather than making the best of our American emphasis on success and competition, unethical sport perverts these values.

It is time we who care about sport recognize the dangers in what sport has become and strive to change it. Above all, we must realize, to win by going outside the rules and the spirit of the rules is not really to win at all.

17

Despite the Positive Rhetoric about Women's Sports, Female Athletes Face a Culture of Sexual Harassment

Leslie Heywood

Last October, Nike and the Partnership for Women's Health at Columbia University announced Helping Girls Become Strong Women, an alliance formed in response to an on-line survey conducted by *Seventeen* and *Ladies' Home Journal.* That survey found that 50 percent of the 1,100 girls polled reported feeling depressed at least once a week; 29 percent felt somewhat or very uncomfortable with their bodies; and close to 50 percent were unhappy with their appearances.

The alliance stresses sports as a major solution to those problems. It echoes a landmark study written under the auspices of the President's Council on Physical Fitness and Sports, which also emphasized the benefits of sports for girls and women. That report cited, for example, the way sports disprove gender stereotypes about female weakness and incompetency, and the ways in which they foster better physical and mental health, self-esteem, and skills such as leadership and cooperation.

Certainly, sports can help with some of the problems faced by young girls and women. And female participation in sports has greatly increased in the years since the 1972 passage of Title IX of the Education Amendments, which barred schools

Source: Leslie Heywood, "Despite the Positive Rhetoric about Women's Sports, Female Athletes Face a Culture of Sexual Harassment," *The Chronicle of Higher Education* (January 8, 1999), pp. B4–B5. Reprinted by permission.

and colleges receiving federal funds from discriminating against women. High-school girls' participation in sports grew from 300,000 in 1972 to 2.25 million in 1995, and today, one in three women in college participates in competitive sports.

But there is another, less-discussed side to the story. A discrepancy exists between the increasing equality and respect for female athletes on the one hand, and, on the other, behavior within the athletics culture that shows profound disrespect for female competitors.

For example, old assumptions that women who excel at sports are really more like men (and must, therefore, be lesbians, because they're not conventionally feminine) are rearticulated in the kind of "lesbian baiting" of female coaches and athletes that happens on many campuses.

In her book *Coming on Strong* (Free Press, 1994) the women's sports historian Susan K. Cahn discusses the recent rumor circulated among coaches that an anonymous list had been mailed to prospective high-school recruits identifying programs as lesbian or straight. "Oddly," Cahn writes, "concerns about lesbianism in sports may even have increased, in inverse relationship to the greater acceptance of women's sports in general." Such concern shows a profound disrespect, because it assumes that good athletes are not "real women," and that lesbianism is something to fear, which undermines the fundamental dignity and worth of all female athletes and fosters a homophobia that may discourage women from participating in sports.

Other denigrating coaching practices—although they are officially discouraged—include mandatory weigh-ins and criticizing athletes about their weight. Many coaches are inordinately preoccupied with what their female athletes eat, and subject them to public ridicule about their diets and bodies. One group of athletes, from an athletically successful university in the South, told me about a coach who dubbed one of his athletes "Janie Snax" because he thought she was overweight (she weighed 125 at 5 feet 8 inches tall), and had the male athletes make fun of her every time she tried to eat anything. I have heard similar tales on many campuses.

Such practices, though disturbing, may stem from assumptions about women's "natures" that are widely accepted. In a recent issue of *The Nation,* in "The Joy of Women's Sports," Ruth Conniff applauds Anson Dorrance, who has coached the women's soccer team at the University of North Carolina at Chapel Hill to 15 national championships, for being responsive to women athletes by making changes in his coaching style. Conniff quotes Dorrance as saying, "You basically have to drive men, but you can lead women. . . . I think women bring something incredibly positive to athletics. They are wonderfully coachable and so appreciative of anything you give them."

Two weeks after the *Nation* article appeared, *The Chronicle* and other news media reported a sexual-harassment lawsuit filed by two of Dorrance's former players, Debbie Keller (now a player on the national woman's soccer team) and Melissa Jennings. They charge that he "intentionally and systematically subjected his players to inappropriate conduct and unwelcome harassment and thereby created a hostile environment at U.N.C." The suit alleges that Dorrance made uninvited sexual advances, monitored players' whereabouts outside of practice, and sent them harassing e-mail messages.

The idea that women are "wonderfully coachable and so appreciative" has a sinister ring in light of these charges (which Dorrance has denied), and highlights some questionable assumptions underlying the positive rhetoric about women in sports. Gender-based assumptions like Dorrance's, such as the idea that women are more "coachable"—that is, open and manipulable—and that they are "appreciative" of whatever attentions the coach chooses to give them, may lead to unethical behavior such as that cited in the charges against Dorrance.

Yet the issues of coaches' behavior toward female athletes—what is acceptable and what is not—has been swept aside, and reports of the lawsuit against Dorrance have had no effect on recruiting for the U.N.C. women's soccer team. One of the nation's top soccer recruits, in a recent article in *College Soccer Weekly,* said that the allegations weren't "an issue"; that the lawsuit, in her opinion, "doesn't exist."

That kind of dismissal is a common response when a female athlete comes forward with charges of sexual harassment. As is the case at U.N.C., teams often rally around the coach and ostracize the accuser, creating an environment in which most women are afraid to speak out. In the November 14 issue of *USA Today,* Dorrance noted that there was a "silver lining" to the lawsuit in that it "unified the team very quickly." High-profile cases such as this one, in which the news media seem to stress support for the coach rather than for the athlete, communicate to other athletes that if they speak out, they will be brushed aside and disbelieved.

In fact, sexual harassment and abuse of female athletes are part of the reality of women's sports. The executive director of the Women's Sports Foundation, Donna Lopiano, has written on the foundation's site on the World Wide Web: "Sexual harassment or even sexual assault is a significant problem in school and open amateur sport settings across the country that often goes unreported."

Michelle Hite, an athlete who competed in track in the mid-'90s at a major Division I university, told me that "one of the reasons I gave up my athletics scholarship was because of the sexual harassment that I felt was as much a part of my athletics routine as practice was." Hite and her teammates cite coaches' preoccupations with their bodies and weight, inappropriate comments about their bodies and their sexuality (and policing of that sexuality, such as forbidding athletes to have romantic relationships), direct sexual come-ons from members of the coaching staff, and romantic relationships between coaches and athletes—which were destructive and disruptive to the athletes involved and to the team as a whole.

It wasn't until recently, however, that romantic relationships between coaches and athletes were seen as a problem. When Mariah Burton Nelson wrote *The Stronger Women Get, the More Men Love Football* (Harcourt Brace, 1994), she found that harassment was a part of everyday reality in sports culture. "Some of the 'best' male coaches in the country have seduced a succession of female athletes," she writes. "Like their counterparts in medicine, education, psychotherapy, and the priesthood, coaches are rarely caught or punished."

In a crucial first step, most athletics organizations have drawn a hard line against such behavior. In his 1994 article "Ethics in Coaching: It's Time to Do the Right Thing" in *Olympic Coach* magazine, William V. Nielsens, of the U.S. Olympic Committee, wrote: "One of the most pressing issues today that needs to be addressed concerning coaching ethics is sexual abuse and harassment." The Women's Sports Foundation and WomenSport International have developed extensive antiharassment and training guidelines for coaches. In Canada, various sports organizations have joined to create the Harassment and Abuse in Sport Collective.

Athletics departments also claim to be sensitive to these issues, but it remains unclear how much action they have taken beyond paying lip service to the problem. Some more-progressive campuses have established preventive measures, such as educational training for coaches and athletes. The University of Arizona, for instance, has implemented an extensive education and support system, which includes seminars prepared for coaches by affirmative-action officers. The seminars specifically deal with the multifaceted nature of sexual harassment, and include case studies and "real-life scenarios" to clarify what exactly constitutes harassment. Freshman orientation for athletes covers "social issues" like harassment, unethical coach/athlete relationships, and eating disorders. This is supplemented by orientation for parents that lets them know about potential problems that may develop in their daughters' athletics careers, and the resources that are available to these young women.

There are several problems, though, with such prevention and treatment strategies at even the most progressive campuses. The first is that almost all such education programs are initiated by affirmative-action offices, rather than originating in the athletics departments themselves. The Women's Sports Foundation recommends that athletics departments have their own policies and programs, because there is so much more personal contact and interaction in the world of athletics than in ordinary teacher-student relationships.

Furthermore, typical seminars given by affirmative-action offices involve outsiders coming in to lecture individuals who are caught up in an athletics culture that doesn't always take such education seriously. In fact, a conflict exists between athletics, which values winning at all costs, and "sensitivity training," which many athletes see either as distracting or as not applying to them.

It is hard to convince coaches and athletes that the problems of female athletes are real and significant: After all, what does the self-esteem of a few girls matter when we've got to go out and win the big game? The women themselves, who may feel that achieving success and respect is bound up with gaining the approval of coaches, view the people who come to talk about harassment as an intrusion or distraction from the larger goal of athletics success.

Many sports administrators also assume that the athlete herself will report any abuses to the proper authorities. But many women rightly believe that doing so would bring about reprisals, such as being ostracized by their teammates and coaches, and being given less playing time.

The problems are complicated, tied up as they are with assumptions inherent in the athletics culture itself. If we really want to create an environment that is supportive to all athletes, we need to change traditional cultural assumptions about which athletes and which sports are most valuable. As continual debates about Title IX reveal, despite the widespread acceptance of female athletes, in many universities male athletes are still seen as "the real thing," the more-valued players. Over all, universities trivialize issues such as harassment, because allegations are perceived as detracting from "business as usual"—that is, producing winning men's teams.

According to the Women's Sports Foundation, every sports organization, from university athletics departments to youth leagues, should have and implement its own code of ethics and conduct for coaches. Creating a climate that fosters open discussion about sexual harassment also is crucial, so that athletes feel authorized and safe in speaking out.

Often, athletes believe that they will be accused of consenting to sexual relations with coaches, or of making up incidents of harassment. Many athletes also feel ashamed to talk about sexual issues publicly. But harassment is an issue of power, not of sex, and college and university policies need to make that distinction clear.

Parents and athletes also should look for schools and colleges with education programs that inform coaches clearly about what kinds of behavior won't be tolerated, and that inform athletes of their rights and the recourse available to them if they should encounter harassment. If parents and athletes show a preference for institutions with such programs, others will follow suit. But the programs need to go beyond lip service and show real support for women who file complaints, by showing zero tolerance for harassment and not—as has historically been the case—immediately leaping to the coaches' defense.

Sports are great for women. Some of my best experiences have been, and continue to be, in competitive sports. But for sports to really improve self-esteem and provide character building, camaraderie, and learning, greater attention needs to be paid to coaching, the assumptions that coaches sometimes make about female athletes, and how much control coaches should have over female athletes' lives. If we want women to truly benefit from participation in sports, we need to find ways to prevent their exploitation.

18

Out of Bounds

The Truth about Athletes and Rape

Jill Neimark

Meg Davis was gang-raped in the spring of her freshman year by seven members of the university's football team—guys she used to hang out with at fraternity parties. "I knew the guys I 'buddied' with sometimes had group sex, and that they even hid in a closet and took pictures of the event," she says now, "but I never thought it would happen to me." She was sexually assaulted for nearly three hours. She blacked out as she was being sodomized, and came to later with a quarterback's penis in her mouth. When she tried to push him off, he shouted, "Hey, what are you doing? I haven't come yet!" Back at the dorm that night, she says, "I took shower after shower. I stayed in until there was no hot water left. I felt so dirty. Even so, I didn't call what happened to me rape. These were guys I knew. It wasn't until I went to a woman's center in town that someone explained I'd been gang-raped."

Men have been raping in gangs for centuries, from Russian soldiers in Germany and American soldiers in My Lai, to the infamous gang of boys "wilding" in New York's Central Park in 1989. When we think of group rape, it is exactly those packs of men who come to mind. But these days a disproportionate number of gang rapes are being committed by men whom we look to as our heroes, whom we laud and look up to for their grace and power and seeming nobility: young male athletes.

Psychologist Chris O'Sullivan, Ph.D., of Bucknell University in Lewisburg, Pennsylvania, studied 26 alleged gang rapes that were documented between 1980 and 1990, and found that fraternity groups committed the highest number, followed by athletic teams. In addition, she found that "the athletes who do this are usually on a star team, not just any old team. It was the football team at Oklahoma, the basketball team at Minnesota, the lacrosse team at St. John's." It seems to be our most privileged athletes-the ones, by the way, most sought after by women—who are often involved in gang rape.

From June 1989 to June 1990, at least 15 alleged gang rapes involving about 50 athletes were reported. Among the most publicized cases: At Berkeley, a freshman claimed she was raped and sodomized in a dark stairwell, among shards of a shattered light bulb, and then dragged by her assaulter—a member of the football team—to his room, where three teammates joined him. In Glen Ridge, New Jersey, four high-school athletes—all of them former football teammates—have been charged with wielding a small baseball bat and a broomstick to rape a seventeen-year-old slightly retarded girl. In Washington, D.C., a seventeen-year-old girl maintained, four members of the Washington Capitals hockey team assaulted her after the team was eliminated at the Stanley Cup play-offs (but none were indicted by a grand jury); and at St. John's University in New York, five members of the lacrosse team (plus one member of the rifle club) were accused of raping a student.

In spite of surging publicity about the phenomenon, athletes accused of rape usually escape with little more than a reprimand. Virtually every athlete accused of participating in a gang rape insists that it was not rape: He says the victim wanted group sex. *She asked for it.* Juries and judges seem to agree, for charges are often dropped. Pressing charges is crucial for a rape victim's recovery. "A guy gets suspended for half a season and then he's back," notes Ed Gondolf, Ed.D., a sociologist at the Indiana University of Pennsylvania and author of *Man Against Woman: What Every Woman Should Know About Violent Men* (Tab Books, 1989). In the occasional gang-rape cases that proceed to prosecution, notes Claire Walsh, Ph.D., director of Campus and Community Consultation, an organization in St. Augustine, Florida, that specializes in presenting rape-prevention workshops across the country, "convictions are very difficult and rare."

"This act is so heinous," explains Dr. Walsh, "that we don't want to admit we have this kind of brutality in our culture. We don't want to believe our athletes are capable of this. So we immediately rename it, call it group sex, and perform a character assassination on the victim. It's her fault—no matter what the circumstances." What professionals involved in studying gang rape are beginning to understand is that there seems to be something very specific about the gloriously physical, sometimes brutal camaraderie of team sports that can set the stage for a brutal act.

One clue to the trigger for such an act may lie in the dynamics of the team experience itself. You don't find gang rape among tennis players or swimmers or those who participate in other solo sports. According to Bernice Sandler, Ph.D., director of the Project on the Status and Education of Women at the Association of American Colleges, it is athletes on football, basketball, and hockey teams who are most prone to group rape. Athletes who work and play together—hours each day, for months and years—become profoundly bonded. I remember my first, and only, outsider's taste of this bond: I was the sole woman attending a stag party for former rowers on the Yale crew team. I was to play waitress. The men wore nothing but loincloths. They were told to gulp down as many shots of whiskey as they could when they walked in the door. Then they slathered one another with mud and beer and spent much of the evening wrestling with a kind of wild, erotic joy. These guys never once talked about women. I went home shaken but, I admit, also envious. I knew I would never experience that raw, physical abandon with my own sex.

One rape victim recalls a similar experience. The group of athletes and fraternity brothers who later raped her, she said, used to dance a tribal dance in a darkened room, finally collapsing on one another in a heap. The "circle" dance, as it was called, was ecstatic and violent. "They'd be jumping up and pounding the ceiling and singing a song that began, 'When I'm old and turning gray, I'll only gang-bang once a day.'"

Most psychologists believe that powerful male bonding is the essence of gang rape—that, in fact, the men are raping for one another. Peggy R. Sanday, Ph.D., University of Pennsylvania anthropologist and author of *Fraternity Gang Rape* (NYU Press, 1990), explains: "They get a high off doing it with their 'brothers.'" The male bonding in these groups is so powerful and seductive that, says Dr. Walsh, "one man leads and the others follow because they cannot break the male bonds." Those men present who don't rape often watch—sometimes even videotaping the event. And, explains Gail Abarbanel, L.C.S.W., director of the Rape Treatment Center at Santa Monica Hospital in California, "There has never been a single case, in all the gang rapes we've seen, where one man tried to stop it." Even the voyeur with a stab of guilt never reports his friends. "That's the crux of the group rape," explains Abarbanel. "It's more important to be part of the group than to be the person who does what's right."

But there is more to team gang rape than male bonding. These athletes see the world in a special way—a way that actually legitimizes rape. They develop a powerful subculture founded on aggression, privilege, and the scapegoating of women. Friendship is expressed through hostile teasing one player calls "busting." And, according to Dr. O'Sullivan, "Sports fosters this supermasculine attitude where you connect aggression with sexuality. These men see themselves as more sexual because they're more aggressive. I talked to one pro-basketball player who says that for years he raped women and didn't know it. Sex was only satisfying if it was a conquest."

According to Dr. Gondolf, who was also a football player, "For some athletes, there's an aggression, a competition, that's heightened in team sports. You come off the field and your adrenaline is still flowing, you're still revved up, and some of these guys may expect to take what they want by force, just like they do on the field." Dr. Gondolf says that he recalls certain moments from his time as a player, "where the whole team was moving as one, where we become part of a collective whole, rather than individuals."

Within that collective whole, according to experts and some athletes themselves, one way the men can demonstrate their power is by scapegoating women. "There was a lot of classic machismo talk," recalls Tommy,* now 24, who played on the football team at Lafayette College in Pennsylvania. "The talk was very sexist, even threatening. I recall some guys sharing that they were really drunk as a big excuse for having sex with a girl everyone thought was a dog. The guy would say, 'I had my beer goggles on.' He'd act like he was embarrassed, but the fact was he did have sex, so it was a bragging kind of confession."

The pressure to score is powerful. Months after one gang rape had taken place, one of the men who had participated in it was still uneasily lamenting his impotence that night. Dr. Gondolf recalls how some men tended to talk about scoring on and off the field as if they were the same thing: "Abuse of women became the norm—not necessarily out of meanness, but because we saw the person as an opponent, an object to be maneuvered. Because the camaraderie among us was so important, we never questioned or challenged one another when these things came up. I remember hearing about forced sex, group sex, naked showers with women, and the tendency was to shrug your shoulders or chuckle. The locker-room subculture fed on itself."

And when the adrenaline rush of the field does get translated to a sexual assault, Dr. Gondolf theorizes, "a high definitely takes over during the rape, and it has a neutralizing effect. There is enough momentum present that it negates any guilt, fear, or doubt. The man thinks to himself, 'Oh, we're just having a good time, nobody's gonna get hurt.' It's the same rationalization men use when they beat or abuse their wives: 'She had it coming, she asked for it, she didn't get hurt that bad, I was drunk, it wasn't my fault.'"

What is perhaps most difficult to comprehend about gang rape is that the men involved *don't* feel guilty; they don't see this act of group violence as rape. Mary Koss, Ph.D., a University of Arizona psychologist, studied over 6,000 students at 32 universities and found that 1 of 12 college males admits to acts legally defined as rape or attempted rape, and yet only 1 out of 100 admits they have raped or attempted rape. "Of the one hundred thirty-one men who had committed what we would legally define as rape," says Dr. Koss, "84 percent argued that what they did was definitely not rape."

In many of the team-gang-rape cases around the country, the athletes involved readily, almost eagerly, admitted they'd had sex with the victim. In fact, they seemed to offer up their confessions as juicy tidbits. One witness in a case against members of the Kentucky State football team, in which all the men were found not guilty, testified that guys had lined up in the hall holding their crotches and saying, "Me next." And in an Oklahoma case, a player testified that he saw three former teammates—who were also subsequently acquitted—take turns having sex with a screaming girl, saying, "If we have to, we're going to take some from her." In many of the cases the athletes described how they viewed their victim as different from other women: cheap, a slut, a whore. Many quoted the old cliché, "When she says no, she really means yes." Usually they'd heard she was "easy"—sometimes because a teammate had already slept with her. At Kentucky, a teammate testified that he'd had oral sex with the victim three days before the alleged rape. "Any woman who would do that would do anything," he'd said. In fact, according to Dr. O'Sullivan, "Some of these guys are really sweet. They can be very nice to other women in their lives. But once a woman is in this category, it's almost as if she isn't a human being. All their beliefs say it's okay to abuse her."

I found the same disturbing paradox when I interviewed athletes. When confronted with the abstract idea of rape, these men use words like "shattering, disgusting, immoral." (Jay,* 25, a former football player at the University of Rochester, said, "I'll tell you something, I'd never even dream of doing anything like that, it makes me sick to my stomach.") But if they personally know of a case involving their teammates, they're curiously lenient and forgiving. A former starting quarterback at Lafayette College recalled rumors of a gang rape by his teammates on campus. "From what I understand she came on to one of the guys. Not that this justifies it, but she did like one of the guys who allegedly raped her, and she was willing to come up to the room with him." Even when I interviewed an old friend of mine formerly on an Ivy League track team, he mentioned offhandedly that some members of his team had shared a girl with a baseball team in Alabama, which "offered" her to the visitors. My friend never questioned whether it might have been rape: He assumed the girl was willing.

One possible reason for the astounding lack of guilt among athletes who rape is the special privilege accorded a star athlete—and the constant female adoration he attracts. "The 'hotshot syndrome' is inevitably part of team sports," says Dr. Gondolf. "If you're an athlete in college, you're given scholarships, a nice dorm, doctors, trainers, a lot of support and attention and cheerleaders who ogle you. That sense of privilege influences you, and some guys may then think, 'I deserve something for this, I can take women, the rules don't apply to me.' They feel they're above the law."

"I used to have girls call me up," says former quarterback Jay, "and say, 'I go to football games and watch you, I look at your picture in the program, I'm writing a paper on you.' It happened all the time. You get this attitude where you can do anything you want and nobody is every going to say anything to you."

Coaches and universities contribute to the athlete's unique sense of entitlement. As Dr. Walsh notes, "When we're talking about athletic teams and gang rape, we see how, time after time, the entire community comes to the support of the team. Athletes are very important in the fabric of a campus or town. They keep alumni interested, and produce money for the community."

Says one outraged father of a seventeen-year-old rape victim, "The college threatened her. They told her if she went to the police her name would be in the paper, and her grandparents, who lived in a neighboring town, would see it. She went to the assistant dean, who never told the dean. He simply made an investigation himself, and wrote her a few months later saying the investigation had led nowhere and he was going to close the matter. The police chief even bragged to me that he'd worked hard to cover it up. As for the boys who raped her, they admitted having sex, but said she was a slut—she'd asked for it. It didn't matter that she'd gone on less than a dozen dates in her life."

Coaches also do their best to help their "boys" slip through the adverse publicity unpunished. Perhaps that's not too surprising, since the coaches themselves are often former players. "Twenty years ago someone could have talked to *me* about all this stuff," confessed Ray Tellier, former football coach and facilitator of campus discussions on rape at the University of Rochester. And three years ago, Bobby Knight, basketball coach at Indiana University, created an uproar by telling broadcaster Connie Chung: "I think that if rape is inevitable, relax and enjoy it."

The attitude of juries is often similarly lenient: Sergeant Danny Conway, a detective in Frankfort, Kentucky, who prosecuted the gang-rape case at Kentucky State University, recalls his fury when the five players prosecuted for rape were set free. "We charged five men on the football team—although there must have been more, because there were semen samples that didn't belong to any of the five. All of them said she was a willing participant, because she had snuck into the dorm with one of them, And all of them were dismissed. These guys made sport of it. In the trial they were giving one another high-fives and holding their fists up in the air and saying, 'First I got her, then he got her,' and they were smiling at one another in open court. The jury didn't seem fazed at all. Their decision tore me to pieces. It never seemed to faze them that this was a young lady whose life was probably ruined."

In the past few years those entrenched attitudes have finally, slowly, begun to be challenged. "At least now we recognize how often gang rape occurs," notes Dr. Walsh. Many universities and fraternities have begun education programs about rape, and Santa Monica's Rape Treatment Center offers an educational video that is being distributed across the country, starring Susan Dey and Corbin Bernsen of *L.A. Law*. At Syracuse University in New York, where last year six rapes were reported in the first five weeks of the school year, activists have formed a group called SCARED (Students Concerned About Rape Education). And New York recently passed a law that requires freshman rape orientation for schools receiving state funds.

New studies are showing that there is no such thing as a typical rape victim. Many women who are raped in college are virgins, according to Mary Koss's study—and the vast majority (75 to 91 percent) of rape victims cannot be differentiated from nonvictims in terms of risk factors like personality or circumstance. Women are often raped in the "honeymoon" period, however: those first few months of school when they're learning to negotiate their new world. And drinking is almost always involved; in fact, states Dr. Walsh, "alcohol is used deliberately to impair the woman." At parties, punch is massively spiked with liquor—to the point where some rape victims complain that they had only two drinks before they passed out drunk. One victim at San Diego State University recalls asking for a nonalcoholic beverage. Instead she was brought punch spiked with Everclear, a 95-percent-alcohol drink that is illegal in California.

But if outside observers have difficulty finding common attributes among victims of team rape, it seems clear that the men themselves have an unspoken code that divides women into classes—the nice-girl girlfriend and the party-girl rape victim. The scary part is that the cues are so hidden most women are completely unaware of them—and the rules may be different among different teams, different campuses, different locker rooms. Athletes will sometimes let drop a few clues: Usually a woman is more vulnerable if she's had sex with one of the group before; if she's buxom, wears tight clothes and lots of makeup; if she's from a college that has a certain reputation.

One fraternity actually stuck colored dots on women's hands as they came to a party, color-coded to indicate how "easy" each woman was. It's that kind of hidden code that has more and more colleges warning young women to stay away altogether from the fraternity and house parties where athletes and their buddies gather—just as one must avoid dark alleys at night. Dr. Gondolf explains: "Athletes are so tangled up in their glory and their privilege, and they get such big benefits for it. We need women to prompt them to check up on one another." But that is only half the answer.

In the case of gang rape, almost all college women are so devastated they drop out of school. "These are overwhelming rapes, and the trauma is profound," explains Abarbanel. "A lot of these women are freshmen who are just beginning to test their independence. They have hopes and dreams about college and achievement, meeting new people, a career, a future. After gang rape, everything that college means is lost to them. They're afraid to be alone, afraid of a recurrence. And since these are often men they know, the sense of betrayal is very profound."

In some cases, says Dr. Sanday, a woman may have subconsciously been courting danger. She knows she should avoid certain parties, be careful about her drinking, come and leave with friends. But she's looking for power, on male territory. "We all, at certain times in our life, test ourselves. It's like going into the inner city on a dare. These women are using the men that way. They want to court and conquer danger. And legally and morally, they have a right to go and have sex with whomever they want, without being gang-raped."

One of the most important ways to prevent rape may be to understand what the word means. Many men and women don't know that the law *requires* that a woman give consent to sexual intercourse. If she's so inebriated that she can't say yes, or so frightened that she won't say no, the act is rape.

But just knowing that distinction is not quite enough; the seeds of team gang rape are buried deep, even subconsciously, in the athletic culture. Dr. O'Sullivan tells of an incident outside the courtroom of the Kentucky State football-team trial. According to her, "We were all standing by the candy machine, and some guy mentioned that it was broken. And Big Will, a huge man who had charmed everybody, and who was testifying on behalf of his dormmate, said, 'I'll make it work. Everybody always does what I want.' And everybody laughed. I couldn't believe it. This is exactly the kind of attitude that can lead to the rape." The perception that force is "okay," that it is masculine and admirable, is really where gang rape begins—and where the fight against it will have to start.

NOTE

*Name has been changed.

19

Crime and Athletes

New Racial Stereotypes

Richard E. Lapchick

It is ironic that as we begin a new millennium, hopeful that change will end the ills such as racism that have plagued our society throughout past centuries, more subtle forms of racism in sport may be infecting American culture.

Polite white society can no longer safely express the stereotypes that so many believe about African Americans. Nonetheless, surveys show that the majority of whites still believe that most African Americans are less intelligent, are more likely to use drugs and be violent, and are more inclined to be violent against women.

However, sport as it is currently being interpreted, now provides whites with the chance to talk about athletes in a way that reinforces those stereotypes about African Americans. With African Americans dominating the sports we watch most often (77 percent of the players in the National Basketball Association, 65 percent in the National Football League, 15 percent in Major League Baseball—another 25 percent are Latino). African Americans comprise 57 percent of the students playing National Collegiate Athletic Association (NCAA) Division I basketball and 47 percent of those playing NCAA Division IA football. Whites tend to "think black" when they think about the major sports.

Many athletes and community leaders believe that the public has been unfairly stereotyping athletes all across America. The latest, and perhaps most dangerous, stereotype, is that playing sport makes athletes more prone to being violent and, especially, gender violent.

Source: Richard E. Lapchick, "Crime and Athletes: New Racial Stereotypes," *Society* 37 (March/April 2000), pp. 14–20.

Rosalyn Dunlap, an eight-time All-American sprinter who now works on so-cial issues involving athletes, including gender violence prevention, said, "perpetra-tors are not limited to any category or occupation. The difference is that athletes who rape or batter will end up on TV or in the newspapers. Such images of athletes in trouble create a false and dangerous mindset with heavy racial overtones. Most other perpetrators will be known only to the victims, their families, the police and the courts."

On our predominantly white college campuses, student athletes are being char-acterized by overwhelmingly white student bodies and faculties while they are being written about by a mostly white male media for a preponderance of white fans.

At an elite academic institution, I asked members of the audience to write down five words they would use to describe American athletes. In addition to listing positive adjectives, not one missed including one of the following words: dumb, violent, rapist, or drug user!

In the past two years, I have met with NBA and NFL players as well as college-student athletes on more than a dozen campuses. There are a lot of angry athletes who are convinced the public is characterizing them because of the criminal acts of a few.

Tom "Satch" Sanders helped the Boston Celtics win eight world champion-ships. Sanders noted, "If they aren't angry about their broad brush depiction, they should be. The spotlight is extremely bright on athletes; their skills have made them both famous and vulnerable. Their prominence means they will take much more heat from the media and the public for similar situations that befall other people with normal lives."

He is now vice president for player programs for the NBA. That office helps guide players off the court to finish their education, prepares them for careers after basketball, and helps those that may have problems adjusting to all the attention that goes to NBA stars.

Many American men have grown to dislike athletes. Given the choice, a typi-cal man might want the money and the fame but knows it is unattainable for him. After reading all the negative stories about athletes, he doesn't want to read about Mike Tyson complaining about being treated unfairly when Tyson has made a re-ported $100 million in his post-release rehabilitation program; or about the large number of professional athletes signing contracts worth more than $10 million a year.

The anger of some white men extends to people who look or act differently than themselves. They are a mini-thought away from making egregious stereotypes about the "other groups" they perceive as stealing their part of the American pie.

Big-time athletes fit the "other groups." Whether it is an African American athlete or coach, or a white coach of African American athletes, when something goes wrong with a player, the national consequences are likely to be immediate.

Sanders expanded on this. "Everyone feels that athletes have to take the good with the bad, the glory with the negative publicity. However, no one appreciates the broad brush application that is applied in so many instances. Of the few thousand that play sport on the highest level, if four or five individuals in each sport—particularly if they are black—have problems with the law, people won't have long to wait before some media people are talking about all those athletes."

Here is the equation we are dealing with as stereotypes of our athletes are built. Fans, who are mostly white, observe sport through a media filter which is overwhelmingly made up of white men. There are 1,600 daily newspapers in America. There are only four African American sports editors in a city where there are professional franchises and 19 African American columnists. Both numbers, as reported at the recent conference of the National Association of Black Journalists, have almost doubled since 1998 and represent a positive sign. Nonetheless, there are no African American sports writers on 90 percent of the 1,600 papers!

I do not, nor would I ever, suggest that most or even many of the white writers are racist. However, they were raised in a culture in which many white people have strong beliefs about what it means to be African American.

The obvious result is the *reinforcement* of white stereotypes of athletes, who are mostly African American in our major sports.

According to the National Opinion Research Center Survey, sponsored by the National Science Foundation for the University of Chicago, whites share the following attitudes:

- 56 percent of whites think African Americans are more violent;
- 62 percent think African Americans are not as hard working as whites;
- 77 percent of whites think most African Americans live off welfare;
- 53 percent think African Americans are less intelligent.

It can be expected that some white writers learned these stereotypes in their own upbringing. When they read about an individual or several athletes who have a problem, it becomes easy to leap to the conclusion that fits the stereotype. Sanders said, "Blacks in general have been stereotyped for having drugs in the community as well as for being more prone to violence. However, now more than ever before, young black athletes are more individualistic and they resist the 'broad brush.' They insist on being judged as individuals for everything." But even that resistance can be misinterpreted by the public and writers as merely being off-the-court trash-talking.

SPORTS' SPECIFIC PROBLEMS

There are, of course, problems in college and professional sports. For the purposes of this chapter, I will only deal with those that involve problems and perceptions of athletes.

Our athletes are coming from a generation of despairing youth cut adrift from the American dream. When the Center for the Study of Sport in Society started in 1984, one of its primary missions was helping youth balance academics and athletics. Now, the issue for youth is balancing life and death.

We are recruiting athletes:

- who have increasingly witnessed violent death. If one American child under the age of 16 is killed every two hours with a handgun, then there is a good chance that our athletes will have a fallen family member or friend. More American children have died from handguns in the last ten years than all the American soldiers who died in Vietnam. Tragedies in places like Paducah, Kentucky, and Littleton, Colorado, have shown us that violent deaths are not limited to our cities.
- who are mothers and fathers when they get to our schools. There are boys who helped 900,000 teenage girls get pregnant each year so we are increasingly getting student-athletes who will leave our colleges after four years with one or more children who are 4–5 years old.
- who have seen friends or family members devastated by drugs.
- who have seen battering in their home.
- who were victims of racism in school. Three-quarters (75 percent) of all students surveyed by Lou Harris reported seeing or hearing about racially or religiously motivated confrontations with overtones of violence very or somewhat often.
- who come home alone: 57 percent of all American families, black and white alike, are headed by either a single parent or two working parents.

We desperately need professionals on our campuses who can deal with these nightmarish factors. The reality is that few campuses or athletic departments have the right people to help guide these young men and women into the 21st century. So what are our problems?

ACADEMIC ISSUES IN COLLEGE SPORT

Academically, we get athletes who have literacy problems. The press discusses that student-athletes have literacy problems extensively throughout the year as if it were a problem unique to athletes. However, it is rarely reported—and never in the sports pages—that 30 percent of *all entering freshmen* must take remedial English or math.

Academically, we get athletes who will not graduate. It is—and always should be—an issue for college athletics to increase the percentages of those who graduate from our colleges. However, the demographics of college have now changed to the point where only 14 percent of entering freshmen graduate in four years. If an athlete does not graduate in four years, some call him dumb; others say the school failed him. Few note that he may be typical of college students.

Don McPherson nearly led Syracuse to a national championship when he was their quarterback in the 1980s. After seven years in the NFL and CFL, McPherson worked until recently directing the Mentors in Violence Prevention (MVP) Program. MVP is the nation's biggest program using athletes as leaders to address the issue of men's violence against women.

McPherson reflected on the image of intelligence and athletes. "When whites meet an uneducated black athlete who blew opportunities in college or high school, they think he is dumb. They don't question what kind of school he may have had to attend if he was poor, or how time pressures from sport may have affected him. If they don't make it as a professional athlete, they're through without a miracle.

"I met lots of 'Trust Fund Babies' at Syracuse. They blew opportunities. No one called them dumb, just rich. We knew they would not need a miracle to get a second chance.

"I played at Syracuse at a time when being a black quarterback had become more acceptable. But the stereotypes still remained. As a player, people still remember me as a great runner and scrambler. I had not dented their image of the physical vs. intelligent black athlete."

This was in spite of the fact that McPherson led the nation in passing efficiency over Troy Aikman and won the Maxwell Award. He won many awards but Don McPherson was most proud of being the nation's passing efficiency leader. "I should have shattered the image of the athletic and mobile black quarterback and replaced it with the intelligent black quarterback. Unfortunately, stereotypes of football players, mostly black, still prevail. They make me as angry as all the stereotypes of black people in general when I was growing up."

McPherson wore a suit to class and carried the *New York Times* under his arm. He was trying to break other images of African American men and athletes. But McPherson said that those whites who recognized his style were both "surprised and said I was 'a good black man' as if I was different from other black men. Most students assumed I was poor and that football was going to make me rich. Like many other blacks on campus, I was middle class. My father was a detective and my mother was a nurse."

There is a common belief that student-athletes, especially those in the revenue sports, have lower graduation rates than students who are not athletes. The facts do not bear this out. Yet it is difficult to get accurate reporting.

- Irrespective of color or gender, student-athletes graduate at higher rate than non–student-athletes.
- White male Division I student-athletes graduate at a rate of 58 percent vs. 57 percent for white male nonathletes. African American male Division I student-athletes graduate at a rate of 42 percent vs. 34 percent for African American male nonathletes.
- White female Division I student-athletes graduate at a rate of 70 percent while 61 percent of white female nonathletes graduate. African American female Division I student-athletes graduate at a rate of 58 versus only 43 percent of the African American female nonathletes.

The disparities, however, remain when we compare white to African American student athletes:

- White male Division I basketball student-athletes graduate at a rate of 52 percent versus a 38 percent graduation rate for African American male Division I basketball student-athletes, still higher than the 34 percent grad rate for African American male nonathletes.
- White female Division I basketball student athletes graduate at a rate of 71 percent while only 57 percent of African American female Division I basketball student-athletes graduate.

College sport does not own these problems. They belong to higher education in general and its inheritance of the near bankruptcy of secondary education in some communities. The publication of graduation rates, long feared by athletic administrators, at once revealed those scandalous rates, but also showed what poor graduation rates there were for all students of color. It turned out that our predominantly white campuses were unwelcoming environments for all people of color.

African American student-athletes arrive on most campuses and see that only seven percent of the student body, three percent of the faculty, and less than five percent of top athletics administrators and coaches look like them. Unless there is a Martin Luther King Center or Boulevard, all of the buildings and streets are named after white people.

In many ways, the publication of graduation rates for student-athletes helped to push the issue of diversity to the forefront of campus-wide discussions of issues of race, ethnicity, and gender. Educators finally recognized what a poor job they were doing at graduating all students of color.

DRUGS AND ALCOHOL IN SPORT

We will get athletes who use drugs. CNN Headline News will understandably run footage of every name athlete who is arrested with drugs. It has become a common belief that athletes have a particular problem with drug and alcohol abuse. Reoccurring problems of athletes like Darryl Strawberry reinforce this image but facts do not bear this out.

According to an extensive *Los Angeles Times* survey of athletes and crime committed in 1995, a total of 22 athletes and three coaches were accused of a drug-related crime in 1995. That means that, on average, we read about a new sports figure with a drug problem every two weeks! Anecdotally, those numbers have seemed to continue in succeeding years. Each new story reinforces the image from the last one.

Their stories are and surely should be disturbing. But those stories are rarely, if ever, put in the context of the 1.9 million Americans who use cocaine each month or the 2.1 million who use heroin throughout their lives. A total of 13 million people (or a staggering 6 percent of the American population) use some illicit drug each month. When you look at the 18–25 male age group in general, the percentage leaps to 17 percent. Twenty-two athletes represent a small fraction of a single percent of the more than 400,000 who play college and professional sports in America.

The NBA's drug policy with the potential of a lifetime ban is generally recognized as a model for sports. The policy may have stopped a substance abuse problem that existed before its inception.

Now players recognize that using so-called "recreational" drugs can seriously hurt their professional abilities in one of America's most competitive professions. Don McPherson emphasized the point that "our personal and professional lives have to be clean and sharp. We cannot afford to lose the competitive edge or our careers will be cut short. There are too many talented young men waiting to step in our shoes."

The NBA's Sanders insists that African American athletes are still being stereotyped as drug users because "blacks in general have been stereotyped for having drugs in the community. . . . I know they [athletes] are hurt by the broad brush" used by the public when it come to African American athletes.

In the same *Los Angeles Times* survey, 28 athletes and 4 coaches had charges related to alcohol. None of these 32 cases were put in the context of the 13 million Americans who engage in binge drinking at least 5 times per month. Yet we read about a new athlete with an alcohol problem every 11 days. Such images can surely create a building sense of problems in athletics if they are not viewed in the context of society.

McPherson remembered being "shocked" when he arrived on Syracuse's campus to see how much drinking went on each night among students in general. He felt compelled to call football players he knew on other campuses. "It was the same everywhere. Now when I go to speak on college campuses I always ask. It is worse today. Athletes are also part of that culture, but insist that practice and academics crowd their schedules too much to be in bars as often as other students."

ATHLETES AND VIOLENCE

We are getting athletes who have fights during games, in bars, and on campus. Is there a link between the violence of a sport and one's actions away from that sport? There is certainly a growing body of public opinion that assumes that there is. Media reports regularly imply that the violence of sport makes its participants more violent in society.

Are sports any more violent today than 20 years ago when no one would have made such an assertion? Or is it the fact that our streets and our schools surely are more violent. According to the National Education Association, there are 2,000 assaults *in our schools every hour of every day!* It is an ugly phenomenon that is neither bound by race, class, geography, nor by athlete vs. nonathlete.

We do have athletes who are the perpetrators in cases of gender violence. In the wake of the O.J. Simpson case, any incident involving an athlete assaulting a woman has received extraordinary publicity. The individual cases add up to the mindset stereotype of 1999: athletes, especially basketball and football players, are more inclined to be violent towards women than nonathletes.

Joyce Williams-Mitchell is the executive director of the Massachusetts Coalition of Battered Women's Service Groups. As an African American woman, she abhors the imagery of athletes being more prone to be violent against women. "It is a myth. The facts do not bear this out. All the studies of patterns of batterers; defined by occupation point to men who control women through their profession. We hear about police, clergy, dentists, and judges. I only hear about athletes as batterers when I read the paper. They are in the public's eye. Men from every profession have the potential to [be] batterers."

There have been, of course, too many cases of athletes committing assaults on girls and women.

However, there has never been a thorough, scientific study conclusively showing that athletes are more inclined than others to commit assaults. The only study that comes close was written by Jeffrey Benedict, Todd Crossett, and Mark McDonald. It was based on 65 cases of assault against women over three years on 10 Division I campuses. Thirteen of the cases involved athletes; seven were basketball or football players.

In spite of the authors pointing out the limitations of both the small numbers and the fact that they did not control for use of alcohol, tobacco, and the man's attitude toward women (the three main predictors of a male's inclination to gender violence), the press regularly quotes their study without qualification. Media reports never state that it is a study that came up with 13 athletes over three years. They simply say that the study concluded that nearly 20 percent of all campus assaults are committed by student-athletes and most are committed by basketball or football players. Rosalyn Dunlap underlines that "This is a racially loaded conclusion. When I was a student-athlete at the University of Missouri, I never thought of keeping myself safe from a 260-pound football player anymore than any other man on the street. In fact, male athletes on campus protected me."

Here is some critical data usually missing in the debate about athletes and violence against women.

- In 1994, 1,400 men killed their significant others. O.J. Simpson was the only athlete accused of murder.
- In 1998, an estimated three million women were battered and close to one million were raped. According to various reports in the press over the past five years, between 70 and 100 athletes and coaches have been accused of assault against a woman each year.
- In data released in 1999 in *The Chronicle of Higher Education*'s annual campus crime survey, there were 1,053 forcible sex offenses in 1997. Less than 35 student-athletes were arrested.

Gender violence is a serious problem of men in America. The cost of crime to America is pegged at $500 billion per year according to a National Institute for

Justice research report for the Justice Department released in March 1996. Gender assault and child abuse account for $165 billion—more than one-third of that total! Men who beat their significant others are statistically also likely to beat their children.

Dunlap, who works with McPherson to create more awareness about the issue, said, "There are no men who should be exempted from being educated about the issue of gender violence although many believe they are. It is a problem for naval commanders, day care providers, fraternities, guys at a bar, in corporations, in halls of higher education and, yes, on athletic teams. But no more so on athletic teams."

There have been numerous cases in corporations in which women brought suits against the corporation for harassment and/or assault. The *Boston Globe* gave extensive coverage to the case in which there were 16 formal legal complaints for incidents from sexual harassment to rape at Astra USA, Inc., a chemical company. Mitsubishi had a suit against it placed by 29 women for the same reasons. No stories about Astra suggested that working in a chemical company produced this climate. At Mitsubishi, no one suggested that any relationship to the manufacturing process is a link to gender assault. So why do stories about athletes imply such a linkage to athletics? Does it fit white America's racial imagery?

McPherson believes it does.

Football and basketball mean black. When the public talks about gender violence and athletes, it talks black. No one discusses the problems of golfer John Dailey or Braves manager Bobby Cox. Warren Moon was another story altogether.

Problems about athletes hit the papers and people think they detect a pattern because of the seeming frequency. But no one else's problems get in the papers. How do we make legitimate comparisons?

With Astra and Mitsubishi, we look at the corporate climate and don't generalize about individuals. But with athletes, especially black athletes, we look at players and look for patterns to add up.

Some observers say athletes are trained to be violent and we can expect that to carry over into our homes. If this is true about training, then what about the training we give to police, the Army, Air Force, Navy, and Marines to use lethal force. Will they come home and kill? McPherson adds, "There is no logic to connect these cases but we do fit our stereotypes of African Americans with such images when we carry through the implication for athletes."

With all the recent publicity about the horrors of gender violence, it would be easy to forget that it was America's big, dirty secret until the notoriety surrounding the O.J. Simpson case. Few were willing to talk about gender violence. But we can never change if we do not confront this disease that is devouring our communities. The same unwillingness to confront racism diminishes society's ability to eradicate it.

Neither were being realistically discussed on college campuses nor in corporate board rooms. We are paying a horrible human price as we realize that society rarely told men that their dominating and controlling actions against women have helped create a climate in which there is a seemingly uncontrollable tidal wave of men's brutality against women.

Athletes should take a leadership role on this, just as they have on drug abuse and educational opportunities. In 1990, Louis Harris completed a landmark study which showed that our children desire to participate in changing their society and viewed athletes as their first choice in terms of who they wanted to give them socially relevant messages.

The MVP Program, organized in 1992 by Northeastern University's Center for the Study of Sport in Society, has been on more than 55 campuses over the last seven years training male athletes to be spokespeople on the issue of gender violence. Each of those schools has become proactive on an issue that has hurt so many women and their families. Don McPherson worked full-time for MVP for several years.

Our society is unraveling at a breakneck pace and McPherson insists "we have do more to help our youth survive by including our athletes rather than excluding them in helping our youth. The stereotyping of our athletes does not help. We need to be ready with facts to dispute the easy labels."

McPherson and Sanders both argue vigorously that America's athletes not only don't fit the emerging stereotypes about athletes and crime but that the vast majority of professional athletes are extremely positive individuals. Sanders said, "When I look at the many NBA players who have their own foundations and who are very involved with giving back to the communities where they play and where they came from, I know they are hurt by the stereotypes." McPherson asserts that "most of the players in the NFL are deeply religious, family-centered men who are constantly giving back to their communities with time and money."

Rosalyn Dunlap wonders when the public and the media will stop being cynical about athletes.

> I hear so many people say that if athletes do some thing in the community that they do it for publicity. Why can't we accept that athletes want to help?
>
> Sport and those who play it can help educate us and sensitize us. While we can't ignore the bad news, we should also focus on the overwhelming good news of what athletes do to make this a better world.

What is the power of sport? Lin Dawson, a ten-year NFL veteran who has spent much his post-playing career in efforts to improve race relations, said,

> Sports can bring good news that can lift the weight of the world. That is a powerful gift to possess, one we all share when we use it in the most noble way we can—to lift the spiritual poverty that hovers over our children. That spirit is the antidote to the loneliness and the feeling of being unwanted that so many young people are burdened with.
>
> We can give them the richness of spirit that comes with being part of a real team, being interdependent and being able to count on a brother or a sister in a time of need.

Sports figures are in a unique position to affect change. Among them are a few who have dramatically hurt the image of the vast majority. Dawson, who is now the chief operating officer of the National Consortium for Academics and Sport, added, "the community needs positive role models now more than ever. They can help young people to believe in what they cannot yet see. Our children need faith considering what they do see in their communities."

The distortions about our athletes and the crimes that a few of them commit need to be put in their real social context. The misleading perceptions need to be corrected so we can focus on the truth and what is really necessary. In that way, we can help America live up to the dream that Jackie Robinson created for us more than 50 years ago.

* FOR FURTHER STUDY *

Beller, Jennifer M., and Sharon Kay Stoll. 1993. "Sportsmanship: An Antiquated Concept." *Journal of Physical Education, Recreation and Dance* 64 (August):74–79.

Benedict, Jeffrey, and Alan Klein. 1997. "Arrest and Conviction Rates for Athletes Accused of Sexual Assault," *Sociology of Sport Journal* 14 (1):86–94.

Black, Terry, and Amelia Pape. 1997. "The Ban on Drugs in Sports: The Solution or the Problem?" *Journal of Sport and Social Issues* 21 (February):83–92.

Brackenridge, Celia. 1997. "'He Owned Me Basically . . .': Women's Experience of Sexual Abuse in Sport," *International Review for the Sociology of Sport* 32 (June):115–130.

Brackenridge, Celia, and Sandra Kirby. 1997. "Playing Safe: Assessing the Risk of Sexual Abuse to Elite Child Athletes," *International Review for the Sociology of Sport* 32 (December):407–418.

Crosset, Todd W., Jeffrey R. Benedict, and Mark A. McDonald. 1995. "Male Student Athletes Reported for Sexual Assault: A Survey of Campus Police Departments and Judicial Affairs Offices," *Journal of Sport and Social Issues* 19 (May):126–140.

Eitzen, D. Stanley. 1996. "The Paradox of Sport: The Contradictory Lessons Learned," *The World & I* 11 (July):307–321.

Eitzen, D. Stanley. 2000. "Sport and Social Control." Pp. 370–381 in *Handbook of Sport Studies,* Jay Coakley and Eric Dunning (eds.), (London: Sage).

Eitzen, D. Stanley. 2003. *Fair and Foul: Beyond the Myths and Paradoxes of Sport,* 2nd ed. (Lanham, MD: Rowman and Littlefield), chapter 4.

Hughson, John. 1998. "Among the Thugs: The 'New Ethnographies' of Football Supporting Cultures," *International Review for the Sociology of Sport* 33 (March):43–58.

Miedzian, Myriam. 1991. *Boys Will Be Boys: Breaking the Link Between Masculinity and Violence* (New York: Doubleday).

Nack, William, and Don Yaeger. 1999. "Every Parent's Nightmare," *Sports Illustrated* (September 13):40–53.

Palmer, Catherine. 2001. "Outside the Imagined Community: Basque Terrorism, Political Activism, and the Tour de France," *Sociology of Sport Journal* 18 (2):143–161.

Priest, Robert F., Jerry V. Krause, and Johnston Beach. 1999. "Four-Year Changes in College Athletes' Ethical Value Choices in Sports Situations," *Research Quarterly for Exercise and Sport* 70 (June):170–178.

Shields, David Lyle Light, Brenda Jo Light Bredemeier, Douglas E. Gardner, and Alan Bostrom. 1995. "Leadership, Cohesion, and Team Norms Regarding Cheating and Aggression," *Sociology of Sport Journal* 12 (3):324–336.

Swift, E. M. 1999. "Breaking Point: Years of Greed and Corruption Have Caught Up at Last with the International Olympic Committee," *Sports Illustrated* (February 1):32–37.

Volkwein, Karen A. E., Frauka I. Schnell, Dennis Sherwood, and Anne Livesey. 1997. "Sexual Harassment in Sport: Perceptions and Experiences of American Female Student-Athletes," *International Review for the Sociology of Sport* 32 (September):283–296.

Young, Kevin. 2000. "Sport and Violence." Pp. 382–407 in *Handbook of Sport Studies,* Jay Coakley and Eric Dunning (eds.), (London: Sage).

Zaichkowsky, Leonard D. 2000. "The Dark Side of Youth Sports: Coaches Sexually Abusing Children," *USA Today* 128 (January):56–58.

PART SEVEN

Problems of Excess: Big-Time College Sport

Interschool sports are found in almost all American schools and at all levels. There are many reasons for this universality. Sports unite all segments of a school and the community or neighborhood they represent. School sports remind constituents of the school, which may lead to monetary and other forms of support. School administrators can use sport as a useful tool for social control. But the most important reason for the universality of school sports is the widespread belief that the educational goals are accomplished through sport. There is much merit to this view; sports do contribute to physical fitness, to learning the value of hard work and perseverance, and to being goal-oriented, There is some evidence that sports participation leads to better grades, higher academic aspirations, and positive self-concept.

However, there also is a negative side to school sports. They are elitist, since only the gifted participate. Sports often overshadow academic endeavors (e.g., athletes are disproportionately rewarded and schools devote too much time and money to athletics that could be diverted to academic activities). Where winning is paramount—and where is this not the case?—the pressure becomes intense. This pressure has several negative consequences, the most important of which is that participants are prevented from fully enjoying sport. The pressure is too great for many youngsters. The game is work. It is a business.

The pressure to win also contributes to abuse by coaches, poor sportsmanship, dislike of opponents, intolerance of losers, and cheating. Most significant, although not usually considered so, is that while sport is a success-oriented activity, it is fraught with failure (losing teams, bench warmers, would-be participants cut from teams, the humiliation of letting down your teammates and school, and so on). For every ego enhanced by sport, how many have been bruised?

While this description fits all types of schools, big-time college sports deserve special attention, for they have unique problems. Athletes in these settings are ath-

199

letes first and students second; thus they are robbed of a first-class education. They are robbed by the tremendous demands on their time and energy. This problem is further enhanced by athletes being segregated from the student body (in classes, majors, and in eating and living arrangements); thus they are deprived of a variety of influences that college normally facilitates.

Another problem of college sports is that they tend to be ultraelitist. The money and facilities go disproportionately to the male athletes in the revenue-producing sports rather than to intramurals, minor sports, and club sports.

The greatest scandal involving college sports is the illegal and immoral behavior of overzealous coaches, school authorities, and alumni in recruiting athletes. In the quest to bring the best athletes to a school, players have been given monetary inducements, sexual favors, forged transcripts, and surrogates to take their entrance exams. In addition to the illegality of these acts, two fundamental problems exist with these recruiting violations: (1) Such behaviors have no place in an educational setting, yet they are done by some educators and condoned by others, and (2) these illicit practices by so-called respected authorities transmit two major lessons—that greed is the ultimate value and that winning supersedes how one wins.

Finally, the win-at-any-cost ethic that prevails in many of America's institutions of higher learning puts undue pressure on coaches. They must win to keep their jobs. Hence, some drive their athletes too hard or too brutally. Some demand total control over their players on and off the field. Some use illegal tactics to gain advantage (not only in recruiting but also in breaking the rules regarding the allowed number of practices, ineligible players, and unfair techniques). But coaches are not the problem. They represent a symptom of the process by which school sports are big business and where winning is the only avenue to achieve success.

The chapters of part 7 reflect on these problems and offer solutions. The first chapter by English professor, Murray Sperber, examines some of the issues of big-time college sports. The second selection, by D. Stanley Eitzen, uses the metaphor of slavery to show how big-time college athletes are exploited. The final selection, by Alisa Solomon, examines women's college sport, assessing the degree to which it follows the male model.

20

College Sports

Winners and Losers

Murray Sperber

Winning has always been important in college sports, one historian of higher education noting, "The games had to be won. Americans lacked a psychology for failure."
The 1970s began with a U.S. president in office who regularly quoted the maxim,
"Winning isn't everything, it's the only thing." In that decade and the following one,
the college sports obsession with victory often undermined the educational objectives of university administrators, as well as the health and welfare of the workers in
the college sports industry, the multitude of vocational student-athletes.

$*$ $*$ $*$

> The State of Indiana has a love affair with basketball, and Bob Knight, IU's
> coach, was a legend long before I arrived [in 1987 to become president of Indi-
> ana University]. In my first year I learned an essential lesson: Intercollegiate
> athletics can be an all-consuming diversion from the academic goals of a univer-
> sity president. . . .
>   How would an Ivy League type, who came from the East Coast and wore
> bow ties, react to basketball as the Hoosier lifeblood? Many asked that question.
>   —Thomas Ehrlich, former president of Indiana University

In this memoir, Ehrlich maintained that he understood college basketball before he arrived in Indiana, but, considering his academic background, his claim is

Source: Murray Sperber, *Beer and Circus: How Big-Time College Sports Is Crippling Undergraduate Education* (New York: Henry Holt & Company, 2000): pp. 23–32.

dubious, and subsequent events revealed his ignorance about the game. During the first year of Ehrlich's presidency, Bob Knight appeared on a national television program on the topic of job stress; Knight was asked by Connie Chung how he handled the intense pressure involved in coaching a big-time college basketball team. He compared the pressure to rape, noting that "if rape is inevitable, relax and enjoy it." That a high-profile public figure could make such a remark in 1988 mainly revealed the isolated, macho world in which Knight lived, his obliviousness to the women's movement of the previous decades and to the feelings of most Americans on the subject of rape. But Knight had recently won his third NCAA men's basketball championship and had become the emperor of Indiana, living in his high castle.

Predictably, many IU faculty members protested to Knight's boss, the IU president, about the coach's remark. Ehrlich issued a mild statement mainly indicating that Knight's views did not represent the views of Indiana University. This enraged the megalomaniacal coach, and he threatened to leave IU and accept an offer from the University of New Mexico, which was at the time looking for a new coach. As Ehrlich wrote, "The matter was on the front page of every paper in the state" of Indiana, and precipitated a huge public debate concerning the pros and cons of keeping Bob Knight at IU. In the end, Ehrlich backed down, apologized to Knight, helped convince the coach to stay at IU, and, in so doing, blighted his presidency. (In his memoir, Ehrlich avoids the negative parts of the story, blandly commenting, "Knight stayed at IU and the crisis passed.")

Forever after this incident, a majority of IU faculty viewed Ehrlich as weak and ineffectual, and they would not cooperate with his policy initiatives. In addition, constantly reminding the faculty of Ehrlich's capitulation to the basketball coach were newspaper photos, as well as TV shots, of the president sitting in the IU section at every home game, wearing a silly cream and crimson suit (IU's colors) and cheering his lungs out for the "Hurrying Hoosiers." Ehrlich hung on for six more years, and then terminated his failed presidency, which had been moribund from the day he revealed who possessed actual power at Indiana University: the coach, not the president.

Would Ehrlich have acted differently if he had not been mired in the academic culture and had known something about college basketball or, at the minimum, had consulted with someone who did? Probably so. Ehrlich could have called Knight's bluff; he could have summoned the coach to his office and said, "Bob, I think that you will love it in 'The Pit' [the nickname for the University of New Mexico arena]. Bob, you will particularly love recruiting for the Lobos [by all accounts, Knight hates recruiting]. Bob, you will have the pick of all those blue chip players who come out of New Mexico high schools [almost none do; New Mexico is not Indiana where, in the 1980s, Knight 'gathered' rather than recruited]. And Bob, what you will particularly like is going into the L.A. ghetto as all Lobo coaches have to do, and taking what remains after UCLA and other Pac-10 schools get the cream of the crop, and also after Tark the Shark gets his guys for UNLV. Bob, you will love the prospects that are left, the most academically and socially marginal players around. They are exactly the kind of athletes who respond to your yelling and your regimented style. Take the Lobo job, Bob, it's perfect for you."

But knowing nothing about college basketball, Ehrlich never made this speech. Instead he trusted his academic training to help him survive the situation. It didn't. A faculty member who provided a back channel for Ehrlich and Knight remarked on the enormous distance between the president's world and the coach's, and how "Ehrlich spoke of Knight as if he were a member of a different social class from himself . . . whose behavior was bound to be different from his own." However, to be fair to Ehrlich, probably his presidency was doomed before he ever set foot in the state of Indiana. Not only was he an outsider by birth and background, but, as an academic, he was an outsider within his own highly collegiate university. He never understood the majority culture at IU, and after he alienated his natural allies—the faculty, his fellow academics—the game was over.

In analyzing the Ehrlich-Knight confrontation, two higher education writers commented that it "reinforced a basic research finding: When a president deals with college sports, three things can happen, and two of them are bad." The only good outcome is if the president's university has a winning team in a high-profile sport; then the CEO can ride the wave of victory and good feeling, garnering lots of student, alumni, and fan support. Bad things happen if the president has a nasty public confrontation with a prominent coach, or an athletic director, or an athlete (for example, a quarterback flunking out of school); a confrontation will set off a firestorm of negative comments from fans on- and off-campus, as occurred in the Ehrlich-Knight encounter. Worse things occur when a scandal envelops a university athletic department, particularly one involving popular coaches or players; then the media arrive on campus, and soon the headlines blare such news as, SECRET SLUSH FUND FOR BIG-TIME U ATHLETES. The president, as the person in charge of the university, must investigate, try to clean up the mess, assure the various university constituencies that such scandals will never occur again . . . ad infinitum.

* * *

> Rarely does a day pass when the daily newspaper doesn't contain some story of recruiting or ethical violation in some athletic department in some grove of academe.
>
> —Ira Berkow, *New York Times* columnist

Berkow offered his comments after surveying the long river of college sports scandals during the 1970s and 1980s. Like all steady flows, the river contained some prodigious pieces of flotsam and jetsam. Berkow cited the case of Dexter Manley, the NFL All-Pro end who admitted that he had entered Oklahoma State University in 1977 unable to read or write, played there for four years, and left still "illiterate." Other commentators highlighted the early-1980s scandal at the University of New Mexico, where, for a number of years, the basketball coach arranged for players to receive academic credit for extension and summer school courses that they never took (the Lobos coach wanted to ensure the playing eligibility of the academically marginal athletes that President Ehrlich should have reminded Bob Knight about).

And by the late 1980s, with the river flowing faster, a book about corruption in the Southern Methodist University football program summed up the situation with its title, *A Payroll to Meet.* (The polluted river rotted on through the 1990s, with illegal pay scandals at many schools, including Texas Tech and Michigan State, and the decade ended with academic messes in the athletic departments of the University of Minnesota and the University of Tennessee.)

During all these years, the NCAA possessed police powers but patrolled the river in canoes, not speedboats. "Consequently," as one sports authority wrote, "close observers of the college sports scene, including coaches and athletes, estimated that only a small fraction of the total violations resulted in punishment by the NCAA." Some observers maintained that the NCAA did not really want to clean up intercollegiate athletics; instead, mainly for PR reasons, it pulled out the especially putrid programs but let most other offenders float along.

Supplying the players with academic and financial favors while in school constituted two major areas of dishonesty, but enticing them to enroll—the recruiting process—produced another large cesspool. In 1988, an authoritative preseason football guide divided cheating in Division I-A recruiting into three categories and sets of percentages: (a) 15 to 20 percent of all programs made illegal offers of cash and/or goods to recruits; (b) 65 percent assured an athlete's "social comfort and/or academic success if he signs"; (c) 15 to 20 percent "occasionally bend a rule" to sign a player. Therefore, all schools cheated in one way or another. If 100 percent was the total in football, then basketball, with many shady coaches and hungry players, easily reached that number and, if it had been possible, would have surpassed it. The recruiting scandals continued through the 1990s, involving such "usual suspects" as Louisiana State and Louisville, and "new kids" southeast Missouri State and Weber State.

Another important area of athletic department deception, one almost unknown to the public but familiar to university administrators, was fiscal. Throughout the 1970s and 1980s, cases of athletic directors and coaches committing fraud emerged, but more systemic and outrageous were the overspending practices of almost all athletic departments. During these years, even as college sports revenues increased significantly, expenses rose faster, generating huge amounts of red ink. According to the NCAA's own financial reports, the vast majority of its members lost money on their college sports programs, often millions of dollars a year; however, because the NCAA allowed athletic departments to engage in "creative accounting," outside experts calculated the real losses as at least three times higher than the reported figures. Moreover, universities had to cover these annual deficits with funds that could have gone to academic departments, student scholarships, or other educational objectives.

Athletic department mismanagement, lavish spending, and waste caused most of the annual losses, but university officials, including presidents, were extremely reluctant to assert control over athletic department finances. Nasty and debilitating confrontations with ADs (athletic directors) and coaches—the people benefitting most from the overspending—constituted the first "bad thing" that happened "when a president deals with college sports." As a result, when the 1990s economic boom pumped even more dollars into athletic department coffers, the annual deficits continued to increase.

Coaches and ADs profited from this system, but how did the athletes fare? Tales of corrupt jocks filled the media from the 1970s to the end of the century and beyond, but the NCAA and other sponsors of intercollegiate athletics always argued that the media focused too much on jocks on the take and ignored the multitude of honest athletes who, without attention, played their sports and went to class. The NCAA and member schools have long called these undergraduates "student-athletes."

Isiah Thomas, a college and NBA star in the 1980s, and now a pro basketball executive, commented:

> When you go to college, you're not a student-athlete but an athlete-student. Your main purpose is not to be an Einstein but a ballplayer, to generate some money, put people in the stands. Eight or ten hours of your day are filled with basketball, football. The rest of your time you've got to motivate yourself to make sure you get something back.

The situation that Thomas described resulted from a key event in the history of intercollegiate athletics, one that transformed the majority of student-athletes into athlete-students: in 1973, the NCAA changed athletic scholarships from guaranteed four-year awards to one-year renewable grants. From their inception, the four-year deals had ensured some institutional commitment to an athlete's education; whether the player became an all-American, a benchwarmer, or never suited up due to injury, he or she could continue in college on scholarship. But coaches despised the four-year grants—from their viewpoint, they wasted far too many scholarship slots on athletes "who didn't work out"—who didn't help the team win—and the coaches pressured the NCAA into changing all athletic scholarships to one-year awards, renewed or canceled every July 1. After the rule came on line, at most NCAA schools, coaches made the annual decisions on their players, generally renewing or cutting on the basis of athletic ability.

The one-year grants gave coaches enormous power over their athletes, and, throughout the 1970s and 1980s, as college sports became more popular and the rewards of winning ever more lucrative, particularly for coaches, in the form of enhanced contracts and endorsements, their demands on their athletes escalated. In previous eras, every college sport had an off-season during which some athletes caught up on their studies, and others just relaxed and recuperated. However, in the 1970s and 1980s, as weight-training and other conditioning methods became an essential part of athletics, the off-season disappeared from the college sports calendar. Then, in-season leisure time for athletes became briefer, to the point where, in the early 1990s, observers noted that because college athletes "can expect to spend . . . 50 hours or more each week in their sport, coaches generally expect the hours required for team-related tasks [meetings, videotape viewing, etc.] . . . to be taken from leisure time, which they often consider a low priority."

For many generations, the lives of college athletes in big-time programs had resembled those of regular vocational students. In the 1970s and 1980s, when many other students edged out of their "dominant subcultures," most athletes withdrew further into their vocational mode, to the point where even the proponents of intercollegiate athletics worried about the intense daily pressure placed upon the jocks. In 1991, a nationally published guidebook for college athletes and their parents began chapter one with:

> The label of student-athlete says it all. A college student who is also an athlete is asked to live two roles and be two people in one. No other college students are identified in this hyphenated way—no others are pulled in two completely different directions. No other students are asked to be one person for half the day and someone else the other half.

Without realizing it, authors Stephen K. Figler and Howard F. Figler placed student-athletes in the traditional vocational category. However, contrary to their assertion, many other students "are pulled in two completely different directions," and endure split lives—all those men and women who work at full-time jobs and also attend college full-time, as well as all those who are parents and must divide their lives among family, school, and job obligations. (By the early 1990s, vocational students comprised over 50 percent of the national undergraduate population, but, ironically, demographers excluded student-athletes from that pool; the demographers, not recognizing that athletic scholarships were payments-in-kind for full-time sports jobs, counted athletes as regular students.)

The Figlers, even if they never used the term *vocational,* expressed the athletes' dilemma in the same way that university counselors described the lives of stressed-out vocational students: Instead of the full-time job or family, "The team demands so much of your time that you cannot perform . . . in courses that you want or need for your future." In addition, the outside pressure constricts your daily life, and narrows your college experience; for athletes this occurs because "coaches arrange aspects of your life (such as meals, housing, [etc.] . . .) so that you will interact primarily with other athletes, and thus be more completely under the control of the coaching staff."

Similar to highly stressed vocationals, intercollegiate athletes tended to remain within their own group, directed by their coaches' extreme emphasis on sports and frequent neglect of everything else, including academics. Coaches phrased their priorities more positively, usually invoking the word *commitment,* as in demanding an athlete's *commitment to the program.*

The Figlers explained "commitment" in a section titled, "Winning versus Your [Athletes'] Welfare": "Coaches feel that the time commitment they demand of athletes is necessary in order to have a winning team." Yet, these writers never discussed the benefits to coaches in high-profile sports who win consistently: annual incomes that in 1991 averaged $300,000 (and today average closer to $600,000, with an increasing number of coaches topping $1 million annually). Winning coaches receive among the highest salaries at their universities, but their supplementary earnings—endorsements of sneakers and other products, lucrative summer camps, public-speaking engagements, and so forth—generate an even larger proportion of their annual incomes. All aspects of their jobs depend on winning; for example, no trade association ever paid a losing coach $20,000 to speak at its convention.

Fred Akers, a NCAA Division I-A head football coach from the 1970s to the early 1990s, explained the process: "The more you win, the bigger the bucks. But you can never win enough—I won at UT [University of Texas at Austin] but got fired for not winning more." Akers then went to Purdue, but had some losing seasons there and was fired again. He commented: "I was out of step. Most coaches believe that the best way to win is to put their players in the most intense training possible. Keep at 'em from dawn to dusk and into the night. I never did that, I didn't feel it was fair to my guys, I wanted them to go to class and have time to study. But I'm not in college coaching anymore."

Nevertheless, college athletes are not entirely the victims of obsessed coaches; the jocks have long participated in their fates. If they possess the talent to win an athletic scholarship, they enter university hoping to star at the college level and then move up to the professionals. As a result, many college athletes regard their university years primarily as minor league training for the pros and secondarily as an opportunity for an education. That only a small percentage of collegiate athletes ever achieve their pro sports dream is irrelevant to its power over them and its role in shaping their lives at school, especially their willingness to devote so many hours a day to athletics.

In 1991, the NCAA instituted a rule that provided a basic test of the athletes' and the coaches' commitment to their sports, as well as the NCAA's commitment to reform. Under pressure from the critics of college sports, including such members of Congress as Bill Bradley and Tom McMillen (authentic student-athletes in their college days), the NCAA moved to control the excessive number of hours that intercollegiate athletes spent in their sports and, by implication, not in their studies. The association passed a rule limiting "a student-athlete's participation" in his or her sport "to a maximum of four hours per day and twenty hours per week." The NCAA hailed the rule as one of the most important pieces of legislation in its history, and even some critics were impressed.

Unfortunately, the rule contained an immense loophole: The NCAA defined the four daily/twenty weekly hours as "mandatory time" required by coaches; however, the rule allowed athletes to spend as many hours per week as they wanted in "voluntary" sports activities, for example, informal practices, weight-training, conditioning, and so forth. Even the NCAA's PR director admitted that "under the new rules, athletes can practice more than twenty hours a week. One hundred hours a week if they want, if it's *voluntary*."

Immediately, the line between mandatory and voluntary blurred. The coaches kept time sheets on the hours that they required their players to be on the practice field or court—and the totals never exceeded four daily or twenty weekly. But the coaches also *encouraged* their athletes to *volunteer* to do all the other activities related to sports success. During the first year of the rule, Jerry Eaves, an assistant basketball coach at Howard University, admitted that in his and other sports the athletes "are still doing everything that takes up the same amount of time" as before; "they're still running" the same training distances, "they're still doing maximum physical conditioning," and also "they're playing" so-called pickup games to supplement official practices.

Many athletes also regarded the four-and-twenty–hour rule as a sham, and they felt that voluntary/mandatory merged into one time unit. A Division I men's volleyball player remarked that, beyond the mandatory hours in afternoon practices, the other functions are voluntary, "but it's not like you don't have to show up if you don't want to. We work out as much or even longer now than we did before the rule. . . . Also each of us wants playing time and needs to keep ahead of everyone else. We know that the coaches totally monitor who is doing the voluntary work. Guess which players the coaches put in the starting lineup?"

The NCAA four-and-twenty–hour rule continued through the 1990s, obeyed so little that in the fall of 1999, *USA Today* published a routine item on USC football player R. Jay Soward, in his team's doghouse because he "was a no-show at workouts that officially were voluntary but were attended by nearly every player on the team." Soward's absence "didn't sit well with Trojans coach Paul Hackett," and resulted in people "in the program questioning his [Soward's] work ethic and commitment." Apparently, no one told USC that they were supposed to pretend to obey the NCAA rule, not openly discuss their flaunting of it with a reporter on a national newspaper.

But from its inception, with the inclusion of the "voluntary" loophole, the four-and-twenty–hour rule was never a serious reform, and mainly revealed the hypocrisy of the NCAA, as well as its bureaucratic impulse—coaches rightly complain about the burdensome time sheets that they must fill out for the NCAA, serving no "real world" purpose whatsoever.

Yet, in a symbolic sense, the four-and-twenty–hour rule captures the essence of the modern NCAA: its PR pretense of guarding the welfare of student-athletes versus the reality of its high-powered promotion of a billion-dollar-a-year college sports business, and its lack of concern for the workers in that industry. Joe Abunasser, a former NCAA Division I assistant basketball coach, commented: "The irony of the entire organization [the NCAA] is that its proclaimed intention is to regulate and reform college athletics, when in reality it is the cause of the corruption."

Propelling the NCAA's corruption is the almighty dollar. From a wealthy organization in the 1970s and 1980s, the association, thanks to television's insatiable appetite for college sports programming, moved into the billionaire range in the 1990s. As a result, the NCAA became an essential part of sports media programming, with the total revenue from college football and basketball games exceeding that of the richest professional leagues in the world.

21

The Big-Time College Sports Plantation and the Slaves Who Drive It

D. Stanley Eitzen

> The plantation owner of old couldn't stay in business were he to divest himself of slaves. Slaves were the production engines of production.
> —Walter Mosley in *Workin' on the Chain Gang*

Many youths dream of playing football or basketball for a university with a big-time sports program. They want to be part of the pageantry, glory, excitement of intense competition, shared sacrifice, commitment to excellence, bonding with teammates, and to be the object of adoring fans. Not incidentally, they would also receive an all-expenses-paid college education, which, if a professional sports career does not work out, would open other lucrative career opportunities. Many observers of big-time college sports accept this idealized version, but just how glamorous is participation in athletics at this level? Are the athletes as privileged as it appears?

There is a dark side to big-time college sports. To show this, let me use the metaphor of big-time college sports as a plantation system. I admit at the outset that this metaphor is overdrawn. Big-time college sports is not the same as the brutalizing, inhumane, degrading, and repressive institution of slavery found in the antebellum South. Nevertheless, there are significant parallels with slavery that highlight the serious problems plaguing collegiate athletics. Thus, the plantation/slavery metaphor is useful for understanding the reality of the big-time college sports world.

Source: This is a revised and updated version of D. Stanley Eitzen, "Slaves of Big-Time College Sports," *USA Today: The Magazine of the American Scene* 120 (September 2000), pp. 26–30. Used with permission.

There is the organization—the National Collegiate Athletic Association (NCAA)—that preserves the plantation system, making and enforcing the rules to protect the interest of the individual plantation owners. The plantations are the football and men's basketball factories within the universities with big-time programs. The overseers are the coaches who extract the labor from the workers. The workers are owned by the plantation and, much like the slaves of the antebellum South, produce riches for their masters while receiving a meager return on the plantation's profits.

Many observers of big-time college sports, most certainly the coaches and players, would argue vehemently with this assertion that big-time college athletes are slaves in a plantation environment. After all, the athletes not only choose to participate, they want desperately to be part of big-time sport. Moreover, they have special privileges that separate them from other students (much like what house slaves received, when compared to field slaves of the Old South), such as more and better food, special housing arrangements, favorable handling in registration for classes, and, sometimes, generous treatment when they cross the line. Also, the athletes, unlike slaves, can leave the program if they wish.

If participation is voluntary and the athletes want to be part of the system, what is the problem? My argument that these athletes are slaves in a plantation system, whether they realize it or not, involves several dimensions: The athletes (slaves) are exploited economically, making millions for their masters but provided only with a subsistence wage of room, board, tuition, and books; they are controlled with restricted freedoms; they are subject to physical and mental abuse by overseers; and the master-slave relationship is accepted by the athletes as legitimate. I begin my argument with demonstrating that big-time college football and men's basketball bring in large sums to the "plantations" while severely limiting the wages of the workers.

THE PLANTATION PROFITS FROM THE WORK OF SLAVES

The governing body of big-time college sports, the NCAA, is caught in a huge contradiction—trying to reconcile a multibillion-dollar industry while claiming that it is really an amateur activity. That it is a huge money-making industry is beyond dispute.

- The major conferences have an eight-year package (ending in 2006) worth $930 million with ABC to televise the Bowl Championship Series (BCS) at the conclusion of the football season. Each team playing in a BCS game now receives about $15 million and with this new contract, each team will receive about $17 million in the final years of the agreement. Since the teams share these monies with their conference members, the 62 schools involved will share approximately $116 million annually.
- The NCAA has signed a $6.2 billion, 11-year deal giving CBS the rights to televise its men's basketball championship (that's $545 million a year). The NCAA also, of course, makes money from advertising and gate receipts for this tournament. To enhance gate receipts the finals are always scheduled in huge arenas with seating capacities of at least 30,000, rather than normal basketball-sized venues.

- Universities sell sponsorships to various enterprises for advertising. The athletic department of the University of Colorado, for example, has 50 corporate sponsors. Its major sponsor is Coors Brewing Company, which has a $300,000 advertising package for scoreboard, radio and TV advertising, and a sign on the mascot's trailer. That university also named its basketball arena the Coors Events Center in return for a $5 million gift.
- Several football and basketball coaches are paid in excess of $2 million in overall compensation (base salary, television and radio, shoe company stipends).
- An estimated $2.5 billion a year in college merchandise is sold under license, generating about $100 million to the schools in royalties. The University of Michigan receives the most income from this source—about $6 million annually.
- The dominant schools have lucrative deals with shoe companies (Nike, Reebok, Adidas) worth millions to each school in shoes, apparel, and cash. For example, in 2001 the University of North Carolina at Chapel Hill signed an eight-year agreement with Nike worth about $3.2 million annually.
- The top programs have annual athletic budgets from $60 to $80 million. At Ohio State in 2002–03, the football team cleared a profit of $22 million and men's basketball made $9 million, and also made over $4 million from the sale of merchandise.
- In 2003 Ohio State played at the University of Michigan before more than 112,000 spectators. If those fans paid an average of $30 a ticket (doubtless a low estimate), that single game brought in $3.36 million not counting money from parking, concessions, and television rights.

Obviously, big-time athletic programs are commercial enterprises. The irony is that while the sports events generate millions for each school, the workers are not paid. Economist Andrew Zimbalist has written that: "Big-time intercollegiate athletics is a unique industry. No other industry in the United States manages not to pay its principal producers a wage or a salary." The universities and the NCAA claim that their athletes in big-time sports programs are amateurs and that, despite the money generated, the NCAA and its member schools are amateur organizations promoting an educational mission. This amateur status is vitally important to the plantation owners in two regards. First, by schools *not* paying the athletes what they are worth their expenses are minimized, thus making the enterprises more profitable. And, second, since athletic departments and the NCAA are considered part of the educational mission, they do not pay taxes on their millions from television, sponsorships, licensing, the sale of sky boxes and season tickets, and gate receipts. Moreover, contributions by individuals and corporations to athletic departments are tax deductible.

THE INJUSTICE OF AMATEURISM

To keep big-time college sports "amateur," the NCAA has devised a number of rules that eliminate all economic benefits to the athletes: They may receive only educational benefits (i.e., room, board, tuition, fees, and books); cannot sign with an agent and retain their eligibility; cannot do commercials; cannot receive meals, clothing, transportation, or other gifts from individuals other than family members; and their relatives cannot receive gifts of travel to attend games or other forms of remuneration.

These rules reek with injustice. Athletes can make money for others, but not for themselves. Their coaches have agents as may students engaged in other extracurricular activities but the athletes cannot. Athletes are forbidden to engage in advertising, but their coaches can readily endorse products for generous compensation. Corporate advertisements are displayed in the arenas where they play but with no payoff to the athletes. The shoes and equipment worn by the athletes bear very visible corporate logos, for which the schools are compensated handsomely. The athletes make public appearances for their schools and their photographs are used to publicize the athletic department and sell tickets, but they cannot benefit.

The schools sell memorabilia and paraphernalia that incorporate the athletes' likenesses, yet only the schools pocket the royalties. The athletes cannot receive gifts but coaches and other athletic department personnel receive the free use of automobiles, country club memberships, housing subsidies, etc.

Most significantly, coaches receive huge deals from shoe companies (e.g., Duke coach Mike Krzyzewski, has a fifteen-year shoe endorsement deal with Adidas, which includes a $1 million bonus plus $375,000 annually), while the players are limited to wearing that corporation's shoes and apparel. An open market operates when it comes to the pay for coaches resulting in huge pay packages for the "golden glamour coaches but not so for star players. When a coach is fired or resigns he often receives a parachute," which sometimes is in the multimillion dollar category, while players who leave a program early receive nothing but vilification for being disloyal. When a team is invited to a bowl game it means an extra month of practice for the athletes while head coaches, depending on the bowl venue, receive generous bonuses. A university entourage of administrators and their spouses accompany the team to the bowl game with all expenses paid while the parents and spouses of the athletes have to pay their own way.

As an extreme example of the discrepancy in pay for college athletes, an analysis of the economic impact of basketball star Patrick Ewing to Georgetown University during his four years there shows that he brought more than $12 million to the university (a tripling of attendance, increased television revenues, and qualifying for the NCAA tournament each year). Meanwhile the cost to Georgetown for Ewing's services totaled only $48,600—providing a tidy profit of $11,951,400 for the university. A study by an economist over a decade ago found that top-level college football players at that time generated a net gain (subtracting room, board, tuition, and books) of more than $2 million over a four-year period.

What exactly are the wages of average college athletes in the big-time sports? The answer is a bit complicated since athletes who do not graduate have not taken advantage of their tuition, so they have played only for their room and board. Also, there is a significant difference in tuition costs between state and private universities. Economist Richard G. Sheehan has calculated the hourly wage of big-time college players taking these considerations into account and assuming a workload of 1,000 hours per year. The best pay received, he found, occurred at private schools with high graduation rates for the athletes; the lowest pay at state schools with low graduation rates. Duke, for example paid an equivalent of $20.37 an hour for its football players, while Texas–El Paso paid $3.51. The median wage at all big-time schools for basketball players was $6.82 an hour and $7.69 an hour for football players. Now compare these wages with their coaches, assuming they also work 1,000 hours annually. A coach with a $1 million package makes $1,000 an hour; a coach with a $250,000 package only $250 an hour. Meanwhile, the workers—whose health is jeopardized by participation in hazardous sports—make a relative pittance and even then not in the form of money but in "free" room, board, and tuition. So it is, that the work of the big-time college athletes, just like the slaves on the antebellum plantations, allows the masters to accumulate wealth at their expense.

RESTRICTIONS ON THE RIGHTS AND FREEDOMS OF THE SLAVES

Slaves, by definition, are not free. The slaves of the antebellum era did not have the right to assemble or to petition. They did not have the right to speak out or freedom of movement. Those conditions characterize today's college athletes as well. The NCAA, the schools, and the coaches restrict the freedom of the athletes in many ways. By NCAA fiat, once athletes sign a contract to play for a school, they are bound to that school. They make a four-year commitment to that college, yet the school makes only a one-year commitment to them. If an athlete wishes to play for another big-time school, he is ineligible for one year (two years if their former coach refuses to release the athlete from his contract). Yet if a coach wants to get rid of an athlete, the school is only bound to provide the scholarship for the remainder of that academic year. Coaches, on the other hand, can break their contracts, and immediately coach another school. Richard Sheehan illustrates how unfair this rule is for athletes, when they are compared with nonathlete students: "Suppose you accept a scholarship from Harvard to study under a Nobel laureate who then takes a position at Yale. Are you under any obligation to attend Harvard and not attempt to matriculate at Yale? This NCAA regulation, like many others, gives schools options and gives athletes nothing."

The right to privacy is invaded routinely when it comes to athletes. College athletes—but not their coaches, teachers, administrators, or other students—are subject to mandatory drug testing. Personnel from the athletic department watch athletes in their dorms and locker rooms, either in person or on closed-circuit television, for "deviant behaviors." Bed checks are not uncommon. Sometimes there are "spies" who watch and report on the behaviors of athletes in local bars and other places of amusement.

Freedom of choice is violated when athletes are red-shirted (i.e., held from play for a year) without their consent. Athletes may have little or no choice in what position they play. They may be told to gain or lose weight, with penalties for noncompliance. Coaches may demand mandatory study halls. They may determine what courses the athletes will take and their majors. Robert Smith, formerly a running back for the Minnesota Vikings, was a pre-med student and star athlete at Ohio State University. To meet his pre-med requirements Smith needed a laboratory course that conflicted with football practices twice a week. The coaches insisted that football take precedence and that he must drop the course. To Smith's credit, he took the course and did not play football that year.

A number of coaches insist that their athletes avoid political protest. Some paternalistic coaches prohibit their athletes from associating with individuals or groups that they feel will have a negative influence on their players. Certain coaches demand dress codes and may even organize leisure-time activities that everyone must attend. University of Colorado basketball coach Ricardo Patton, for example, has included among his mandatory team activities: touring a prison, attending church services, sleeping together on cots in the gym for a week, and practicing at six in the morning. During slavery, the masters imposed their religious beliefs on to their slaves. In today's sports world, team chaplains, chapel services, Bible study, and team prayers are commonplace. Ricardo Patton, coach at a public university, for example, concludes each practice with the players holding hands in a circle while Patton or a player he calls upon leads the team in prayer. He claims that participation is voluntary. Sportswriter Mike Littwin of the *Denver Rocky Mountain News* argues that the practice is anything but voluntary: "According to the argument, players, whose playing time and scholarship are dependent upon the coach's whim, are free to pray or not to pray with him. Here's what I believe: Anyone who thinks that when the coach says it's time to pray that it's somehow voluntary ought to pray for more wisdom. It is inherently coercive. It's about as voluntary as when the coach tells you to run laps. You're not the coach for 60 minutes of practice and then not the coach once you kneel on the floor."

OPPRESSION, BRUTALITY, AND TERROR: KEEPING SLAVES IN THEIR PLACE

Although not a universal trait of coaches, instances of physical and mental cruelty toward players occur all too frequently. Bob Knight, the highly successful basketball coach at Indiana University and now Texas Tech once stopped the videotape of a game to say to one of his players: "Daryl, look at that. You don't even run back down the floor hard. That's all I need to know about you, Daryl. All you want to be out there is comfortable. You don't work, you don't sprint back. Look at that! You never push yourself. You know what you are Daryl? You are the worst f———pussy I've ever seen play basketball at this school. The absolute worst pussy ever. You have more goddamn ability than 95 percent of the players we've had here but you are pussy from the top of your head to the bottom of your feet. An absolute f_____ pussy."

When University of South Carolina football coach Lou Holtz was at Notre Dame University, one of his players, Chet Lacheta, made several mistakes in practice. In Lacheta's words: "[Holtz] started yelling at me. He said that I was a coward. He said that I should find a different sport to play and that I shouldn't come back in the fall. He was pretty rough. . . . First he grabbed me by my face mask and shook it. Then he spit on me."

On the return trip from a road game coaches may punish their players by having the bus driver let them off several miles from the school. Another tactic is to schedule practices at inconvenient times such as 2 A.M. or on holidays. Coach Bob Knight schedules some holiday practices, without telling the players when to report for the next practice. Consequently, they must wait by their phones to hear from the manager about the practice schedule. If not, they will incur the wrath of their autocratic boss. These acts of control are similar to those used by the military to train recruits. As sociologist Philip Slater has observed: "Exposure to random punishment, stress, fatigue, personal degradation and abuse, irrational authority, and constant assertions of one's worthlessness as a human being [are] all tried-and-true techniques of 'reeducation' used by totalitarian regimes." In effect, these are powerful means to create and maintain obedient slaves.

THE SLAVE MENTALITY

Historians George Fredrickson and Christopher Lasch have stated that the real horror of slavery was that many of the slaves "mentally identified with the system that bound and confined them." This is an especially troubling aspect of the plantation system that is big-time college sport. Jerry Farber's description of students in his classic 1960s critique of higher education, "The Student as Nigger," aptly describes athletes as well: "They're pathetically eager to be pushed around. They're like those old greyheaded house niggers you can still find in the South who don't see what all the fuss is about because Mr. Charlie 'treats us real good.'"

Sport sociologist George H. Sage provides some of the reasons why athletes rarely resist the authoritarian and unjust regime under which they labor:

A question may be raised about the lack of protest from intercollegiate athletes about the prevailing conditions under which they labor. In one way it can be expected that the athletes would not find anything to question: they have been thoroughly conditioned by many years of organized sport involvement to obey athletic authorities. Indeed, most college athletes are faithful servants and spokespersons for the system of college sport. They tend to take the existing order for granted, not questioning the status quo because they are preoccupied with their own jobs or making the team and perhaps gaining national recognition. As a group, athletes tend to be politically passive and apathetic, resigned to domination from above because, at least partly, the institutional structure of athletics is essentially hostile to independence of mind. Hence, athletes are willing victims whose self-worth and self-esteem have largely become synonymous with their athletic prowess. Their main impulse is to mind their own business while striving to be successful as athletes.

Another reason for the docility and submissiveness of athletes is that they are politically disenfranchised. Athletes who challenge the athletic power structure risk losing their scholarships and eligibility. Athletes who have a grievance are on their own. They have no union and no arbitration board. The coaches, athletic directors, and ultimately the NCAA have power over them as long as they are scholarship athletes. Their only option is to leave the plantation. If they do quit, they are often viewed by others as the problem. After all, most accept the system. Those who quit are not seen as victims but as losers. So powerful is the socialization of athletes, even those who quit are likely to turn their anger inward, regarding themselves as the problem.

Others may tolerate the oppressive system because they see it as the only vehicle for becoming a professional athlete. If they were to become professional athletes, the rewards are substantial. However, making it to the pros is just a dream except for the most-talented few. Of the thousands of players eligible for the National Football League draft each year, only 336 are drafted and about 160 actually make a final roster. Fewer than one-half of 1 percent of all Division I male basketball players make it to the National Basketball Association.

DISMAL GRADUATION RATES

Since most college athletes never play at the professional level, the attainment of a college degree is a crucial determinant for their upward mobility, and thus a rationale for tolerating the unjust plantation system. But graduation from college, while not the long shot of becoming a professional athlete, is also a bad bet.

The 1999 report on graduation rates compiled by the National Collegiate Athletic Association (NCAA), examined Division I athletes who enrolled as freshmen in 1996 to determine how many had graduated after six years (athletes who left school in good academic standing were not counted in the results). The data show that while the overall graduation rate for all male students at Division I schools was 56 percent, the rate for football players was 54 percent and 44 percent for male basketball players. While some programs are exemplary (Notre Dame graduated 81 percent of its football players, and Stanford graduated 100 percent of its men's basketball players over the six-year period); others are not. Among top-rated basketball programs, Arizona graduated only 23 percent, while Connecticut and Maryland graduated 27 percent.

There are several reasons for the relatively low graduation rates for big-time college athletes. Compared to nonathletes they are less prepared for college. On average, they enter college in the bottom quarter of the freshman class (based on SAT scores). Football and men's basketball players in big-time sports programs are more than six times as likely as other students to receive special treatment in the admissions process, that is, they are admitted *below* the standard requirements for their universities. Second, athletes spend 30 to 40 hours a week on their sport, which is demanding, as well as physically and mentally fatiguing. Third, an anti-intellectual atmosphere is common within the jock subculture. Finally, some athletes attend college, not for the education, but because they believe it will lead to a professional career. In this regard, Iowa State football coach Jim Walden has said: "Not more than 20 percent of the football players go to college for an education."

Not only do typical athletes in big-time sports enter at an educational disadvantage, they often encounter a diluted educational experience while attending their schools. Coaches, under the intense pressure to win, tend to diminish the student side of their athletes by counseling them to take easy courses, to choose easy majors, and to enroll in easy courses from professors friendly to the athletic department. Some of the more unscrupulous have altered transcripts, given athletes answers to tests, staged phantom courses, and hired surrogate test takers. In one infamous case of academic fraud, a tutor for the University of Minnesota athletic department wrote more than 400 papers for basketball players over five years. Even with that help only 23 percent of the players recruited since 1986 to play basketball at that university have graduated, the worst rate of any Big Ten basketball team during that period.

Some ill-prepared and/or unmotivated athletes manage to stay eligible without being educated. Dexter Manley, for example, testified before a Senate committee that he had played football four years at Oklahoma State University only to leave illiterate. As Cynthia Tucker, editor of the *Atlanta Constitution* editorial page, writing about exploited basketball players but applicable to football players as well, said: "So those college basketball players you're watching on the court desperately need to earn degrees. If they don't, they'll be left with little more than shattered 'hoop dreams.'" When less than 40 percent of the black basketball players do not leave college with a degree something is drastically amiss. The uneducated have been exploited by their schools and when used up, the schools turn to another crop to exploit. As columnist George Will has argued: "College football and basketball are, for many players, vocations, not avocations, and academics are unsubstantiated rumors."

Reexamining the plantation/slave metaphor, athletes voluntarily enter into an unjust arrangement. Nevertheless, there are important similarities that college sport shares with slavery. The plantation system as represented by the NCAA and the individual (school) plantations benefit handsomely from the work of the athletes. The athletes, meanwhile, like slaves, are bound to the plantation by the plantation's rules. They are dominated, managed, and controlled. They take orders. They do not receive a wage commensurate with their contribution to the economic return. They are sometimes mistreated physically and mentally by their overseers. They are denied the rights and freedoms of other citizens and they have no real democratic recourse to right an unjust system.

CHANGING THE PLANTATION SYSTEM

The obvious starting point for changing the "plantation" system is to pay athletes in the revenue-producing sports fair compensation for the revenues they generate. Athletes should receive a monthly stipend for living expenses, insurance coverage, and paid trips home during holidays and for family emergencies. Media basketball commentator Dick Vitale suggests a modest plan to make the system somewhat fairer.

He says that the NCAA should invest a billion of its $6.2 billion deal to broadcast the NCAA men's basketball tournament and pay the athletes $250 a month. *Sports Illustrated* writer E. M. Swift responded: "Is Vitale right on the money? You make the call. For now, as the NCAA continues to treat its athletes with supercilious contempt while reaping GNP-sized windfalls from their labor, you can at least say this for scholarship athletes: They're getting a free education in no-holds-barred capitalism."

The time has come to end the pretense that players in big-time college sports are amateurs. They are paid through a scholarship but far from a just or living wage in this world of big-time sports megabucks.

Second, maximize the probability that athletes receive a legitimate education and graduate. The late Ernest L. Boyer, former president of the Carnegie Foundation for the Advancement of Teaching, said: "I believe that the college sports system is one of the most corrupting and destructive influences on higher education. It is obscene, and there is no way to put an educational gloss on this enterprise." In short, as currently structured, big-time sports are not compatible with education.

To emphasize education and replace athlete-student with student-athlete, I suggest the following: Do not admit athletes who do not meet the minimum entrance requirements for admission and retention. Eliminate freshman eligibility so that incoming students have time to adjust to the demanding and competitive academic environment. Provide remedial classes and tutoring as needed. Reduce the time demands on athletes by eliminating spring football practice, starting the basketball season at the beginning of second semester, and holding the weekly time devoted to sport at 20 hours. Include among the criteria for evaluating coaches, the humane treatment of players, and, most critically, the proportion of their athletes who graduate in six years.

Third, establish a comprehensive athletes' Bill of Rights to ensure a nonexploitive context. At a minimum these "Rights" should include:

- The right to transfer schools. Athletes who transfer should be eligible to play the next school year, not the current stipulation that they must wait a year with no athletic scholarship aid.
- The right to a four-year scholarship, not the one-year renewable at the option of the coach as is the current NCAA policy. Those athletes who compete for three years should be given an open-ended scholarship guaranteeing that they will receive aid as long as it takes to graduate.
- The rights that other college students have (freedom of speech, privacy rights, protections from the physical and mental abuse of authorities, and the fair redress of grievances). There should be an impartial committee on each college campus, separate from the athletic department, that monitors the behavior of coaches and the rules imposed by them on athletes to ensure that individual rights are guaranteed.
- The right of athletes to consult with agents concerning sports career choices.
- The right of athletes to make money from endorsements, speeches, and the like. Walter Byers, former executive director of the NCAA, has stated that

athletes should have the same financial opportunities as other students, arguing that "The athlete may access the marketplace just as other students exploit their own special talents, whether they are musicians playing on weekends, journalism students working piecemeal for newspapers, or announcers for the college radio station filing reports for CNN radio."

Big-time college sport presents us with a fundamental dilemma. We like the festival, pageantry, exuberance, excitement, and the excellence, but are we then willing to accept the hypocrisy, scandal, and exploitation that go with them? To date, the plantation system is not challenged as the college presidents and various NCAA committees make timid and tepid cosmetic changes. As a beginning to the real reform of the oppressive system, we need to understand who benefits and who is exploited. The plantation/slave metaphor illuminates the injustices of the system in stark reality. Seeing it this way should create an urgency among educators to make real changes. The time is ripe for bold action to transform big-time college athletics so that it can be part of the educational vision of the university *without* the shame and the sham that characterize it now.

22

Guys and Dollars

Women Still Trail in the Greed Game of College Sports

Alisa Solomon

Is women's collegiate sports as corrupt as men's? Have the enormous gains in opportunities for female athletes over the last three decades led inevitably to skewed academic priorities, recruitment cheating, grade-fixing, and other infractions that for years have flowed as freely in men's programs as beer in the stands? Has the liberal feminist push for inclusion merely elbowed gender balance into an inherently corrupt value system of greed that hasn't otherwise been questioned? And why all the hand-wringing when it's women who break the rules?

First, says Tara VanDerveer, the Stanford and former U.S. Olympic coach who will be inducted into the Women's Basketball Hall of Fame later this month, it makes little sense to compare women's iniquities to those of their brothers.

"We're still horse and buggy compared to men's sports," she says. "There are definitely pressures in the women's games, but not nearly like those men have." The TV contract with the NCAA for the women's Final Four, for example, is $200 million—colossal considering the absence of any television coverage only a few years ago, but puny next to the boys' beefy $6.1 billion CBS deal. What's more, VanDerveer points out, "When men's teams make it to the finals, money goes to their conference and their teams. Winning for them is tied to money. The women's tournament doesn't have any such deal."

Source: Alisa Solomon, "Guys and Dollars: Women Still Trail in the Greed Game of College Sports," *Village Voice* (April 10–16, 2002).

By any statistical measure currently available, women have not stooped as low as guys under the weight of the pressure to win at all costs. The most egregious infractions are still most often found in football and men's basketball. For instance, Bobby Knight-style basketball coach Cheryl "Mad Dog" Littlejohn was fired last May by the University of Minnesota in the wake of allegations of NCAA violations, but her alleged crimes were petty compared to the academic scandal that put men's basketball there on probation for four years: A college tutor had written some 400 papers for 18 players over five years.

Similarly, while steroid use by girls is climbing, it is nowhere near the one-in-40 level among teenage boys. Meanwhile, women athletes' college graduation rates far surpass men's: The average for last month's women's Final Four teams was 66 percent; on the men's side, it was 32 percent. Men far exceed women, too, when it comes to gambling on sports—even on games in which they're involved.

In sum, while problems are rife in the megabuck men's wide world of sports, it's no wonder that they are emerging at a rate parallel to the growth in women's still more circumscribed world. And women are far from closing the gap. "It will take us eons and eons to get to a point where our culture will allow a woman professional athlete to be a Darryl Strawberry," says Mary Jo Kane, a professor and director of the Tucker Center for Research for Women in Sport at the University of Minnesota. "Women's sports is not about to produce a Jayson Williams. We're not even in the same universe. A little trash-talking is a whole lot different from manslaughter and obstruction of justice." But, she's quick to add, "I don't want to sound all pious about how women are not supposed to be as corrupt as men. That's a morality argument that does more harm to women than exposure to corruption does. This isn't about women, but about the institution of sport. The issue isn't gender, it's greed."

Fair enough. But assumptions about supposed differences between men's and women's values constantly creep into the discourse. In part, that's the piety Kane bristles at—the sexist idea that women are by nature upright and innocent and must be protected from the sinister forces men are just born more fit to handle.

The *New York Times* editorial board warned women during the Final Four to steer clear of "the win-at-any-cost philosophy that has deformed men's collegiate basketball and most of the schools that field the perennial powerhouse teams." With stolid sanctimoniousness, the *Times* cautioned: "As the popularity of the women's game grows, coaches, parents and athletic directors will need to work hard to keep their sport in perspective." That's not wrong, of course. You just have to wonder why the *Times* isn't railing constantly at the distortions already brought to fruition by men. Corruption must really be avoided, the editorial seems to say, because now even women are in danger of being tainted. And, as coach VanDerveer quips, "We like our women pure, don't we?"

Taking the analysis further, the author and former pro basketball player Mariah Burton Nelson argues in her book, *The Stronger Women Get, the More Men Love Football*, that instead of being influenced by what women bring when they enter previously all-male precincts, men exaggerate their masculinity. The mechanism operates even around a development as negative as corruption, suggests Ellen Staurowsky, a sports sociologist at Ithaca College and co-author of *College Athletes for Hire: The Evolution and Legacy of the NCAA Amateur Myth.* "Athletes have been required to legitimate themselves as athletes within a value system that says you have to be brutish and willing to do anything to win," she explains. "Of course women are capable of doing that. So they chase the phantom of legitimacy, and the bar keeps moving. Masculine culture gets hyper-masculinized, and the stakes keep getting higher and higher. Women are constantly in pursuit, and men never turn around to see that women might have something to offer, that they might have some authority. That dynamic doesn't produce what I would call progress."

If that sounds too abstract, ask Christine Grant, women's athletic director at Iowa from 1973 until 2000, how it plays out in real life. During more than three decades in collegiate competition as well as in international field hockey, she has seen women get shut out of decision-making even as their access has expanded on playing fields. When, in the early 1980s, the NCAA supplanted the Association of Intercollegiate Athletics for Women (for which Grant served a term as president) and forced a merger of men's and women's athletics programs, Grant recalls, "We thought that together the women and the men would rethink what college sport could be, that we would bring the best from both worlds to create the best college experience imaginable for male and female athletes." Instead, women were frozen out of leadership, and what Grant calls "the alternative model" the AIAW represented never got a fair hearing.

Indeed, according to research by R. Vivian Acosta and Linda Jean Carpenter, the number of female coaches and athletic directors has declined steadily. While, in 1972, 90 percent of women's teams were coached by women, today that figure has dropped to 45.6 percent. Today, men head up 82.8 percent of athletic departments.

The AIAW system—keeping scholarships need-based, or at least limiting them to tuition only; developing all sports that students wanted to participate in on an equal level instead of favoring football or other mega-programs; allowing athletes to transfer and keep playing their sport; emphasizing athletes' academic lives and requiring them to meet the same admissions requirements as all other students—was thrown out altogether. "Women were muted in the NCAA and couldn't effectuate change," says Grant. "Women's sport headed down the same path as men's."

How could it be otherwise, when schools troll for more and more dollars by big Division I-A programs at which male coaches earn salaries upward of $1 million, and women's teams have to swim in the same waters? Still, the Knight Foundation Commission on Intercollegiate Athletics has been trying to rein in the runaway jockocracy. "The pressures that have corrupted too many major athletic programs are moving with inexorable force," the commission's report of last May warns, and the near future may see ever more widespread "weakened academic and amateurism standards, millionaire coaches and rampant commercialism, all combined increasingly with deplorable sportsmanship and misconduct."

The commission lists a number of recommendations. They sound a lot like the principles of the long-buried AIAW.

✳ FOR FURTHER STUDY ✳

Adler, Patricia A., and Peter Adler. 1991. *Backboards and Blackboards: College Athletics and Role Engulfment* (New York: Columbia University Press).

Books, Dana D., and Ronald C. Althouse (Eds.). 2000. *Racism in College Athletics: The African American Athlete's Experience,* 2nd ed. (Morgantown, WV: Fitness Information Technology).

Bower, William G., and Sarah A. Levin. 2003. *Reclaiming the Game: College Sports and Educational Values* (Princeton, NJ: Princeton University Press).

Byers, Walter, with Charles Hammer. 1995. *Unsportsmanlike Conduct: Exploiting College Athletes* (Ann Arbor: University of Michigan Press).

Eitzen, D. Stanley. 2000. "Racism in Bit-Time College Sport: Prospects for the Year 2020 and Proposals for Change," in *Racism in College Athletics: The African American Experience,* 2nd ed., Dana D. Brooks and Ronald C. Althouse (Eds.) (Morgantown, WV: Fitness Information Technology).

Meggyesy, David. 2000. "Athletes in Big-Time College Sports," *Society* 37 (March/April):24–28.

Sack, Allen L., and Ellen J. Staurowsky. 1998. *College Athletes for Hire: The Evolution and Legacy of the NCAA's Amateur Myth* (Westport, CT: Praeger).

Shulman, James L., and William G. Bowen. 2001. *The Game of Life: College Sports and Educational Values* (Princeton, NJ: Princeton University Press).

Sokolove, Michael. 2002. "Football Is a Sucker's Game," *The New York Times Magazine* (December 22):36–41,64,68–71.

Wyatt, Joe B. 1999. "Our Moral Duty to Clean Up College Athletics," *The Chronicle of Higher Education* (August 13):A56.

Yaeger, Don, and Douglas S. Looney. 1993. *Under the Tarnished Dome: Notre Dame Betrayed Its Ideals for Football Glory* (New York: Simon and Schuster).

Yaeger, Don, and Alexander Wolff. 1997. "Troubling Questions," *Sports Illustrated* (July 7):70–79.

Zimbalist, Andrew. 1999. *Unpaid Professionals: Commercialism and Conflict in Big-Time College Sports* (Princeton, NJ: Princeton University Press).

PART EIGHT

Problems of Excess: Sport and Money

A dilemma that characterizes professional sport and much of what is called amateur sport in the United States has been described by journalist Roger Kahn: "Sport is too much a game to be a business and too much a business to be a game."[1] The evidence indicating a strong relationship between sport and money is overwhelming. Consider the following facts for 2000:[2]

- The sports industry in the United States generated $212.53 billion, twice as much as the automobile industry generated.
- Legal gambling on sports amounted to $18.55 billion. Another $100 billion is bet legally and illegally in the United States annually.
- Team operating expenses for the four major professional leagues was $19.23 billion.
- Sports advertising amounted to $28.25 billion.
- Media broadcast rights cost $10.57 billion.
- Facility construction for the year cost $2.49 billion.
- Gate receipts for spectator sports were $22.57 billion.
- Sports spectators spend $44.47 billion for transportation, accommodations, and meals.
- Medical treatment for athletes costs $4.1 billion.
- Some universities in 2003 had annual athletic budgets in the $60 to $80 million range.

There is no longer any question that sport is a business.

Money is often the key motivator of athletes. Players and owners give their primary allegiance to money rather than to the sport or to the fans. Modern sport, whether professional, big-time college, or Olympic, is "corporate sport." The original purpose of sport—pleasure in the activity—has been lost in the process. Sport has become work. Sport has become the product of publicity agents using superhype methods. Money has superseded the content as the ultimate goal. Illicit tactics are commonplace, because winning translates into more revenues. In short, U.S. sport is a microcosm of the values of U.S. society. Journalist Roger Angell has said of baseball what is applicable to all forms of corporate sport.

> Professional sports now form a noisy and substantial, if irrelevant and distracting, part of the world, and it seems as if baseball games taken entirely—off the field as well as on it, in the courts and in the front offices as well as down on the diamonds—may now tell us more about ourselves than they ever did before.[3]

The selections in part 8 illustrate the problems and issues involving the impact of money on sports. The first two examine the money machines in automobile racing and the NFL, respectively. The third selection, by economists Roger G. Noll and Andrew Zimbalist, examines the issues and debates surrounding the public financing of stadiums for professional teams. The final selection, by D. Stanley Eitzen, demythologizes the common belief that sport is a path to upward social mobility.

NOTES

1. Roger Kahn, quoted in CBS Reports, "The Baseball Business," television documentary, narrated by Bill Moyers (1977).

2. David Broughton, Jennifer Lee, and Ross Nethery, "Numbers Show Sports Ranks Among Best for Big Business," *Fort Collins Coloradoan* (January 16, 2000), p. D1, first published in *Sports Business Journal.*

3. Roger Angell, "The Sporting Scene: In the Counting House," *New Yorker* (May 10, 1976), p. 107.

23

NASCAR

A Big Money Machine

Paul Newberry

Stock car racing has made huge strides from its beginnings on the sands of Daytona Beach, squeezing in alongside football, baseball, and basketball as one of the nation's sporting passions.

Television ratings keep going up. Grandstands are packed with hundreds of thousands of die-hard fans.

Still, the good ol' boys are clinging to their roots.

Confederate banners flap in the infield breeze.

Cutoff jeans, beer-packed coolers, and sunburns remain the symbols of a true fan.

And the buck stops with the France family, just as it has for more than a half-century.

NASCAR is an anomaly—a major sport that is essentially ruled by one set of kinfolk. The late Bill France Sr. founded NASCAR in 1948, giving a bunch of ex-moonshine runners a place to display their driving skills. When he retired, the organization was turned over to sons Bill Jr. and Jim. The next generation, Brian France and Lesa France Kennedy, is in place.

The strict control—France supporters call it a "benevolent dictatorship"—has been a major reason for NASCAR's surge in popularity.

While other sports became a cesspool of warring factions, the Frances could make their decisions freely. No player unions. No hardheaded owners. It's their way or the highway.

Source: Paul Newberry, "NASCAR a Big Money Machine," part one of a three-part series. Associated Press (December 25, 2002).

"I think my family and NASCAR have been terrific partners," Kennedy said. "You especially have to look to the second generation, my father and my uncle. They have given life to the sport."

But their control also has sparked some grumbling in the garage: Is everyone getting a fair share?

- Drivers race for more than nine months a year and put their lives on the line every time they get behind the wheel, yet don't even get a pension from NASCAR.
- Car owners struggle to contain increasing costs, woo sponsors in a sluggish economy, and grovel for a larger share of the NASCAR-distributed pot.
- The cost of a ticket has grown to the highest in sports.

Of course, the France family likes things just the way they are.

"Having a dictatorship is not a bad thing," longtime driver Darrell Waltrip said with a chuckle, "if you're the dictator."

Certainly, the Frances aren't the only people getting rich. Kyle Petty, son of the greatest driver the sport has known, made $88 a week when he started racing. Now, seven-figure salaries are common.

But no one has claimed a greater share of the money than the France family, through a complex web of companies, subsidiaries, and affiliates.

They run NASCAR, wielding enormous power with sanctioning fees, scheduling, and the final word on how the billions in TV dollars are split up. They also control International Speedway Corp. (ISC), a publicly traded company that owns or has a stake in 12 of the circuit's 23 tracks, including Daytona and Talladega.

"Imagine if [NFL-commissioner] Paul Tagliabue owned half the stadiums where the Super Bowl was played," said Timothy Sullivan, a Southern Illinois University economist who has studied NASCAR.

ISC also runs the radio network that broadcasts races, as well as the concessions company that sells soft drinks and hot dogs at its tracks. Licensing fees on everything from T-shirts to racing-themed restaurants also put money in the France coffers.

The Frances own about 62 percent of ISC stock, Kennedy said. With shares trading about $38 in mid-December, their stake was worth more than $1.2 billion. That doesn't even include NASCAR, a private enterprise that declines to reveal its bottom line.

"They basically monopolized the sport," said Hadrian Shaw, a California-based analyst who has studied the business side of NASCAR. "A lot of money gets washed, blurred and confused. When you finally boil it down, they're very successful."

Bruton Smith, whose Speedway Motorsports Inc., owns six tracks, says NASCAR collects more than $2 million on every race weekend through sanctioning fees, its cut of the TV money, and other items. This year, for instance, NASCAR doubled the "inspection" fee—basically an entry fee—to $3,400 per car at each race. If a team wrecks the car in practice and uses a backup, that's another $3,400. In all, that revenue stream brings about $5.5 million to NASCAR.

Where does all the money go? A lot is used for safety and testing programs. In January, NASCAR will open a $10 million research center near Charlotte, N.C., where more than 50 workers will study how to curb serious injuries in an inherently dangerous sport.

Just getting by each week is costly for NASCAR, according to its president, Mike Helton.

"We run the races and police the races and move 75 people around every race weekend from track to track to track," he said. "The hardware just for the Winston Cup series takes five trailers to move around. I don't think NASCAR is being unfair with the balance of economics."

Forbes magazine estimated that brothers Bill and Jim France are billionaires, putting them among the 400 richest people in America.

After their father stepped aside, they forged a hugely successful partnership: Bill Jr. runs NASCAR, younger brother Jim controls ISC. Their business acumen is unquestioned, their hold on the sport essentially unchallenged, even though they have let an outsider, Helton, into their inner circle for the first time.

Helton serves on an otherwise all-France board: Bill Jr., Jim, Brian, and Lesa. No drivers or car owners are allowed in, at least not officially. In NASCAR parlance, they are "independent contractors."

"Certainly, they run this place like a dictatorship," car owner Bill Davis said. "It's their deal. They started it. And they've done a fabulous job of growing the sport. We probably have more than we ever thought we would have."

Rick Burton, director of the University of Oregon's Warsaw Sports Marketing Center, compares the family to Pete Rozelle, who almost single-handedly transformed the NFL into its leading role.

"I think it really comes down to two words: strong leadership," Burton said.

But some question if enough money is trickling down.

"I just don't think that Bill Sr. would have been quite this greedy," said Dave Marcis, now retired after a career that included 881 starts and $7.2 million in winnings. "I believe he probably would have seen to it that the drivers got a little more."

Shaw, in a study conducted for Kagan World Media, projected that nearly $1.9 billion in revenues would flow through NASCAR in 2002. He also found that Winston Cup drivers get a much smaller share of the revenues than athletes in the four major team sports.

NFL players are assured of about half the total revenue under their salary-cap arrangement. The figure is around 60 percent for major league baseball, 63 percent for the NHL and 57 percent for the NBA, Shaw said.

In NASCAR, driver salaries are harder to pin down. In addition to guaranteed contracts, drivers bolster their pay with a percentage of the winnings, merchandise deals, and personal-service contracts with sponsors. The late Dale Earnhardt essentially became the richest driver by selling more T-shirts than anyone else.

Waltrip, now a TV analyst, estimates the top four or five drivers are taking home at least $8 million to $10 million annually, the rest of the upper echelon is in the $5 million–$8 million range, and even the back markers are making around $3 million.

It's hard to feel sorry for millionaires. Still, assuming the 40 or so Winston Cup regulars are making an average of $5 million a year, that means they take home no more than 12 percent of the Shaw-projected revenues.

The numbers are skewed because there are more players on just one NFL roster than you'll find in a Winston Cup race.

But it doesn't hurt that NASCAR has set up a system where driver salaries aren't its concern.

"Our sport is unique in that there's an ability to make an enormous amount of money, but it's all competition driven," Helton said. "If you perform well, you benefit. That's the mainstay of our success. I think it's going to stay that way."

No one balks at that arrangement with a unified voice, but there are a few signs of dissension. Longtime star Rusty Wallace contends Winston Cup drivers should get the big contracts of other sports.

The racing season begins in early February and runs until mid-November, with events on all but three weekends. And there are testing sessions to get the car running well, and promotional appearances for sponsors and fans.

"Compared to other sports, we've got a long way to go," Wallace said. "We're out there for four or five hours a race, 36 or 38 weeks a year. In a perfect world, we would be making more money."

Helton concedes NASCAR has the upper hand over drivers who put on the show each weekend.

"The desire of drivers to become part of Winston Cup is fairly significant now," he said. "That's a good thing for us. If a driver doesn't think he has a good deal, he has a choice [to leave]. And we have a lot of other guys who want to do it for a living."

Sullivan said NASCAR benefits from a "cultural psychology."

"A lot of these guys are used to driving on Friday nights at all these different small tracks," he said. "To make a million dollars driving a car, they can't imagine complaining about something like that."

Maybe they should. It's the individual teams, not NASCAR, that provide everything from 401(k) plans to health insurance.

Longtime car owner Robert Yates, who has a payroll of 160, said his team pays some $2 million in insurance premiums before it even leaves the garage.

"I wish there was a little more money on this side of the fence," he said.

Bill France Jr. doesn't want to get mixed up in that discussion, saying the teams should control their costs. Again, those words: "independent contractors."

"What's a tire-changer getting?" France said before a July race at Daytona. "That's not up to NASCAR. This is America."

France, who has been in poor health, was not available to comment on other financial issues, said NASCAR spokesman Jim Hunter, who referred all questions to Helton. Jim France did not reply to several requests for an interview; Kennedy spoke on behalf of ISC, where she is an executive vice president.

Car owner and driver Brett Bodine thinks NASCAR should consider setting aside money for pensions that would benefit not only the drivers but also crew members.

"Does it fall under NASCAR to set up a pension or does it fall to the team?" Bodine said. "Well, you have to be a member of NASCAR to be here. I'd like to see that looked at."

A pension would have helped Bobby Allison, who won 84 races—third-most in Winston Cup history—before a wreck ended his career. At the time, NASCAR covered only $50,000 of his medical bills; Allison was wiped out financially when the cost soared to more than $200,000.

Today, NASCAR provides a $500,000 umbrella policy for drivers injured in a race. Still, Allison blames himself more than NASCAR for making bad business decisions when he was at the pinnacle of the sport.

"I should have made sure I took care of my earnings and had the proper insurance," he said. "I didn't do that."

PGA Tour golfers have benefitted from a pension plan since 1983. Under current projections, Tiger Woods would be eligible for up to $300 million in deferred compensation beginning at age 60 if he became fully vested. Even a 26-year-old golfer who started in 2001, played 17 seasons, and averaged 75th on the money list could stockpile an account of nearly $43 million—without ever winning a tournament.

Helton said NASCAR has looked at the pension issue but hasn't found a system that makes financial sense.

"It goes back to the fact that, from NASCAR's perspective, they're not employees of NASCAR," he said. "They're employees of the race team."

Thirty years ago, some of the sport's biggest names—including Richard Petty and Allison—tried to form the Professional Drivers Association.

"We were going to try to get a retirement benefit program, insurance, health protection, things that a lot of professional sports and businesses already had," Allison said.

Bill France Sr. ignored the PDA, and it quickly collapsed.

"We were more competitors than we were comrades,"Allison said. "The few guys that were making good money were taking care of their own stuff and not worrying about the rest of the guys down the line."

Today, there's still no union, and Helton said there's no need for one.

"Every owner, every team member in that garage, has a voice that's loud and clear to us," he said.

Still, a couple of battles could be looming—on dividing TV money and a lawsuit over the NASCAR schedule.

Fox and NBC just finished the second of six years in a landmark $2.8 billion contract with NASCAR. When it was signed, some drivers and owners wanted the formula revised. The Frances refused, sticking with the split of 65 percent to the tracks, 25 to the car owners, and 10 percent for NASCAR itself.

Considering the France-affiliated tracks host half of the 36 races, the family steered more than 40 percent of the TV money in its direction—the biggest cut of all.

Kyle Petty calls the arrangement "a decent starting point," indicating it could be reopened in three of four years.

Helton said no changes are imminent. He pointed out the ISC had only two tracks—Daytona and Talladega—when the formula began, so NASCAR is not playing favorites. He also said track owners deserve most of the TV money for investing in facilities that weren't always lucrative.

Petty agrees.

"No one was complaining 10 or 12 years ago when NASCAR was going in and buying these tracks to keep them from going out of business," he said.

Can the Frances maintain their grip? A new generation of stars, including 2002 Winston Cup champion Tony Stewart, are making more money in a year than the oldtimers did in a career.

"NASCAR is having a harder and harder and harder time controlling this young breed of drivers we've got right now," Waltrip said. "If they can't control that, then there's a chance there's going to be some cracks in other parts of the armor."

AT A GLANCE

- **History**—William H. G. "Bill" France founded the National Association for Stock Car Auto Racing (NASCAR) in 1948 to organize and promote a sport that had been run in a ragtag fashion throughout the Southeast. He also founded International Speedway Corp. (ISC), a company that built two of the sport's most prominent tracks: Daytona International Speedway in 1959 and Talladega (Ala.) Superspeedway in 1969.
- **Family matters**—When France retired, he ceded power to his two sons. Bill France Jr. became NASCAR president, while Jim France took over as executive vice president and secretary, as well as president of ISC. The France family essentially controls NASCAR, though Mike Helton became the first non-family member to run day-to-day operations when he was installed as president in November 2000. Bill Jr. is now chairman of a five-member board of directors that includes his brother, Jim, children Brian France and Lesa France Kennedy, and Helton. ISC is a publicly traded company in which the France family controls approximately 62 percent of the stock, worth an estimated $1.2 billion.
- **Structure**—The Winston Cup series is the sport's highest level. NASCAR also runs two major support series, Busch and Craftsman Truck, that help develop drivers.
- **Schedule**—NASCAR modernized its schedule in 1972 and now runs 36 Winston Cup races around the country. The 2003 season begins with the February 16 Daytona 500, its premier race, and ends with a November 16 race at Homestead-Miami Speedway. Eighteen of those races are run at tracks that are owned or have a financial connection to ISC.

- **Television**—NASCAR completed the second season of a six-year, $2.8 billion deal with Fox and NBC. All Winston Cup races are televised live on the national networks or their cable partners. In 2002, NASCAR became the first sport since the NGA in 1995–1996 to have back-to-back years in which ratings increased.
- **On the Web**—NASCAR's official site is www.nascar.com. ISC's official site is www.iscmotorsports.com.

—The Associated Press

24

The NFL Machine

Tom Lowry

In this era of bad-boy businessmen and the corporate perp walk, it's hard to imagine any CEO commanding a police escort—unless he's cuffed in the backseat of a patrol car. Still, that's what is waiting for Paul Tagliabue as his private jet touches down in Tampa in early December. Why the rock-star treatment? Simple. From September to February, this bookish 62-year old with the button-down look of a corporate lawyer controls the passion of America—the 32 teams of the NFL. Besides, he can get Super Bowl tickets.

There are hours to go before the Tampa Bay Buccaneers face the Atlanta Falcons, but Tagliabue hops into a black Lincoln Town Car buffered by two police cruisers. As sirens blare and lights flash, the commissioner's car is guided through pregame traffic directly into the caverns beneath Raymond James Stadium. Fans treat him like a celebrity, too. "Hey commish, over here," shouts one Warren Sapp wannabe in a bright-red No. 99 jersey as he snaps a photo. The 6-foot, 5-inch Tagliabue signs autographs and chats with security guards before strolling out onto the lush field to watch warm-ups. He quickly notes that the socks of Falcons star quarterback Michael Vick are scrunched down around his ankles in violation of league rules. They are pulled up tightly by kickoff time.

Sometimes a quarterback finds himself in a sweet spot where everything works just right, week after week. Tagliabue in 2002, and now heading into the Super Bowl on Jan. 26 in San Diego, is in that kind of groove. Behind him is a thrilling, anyone-can-

Source: Tom Lowry, "The NFL Machine," *Business Week* (January 27, 2003), pp. 86–91, 94.

win season and a white-knuckle postseason. Ahead is a media empire in the making. The National Football League recently signed a $2 billion satellite-TV deal. There are three years left on an $18 billion network and cable contract. Twenty spanking-new football-only stadiums have been built or renovated in the past 10 years, thanks to the league's deft use of the bond market. Sponsors keep queuing up to get a piece of the NFL brand. Harmony reigns among players and owners. And heck, as John Madden might say, this is in the middle of an economic slump.

Maybe one reason for Tagliabue's championship season in the face of a stubborn downturn is that the NFL is not exactly a model of capitalism. The commissioner has made it his mission to distribute equally as much of the league's revenues as possible among the teams of the National Football Conference and the American Football Conference. "We're 32 fat-cat Republicans who vote socialist," Baltimore Ravens owner Art Modell quipped recently. It doesn't hurt that players have agreed to a hard cap on salaries and few guarantees. "I don't see this as us vs. the owners, but instead it's us vs. all the other entertainment choices out there; the movies, music, theater," says Gene Upshaw, the former Oakland Raider and Hall of Famer who represents 2,000 players as executive director of the NFL Players Association.

To understand the success of the business that Tagliabue has built and runs with almost military precision, take a look at the season just past. It started in early September, when the commish and his marketing team were able to persuade New York City to shut down Times Square during rush hour on a workday for a kickoff concert featuring Jersey rockers Bon Jovi. Half a million people turned out.

By the final regular-season weekend at the end of December, 19 teams still had a shot at the playoffs and a record 24 games had been decided in overtime. Those photo finishes helped boost TV viewership by 5 percent over 2001, inching closer to the NFL's recent peak in 1999. An average of 15.8 million viewers this season tuned in to any one game on the networks, according to Nielsen Media Research. For a league that loves to boast about competitive balance, it couldn't have been a more satisfying finale. "They wanted parity. They sure got parity," says Richard A. Bilotti, a media analyst at Morgan Stanley.

Life looks like a cakewalk for the 83-year-old NFL these days, but it's not as if the league hasn't had its issues. Grumbling that the game had gone flat led to the birth in 2001 of the testosterone-infused XFL—a smash-mouth spectacle featuring cheerleaders dressed like showgirls. But this production of World Wrestling Entertainment and NBC proved too staged, too self-parodying, and maybe even too violent to turn the curious into fans.

Not that violence isn't a good part of the NFL's appeal on-field—and a problem for the league off-field. The controversial 1998 book *Pros and Cons: The Criminals Who Play in the NFL* cited research showing that one in five players during the 1996–97 season had been charged with a serious crime at one time. "These guys are the gladiators of modern culture," says sports media consultant Neal Pilson. "And with that come pluses and minuses associated with players who are larger than life." It doesn't help that a string of crummy calls by refs in recent games have fans, owners, coaches, and players riled up. But most of the focus has been where it should be: between the chalk lines.

Beyond the compelling action on the turf, the NFL, already widely considered the most successful and opportunistic of the pro leagues, has struck half a dozen or so blockbuster business deals in the past year. The moves, from the new $2 billion, exclusive satellite television deal with DirecTV (triple the value of the previous pact) to a $300 million sponsorship by Coors, underscore how pro football has been able to leverage its mass following to double revenues in five years, to $4.8 billion in 2002. By comparison, the valuable cable networks at media giant Viacom, such as MTV and Nickelodeon, had revenues totaling $4.3 billion in 2001.

The NFL estimates that revenues will grow by an additional $1 billion over the next three years. "When [Tagliabue's predecessor] Pete Rozelle ran the league, it was a football business and a good one," says Paul J. Much, a senior managing director of investment firm Houlihan Lokey Howard & Zukin. "Now it's truly an entertainment business." Says Tagliabue: "In 1989, I inherited a great structural underpinning, the equal sharing of TV money. We've added three more pillars to that: branching into new media, including satellite TV; creating a narrow band between player salary cap and floor; and using our growing TV revenues to ensure that new stadiums could be financed."

As evidence of the faster march into showbiz and the push into distribution, *Business Week* has learned that the NFL will hire Steve Bornstein, 50, one of the architects of ESPN and a former top executive at Walt Disney Co., to be in charge of TV and media. Bornstein will also be CEO of a 24-hour, NFL-owned, digital cable channel devoted to football—though the only games shown will be classics. The channel, which will include news and commentary, will launch later this year.

Also in the works are plans to sell the league's rich archives through a video-on-demand service that will allow fans to watch old game footage for a fee. In addition, Tagliabue is expected soon to announce a deal with Time Inc. to put out an NFL magazine. and ESPN is nearing a deal with the NFL Films unit to help develop two original movies.

Unlike other leagues with big corporate owners such as AOL Time Warner, News Corp., and Walt Disney, no company has ever owned an NFL club. The league maintains that individuals care more about winning and corporations care more about their shareholders—not that there's anything wrong with that. NFL ownership groups are restricted to 25 people, with the principal owner holding at least a 30 percent stake. And an owner can borrow only $125 million against the value of the team. By contrast, the free-spending lords of baseball were allowed to tap an MLB-backed loan pool almost at will—jacking up the teams' collective debt to $3.5 billion today from $598 million in 1993.

In the NFL, strict oversight ensures that the 32 teams equally divide about 63 percent of total revenues. That helps level the playing field when it comes to buying top talent. In fact, the combined revenues of the top eight richest teams is just 28 percent more than the eight teams on the low end. The NFL closely guards revenue and earning numbers, but it is widely believed that almost every team turns an operating profit. In baseball, by contrast, revenue is largely dependent on how much teams derive from local broadcasting contracts, not national deals. In 2001, the local revenues generated by the richest team, the New York Yankees, were $218 million. The poorest team, the Montreal Expos, took in just $9.7 million.

Jerry Jones, 60, the hands-on owner of the Dallas Cowboys since 1989 and one of the most aggressive businessmen in the league, takes the view that sharing revenue is all well and good but that teams need to seize their own marketing opportunities. In fact, the NFL has sued Jones over his aggressive local sponsorship deals. Still Jones doesn't seem bitter and likens owning a team to acquiring a piece of art. "You're not going to see an inordinate amount of annual return on your money," he says. "It's all in the potential appreciation."

On the other hand, revenue guarantees have been swiftly driving up the value of an NFL franchise. In 2000, advertising executive Daniel Snyder, 38, shelled out a record $800 million for the Washington Redskins and its stadium. Previous owner Jack Kent Cooke paid $300,000 for a 25 percent stake in the 'Skins in the early 1960s. The newest owner is Arthur M. Blank, 60, the retired co-founder of Home Depot. Last year, he spent $545 million for the Atlanta Falcons, which had the league's second-lowest attendance record—an average of 52,000 a game. Previous owner Rankin M. Smith Sr. paid $8.5 million in 1965.

H. Wayne Huizenga, 65, owner of the Miami Dolphins and ProPlayer Stadium, used to own MLB's Florida Marlins and the NHL's Florida Panthers. After losing more than $100 million collectively, he sold both. "[The NFL] is the only thing that makes sense in sports today," he says. Huizenga, who is chairman of several real estate companies and serves on the board of AutoNation Inc., says the disparity of local revenues in baseball and hockey makes it impossible to compete if you're not in the TV-rich market of New York City. "I keep hearing about the Yankees dynasty. It makes me sick. Put me in that local TV market, and I would have had a dynasty, too," says Huizenga. He won't disclose the Dolphins' financials but says: "We do make some money."

One of the most important changes in the economics of the league has been new stadiums. "It's been the biggest transformation in the balance sheet of the NFL since I've been commissioner," says Tagliabue. With criticism of public funding for stadiums growing louder, the owners in 1999 authorized the league to go to Wall Street to sell bonds, the proceeds from which would be used to lend money for construction at low interest rates. So far, $650 million in such loans has helped build or renovate eight stadiums, including Gillette Stadium in Foxboro, Mass., and Lincoln Financial Field in Philadelphia, which opens next season. Gone is the emptiness of yesteryear's cold concrete shells. The new stadiums—adult theme parks, really—create fresh revenue streams from sources such as luxury suites, club seats, high-tech signage, restaurants, and shops.

Still, the league faces sizable risks. More than 50 percent of revenues comes from the money television pays for the rights to show NFL games. The league is in year five of an eight-year, $18 billion package with ABC/ESPN, CBS, and Fox. But all three are part of media companies that have just endured one of the worst ad recessions in decades. When renegotiation time rolls around, it remains to be seen whether they will pony up as much as they have in the past. For example, News

Corp., owner of Fox, in February announced a nearly $1 billion write-off from losses associated with its sports contracts.

Morgan Stanley last year estimated that media companies would lose a combined $2 billion on the NFL over the term of their deals. Still, as part of the current pact, the league has until February 15 to renegotiate terms or extend the contract. Or it can just wait for it to expire in three years. "The networks are between a rock and a hard place because they are bleeding money, but they want to have the NFL as a platform to promote the rest of their schedules to that enormous audience," says Morgan Stanley analyst Bilotti. ESPN will be the only one to make money on the current deal—an estimated $50 million profit, according to Morgan Stanley—in large part because it can get revenues from both advertising and hefty fee increases it charges cable and satellite operators.

NBC, a unit of General Electric Co., walked away from football in 1998, refusing to cough up for new rights after 34 years of broadcasting AFC (and earlier, AFL) games. CBS, which in 1994 lost the NFC to Fox, won the AFC contract by shelling out $4.1 billion over eight years. Executives at NBC, who also passed on an NBA contract last year, say privately that they have no regrets. They estimate that the net would have lost upwards of $1 billion if it had kept the NFL. "Look," says one network executive, "NBC was the No. 1 network in terms of ratings when they walked away, and they still are. In other words, if you don't have it, it doesn't kill you."

The fear in NFL offices is that other nets, pressured by parent companies, will take the NBC line in three years. "Will the next negotiation be a difficult one? Sure," says Howard Katz, president of ABC Sports, home of *Monday Night Football,* which has struggled with declining ratings, though viewership was up 4 percent this season over last.

So Tagliabue is already talking to the nets about flexible scheduling that would allow last-minute switches to more competitive games on Monday night. An additional prime-time game on Sunday is also under consideration. Such ideas aren't going over too well with Fox and CBS, which don't want to give up a daytime game to rival ABC/ESPN. The only certainty next time around, network execs say, is that there must be plans in place for a Los Angeles team.

More viewers, yes. But not all football, all the time. Talk about expanding the NFL's presence on TV fuels worries about consumers reaching a saturation point. "We're always concerned about commoditizing the NFL," says Chief Operating Officer Roger Goodell, 43, son of the late New York Senator Charles Goodell and thought to be the leading candidate to succeed Tagliabue. "But we still see extraordinary demand for what we offer. It's the best reality TV going."

At the same time that the TV contract expires, so does the league's labor agreement. The NFL is widely seen as having the most favorable player deal in pro sports, with average salaries at $1.2 million. True, the average NBA salary is $4.5 million. But don't cry too hard for the footballers, many of whom get fat signing bonuses not figured into that average salary. Philadelphia Eagles quarterback Donovan McNabb, the league's highest-paid player, for one, will make $21.7 million this year, almost all of it from his signing bonus. While the salary cap has been instrumental in bringing parity to the league, there is a downside: Teams sometimes must cut veteran players, alienating fans.

Overall, though, the league has a highly dedicated following. Despite some erosion of support in the face of so many other entertainment options, NFL fans remain the most loyal of any sport, followed by those of the NBA, then baseball and hockey, according to a newly released index for consultant Brand Keys Inc. One big reason so many are so hot for football is gambling. An estimated $560 million is wagered on NFL games each year in Nevada alone, the only state where sports betting is legal. Estimates of illegal betting, of course, go into the billions.

To understand the roots of the NFL's powerful and enduring brand, you have to go back to 1960 when new Commissioner Rozelle, then 33, persuaded Washington to pass the Sports Broadcasting Act. That allowed leagues to sell broadcast rights as a package and gave them much more clout in negotiating favorable contracts. The first NFL deal was reached a short time later with CBS, which agreed to pay $4.6 million, split among the teams.

Rozelle is credited with transforming modern sports by marrying games with TV, and needless to say, when he retired in 1989, his were big shoes to fill. The differences between Rozelle and Tagliabue, who was hired to replace him, could not have been more striking. Rozelle, a tanned Southern Californian and former PR man, had the gift of schmooze. Jersey City-born Tagliabue, who played basketball at Georgetown and had been the NFL's outside lawyer at the Washington firm of Covington & Burling, was seen as stiff and reticent.

But Tagliabue's methodical, lawyerly approach has served the league well, say those who have worked with him. He sweats every detail. His office in the NFL's Park Avenue headquarters in Manhattan is littered with yellow legal pads on which he often diagrams his strategies. And his interests extend well beyond the gridiron. In fact, the commish will actually read the front section of the *New York Times,* where his brother John is a highly regarded foreign correspondent, before digging into the sports pages. A former Pentagon policy analyst during the Johnson years, Tagliabue is just as conversant with America's Mideast policy as he is with the NFL's ban on the supplement ephedrine.

While Rozelle may have delivered the NFL to the media altar, it is Tagliabue who has made the union a lasting success. He studies the media, lunches regularly with Rupert Murdoch, and is a frequent guest of investment banker Herb Allen at his annual gathering of moguls. And with an annual salary and bonus totaling $8.5 million, Tagliabue is indeed a member of the media elite.

Robert Kraft, who made his fortunes in paper and packaging and has owned the New England Patriots for nine years, is one of the beneficiaries of Tagliabue's innovative reign. Kraft's new Gillette Stadium, which cost $345 million and was partially financed by the league's novel bond scheme, features two large clubhouses—sponsored by Fidelity Investments—that boast working fireplaces, chef stations, and several bars. There is a McDonald's above each end zone. The stadium has a capacity of 68,000 with 6,000 club seats in midfield that go for as much as $6,000 apiece for

10 years. More than 50,000 fans have put down a deposit to be on a waiting list for season tickets.

On the last weekend of the regular season, as the Super Bowl defending champion Patriots host the Dolphins in a game with crucial playoff implications, Kraft seems practically giddy. The sellout crowd is supercharged with adrenaline after fighter jets perform a scorching fly-by timed to the last note of *The Star Spangled Banner.* Following the kickoff, the 61-year-old Kraft, who had open-heart surgery last summer, runs from the field to take his place up in the owner's suite. He gazes out across what he calls "my new home,"a far cry from the expanse of rickety aluminum bench seats at the old Foxboro stadium. As the Patriots contain the Dolphins on the first set of downs and the crowd roars, Kraft rises from his seat—a Caesar before his legions—waving his arms to signal: "Louder, louder." The stadium erupts, and a smiling Kraft turns to a guest and like a school kid at his first game, shouts: "Is this cool, or what?"

The Patriots come from behind to beat the Dolphins in overtime. But a win later that Sunday by the New York Jets ends the postseason hopes of Kraft and New England. Emperor one minute, off the throne the next. That's the way it is in the frenzied, fast-money empire called the NFL.

How the NFL Levels the Playing Field
Total league revenues in 2002: $4.8 Billion

$2.5 BILLION (52%) comes from network- and cable-TV contracts and is split by the 32 teams, giving each $78 million.

$200 MILLION (4%) comes from DirecTV's Sunday Ticket, merchandise, NFL Films syndication fees, and sponsorships. It is divided equally. Each team gets $6.2 million.

$1.1 BILLION (22%) comes from ticket revenues. $350 million of it is put into a visitors pool and split evenly. Each team gets $10.9 million.

$1 BILLION (22%) comes from local sponsorships, luxury suites, broadcasting, parking and concessions. It is retained by the individual clubs.

Other Leagues Share a Lot Less of the Wealth

League	Revenues (2002)	Percent Shared Equally
NFL	$4.89 billion	63%
MLB	$3.5 billion	20%
NBA	$3.0 billion	35%
NHL	$2.0 billion	9%

The result: $3 billion (63%) divided evenly among teams. Of that amount, there is a cap on how much can be spent on players' salaries and benefits—and a minimum that must be spent. In 2002, the cap was $83 million per club, the minimum $72.5 million. This system has created the most level playing field in pro sports.

25

Sports, Jobs, and Taxes

Are New Stadiums Worth the Cost?

Roger G. Noll and Andrew Zimbalist

America is in the midst of a sports construction boom. New sports facilities costing at least $200 million each have been completed or are under way in Baltimore, Charlotte, Chicago, Cincinnati, Cleveland, Milwaukee, Nashville, San Francisco, St. Louis, Seattle, Tampa, and Washington, D.C., and are in the planning stages in Boston, Dallas, Minneapolis, New York, and Pittsburgh. Major stadium renovations have been undertaken in Jacksonville and Oakland. Industry experts estimate that more than $7 billion will be spent on new facilities for professional sports teams before 2006.

Most of this $7 billion will come from public sources. The subsidy starts with the federal government, which allows state and local governments to issue tax-exempt bonds to help finance sports facilities. Tax exemption lowers interest on debt and so reduces the amount that cities and teams must pay for a stadium. Since 1975, the interest rate reduction has varied between 2.4 and 4.5 percentage points. Assuming a differential of 3 percentage points, the discounted present value loss in federal taxes for a $225 million stadium is about $70 million, or more than $2 million a year over a useful life of 30 years. Ten facilities built in the 1970s and 1980s, including the Superdome in New Orleans, the Silverdome in Pontiac, the now-obsolete Kingdome in Seattle, and Giants Stadium in the New Jersey Meadowlands, each cause an annual federal tax loss exceeding $1 million.

Source: Roger G. Noll and Andrew Zimbalist, "Sports, Jobs, and Taxes: Are New Stadiums Worth the Cost?" *Brookings Review* 15 (Summer 1997), pp. 35–39. Reprinted by permission.

State and local governments pay even larger subsidies than Washington. Sports facilities now typically cost the host city more than $10 million a year. Perhaps the most successful new baseball stadium, Oriole Park at Camden Yards, costs Maryland residents $14 million a year. Renovations aren't cheap either: The net cost to local government for refurbishing the Oakland Coliseum for the Raiders was about $70 million.

Most large cities are willing to spend big to attract or keep a major league franchise. But a city need not be among the nation's biggest to win a national competition for a team, as shown by the NBA's Utah Jazz's Delta Center in Salt Lake City and the NFL's Houston Oilers' new football stadium in Nashville.

WHY CITIES SUBSIDIZE SPORTS

The economic rationale for cities' willingness to subsidize sports facilities is revealed in the campaign slogan for a new stadium for the San Francisco 49ers: "Build the Stadium—Create the jobs!" Proponents claim that sports facilities improve the local economy in four ways. First, building the facility creates construction jobs. Second, people who attend games or work for the team generate new spending in the community, expanding local employment. Third, a team attracts tourists and companies to the host city, further increasing local spending and jobs. Finally, all this new spending has a "multiplier effect" as increased local income causes still more new spending and job creation. Advocates argue that new stadiums spur so much economic growth that they are self-financing: Subsidies are offset by revenues from ticket taxes, sales taxes on concessions and other spending outside the stadium, and property tax increases arising from the stadium's economic impact.

Unfortunately, these arguments contain bad economic reasoning that leads to overstatement of the benefits of stadiums. Economic growth takes place when a community's resources—people, capital investments, and natural resources like land—become more productive. Increased productivity can arise in two ways: from economically beneficial specialization by the community for the purpose of trading with other regions or from local value added that is higher than other uses of local workers, land, and investments. Building a stadium is good for the local economy only if a stadium is the most productive way to make capital investments and use its workers.

In our 1997 book, *Sports, Jobs, and Taxes,* we and 15 collaborators examine the local economic development argument from all angles: case studies of the effect of specific facilities, as well as comparisons among cities and even neighborhoods that have and have not sunk hundreds of millions of dollars into sports development. In every case, the conclusions at the same. A new sports facility has an extremely small (perhaps even negative) effect on overall economic activity and employment. No recent facility appears to have earned anything approaching a reasonable return on investment. No recent facility has been self-financing in terms of its impact on net tax revenues. Regardless of whether the unit of analysis is a local neighborhood, a city, or an entire metropolitan area, the economic benefits of sports facilities are de minimus.

As noted, a stadium can spur economic growth if sports is a significant export industry—that is, if it attracts outsiders to buy the local product and if it results in the sale of certain rights (broadcasting, product licensing) to national firms. But, in reality, sports has little effect on regional net exports.

Sports facilities attract neither tourists nor new industry. Probably the most successful export facility is Oriole Park, where about a third of the crowd at every game comes from outside the Baltimore area. (Baltimore's baseball exports are enhanced because it is 40 miles from the nation's capital, which has no major league baseball team.) Even so, the net gain to Baltimore's economy in terms of new jobs and incremental tax revenues is only about $3 million a year—not much of a return on a $200 million investment.

Sports teams do collect substantial revenues from national licensing and broadcasting, but these must be balanced against funds leaving the area. Most professional athletes do not live where they play, so their income is not spent locally. Moreover, players make inflated salaries for only a few years, so they have high savings, which they invest in national firms. Finally, though a new stadium increases attendance, ticket revenues are shared in both baseball and football, so that part of the revenue gain goes to other cities. On balance, these factors are largely offsetting, leaving little or no net local export gain to a community.

One promotional study estimated that the local annual economic impact of the Denver Broncos was nearly $120 million; another estimated that the combined annual economic benefit of Cincinnati's Bengals and Reds was $245 million. Such promotional studies overstate the economic impact of a facility because they confuse gross and net economic effects. Most spending inside a stadium is a substitute for other local recreational spending, such as movies and restaurants. Similarly, most tax collections inside a stadium are substitutes: As other entertainment businesses decline, tax collections from them fall.

Promotional studies also fail to take into account differences between sports and other industries in income distribution. Most sports revenue goes to a relatively few players, managers, coaches, and executives who earn extremely high salaries—all well above the earnings of people who work in the industries that are substitutes for sports. Most stadium employees work part time at very low wages and earn a small fraction of team revenues. Thus, substituting spending on sports for other recreational spending concentrates income, reduces the total number of jobs, and replaces full-time jobs with low-wage, part-time jobs.

A second rationale for subsidized stadiums is that stadiums generate more local consumer satisfaction than alternative investments. There is some truth to this argument. Professional sports teams are very small businesses, comparable to large department or grocery stores. They capture public attention far out of proportion to their economic significance. Broadcast and print media give so much attention to sports because so many people are fans, even if they do not actually attend games or buy sports-related products.

A professional sports team, therefore, creates a "public good" or "externality"—a benefit enjoyed by consumers who follow sports regardless of whether they help pay for it. The magnitude of this benefit is unknown, and is not shared by everyone; nevertheless, it exists. As a result, sports fans are likely to accept higher taxes or reduced public services to attract or keep a team, even if they do not attend games themselves. These fans, supplemented and mobilized by teams, local media, and local interests that benefit directly from a stadium, constitute the base of political support for subsidized sports facilities.

THE ROLE OF MONOPOLY LEAGUES

While sports subsidies might flow from externalities, their primary cause is the monopolistic structure of sports. Leagues maximize their members' profits by keeping the number of franchises below the number of cities that could support a team. To attract teams, cities must compete through a bidding war, whereby each bids its willingness to pay to have a team, not the amount necessary to make a team viable.

Monopoly leagues convert fans' (hence cities') willingness to pay for a team into an opportunity for teams to extract revenues. Teams are not required to take advantage of its opportunity, and in two cases—the Charlotte Panthers and, to a lesser extent, the San Francisco Giants—the financial exposure of the city has been the relatively modest costs of site acquisition and infrastructural investments. But in most cases, local and state governments have paid over $100 million in stadium subsidy, and in some cases have financed the entire enterprise.

The tendency of sports teams to seek new homes has been intensified by new stadium technology. The rather ordinary cookie-cutter, multipurpose facility of the 1960s and 1970s has given way to the elaborate, single-sport facility that features numerous new revenue opportunities: luxury suites, club boxes, elaborate concessions, catering, signage, advertising, theme activities, and even bars, restaurants, and apartments with a view of the field. A new facility now can add $30 million annually to a team's revenues for a few years after the stadium opens.

Because new stadiums produce substantially more revenues, more cities are now economically viable franchise sites—which explains why Charlotte, Jacksonville, and Nashville have become NFL cities. As more localities bid for teams, cities are forced to offer ever larger subsidies.

WHAT CAN BE DONE?

Abuses from exorbitant stadium packages, sweetheart leases, and footloose franchises have left many citizens and politicians crying foul. What remedy, if any, is available to curb escalating subsidies and to protect the emotional and financial investments of fans and cities?

In principle, cities could bargain as a group with sports leagues, thereby counterbalancing the leagues' monopoly power. In practice, this strategy is unlikely to work. Efforts by cities to form a sports-host association have failed. The temptation to cheat by secretly negotiating with a mobile team is too strong to preserve concerted behavior.

Another strategy is to insert provisions in a facility lease that deter team relocation. Many cities have tried this approach, but most leases have escape clauses that allow the team to move if attendance falls too low or if the facility is not in state-of-the-art condition. Other teams have provisions requiring them to pay tens of millions of dollars if they vacate a facility prior to lease expiration, but these provisions also come with qualifying covenants. Of course, all clubs legally must carry out the terms of their lease, but with or without these safeguard provisions, teams generally have not viewed their lease terms as binding. Rather, teams claim that breach of contract by the city or stadium authority releases them from their obligations. Almost always these provisions do not prevent a team from moving.

Some leases grant the city a right of first refusal to buy the team or to designate who will buy it before the team is relocated. The big problem here is the price. Owners usually want to move a team because it is worth more elsewhere, either because another city is building a new facility with strong revenue potential or because another city is a better sports market. If the team is worth, say, $30 million more if it moves, what price must the team accept from local buyers? If it is the market price (its value in the best location), an investor in the home city would be foolish to pay $30 million more for the franchise than it is worth there. If the price is the value of the franchise in its present home, the old owner is deprived of his property rights if he cannot sell to the highest bidder. In practice, these provisions typically specify a right of first refusal at market price, which does not protect against losing a team.

Cities trying to hold on to a franchise can also invoke eminent domain, as did Oakland when the Raiders moved to Los Angeles in 1982 and Baltimore when the Colts moved to Indianapolis in 1984. In the Oakland case, the California Court of Appeals ruled that condemning a football franchise violates the commerce clause of the U.S. Constitution. In the Colts case, the condemnation was upheld by the Maryland Circuit Court, but the U.S. District Court ruled that Maryland lacked jurisdiction because the team had left the state by the time the condemnation was declared. Eminent domain, even if constitutionally feasible, is not a promising vehicle for cities to retain sports teams.

ENDING FEDERAL SUBSIDIES

Whatever the costs and benefits to a city of attracting a professional sports team, there is no rationale whatsoever for the federal government to subsidize the financial tug-of-war among the cities to host teams.

In 1986, Congress apparently became convinced of the irrationality of granting tax exemptions for interest on municipal bonds that financed projects primarily benefitting private interests. The 1986 Tax Reform Act denies federal subsidies for sports facilities if more than 10 percent of the debt service is covered by revenues from the stadium. If Congress intended that this would reduce sports subsidies, it was sadly mistaken. If anything, the 1986 law increased local subsidies by cutting rents below 10 percent of debt service.

Last year Senator Daniel Patrick Moynihan (D-NY), concerned about the prospect of a tax exemption for a debt of up to $1 billion for a new stadium in New York, introduced a bill to eliminate tax-exempt financing for professional sports facilities and thus eliminate federal subsidies of stadiums. The theory behind the bill is that raising a city's cost from a stadium giveaway would reduce the subsidy. Although cities might respond this way, they would still compete among each other for scarce franchises, so to some extent the likely effect of the bill is to pass higher interest charges on to cities, not teams.

ANTITRUST AND REGULATION

Congress has considered several proposals to regulate team movement and league expansion. The first came in the early 1970s, when the Washington Senators left for Texas. Unhappy baseball fans on Capital Hill commissioned an inquiry into professional sports. The ensuing report recommended removing baseball's antitrust immunity, but no legislative action followed. Another round of ineffectual inquiry came in 1984–85, following the relocations of the Oakland Raiders and Baltimore Colts. Major league baseball's efforts in 1992 to thwart the San Francisco Giants' move to St. Petersburg again drew proposals to withdraw baseball's cherished antitrust exemption. As before, nothing came of the congressional interest. In 1995–96, inspired by the departure of the Cleveland Browns to Baltimore, Representative Louis Stokes from Cleveland and Senator John Glenn of Ohio introduced a bill to grant the NFL an antitrust exemption for franchise relocation. This bill, too, never came to a vote.

The relevance of antitrust to the problem of stadium subsidies is indirect but important. Private antitrust actions have significantly limited the ability of leagues to prevent teams from relocating. Teams relocate to improve their financial performance, which in turn improves their ability to compete with other teams for players and coaches. Hence, a team has an incentive to prevent competitors from relocating. Consequently, courts have ruled that leagues must have "reasonable" relocation rules that preclude anticompetitive denial of relocation. Baseball, because it enjoys an antitrust exemption, is freer to limit team movements than the other sports.

Relocation rules can affect competition for teams because, by making relocation more difficult, they can limit the number of teams (usually to one) that a city is allowed to bid for. In addition, competition among cities for teams is further intensified because leagues create scarcity in the number of teams. Legal and legislative actions that change relocation rules affect which cities get existing teams and how much they pay for them, but do not directly affect the disparity between the number of cities that are viable locations for a team and the number of teams. Thus, expansion policy raises a different but important antitrust issue.

As witnessed by the nearly simultaneous consideration of creating an antitrust exemption for football but denying one for baseball on precisely the same issue of franchise relocation, congressional initiatives have been plagued by geographical chauvinism and myopia. Except for representatives of the region affected, members of Congress have proven reluctant to risk the ire of sports leagues. Even legislation that is not hampered by blatant regional self-interest, such as the 1986 Tax Reform Act, typically is sufficiently riddled with loopholes to make effective implementation improbable. While arguably net global welfare is higher when a team relocates to a better market, public policy should focus on balancing the supply and demand for sports franchises so that all economically viable cities can have a team. Congress could mandate league expansion, but that is probably impossible politically. Even if such legislation were passed, deciding which city deserves a team is an administrative nightmare.

A better approach would be to use antitrust to break up existing leagues into competing business entities. The entities could collaborate on playing rules and interleague and postseason play, but they would not be able to divvy up metropolitan areas, establish common drafts or player market restrictions, or collude on broadcasting and licensing policy. Under these circumstances no league would be likely to vacate an economically viable city, and, if one did, a competing league would probably jump in. Other consumer-friendly consequences would flow from such an arrangement. Competition would force ineffective owners to sell or go belly up in their struggle with better managed teams. Taxpayers would pay lower local, state, and federal subsidies. Teams would have lower revenues, but because most of the costs of a team are driven by revenues, most teams would remain solvent. Player salaries and team profits would fall, but the number of teams and player jobs would rise.

Like Congress, the Justice Department's Antitrust Division is subject to political pressures not to upset sports. So sports leagues remain unregulated monopolies with de facto immunity from federal antitrust prosecution. Others launch and win antitrust complaints against sports leagues, but usually their aim is membership in the cartel, not divestiture, so the problem of too few teams remains unsolved.

CITIZEN ACTION

The final potential source of reform is grassroots disgruntlement that leads to a political reaction against sports subsidies. Stadium politics has proven to be quite controversial in some cities. Some citizens apparently know that teams do little for the local economy and are concerned about using regressive sales taxes and lottery revenues to subsidize wealthy players, owners, and executives. Voters rejected public support for stadiums on ballot initiatives in Milwaukee, San Francisco, San Jose, and Seattle, although no team has failed to obtain a new stadium. Still, more guarded, conditional support from constituents can cause political leaders to be more careful in negotiating a stadium deal. Initiatives that place more of the financial burden on facility users—via revenues from luxury or club boxes, personal seat licenses (PSLs), naming rights, and ticket taxes—are likely to be more popular.

Unfortunately, citizen resistance notwithstanding, most stadiums probably cannot be financed primarily from private sources. In the first place, the use of money from PSLs, naming rights, pouring rights, and other private sources is a matter to be negotiated among teams, cities, and leagues. The charges imposed by the NFL on the Raiders and Rams when they moved to Oakland and St. Louis, respectively, were an attempt by the league to capture some of this (unshared) revenue, rather than have it pay for the stadium.

Second, revenue from private sources is not likely to be enough to avoid large public subsidies. In the best circumstance, like the NFL's Charlotte Panthers, local governments still pay for investments in supporting infrastructure, and Washington still pays an interest subsidy for the local government share. And the Charlotte case is unique. No other stadium project has raised as much private revenue. At the other extreme is the disaster in Oakland, where a supposedly break-even financial plan left the community $70 million in the hole because of cost overruns and disappointing PSL sales.

Third, despite greater citizen awareness, voters still must cope with a scarcity of teams. Fans may realize that subsidized stadiums regressively redistribute income and do not promote growth, but they want local teams. Alas, it is usually better to pay a monopoly an exorbitant price than to give up its product.

Prospects for cutting sports subsidies are not good. While citizen opposition has had some success, without more effective intercity organizing or more active federal antitrust policy, cities will continue to compete against each other to attract or keep artificially scarce sports franchises. Given the profound penetration and popularity of sports in American culture, it is hard to see an end to rising public subsidies of sports facilities.

26

Upward Mobility Through Sport?

The Myths and Realities

D. Stanley Eitzen

Typically, Americans believe that sport is a path to upward social mobility. This belief is based on the obvious examples we see as poor boys and men (rarely girls and women) from rural and urban areas, whether white or black, sometimes skyrocket to fame and fortune through success in sports. Sometimes the financial reward has been astounding, such as the high pay that some African American athletes received in recent years. In 1997 Tracy McGrady, an NBA-bound high school star, bypassed college, signed a $12 million deal over 6 years with Adidas. Golfer Tiger Woods in his first year as a professional made $6.82 million in winnings (U.S. and worldwide) and appearance fees plus signed a series of five-year deals with Nike, Titleist, American Express, and Rolex worth $95.2 million. In 1998 Woods's earnings from endorsements totaled $28 million. Boxer Mike Tyson made $75 million in 1996. It is estimated that Michael Jordan made over $100 million in 1998, including salary, endorsements, and income from merchandise and videos. The recent deals for baseball stars, some exceeding $15 million a year for multiyear contracts, further underscore the incredible money given to some individuals for their athletic talents.

But while the possibility of staggering wealth and status through sport exists, the reality is that dramatic upward mobility through sport is highly improbable. A number of myths, however, combine to lead us to believe that sport is a social mobility escalator.

Source: D. Stanley Eitzen, "Upward Mobility Through Sport? The Myths and Realities," *Z Magazine* 12 (March 1999), pp. 14–19. Reprinted by permission.

MYTH: SPORT PROVIDES A FREE EDUCATION

Good high school athletes get college scholarships. These athletic scholarships are especially helpful to poor youth who otherwise would not be able to attend college because of the high costs. The problem with this assumption is that while true for some, very few high school athletes actually receive full scholarships. Football provides the easiest route to a college scholarship because Division I-A colleges have 85 football scholarships, but even this avenue is exceedingly narrow. In Colorado there were 3,481 male high school seniors who played football during the 1994 season. Of these, 31 received full scholarships at Division I-A schools (0.0089 percent).

Second, of all the male varsity athletes at all college levels only about 15 percent to 20 percent have full scholarships. Another 15 percent to 25 percent have partial scholarships, leaving 55 percent to 70 percent of all intercollegiate athletes without any sport-related financial assistance. Third, as low as the chances are for men, women athletes have even less chance to receive an athletic scholarship. While women comprise about 52 percent of all college students, they make up only 35 percent of intercollegiate athletes with a similar disproportionate distribution of scholarships. Another reality is that if you are a male athlete in a so-called minor sport (swimming, tennis, golf, gymnastics, cross-country, wrestling), the chances of a full scholarship are virtually nil. The best hope is a partial scholarship, if that, since these sports are underfunded and in danger of elimination at many schools.

MYTH: SPORT LEADS TO A COLLEGE DEGREE

College graduates exceed high school graduates by hundreds of thousands of dollars in lifetime earnings. Since most high school and college athletes will never play at the professional level, the attainment of a college degree is a crucial determinant of upward mobility through sport. The problem is that relatively few male athletes in the big-time revenue-producing sports, compared to their nonathletic peers, actually receive college degrees. This is especially the case for African American men who are overrepresented in the revenue-producing sports. In 1996, for example, looking at the athletes who entered Division I schools in 1990, only 45 percent of African American football players and 39 percent of African American basketball players had graduated (compared to 56 percent of the general student body).

There are a number of barriers to graduation for male athletes. The demands on their time and energy are enormous even in the off-season. Many athletes, because of these pressures, take easy courses to maintain eligibility but do not lead to graduation. The result is either to delay graduation or to make graduation an unrealistic goal.

Another barrier is that they are recruited for athletic prowess rather than academic ability. Recent data show that football players in big-time programs are, on average, more than 200 points behind their nonathletic classmates on SAT test scores. Poorly prepared students are the most likely to take easy courses, cheat on exams, hire surrogate test takers, and otherwise do the minimum.

A third barrier to graduation for male college athletes is themselves, as they may not take advantage of their scholarships to obtain a quality education. This is especially the case for those who perceive their college experience only as preparation for their professional careers in sport. Study for them is necessary only to maintain their eligibility. The goal of a professional career is unrealistic for all but the super-stars. The superstars who do make it at the professional level, more likely than not, will not have graduated from college; nor will they go back to finish their degrees when their professional careers are over. This is also because even a successful professional athletic career is limited to a few years, and not many professional athletes are able to translate their success in the pros to success in their post-athletic careers. Such a problem is especially true for African Americans, who often face employment discrimination in the wider society.

MYTH: A SPORTS CAREER IS PROBABLE

A recent survey by the Center for the Study of Sport on Society found that two-thirds of African American males between the ages of 13 and 18 believe that they can earn a living playing professional sports (more than double the proportion of young white males who hold such beliefs). Moreover, African American parents were four times more likely than white parents to believe that their sons are destined for careers as professional athletes.

If these young athletes could play as professionals, the economic rewards are excellent, especially in basketball and baseball. In 1998 the average annual salary for professional basketball was $2.24 million. In baseball the average salary was $1.37 million with 280 of the 774 players on opening day rosters making $1 million or more (of them, 197 exceeded $2 million or more, while 32 of them made $6 million or more). The average salaries for the National Hockey League and National Football League were $892,000 and $795,000, respectively. In football, for example, 19 percent of the players (333 of 1,765) exceeded $1 million in salary. These numbers are inflated by the use of averages, which are skewed by the salaries of the superstars. Use of the median (in which half the players make more and half make less) reveals that the median salary in basketball was $1.4 million; baseball—$500,000; football—$400,000; and hockey—$500,000. Regardless of the measure, the financial allure of a professional sports career is great.

A career in professional sports is nearly impossible to attain because of the fierce competition for so few openings. In an average year there are approximately 1,900,000 American boys playing high school football, basketball, and baseball. Another 68,000 men are playing those sports in college, and 2,490 are participating at the major professional level. In short, one in 27 high school players in these sports will play at the college level, and only one in 736 high school players will play at the major professional level (0.14 percent). In baseball, each year about 120,000 players are eligible for the draft (high school seniors, college seniors, collegians over 21, junior college players, and foreign players). Only about 1,200 (1 percent) are actually drafted, and most of them will never make it to the major leagues. Indeed, only one in ten of those players who sign a professional baseball contract ever plays in the major leagues for at least one day.

The same rigorous condensation process occurs in football. About 15,000 players are eligible for the NFL draft each year. Three hundred thirty-six are drafted and about 160 actually make the final roster. Similarly, in basketball and hockey, only about 40 new players are added to the rosters in the NBA and 60 rookies make the NHL each year. In tennis only about 100 men and 100 women make enough money to cover expenses. In golf, of the 165 men eligible for the PGA tour in 1997, their official winnings ranged from $2,066,833 (Tiger Woods) to $10,653 (Chip Beck). The competition among these golfers is fierce. On average, the top 100 golfers on the tour play within 2 strokes of each other for every 18 holes, yet Tiger Woods, the tops in winnings won over $2 million, and the 100th finisher won only $250,000. Below the PGA tour is the Nike Tour where the next best 125 golfers compete. Their winnings were a top of $225,201 to a low of $9,944.

MYTH: SPORT IS A WAY OUT OF POVERTY

Sport appears to be a major way for African Americans to escape the ghetto. African Americans dominate the major professional sports numerically. While only 12 percent of the population, African Americans comprise about 80 percent of the players in professional basketball, about 67 percent of professional football players, and 18 percent of professional baseball players (Latinos also comprise about 17 percent of professional baseball players). Moreover, African Americans dominate the list of the highest moneymakers in sport (salaries, commercial sponsorships). These facts, while true, are illusory.

While African Americans dominate professional basketball, football, and to a lesser extent baseball, they are rarely found in certain sports such as hockey, automobile racing, tennis, golf, bowling, and skiing. Moreover, African Americans are severely underrepresented in positions of authority in sport—as head coaches, referees, athletic directors, scouts, general managers, and owners. In the NFL in 1997, for example, where more than two-thirds of the players were African American, only three head coaches and five offensive or defensive coordinators were African American. In that year there were 11 head coaching vacancies filled, none by African Americans. The reason for this racial imbalance in hiring, according to white sports columnist for the *Rocky Mountain News* Bob Kravitz is that "something here stinks, and it stinks a lot like racism."

Second, while the odds of African American males making it as professional athletes are more favorable than is the case for whites (about 1 in 3,500 African American male high school athletes, compared to 1 in 10,000 white male high school athletes), these odds remain slim. Of the 40,000 or so African American boys who play high school basketball, only 35 will make the NBA and only 7 will be starters. Referring to the low odds for young African Americans, Harry Edwards, an African American sociologist specializing in the sociology of sport, said with a bit of hyperbole: "Statistically, you have a better chance of getting hit by a meteorite in the next ten years than getting work as an athlete."

Despite these discouraging facts, the myth is alive for poor youth. As noted earlier, two-thirds of African American boys believe they can be professional athletes. Their parents, too, accept this belief (African American parents are four times more likely than white parents to believe that their children will be professional athletes). The film *Hoop Dreams* and Darcey Frey's book *The Last Shot: City Street, Basketball Dreams* document the emphasis that young African American men place on sports as a way up and their ultimate disappointments from sport. For many of them, sport represents their only hope of escape from a life of crime, poverty, and despair. They latch on to the dream of athletic success partly because of the few opportunities for middle-class success. They spend many hours per day developing their speed, strength, jumping height, or "moves" to the virtual exclusion of those abilities that have a greater likelihood of paying off in upward mobility such as reading comprehension, mathematical reasoning, communication skills, and computer literacy.

Sociologist Jay Coakley puts it this way:

> My best guess is that less than 3,500 African Americans . . . are making their livings as professional athletes. At the same time (in 1996), there are about 30,015 black physicians and about 30,800 black lawyers currently employed in the U.S. Therefore, there are 20 times more blacks working in these two professions than playing top level professional sports. And physicians and lawyers usually have lifetime earnings far in excess of the earnings of professional athletes, whose playing careers, on average, last less than five years.

Harry Edwards posits that by spending their energies and talents on athletic skills, young African Americans are not pursuing occupations that would help them meet their political and material needs. Thus, because of belief in the "sports as a way up" myth, they remain dependent on whites and white institutions. Salim Muwakkil, an African American political analyst, argues that

> If African Americans are to exploit the socio-economic options opened by varied civil rights struggles more fully, blacks must reduce the disproportionate allure of sports in their communities. Black leadership must contextualize athletic success by promoting other avenues to social status, intensifying the struggle for access to those avenues and better educating youth about those potholes on the road to the stadium.

John Hoberman in his book *Darwin's Athletes* also challenges the assumption that sport has progressive consequences. The success of African Americans in the highly visible sports gives white America a false sense of black progress and interracial harmony. But the social progress of African Americans in general has little relationship to the apparent integration that they have achieved on the playing fields.

Hoberman also contends that the numerical superiority of African Americans in sport, coupled with their disproportionate underrepresentation in other professions, reinforces the racist ideology that African Americans, while physically superior to whites are inferior to them intellectually.

I do not mean to say that African Americans should not seek a career in professional sport. What is harmful is that the odds of success are so slim, making the extraordinary efforts over many years futile and misguided for the vast majority.

MYTH: WOMEN HAVE SPORT AS A VEHICLE FOR UPWARD MOBILITY

Since the passage of Title IX in 1972 that required schools receiving federal funds to provide equal opportunities for women and men, sports participation by women in high school and college has increased dramatically. In 1973, for example, when 50,000 men received some form of college scholarship for their athletic abilities, women received only 50. Now, women receive about 35 percent of the money allotted for college athletic scholarships (while a dramatic improvement, this should not be equated with gender equality as many would have us believe). This allows many women athletes to attend college who otherwise could not afford it, thus receiving an indirect upward mobility boost.

Upward mobility as a result of being a professional athlete is another matter for women. Women have fewer opportunities than men in professional team sports. Beach volleyball is a possibility for a few but the rewards are minimal. Two professional women's basketball leagues began in 1997, but the pay was very low compared to men and the leagues were on shaky financial ground (the average salary in the American Basketball League was $80,000). The other option for women is to play in professional leagues in Europe, Australia, and Asia but the pay is relatively low.

Women have more opportunities as professionals in individual sports such as tennis, golf, ice-skating, skiing, bowling, cycling, and track. Ironically, the sports with the greatest monetary rewards for women are those of the middle and upper classes (tennis, golf, and ice skating). These sports are expensive and require considerable individual coaching and access to private facilities.

Ironically, with the passage of Title IX, which increased the participation rates of women so dramatically, there has been a decline in the number and proportion of women as coaches and athletic administrators. In addition to the glaring pay gap between what the coaches of men's teams receive compared to the coaches of women's teams, men who coach women's teams tend to have higher salaries than women coaching women's teams. Women also have fewer opportunities than men as athletic trainers, officials, sports journalists, and other adjunct positions.

MYTH: SPORTS PROVIDES LIFELONG SECURITY

Even when a professional sport career is attained, the probabilities of fame and fortune are limited. Of course, some athletes make incomes from salaries and endorsements that if invested wisely, provide financial security for life. Many professional athletes make relatively low salaries. During the 1996 season, for example, 17 percent of major league baseball players made the minimum salary of $247,500 for veterans and $220,000 for rookies. This is a lot of money, but for these marginal players their careers may not last very long. Indeed, the average length of a professional career in a team sport is about five years. A marginal athlete in individual sports such as golf, tennis, boxing, and bowling struggles financially. They must cover their travel expenses, health insurance, equipment, and the like with no guaranteed paycheck. The brief career diverts them during their youth from developing other career skills and experiences that would benefit them.

Ex-professional athletes leave sport, on average, when they are in their late 20s or early 30s, at a time when their nonathletic peers have begun to establish themselves in occupations leading toward retirement in 40 years or so. What are the ex-professional athletes to do with their remaining productive years?

Exiting a sports career can be relatively smooth or difficult. Some athletes have planned ahead, preparing for other careers either in sport (coaching, scouting, administering) or some non-sport occupation. Others have not prepared for this abrupt change. They did not graduate from college. They did not spend the off-seasons apprenticing non-sport jobs. Exiting the athlete role is difficult for many because they lose: (1) what has been the focus of their being for most of their lives; (2) the primary source of their identities; (3) their physical prowess; (4) the adulation bordering on worship from others; (5) the money and the perquisites of fame; (6) the camaraderie with teammates; (7) the intense "highs" of competition; and (8) for most ex-athletes retirement means a loss of status. As a result of these "losses," many ex-professional athletes have trouble adjusting to life after sport. A study by the NFL Players Association found that emotional difficulties, divorce, and financial strain were common problems for ex-professional football players. A majority had "permanent injuries" from football.

The allure of sport, however, remains strong and this has at least two negative consequences. First, ghetto youngsters who devote their lives to the pursuit of athletic stardom are, except for the fortunate few, doomed to failure in sport and in the real world where sports skills are essentially irrelevant to occupational placement and advancement. The second negative consequence is more subtle but very important. Sport contributes to the ideology that legitimizes social inequalities and promotes the myth that all it takes is extraordinary effort to succeed. Sport sociologist George H. Sage makes this point forcefully:

> Because sport is by nature meritocratic—that is, superior performance brings status and rewards—it provides convincing symbolic support for hegemonic [the dominant] ideology—that ambitious, dedicated, hard working individuals, regardless of social origin, can achieve success and ascend in the social hierarchy, obtaining high status and material rewards, while those who don't move upward simply didn't work hard enough. Because the rags-to-riches athletes are so visible, the social mobility theme is maintained. This reflects the opportunity structure of society in general—the success of a few reproduces the belief in social mobility among the many.

* FOR FURTHER STUDY *

Armstrong, Jim. 1999. "Money Makes the Sports Go 'Round," *The Denver Post* (July 25): 1C, 12C.

Atkinson, Michael. 2002. "Fifty Million Viewers Can't Be Wrong: Professional Wrestling, Sports-Entertainment, and Mimesis," *Sociology of Sport Journal* 19 (1):1–24.

Barney, Robert K., Stephen R. Wenn, and Scott G. Marlyn. 2002. *Selling the Five Rings: The International Olympic Committee and the Rise of Olympic Commercialism* (Salt Lake City: University of Utah Press).

Brown, Clyde, and David M. Paul. 2002. "The Political Scorecard of Professional Sports Facility Referendums in the United States, 1984–2000,"*Journal of Sport & Social Issues* 26 (August): 248–267.

Cagan, Joanna, and Neil deMause. 1996. "The Great Stadium Swindle," *In These Times* (August 19):14–17.

Cagan, Joanna, and Neil deMause. 1996. "Buy the Bums Out," *In These Times* (December 9):15–17.

Cagan, Joanna, and Neil deMause. 1998. *Field of Schemes: How the Great Stadium Swindle Turns Public Money into Private Profit* (Monroe, ME: Common Courage Press).

Colatosti, Camille. 1996. "Sports Stadium Ripoffs: Building Neighborhoods or Building Profits," *Dollars and Sense,* No. 206 (July/August):17–21.

Drahota, JoAnne Tremaine, and D. Stanley Eitzen. 1998. "The Role Exit of Professional Athletes," *Sociology of Sport Journal* 15 (3):263–278.

Eckstein, Rick, and Kevin Delaney. 2002. "New Sports Stadiums, Community Self-Esteem, and Community Collective Conscience," *Journal of Sport & Social Issues* 26 (August):235–247.

Eitzen, D. Stanley. 1996. "Classism in Sport: The Powerless Bear the Burden," *Journal of Sport and Social Issues* 20 (February):95–105.

Harvey, Jean, Alan Law, and Michael Cantelon. 2001. "North American Professional Sport Franchises Ownership Patterns and Global Entertainment Conglomerates," *Sociology of Sport Journal* 18(4):435–457.

Hudson, Ian. 2001. "The Use and Misuse of Economic Impact Analysis: The Case of Professional Sports," *Journal of Sport and Social Issues* 25 (February):20–39.

Leonard, Wilbert M., H. 1996. "The Odds of Transiting from One Level of Sports Participation to Another," *Sociology of Sport Journal* 13(3):288–299.

Lewis, Michael. 2001. "Franchise Relocation and Fan Allegiance," *Journal of Sport and Social Issues* 25 (February):6–19.

Rosentraub, Mark S. 1997. *Major League Losers: The Real Cost of Sports and Who's Paying for It* (New York: Basic Books).

_____. 1998. "Why Baseball Needs New York to Just Say No," *The Nation* (August 10/17):20–26.

Sheehan, Richard G. 1996. *Keeping Score: The Economics of Big-Time Sports* (South Bend, IN: Diamond Communications).

Simons, John. 1997. "Improbable Dreams," *U.S. News and World Report* (March 24):46–59.

Simpson, Vyv, and Andrew Jennings. 1992. *Dishonored Games: Corruption, Money, and Greed at the Olympics* (New York: S. P. I. Books).

Zimmer, Martha Hill, and Michael Zimmer, 2001. "Athletes as Entertainers: A Comparative Study of Earnings Profiles," *Journal of Sport and Social Issues* 25 (May):202–215.

PART NINE

Structured Inequality: Sport and Race/Ethnicity

By definition, a minority group is one that (1) is relatively powerless compared with the majority group, (2) possesses traits that make it different from others, (3) is systematically condemned by negative stereotyped beliefs, and (4) is singled out for differential and unfair treatment (that is, discrimination). Race (a socially defined category on the basis of a presumed genetic heritage resulting in distinguishing social characteristics) and ethnicity (the condition of being culturally distinct on the basis of race, religion, or national origin) are two traditional bases for minority group status and the resulting social inequality. Sociologists of sport are interested in the question: Is sport an area of social life where performance counts and race or ethnicity is irrelevant? The three selections in this section examine four racial or ethnic minorities—Native Americans, Asian Americans, Latinos, and African Americans—to answer this question.

The first selection, by journalist Kevin Simpson, seeks an answer to the dilemma posed by the typical behaviors of excellent Native American athletes from reservations: Why do so many who are given scholarships either refuse them or return quickly to the reservation? These responses do not make sense to Anglos because the reservation has high unemployment, a life of dependency, and disproportionate alcohol abuse. Simpson points to these young men being "pulled" by the familiar, by the strong bonds of family, and by their unique culture. They are also "pushed" back to the reservation by social isolation, discrimination, poor high school preparation for college, and little hope for a return on their investment in a college education.

The second selection, by physical educator George H. Sage, provides an overview of racial inequality and sport, focusing on African Americans. The final selection, by journalist Mike Klis, explores the reasons for the declining proportion of African American professional baseball players.

27

Sporting Dreams Die on the "Rez"

Kevin Simpson

Last season, basketball fans followed Willie White everywhere through the unforgiving South Dakota winter. Mesmerized by smooth moves, and spectacular dunks, they watched the most celebrated product of the state's hoop-crazy Indian tribes secure his status as local legend by leading his high school to an undefeated season and state championship.

They would mob him after games in an almost frightening scene of mass adulation, press scraps of paper toward him, and beg for an autograph preferably scribbled beneath some short personal message. White would oblige by scrawling short, illegible phrases before signing. He made certain they were illegible for fear someone would discover that the best prep basketball player in South Dakota could barely read or write.

As the resident basketball hero on the impoverished Pine Ridge Reservation, where there was precious little to cheer about before the state title rekindled embers of Indian pride, White was allowed to slip undisturbed through the reservation school system, until, by his senior year, he could read at only the sixth-grade level. Ironically, the same hero status moved him to admit his problem and seek help. The constant humiliation at the hands of autograph-seekers proved more than he could take.

"I had to face up to it," says White, a soft-spoken 6-foot-4 Sioux who looks almost scholarly behind his wire-rimmed glasses. "I couldn't go on forever like that.

Source: Kevin Simpson, "Sporting Dreams Die on the 'Rez,'" *The Denver Post,* September 6, 1987, pp. 1C, 19C. Copyright 1987 *The Denver Post.* Reprinted by permission.

In school I didn't study. I cheated on every test they gave me. I couldn't read good enough to answer the questions."

After some intense individual help with his reading and writing, this fall White enrolled at Huron (South Dakota) College, where he intends to continue his basketball career and take remedial reading courses. If he manages to play four years and complete his degree, he'll be the first schoolboy athlete from Pine Ridge to do so.

Other than his close friends, nobody thinks he stands a chance. Indians usually don't.

Every year, all over the western United States, promising native American athletes excel in high school sports only to abandon dreams of college, return to economically depressed reservations, and survive on their per capita checks, welfare-like payments from the tribal government, or the goodwill of more fortunate relatives. They waste away quietly, victims of alcohol, victims of inadequate education, victims of boredom, victims of poverty, but nearly always victims of their own ambivalence, caught between a burning desire to leave the reservation and an irresistible instinct to stay.

"We've had two or three kids get scholarships in the eight years I've been here," says Roland Bradford, athletic director and basketball coach at Red Cloud High School, just a few miles down the highway from Pine Ridge. "None have lasted. It's kind of a fantasy thing. In high school they talk about going to college, but it's not a reality. They have no goals set. They start out, things get tough and they come home."

At 6-foot-7 and 280 pounds, Red Cloud's Dave Brings Plenty inspired enough comparisons to the Refrigerator to lure a photographer from *People* magazine out to the reservation. He went to Dakota Wesleyan to pursue his football career, but returned home after suffering a mild concussion in practice. He never played a game. Brings Plenty says he might enroll at a different school sometime in the future, but his plans are vague. For now, he's content to hang out on the reservation and work as a security guard at a bingo parlor.

Some of the athlete-dropouts have squandered mind-boggling potential. Jeff Turning Heart, a long-distance legend on South Dakota's Cheyenne River Reservation, enrolled at Black Hills State College in Spearfish, South Dakota, on a Bureau of Indian Affairs grant in 1980 amid great expectations. He left eight days later.

In 1982, he wound up at Adams State College in Alamosa, Colorado. Longtime Adams State coach Joe Vigil, the U.S. men's distance coach for the 1988 Olympics, says that as a freshman Turning Heart was far more physically gifted than even Pat Porter, the Adams State graduate who now ranks as the premier U.S. runner at 10,000 meters. Both Porter and Vigil figured Turning Heart was on a course to win the national cross-country title—until he left school, supposedly to tend to his gravely ill father in North Dakota. He promised to return in a few days. The story was bogus and Turning Heart never went back.

At Black Hills State, where in 19 years as athletic director and track coach, David Little has seen only one Indian track athlete graduate, Turning Heart wasn't the first world-class, Native American runner to jilt him. Myron Young Dog, a distance man from Pine Ridge who once won 22 straight cross-country races in high school, came to Black Hills after dropping out of Ellendale (North Dakota) Junior College in 1969. Although he was academically ineligible for varsity sports and hadn't trained, Young Dog stepped onto the track during a physical conditioning class and ran two miles in 9:30 "like it was a Sunday jog," according to Little. Three weeks later he entered a 15-km road race and ran away from all the collegiate competition.

It was a tantalizing glimpse of talent ultimately wasted. Little still rates Young Dog as one of the top 10 athletes ever to come out of South Dakota, but in the spring of 1970 he returned to the reservation, never to run competitively again.

It doesn't take many heartbreaks before the college coaches catch on to the risky business of recruiting off the reservations. Although Indian athletes often are immensely talented and given financial backing from the tribe and the BIA—a budgetary boon to small schools short on scholarship funds—they suffer from a widespread reputation as high-risk recruits who probably won't stick around for more than a few weeks.

That's part of the reason so many schools backed off Willie White—that and his reading deficiency. Huron College coach Fred Paulsen, who made White his first in-state recruit in four years, thought the youngster's potential made him worth the risk.

"I hate to stereotype," says Paulsen, "but is he the typical Indian? If Willie comes and doesn't make it, nobody will be surprised. My concern is that he'll go home for the weekend and say he'll be back on Monday. Which Monday?"

Talented Indians are diverted from their academic and athletic career courses for many reasons, but often they are sucked back to subsistence-level life on the reservation by the vacuum created by inadequate education and readily available escapes like drugs and alcohol.

Ted Little Moon, an all-state basketball player for Pine Ridge High School in 1984 and '85, still dominates the asphalt slab outside the school. At 6-foot-6, he roams from baseline to baseline jamming in rebounds, swatting away opponents' shots, and threading blind passes to teammates beneath the basket. He is unmistakable small-college talent.

But Little Moon missed his first opportunity to play ball in college when he failed to graduate from high school. By the following August, though, he had passed his high school equivalency exam and committed to attend Huron College. But when the basketball coach showed up at his house to pick him up and drive him to school, Little Moon said he couldn't go because he had gotten his girlfriend pregnant and had to take care of a newborn son.

He played independent basketball, a large-scale Indian intramural network, until last fall, when he planned to enroll at Haskell Junior College, an all-Indian school in Lawrence, Kansas. He and some friends drank heavily the night before he was to take the bus to Kansas. Little Moon was a passenger in a friend's car when they ran a stop sign and hit another vehicle. He spent four days in jail, missed his bus, and missed out on enrolling at Haskell.

Now he talks of going back to school, of playing basketball again, but there's ambivalence in his voice. He has become accustomed to cashing his biweekly per capita check for $28.50, drinking beer, and growing his own marijuana at a secret location on the reservation. He distributes it free to his friends.

"I guess I'm scared to get away," Little Moon admits. "But also I'm afraid I'll be stuck here and be another statistic. You grow old fast here. If I get away, I have a chance. But I'm used to what I'm doing now. Here, your mom takes care of you, the BIA takes care of you. You wait for your $28.50 and then party. It's something to look forward to.

"I started drinking as a freshman in high school, smoking dope as a sopho-more. I used to get high before practice, after practice. I still do it, on the average, maybe every other day. After I play, I smoke some. It makes you forget what you're doing on the reservation."

At home, alcohol offers whatever false comfort family ties cannot. Then it kills. Two years ago, Red Cloud's Bradford tallied all the alcohol-related deaths he had known personally and came up with some sobering statistics. In 13 years of teaching, 18 of his former students have died in alcohol-related tragedies. Aside from students, he has known an incredible 61 people under the age of 22 who have lost their lives in one way or another to the bottle.

Many died along a two-mile stretch of Highway 407 that connects Pine Ridge with Whiteclay, Nebraska, a depressing cluster of bars and liquor stores that do a land-office business. Three years ago, South Dakota's highway department began erecting metal markers at the site of each alcohol-related fatality. Locals say that if they'd started 10 years ago, the signs would form an unbroken chain along the road. They'd have run out of signs before they ran out of death.

Among Indians nationwide, four of the top 10 causes of death are alcohol-related: accidents, suicides, cirrhosis of the liver, and homicide. Alcohol mortality is nearly five times higher among Indians, at 30 per 100,000 population, than for all other races. According to Dr. Eva Smith of the Indian Health Service in Washington, D.C., between 80 and 90 percent of all Indian accidents, suicides, and homicides are alcohol-related.

Fred Beauvais, a research scientist at Colorado State University, points out that Indians not only start using drugs and alcohol earlier than the general population, but the rate of use also tends to be higher. According to a 1987 study of 2,400 subjects in eight western tribes Beauvais conducted with funding from the National Institute on Drug Abuse, 50 percent of Indian high school seniors were classified as "at risk" of serious harm because of drug and alcohol use. An amazing 43 percent are at risk by the seventh grade. The figure for seniors probably is too low, Beauvais explains, because by 12th grade many Indian students already have dropped out.

He attributes these phenomena not to racial or cultural idiosyncrasies, but to socioeconomic conditions on the reservations.

"Once it becomes socially ingrained, it's a vicious cycle," Beauvais says. "The kids see the adults doing it and they see no alternatives. It's a real trap. For some Indian kids to choose not to drink means to deny their Indianness. That can be a powerful factor."

Even those athletes who excel in the classroom are not necessarily immune to the magnetic pull of alcohol. Beau LeBeau, a 4.0 student at Red Cloud High who has started for the varsity basketball team since he was in eighth grade, recognizes the dangers but speaks of them as if they are elements quite out of his control. He estimates that 90 percent of his friends abuse alcohol.

"I'm going to the best academic school on the reservation," he says. "I should get a good education if I don't turn to drugs and alcohol in the next few years and ruin it for myself. In my room before I go to sleep I think, 'Is this how I'm going to spend the rest of my life? On the reservation?' I hope not."

For all the roadside signs that stand as chilling monuments to death around Pine Ridge, the drinking continues, a false and addictive cure for boredom and futility.

"If they win they want to celebrate," offers Bryan Brewer, athletic director at Pine Ridge High School. "If they lose, that's another excuse to drink. People who didn't make it want to drag the good athletes down with them."

Consequently, the road to a college athletic career sometimes ends before it even begins.

"I'm not opposed to recruiting the Indian athlete," offers Black Hills State athletic director Little. "I'm selective about who I recruit, though. I don't have the answer to the problem and don't know [if] I totally understand the situation. I do know that what's going on now is not working."

Something definitely isn't working in Towoac (pronounced TOI-ahk), in southwestern Colorado, where Indian athletes don't even wait until after high school to see their careers disintegrate. There, on the Ute Mountain Reservation, a multitude of Indian athletes compete and excel up to eighth grade and then quit rather than pursue sports at Montezuma-Cortez High, a mixed-race school 17 miles north of the reservation in the town of Cortez.

They drop out at the varsity level sometimes for academic reasons but often because of racial tension—or what they feel is bias on the part of white coaches. Pressed for particulars, current and former athletes make only vague accusations of negative attitudes and rarely cite specific instances. But how much of the discrimination is real and how much imagined is academic. The perception of discrimination remains, passed down among the athletes almost as an oral tradition.

For instance, today's athletes hear stories like those told by former Cortez High athlete Hanley Frost, who in the mid-1970s felt the wrath of the school administration when he was a sophomore on the basketball team and insisted on wearing his hair long, braided in traditional Indian style. He played four games with it tucked into his jersey but then was told school policy demanded that he cut it off. Eventually, he quit the team and began experimenting with drugs and alcohol.

Frost stated, "Really, it was the townspeople who didn't enjoy having a long-haired Indian on the team. There were a lot of people out there who would rather see their kids in a position on the team an Indian kid has."

"There's something about Towoac that just doesn't sit right." Adds reservation athletic director Doug Call, a Mormon who came to the Ute Mountain Reservation from Brigham Young University. "I don't know if people are afraid or what, but there's a stigma if you live out here."

Those Indians who do participate in sports at the high school level tend to live in Cortez, not on the reservation. An invisible wall of distrust seems to surround Towoac, where most of the young athletes play what is known on reservations as "independent ball," a loosely organized kind of intramural basketball.

"They feel they're not getting a fair chance, I know they do," says Gary Gellatly, the Cortez High School athletic director who once served as recreation director on the reservation. "And I'm sure they have been discriminated against, directly or indirectly. It's tough to get them to compete. Yet you go out there on any weekend and watch those independent tournaments—you'll see kids playing basketball that you've never seen before. But I'm afraid if we start an overt effort to get them to participate you crowd them into a tighter corner. In a sense, not participating because they think they might be discriminated against is a cop-out, but it's been perpetuated by circumstances. Somewhere, something happened that wasn't good."

After massive turnover in the school's coaching staff, some new hires have expressed a desire to see more Indians become involved in the school's sports programs. Bill Moore, the new head football coach, heard the rumors that Indian kids wouldn't even try out for the squad and mailed tryout invitations to much of the student body including as many Indian boys as he could find addresses for. Even so, the turnout hasn't been markedly different from previous years.

"The solution," says varsity basketball coach Gordon Shepherd, "is that something has to give. Cultural groups that remain within themselves don't succeed. For Indians to succeed in white society terms, they have to give up some cultural ethnicity."

Ethnic idiosyncrasies present a whole range of problems—from students' inclination or ability to perform in the classroom to conflicts such as the one currently under way at Jemez Pueblo, a small reservation north of Albuquerque, New Mexico. There, in a hotbed of mountain running, a cross-country coach at a mixed-race school has struggled with athletes who reject modern training techniques for the less formal but highly traditional ways of their ancestors.

On some reservations, Indian student-athletes are merely ill-prepared to cope with the stringent academic demands of college. According to BIA statistics, the average Indian high school senior reads at the ninth-grade level. Of the 20 percent of high school seniors who go on to attempt college, 40 percent drop out.

And with some reservations approaching economic welfare states, students considering college confront a serious question about the value of an education: Why spend four years pursuing a college degree only to return to a reservation that has few or no private sector jobs?

Indians often find themselves without any real ethnic support system in college and become homesick for reservation life and the exceptionally strong bonds of an extended family in which aunts, uncles, and grandparents often live under the same roof. In some tribal cultures, 18- or 19-year olds still are considered mere children and haven't been pressed to formulate long-term goals. It's no coincidence, says an education administrator for the Arapahoe tribe on central Wyoming's Wind River

Reservation, that most successful Indian students are in their mid- to late 20s—when, incidentally, athletic eligibility has gone by the board.

Even the basic incentive of athletics tends to evaporate in a more intense competitive climate far removed from the reservation.

Myron "The Magician" Chavez, a four-time all-state guard from Wyoming Indian High School on the Wind River Reservation, enrolled at Sheridan (Wyoming) College last fall but left school during preseason workouts when he was asked to redshirt. He felt he had failed because he didn't step immediately into a starting position. Jeff Brown, who preceded Chavez at WIHS, had a scholarship offer from the University of Kansas in 1982 but turned it down because he feared he would fail—academically if not athletically.

Dave Archambault, a Sioux who started the athletic program at United Tribes Junior College in Bismarck, North Dakota, has found the fear of failure to be a familiar theme among talented Indian athletes. On the reservations, he points out, athletes become heroes, modern extensions of the old warrior society that disappeared after defeat at the hands of the white man.

"They're kicking butt on the reservation," Archambault explains, "and then all of the sudden they're working out with juniors and seniors in college and getting their butts kicked. They're not held in that high regard and esteem. But they can go back to the reservation any time and get it."

They recapture their high school glory through independent ball, the intramural network among reservations that quenches an insatiable thirst for basketball competition among all age groups. There are tournaments nearly every weekend and an all-Indian national tournament each spring, where the best teams often recruit talent from a wide area by offering modest incentives like cash and expenses. At most levels, though, independent ball resembles extremely organized pickup basketball.

For most Indian athletes, it represents the outer limits of achievement, caught though it is in a void between the reservation and the outside world. It's in that limbo—socially as well as athletically—that most Indians play out their careers.

"There's no way to return to the old way, spiritually and economically," observes Billy Mills, the 1964 Olympic gold medalist at 10,000 meters who grew up on the Pine Ridge Reservation. "It's like walking death—no goals, no commitment, no accomplishment. If you go too far into society, there's a fear of losing your Indianness. There's a spiritual factor that comes into play. To become part of white society you give up half your soul. Society wants us to walk in one world with one spirit. But we have to walk in two worlds with one spirit."

28

Racial Inequality and Sport

George H. Sage

It is said that the history of sport is one that reveals all that has been bad as well as good throughout the history of the United States. This is true for African Americans in sport: sport has simultaneously been a powerful reinforcer of racist ideology and an instrument of opportunity for African Americans.

Unlike the patriarchal ideology that historically barred most women from sport, the ideology underlying racism has not been incompatible with African American sport participation, but it has dictated that African American athletes be subordinate and in certain times and places totally segregated from playing with whites. Still, despite pervasive and systematic discrimination against African Americans, they have played a continuing and significant role in every era of American history. Their involvement can be roughly divided into three stages: (1) largely exclusion before the Civil War, (2) breakthroughs immediately after the Civil War but segregation beginning in the last two decades of the 19th century continuing to the mid-20th century, and (3) integration during the latter 20th century.

THE ERA OF SLAVERY

Social relations among African Americans during the more than 200 years of slavery involved a wide variety of games and sports played among themselves. Many plantation

Source: Reprinted by permission from G. H. Sage, 1998, *Power and Ideology in American Sport,* 2nd ed. (Champaign, IL: Human Kinetics), pp. 88–98.

owners actually encouraged such use of leisure time because it was seen as preferable to other options such as drinking, fighting, and general mischief. They may have also encouraged games and sports to dissuade slaves from plotting acts of insurgency against plantation owners. Sporting social relations between whites and blacks during the slavery era (1619 to 1865) centered on two activities: boxing and horse racing. Holidays and special occasions in the colonial (1607–1789) and antebellum periods were often enlivened with sports and games, especially those on which people could wager. Many plantation owners selected—and even trained—one or more male slaves to enter in boxing matches held in conjunction with festive occasions. The black boxers under such conditions were merely used to entertain their white "masters" and their friends.

Horse racing was another popular sporting event that allowed spectators to bet on the outcome. Horses were, of course, owned by whites, and training was usually done by whites, but African Americans were used as jockeys. There was little status and no significant material reward for jockeying because slave labor of any kind was unpaid; jockeying was viewed as basically mechanical, so slaves were trusted with a task that whites did not care to do anyway. Social relations, then, were seen as distant, with whites in control and African Americans in subordinate roles, pleasing the dominant white groups.

LATTER 19TH CENTURY TO MID-20TH CENTURY

Emancipation had little effect on the social relations between African Americans and whites in sports. Although a number of African Americans played on professional baseball teams in the early years of the National League, Jim Crowism (segregation) gradually raised its ugly head. White players threatened to quit rather than share the diamond with black men. White opponents tried to spike African American players at every opportunity; pitchers aimed at their heads. Finally, in 1888 major league club owners made a gentlemen's agreement not to sign any more African American players. This unwritten law against hiring black players was not violated until 1945 when Branch Rickey, general manager of the Brooklyn Dodgers, signed Jackie Robinson to a contract.[1]

As other professional sports developed, African Americans were likewise barred from participation. This exclusion maintained the segregation of the wider society as well as the segregation of Major League Baseball. One of the many consequences of excluding African Americans from professional sports was to perpetuate privileges for white athletes, who did not have to compete with an entire segment of the population for sport jobs.

Excluding African Americans from white-only professional leagues did not stop them from forming their own teams and leagues. These so-called Negro baseball leagues (that is the term that was used) flourished for more than 40 years; they staged their own versions of the World Series and All-Star Games and produced their own heroes who were idolized in African American communities. All-black basketball teams and leagues succeeded in many cities of the Northeast and Midwest.[2]

African Americans were active in boxing throughout the time of slavery, but they found their aspirations for top prizes blocked when they tried to compete as free men after the Civil War. For example, when John L. Sullivan became the first American heavyweight boxing champion in 1882, he announced that he would fight any contender: "In this challenge, I include all fighters—first come, first served—who are white. I will not fight a Negro. I never have, and never shall." And he never did. One of the greatest heavyweight boxing champions of all time, Jack Dempsey, in his first public statement after he won the championship in 1919, said that he would not under any circumstances "pay any attention to Negro challengers."[3] Despite barriers like these, two African Americans—Jack Johnson and Joe Louis—managed to win the heavyweight championship during the first half of the 20th century.

During the late 19th and early 20th centuries, education in the South was totally segregated, so African American high school and intercollegiate athletes competed against other African American athletes. Although not segregated, schools and colleges in other parts of the country managed to bar most African Americans from high school and college sports teams. Until the 1960s, most African American college athletes played at black colleges in black leagues (known as Negro colleges and Negro leagues), which existed because of institutionalized racial prejudice and discrimination.

Black colleges fielded teams in all the popular sports and played a leading role in promoting women's sports, especially in track and field—Tuskegee Institute (now Tuskegee University) and Tennessee State are prominent examples. They provided opportunities for women before such opportunities were available on predominantly white campuses. Although the educational system was segregated, the so-called Negro colleges provided an avenue of opportunity for many African American athletes—both men and women—though few were ever recognized outside the African American community.[4]

LATTER 20TH CENTURY

The past 50 years have been a time of remarkable change for African Americans in sports. They have become a significant presence at every level of organized sports. From a condition of exclusion from "white" sports, they have passed through periods of tokenism, during which they were admitted in small numbers, to a period of "stacking," during which only specific positions on teams were thought appropriate for them (because racist ideology stereotyped them as having speed, quickness, and jumping ability, but not intellectual and complex thinking ability), to a period of open acceptance in many sports.

Professional Sports

African Americans have gradually assumed a remarkably prominent role in several professional sports. When Jackie Robinson took the field for the Brooklyn Dodgers in 1947, he broke the all-white exclusion barrier of Major League Baseball that had been in place for more than 50 years. The next 10 years were a period of tokenism by which most teams integrated by signing one or two African American players. By 1959, when the Boston Red Sox finally signed an African American player, every major league team was integrated, but even in the mid-1960s, less than 10 percent of all Major League Baseball players were African American. Most African American players were "stacked" at the outfield and infield corner positions of first and third base. Currently about 18 percent of Major League Baseball players are African American, and they are more widely distributed in the various playing positions.

Other popular professional team sports have passed through essentially the same phases as Major League Baseball. Exclusion was largely the situation in professional football before World War II. Then from the 1950s to well into the 1980s, periods of tokenism and "stacking" players into running back, wide receiver, and defensive back positions followed. African Americans have become dominant in the National Football League (NFL) in the 1990s; in 1998 68 percent of NFL players were African American, and they are distributed in all the playing positions (though very few are quarterbacks).

The most striking increase of African Americans in professional sports has taken place in basketball; in the late 1950s, only about 10 percent of National Basketball Association (NBA) players were black. Tokenism and stacking, while present for periods in basketball, were not as conspicuous as in baseball and football. At present, more than 80 percent of NBA players are African American; they dominate at all the positions.

When the two women's professional basketball leagues, the American Basketball League and the Women's National Basketball Association, began their inaugural seasons in 1996 and 1997, more than 75 percent of the players were African American. This reflects the prominent place that African American women have played during the past decade on intercollegiate and U.S. Olympic basketball teams, for it was from these teams that the professional leagues recruited their players.

Intercollegiate Sports

Intercollegiate sports at predominantly white institutions remained segregated, with isolated exceptions, until after World War II. At the University of Michigan, for example, from 1882 to 1945 there were only four black lettermen in football and none in basketball. The impact of World War II in opening up social and economic opportunities for African Americans, the 1954 Supreme Court decision forbidding racially separate educational facilities, and the growing commercialization of collegiate sports led more and more formerly white colleges and universities to recruit talented African American athletes to bolster their teams. Consequently, black colleges lost their monopoly on African American athletic talent. The best athletes found it advantageous to play at predominantly white schools because of greater visibility, especially on television, which boosted their chances for signing professional contracts at the conclusion of their eligibility. Athletic programs at black colleges were rapidly depleted, forcing several schools to drastically modify their athletic programs and some black leagues to disband.

In 1948 only 10 percent of predominately white college basketball teams had one or more African Americans on their rosters. This proportion increased to 45 percent of the teams in 1962 and 92 percent by 1975. Universities in the southern states maintained white-only teams until the latter 1960s. The conversion from segregated to integrated programs in the South is well illustrated by the University of Alabama: In 1968 there were no African Americans on any of its teams, but by 1975 its basketball team fielded an all-black starting lineup.

The percentage of African American athletes has exceeded the percentage of African American nonathletes in higher education for many years. In the late 1990s, less than 6 percent of all students at Division I universities are African American, while overall, 27.5 percent of the scholarship athletes in Division I institutions are African American; 60 percent of the men's basketball players, 37 percent of the women's basketball players, and 42 percent of the football players are African American.[5]

Remaining Barriers to Access

Despite the many opportunities now available in sport for African Americans that did not exist a generation ago, racial inequality in sport has not been eliminated. Many professional and college sports still have very few African American participants. Those sports most closely linked to upper-class patronage and with less spectator interest, and thus less economic impact, have been slow to provide access to African Americans. Both men's and women's professional tennis and golf have conspicuously few African Americans. But socially elite sports are not the only ones still lacking significant African American presence. Auto racing, ice hockey, and soccer are others. Laws that prevent African Americans from being kept out do not assure that they will get in. Ample evidence shows that those who control certain sports have created barriers to black participation, thus reproducing some of the more odious features of racial injustice.

It is important to understand that where barriers to access have been eliminated for African Americans in sports, these changes have not taken place purely from humanitarian concerns. Political, legal, and economic factors have played interlocking roles. The civil rights legislation of the 1960s opened up many sectors of life for African Americans, including sport. Sport opportunities for African Americans in professional sport grew only as discrimination became incompatible with good capitalist financial policy. It was in those team sports in which spectator appeal was strong and growing, and in which the profit motive was foremost, that African Americans were given a chance, and the valuable contributions of outstanding African American athletes in winning championships opened up further opportunities.

It is also important to understand that racism has not been eliminated in sport even though more sports opportunities are available and even though there is more equitable distribution of African Americans in professional and intercollegiate sports. Racial attitudes are not necessarily changed by laws or political and economic pressures. Prejudice, discrimination, and injustice remain, albeit in more subtle, even unconscious, forms. African American athletes, coaches, and sport administrators report that rarely a day goes by that they do not experience racial prejudice or discrimination of some kind. Their accounts have been corroborated by empirical research as well as from testimonials from their white teammates and friends.[6]

LEADERSHIP AND MANAGEMENT OPPORTUNITIES

Employment patterns in sports leadership for African Americans have been similar to that of female sport coaches and administrators. Access for black athletes has expanded greatly in recent years, but very few African Americans—men or women—have been hired for positions high in the sport hierarchy. At the present time, blacks account for less than 5 percent of the key management positions in professional and intercollegiate sports. Racist ideology, stereotypes, and caricatures have portrayed African Americans as lacking the requisite intelligence and rational thinking capabilities for leadership. The same racist ideology claims that whites will not follow black leaders.

Another barrier to leadership positions in sport for African Americans is the dominance of the entrenched white "ol' boys" network. Those who control access to those higher levels can subtly insulate themselves against those with whom they do not wish to associate.[7] Of course, the extent to which any of these factors account for the hiring for any given sport leadership position is hard to determine, but the perpetuation of racial stereotypes and the dominant social network certainly are powerful forces.

In both professional and intercollegiate sports, coaching and administration jobs are under the control of those who have the power for determining who gets selected for the upper-level positions. Statements made by powerful persons in sport organizations suggest racist beliefs play a role in excluding African Americans from administrative positions. In 1987 Al Campanis, an executive for the Los Angeles Dodgers, appeared on the television program *Nightline* and was asked by host Ted Koppel why there are no black managers and general managers in Major League Baseball. Campanis replied that blacks "may not have some of the necessities to be . . . a field manager or perhaps a general manager." In 1992 Marge Schott, owner of the Cincinnati Reds, reportedly said she would rather "hire a trained monkey than a nigger" to work in her front office. These statements, and the hiring practices of those who make hiring decisions for sports organizations, clearly suggest that race has been a factor in those decisions.

As of 1998 there were only three black head coaches in the NFL, and conditions are not promising for improvement. During the 1997 season and before the 1998 season began, the NFL had 11 head coaching openings and none of the jobs were filled by an African American. Twenty-six percent of NFL assistant coaches in 1997 were black, and only four were offensive or defensive coordinators—the most responsible and prestigious coaching positions below head coaching. This in a league in which about 68 percent of the players are black.[8] Major League Baseball has had only a handful of black managers to date, and currently only about 18 percent of the coaches and one of the general managers are African American. In fall 1996, six Major League Baseball manager positions were open; no one was hired from the list of minority candidates. Professional basketball has had the most African American head coaches. In recent years, as many as seven blacks have held these positions at once, but this is in a league with more than 80 percent African American players.

African American coaches are equally scarce in intercollegiate athletics. The first African American to be hired as a head football coach at a major college was Ron Cooper at Eastern Michigan University in 1992. As of spring 1998, less than 8 of 112 head football coaches in NCAA Division I-A are African American. Nearly all African American college coaches are assistants, and most coaching staffs have only one black. Of about 1,220 head coaching positions in NCAA Division I sports, not including the predominantly black colleges, in which African American athletes have a significant presence (football, basketball, track, baseball), less than 5 percent are held by African Americans.[9]

Executive positions in professional and intercollegiate sports continue to elude African Americans. In the commissioner's offices of pro sports, in the front offices of professional clubs, among the top-level NCAA administrators, and among university athletic directors, there are scandalously few African Americans. As of 1998, the NFL has had fewer than six black general managers, and about 10 NBA general managers have been African American. Of more than 20 new general managers hired by Major League Baseball from 1990 to 1998, one was African American. The one bright spot in this otherwise dim picture for baseball was the choice in February 1989 of Bill White, an African American, as the president of the National League.

In 1994 the NCAA's Minority Opportunity and Interests Committee reported that the proportion of black sport administrators at member institutions of the NCAA had changed little over the past four years. Two years later, the situation was much the same. In 1998 only about 5 percent of the athletic directors at NCAA Division I institutions were African American.[10]

African American women who aspire to leadership positions in professional and intercollegiate sports are faced with two obstacles. First, they are victims of racist ideology that militates against their employment. Second, there are fewer women's sports than men's; the opportunities simply do not exist for females—white or black— to coach or manage in professional or intercollegiate sports. But where positions exist for which African American women might be employed, they are not being hired. Only one sport—women's intercollegiate basketball—has a significant number of black female coaches. In 1998 there were about a dozen NCAA Division I basketball teams coached by an African American woman.

The sports leadership situation for African Americans had become so disgraceful in the early 1990s that some of the sport governing bodies and civil rights groups formed committees and task forces to help seek out minorities for management and executive positions and to monitor team hiring. In 1993 the Rainbow Commission for Fairness in Athletics was created by the Reverend Jesse Jackson to reduce racism and gender barriers in the hiring practices of professional and collegiate sport. Substantial and meaningful results have been slow; the ranks of managers, head coaches, and front-office personnel continue to be filled by whites, sometimes using thinly disguised ploys that eliminate African Americans from serious consideration.

SOCIAL MOBILITY THROUGH SPORT FOR AFRICAN AMERICANS

It has often been contended that sport is one of the most responsive social practices for serving as an avenue of upward social mobility for African Americans; indeed, it has been argued that sport has done more in this regard than any other social practice or institution. Although it is certainly true that sport has provided some African American athletes with opportunities for social mobility denied them in other sectors of American life, and a few have become prominent figures in American life— Jackie Robinson, Muhammad Ali, Wilma Rudolph, "Magic" Johnson, Jackie Joyner-Kersee, and others—sport has not moved large numbers of African Americans into higher social-class standing. The rags-to-riches stories of individual, high-profile African American athletes disguise the actual reality of how little social mobility results from sports participation.

There are fewer than 3,400 male professional team sport athletes. There are about 50.2 million American males age 15 to 39 (the age range of most professional athletes), 6.2 million of whom are African Americans. So that makes the odds of an African American male becoming a professional athlete about one in 5,000. Meanwhile, there are 12 times more black lawyers and 15 times more black doctors than there are black professional athletes.

Sociologist Harry Edwards once remarked about an African American's chances of becoming a professional athlete: "You have a better chance of getting hit by a meteorite in the next 10 years than getting work as an athlete." Henry Louis Gates Jr., professor of humanities at Harvard University and an African American, made a similar point: "An African American youngster has about as much chance of becoming a professional athlete as he or she does of winning the lottery. The tragedy for our people, however, is that few of us accept the truth. . . . The blind pursuit of attainment in sports is having a devastating effect on our people."[11] Still, many young African American athletes have bought into the myth that sport is the highway to financial success and upward social mobility. According to a national survey, 51 percent of African American high school athletes believe they can become professional athletes.[12]

African Americans have received an increasing number of athletic scholarships at predominantly white schools since the early 1970s, but this has been a mixed blessing. On one hand, a few athletically talented African Americans have been able to attend and graduate from colleges otherwise inaccessible to them, and this has allowed them to achieve upward social mobility. On the other hand, the evidence is clear and abundant that the athletic talent of many African American college athletes has been exploited by their schools. They have been recruited even though they lacked the academic background to succeed in higher education, and they have been advised into courses that keep them eligible but are dead-end choices for acquiring a college diploma. When their eligibility is used up or they become academically ineligible to compete for the team, they are discarded and ignored by the coaches who recruited them. From 55 percent to 75 percent of African American NCAA Division I football, basketball, and track athletes do not graduate. This represents a much lower rate of graduation than the overall graduation averages in those universities.[13]

The evidence is overwhelming that professional sport cannot provide much in the way of upward social mobility for large numbers of African Americans. Yes, the very few who become professional athletes make a lot of money and become wealthy for a time. But even for those who do become professional athletes, the average professional sports career is very short—less than five years. That's right. The average professional athlete remains at the top level of competition for less than five years.

An athletic scholarship has the potential to help an African American college student from a poor family earn a college diploma, which can then lead to a high-paying position in a professional field or business. But every year thousands of African American college athletes leave college without the diploma. For them, their future occupation will be determined by their educational achievement and by chance, just as it is for other men and women without a college degree.

NOTES

1. Robert Peterson, *Only the Ball Was White: History of Legendary Black Players and All-Black Professional Teams* (New York: Oxford University Press, 1992); Robert Gardner and Dennis Shortelle, *The Forgotten Players: The Story of Black Baseball in America* (New York: Walker 1993); Art Rust Jr., *Get That Nigger Off the Field: The Oral History of the Negro Leagues* (Brooklyn: Book Mail Services, 1992).

2. Ibid.; see also David K. Wiggins, *Glory Bound: Black Athletes in a White America* (Syracuse, NY: Syracuse University Press, 1997).

3. Quoted in John R. Betts, *America's Sporting Heritage* (Reading, MA: Addison-Wesley, 1974), 337; "Dempsey Will Meet Only White Boxers," *The New York Times*, 6 July 1919, 17; see also Arthur Ashe, *A Hard Road to Glory—Boxing: A History of the African American Athlete* (New York: Amistad 1993).

4. David K. Wiggins, "Prized Performers, but Frequently Overlooked Students: The Involvement of Black Athletes in Intercollegiate Sports of Predominately White University Campuses, 1890–1972," *Research Quarterly for Exercise and Sport* 62 (June 1991):164–77, Cindy Himes Gissendanner, "African-American Women and Competitive Sport, 1920–60," in *Women, Sport, and Culture,* edited by Susan Birrell and Cheryl L. Cole (Champaign, IL: Human Kinetics, 1994), 81–92.

5. Kenneth L. Shropshire, *In Black and White: Race and Sport in America* (New York: New York University Press, 1996); see also Othello Harris, "African-American Predominance in Collegiate Sports," in *Racism in College Athletics: The African-American Athletes Experience,* edited by Dana D. Brooks and Ronald C. Althouse (Morgantown, WV: Fitness Information Technology, 1993), 51–74.

6. Timothy Davis, "The Myth of the Superspade: The Persistence of Racism in College Athletics," *Fordham Urban Law Journal* 22, no. 3 (1995): 615–98; Phoebe W. Williams, "Performing in a Racially Hostile Environment," *Marquette Sports Law Journal* 6 (Spring 1996): 287–314; Shropshire, *In Black and White: Race and Sport in America;* John Hoberman, *Darwin's Athletes: How Sport Has Damaged Black America and Preserved the Myth of Race* (Boston: Houghton Mifflin, 1997).

7. Kenneth L. Shropshire "Merit, Ol' Boy Networks, and the Black-Bottomed Pyramid," *Hastings Law Journal* 47 (January 1996): 455–72; see also Bret L. Billet and Lance J. Formwalt, *America's National Pastime: A Study of Race and Merit in Professional Baseball* (Westport, CT: Praeger, 1995).

8. Kenneth L. Shropshire, "Jackie Robinson's Legacy," *Emerge,* April 1997, 60–63; S.L. Price, "About Time," *Sports Illustrated,* 10 June 1996, 69–75; Jarrett Bell, "Tagliabue, Black Assistant Coaches in 'Constructive' Meeting on Hiring," *USA Today,* 25 March 1997, 2C.

9. Steve Wieberg, "Black Coaches Make Mark at Major Schools," *USA Today,* 22 August 1996, 10C; Richard E. Lapchick, *1996 Racial Report Card* (Boston: Northeastern University, Center for the Study of Sport in Society, 1995); Richard E. Lapchick, ed., *Sport in Society: Equal Opportunity or Business as Usual?* (Thousand Oaks, CA: Sage, 1996).

10. Dana Brooks and Ronald Althouse, "Racial Imbalance in Coaching and Managerial Positions," in *Racism in College Athletics: The African-American Athlete's Experience,* 101–42.

11. Henry Louis Gates Jr., "Delusions of Grandeur," *Sports Illustrated,* 19 August 1991, 78.

12. Richard E. Lapchick, "Athletes Learn the Lesson: The Lou Harris Survey," in *Sport in Society: Equal Opportunity or Business as Usual?* edited by Richard E. Lapchick, 174–75.

13. Audwin Anderson and Donald South, "Racial Differences in Collegiate Recruiting, Retention, and Graduation Rates," in *Racism in College Athletics: The African-American Athlete's Experience,* 79–100.

29

Fewer Blacks Step Up to Plate in Pro Baseball

Mike Klis

As he stood in left field for the Anaheim Angels during Game 1 of the World Series last fall, Garret Anderson was surrounded by white friends.

His teammate in center field, Darin Erstad, was white, as was right fielder Tim Salmon. The entire Angels infield of Troy Glaus, David Eckstein, Adam Kennedy, and Scott Spiezio was white. Angels starting pitcher Jarrod Washburn and designated hitter Brad Fullmer were white. Bengie Molina, the catcher, was Latin American.

Had Anderson bothered to notice, he would have seen pretty much what Jackie Robinson saw while playing first base for the Brooklyn Dodgers in the 1947 World Series.

"I don't pay attention to that stuff," said Anderson, the lone African American starting player on the eventually world-champion Angels.

A recently released racial survey, however, revealed numbers that baseball may not be able to ignore.

A little more than 50 years after Robinson broke the color barrier in Major League Baseball, the number of African American players in the big leagues has dropped to its lowest level since 1960.

The Angels are one of seven teams that finished April with just one African American player on the roster. The others were Boston (utility infielder Damian Jackson), St. Louis (backup outfielder Kerry Robinson), the New York Yankees (in-

Source: Mike Klis, "Fewer Blacks Step Up to Plate in Pro Baseball," *Denver Post* (May 11, 2003), pp. 1A, 14A–15A.

jured shortstop Derek Jeter), Houston (backup outfielder Brian Hunter), Montreal (backup outfielder Ron Calloway), and Texas (starting outfielder Carl Everett).

More than 20 baseball players and officials at all levels interviewed for this report say there are a number of factors:

- Baseball is not reaching out in the inner cities to combat the perception that basketball and football offer more glamorous athletic opportunities.
- A lack of facilities, or facilities in poor condition, deters participation in inner cities.
- Real or perceived racism drives young black players away from the sport.
- The increasing cost of equipment and of joining organized leagues makes it difficult for some families to participate.

Regardless of the cause, the numbers tell the story.

"I'm not going to say it hasn't gone unnoticed," said Colorado Rockies pitcher Shawn Chacon.

Chacon is part of a Rockies team that has the most African American players in the majors, with five. The four others are Preston Wilson, Charles Johnson, Darren Oliver, and Jay Payton. Although the Rockies score well in racial equality, what does it say about baseball as an industry when just one team has 20 percent African American players when in 1975, blacks represented 27 percent of all big-league players?

"I tell kids it's an ideal time to be in baseball. Because the best athletes are playing basketball and football," said Rockies scout Orsino Hill, once a professional baseball player and uncle to former all-star Darryl Strawberry.

A recent report by Richard Lapchick for the Institute for Diversity and Ethics in Sport at the University of Central Florida revealed that only 10 percent of major-league players in 2002 were African Americans—the smallest percentage of black baseball players since 1960.

"That's a slap to Jackie and Hank (Aaron) and all the guys who played before us," said veteran Chicago Cubs outfielder Tom Goodwin. "We're not carrying the torch. We've got to keep it burning."

The decrease in the number of African American ballplayers was gradual from its height in the mid-1970s until 1995 when they filled 19 percent of big-league rosters. But since the year of the wildcard and the opening of Coors Field, the number of African American players has dropped nearly by half.

"Our industry, I don't think, is doing a real good job in the inner cities," said San Diego Padres general manager Kevin Towers. "The inner-city kids are playing basketball. They're not playing baseball."

The Lapchick report stated African Americans account for four of five National Basketball Association players and two of every three players in the National Football League.

"One reason why the black athlete isn't playing baseball is because baseball doesn't market their players like they do in the NBA and NFL," Hill said. "The NBA and NFL make sure people know who their players are. Baseball is kind of stuck in this dinosaur way of thinking in that, 'We're the national pastime—every kid wants to play baseball.' That's not the way it is. African American children aren't playing baseball because baseball doesn't appeal to them."

There is no greater irony regarding the gradual disappearance of African American ballplayers than this: In 1997, the year baseball celebrated the 50-year anniversary of Robinson's breaking the color barrier, for his former organization, the Los Angeles Dodgers, opened that season with just one African American player: Wayne Kirby, a backup outfielder.

Fifty years and no progress, at least not statistically.

"What happened that year with the Dodgers was astonishing," Lapchick said.

When decreases are this drastic, they're usually the result of several factors.

LATIN AMERICAN BOOM

The drop in black ballplayers has been exceeded by an even greater decrease in white ballplayers. Since Lapchick began formally reporting on race and gender in all major sports, white ballplayers decreased from 70 percent in 1989 to 58 percent in 1997, although the percentage was back up to 60 last season.

Statistically, the roster spots vacated by the white and black ballplayers have been filled by Latin Americans. Since 1989 the number of Latino ballplayers has more than doubled from 13 to 28 percent.

"Baseball is still the No. 1 sport over there," said the Cubs' Dusty Baker, one of baseball's four black managers. "In America, baseball is not the No. 1 sport. There are about 18 different sports here, with X Games on the rise. Soccer's on the rise."

THE LEBRON JAMES FACTOR

It's not so much that Latin Americans took over big-league roster sports as African Americans forfeited them. Hill, who at 41 is 12 days older than his more famous nephew, Strawberry, grew up in playing in the same southern Los Angeles sandlots where future major-league stars such as Strawberry, Eric Davis, Ozzie Smith, Eddie Murray, and Chris Brown spent their afternoons and evenings. Rockies scouting director Bill Schmidt grew up not far from the area and scouted all the Los Angeles high schools that were once fertile ground for major-league stars.

"Now I can't tell you when's the last time I went to southern L.A. to scout," Schmidt said.

Baseball can't observe somebody who's not there.

"I think communities themselves are a lot different," said Rockies center fielder Wilson, who grew up in South Carolina. "Baseball used to be a community sport where people would get together and play a game. It seems a whole lot harder to get enough guys to play a baseball game. But it only takes four kids to have a pickup basketball game."

More than convenience, African American children see a greater reward in basketball and football. LeBron James didn't have to leave high school to play in basketball games televised on ESPN. In Division I college football and the NFL, African Americans dominate the glamorous skill positions of running back, wide receiver, defensive back and, finally, quarterback.

The NCAA Final Four basketball tournament has become one of the biggest events in sports. When they're through with college, the best basketball and football players go straight to the top professional league.

College baseball games, however, aren't televised until the final rounds of the World Series. If an African American child happens to tune in, he will be lucky to see more than one or two players of his skin color.

"When I scout college baseball games, I'm the only black in the stadium," Hill said. "And I go to Chicago. I go to St. Louis, It's very rare that you see African Americans playing college baseball."

The star college baseball player goes straight to Elmira, N.Y., for the minor leagues. On a bus. With $15 a day meal money and an $850 a month salary.

"Baseball's just not as glamorous as the other sports," Goodwin said.

In baseball, you're drafted, and you're hot stuff for a couple minutes, and the next thing you know, you're gone. A couple years later, your buddies are going, "Whatever happened to that guy?" He went off to the minor leagues for a couple years. And little kids see that.

You look at LeBron James. I don't think his situation hurts basketball, but as far as getting youths to play baseball, that's not going to help us.

Derrick Martin played shortstop and outfield in a Denver-area police athletic league from age 8 until 13, when he decided to specialize in football. An all-state senior cornerback at Thomas Jefferson High School, Martin will play football at the University of Wyoming next year.

"I like baseball; it was fun," Martin said. "But I wanted to concentrate on football. I thought I had a better future in football."

PLAGUED BY POOR FACILITIES

True story. The spring blizzard, coupled with ballfield scheduling conflicts, forced the Denver Montbello High School baseball team to hold several hitting practice sessions this year in the school shower.

"We had two choices," said Montbello baseball coach Herb Sanders. "We either hit in the shower or we didn't hit."

Danny Hall is in his 10th year as the Georgia Tech baseball coach. Although the campus is in downtown Atlanta, Hall didn't sign his first inner-city player until this year, when he lured center fielder Avery Johnson.

Hall said the reason he hasn't recruited more from the inner city is because most of the Avery Johnsons are playing in the suburbs.

"The facilities in the inner city are bad," Hall said. "Nothing to where you say, 'Boy, that's awful,' but 30 miles out of town, Cobb County, every field you see is a castle. Compare it with what else is available in the metro area, and they seem a lot worse. I wish there was a solution."

Improving baseball facilities in the inner cities, however, can become a Catch-22. For years, the Rockies had a "Field of Dreams" program in which their highest-paid players donated enough money to build 49 state-of-the-art youth ballparks in the Denver metro area and beyond. the Rockies began tapering off the program two years ago, however, as they realized that the slogan "If you build it, they will come," may be fine with movies and ghosts, but it only goes so far in real life.

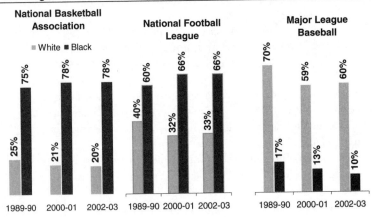

Majorities in the Majors
Percentage of white and black players in three major sports

Source: Institute for Diversity and Ethics in Sport at the the University of Central Florida. Compiled by Thomas McKay. *The Denver Post*.

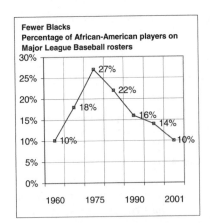

Source: Institute for Diversity and Ethics in Sport at the University of Central Florida. Compiled by Thomas McKay, *The Denver Post*.

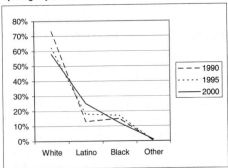

Source: Institute for Diversity and Ethics in Sport at the University of Central Florida. Compiled by Thomas McKay, The Denver Post.

QUESTIONS OF RACISM LINGER

Statistically, it's difficult to charge prejudice as a contributing factor to the decline of African American ballplayers when the percentage of white major-league players also has dropped significantly.

Anecdotally, baseball can also present a strong defense by asking: Wasn't racism stronger in 1975, when 27 percent of big-league players were African Americans, than in 2002, when there were 10 percent? Still, many African American ballplayers can't look at baseball's 100 percent white ownership fraternity and not wonder if true equality exists, just like they can't forget what Dodgers vice president Al Campanis said 16 years ago about how blacks didn't have "the necessities"to manage. Nor can they forget that 10 years ago, Cincinnati owner Marge Schott referred to Davis and Dave Parker by using the N-word.

"There's no question that African Americans believe racism is a factor in baseball," Lapchick said. "Whether it's a reasonable belief, I can't say. But I don't think, in this country's cultural climate, that Marge Schott was alone among owners when she shared her position on race."

MORE COSTS, FEWER INCENTIVES

Sanders believes the nationwide epidemic of African American children living in fatherless family environments has contributed to baseball's participation decline.

Lapchick said that while baseball has improved dramatically in hiring African Americans for management positions, the perception remains there aren't many employment opportunities available to minorities after their playing days are finished.

Many of those interviewed believe the increasing financial commitment of youth baseball has chased away African American children from the ball diamonds.

"It's getting to where it's almost like golf," Payton said.

For its part, Major League Baseball recognizes it is losing African American ballplayers at an alarming rate. It started its Reviving Baseball in Inner Cities (RBI) program in 1989, and today 120,000 children, ages 13 through 18 from 185 cities, participate, according to Tom Brasuell, the commissioner's vice president for community affairs.

There are signs the RBI program is beginning to make a difference. Vic Darensbourg, a relief pitcher on the Colorado Rockies' disabled list, became the first RBI alumnus to reach the majors when he was called up by Florida in 1998.

"It's a good program because it gives kids another sport to love besides basketball and football," said Darensbourg, who played in a Los Angeles RBI league when he was 17.

Perhaps confirming RBI's impact is the recent Lapchick report showing a significant increase in African American players at the Division I college level, from 2.8 percent in 1999 to 6.7 percent in 2001.

Perhaps most promising is the academy Major League Baseball has financially committed to build in Los Angeles. It would be the first of its kind in the United States.

"There's no doubt in my mind that Jackie Robinson breaking the color barrier in 1947 was the most powerful event of the 20th century in all of sports," said Bud Selig, baseball's commissioner. "And there's no question we are starting to see an evolution of the African American ballplayers from what we had in the 1950s and '60s. We need to continue to make progress in promoting baseball to the inner-city kids. We've made progress, but we need more."

The problem with the RBI program and L.A. academy, however, is that they address teenagers. A critical time to capture interest is between the ages of 8 and 12, when most boys get over their fear of the hard, little ball and experience the kind of love that lasts a lifetime.

"Baseball, probably more than any other sport is a game you have to love," Goodwin said. "How many people do you hear say, 'I don't like to watch baseball on TV'? You've got to go out and play it to develop a love for the game. I think it all starts with Little League. We need to have our black children playing Little League. It's kind of late to play baseball in high school."

Hill found out that recruiting junior high kids to baseball can be a waste of time.

"I was at one of my 12-year-old son's basketball games this winter," Hill said. "And I was telling the kids, 'You guys should start focusing on baseball. It's the highest-paying sport, and all the black kids are playing basketball and football. With your athleticism, if you can pick up the baseball skills, you'd be able to skate to the big leagues.' And they all looked at me and went, 'Baseball?' Like I was high on something."

✳ FOR FURTHER STUDY ✳

Brown, Tony N., James S. Jackson, Kendrick T. Brown, Robert M. Sellers, Shelley Keiper, and Warde J. Manuel. 2003. "'There's No Race on the Playing Field': Perceptions of Racial Discrimination Among White and Black Athletes," *Journal of Sport & Social Issues* 27 (May): 162–183.

Bryant, Howard. 2002. *Shut Out: A Story of Race and Baseball in Boston* (New York: Routledge).

Edwards, Harry. 1998. "An End of the Golden Age of Black Participation in Sport?" *Civil Rights Journal* 3 (Fall): 19–24.

Edwards, Harry. 2000. "Crisis of Black Athletes on the Eve of the 21st Century," *Society* 37 (March/April):9–13.

Goldsmith, Pat Antonio. 2003. "Race Relations and Racial Patterns in School Sports Participation," *Sociology of Sport Journal* 20 (2):147–171.

Harrison, C. Keith. 2000. "Black Athletes at the Millennium," *Society* 37 (March/April):35–39.

Hoberman, John. 2000. "The Price of 'Black Dominance,'" *Society* 37(March/April):35–39.

Jamieson, Katherine M. 2003. "Occupying a Middle Space: Toward a Mestiza Sport Studies," *Sociology of Sport Journal* 20 (1):1–16.

Jones, Robyn L. 2002. "The Black Experience Within English Semiprofessional Soccer," *Journal of Sport and Social Issues* 26 (February): 47–64.

Juffer, Jane. 2002. "Who's the Man? Sammy Sosa, Latinos, and Televisual Redefinitions of the 'American' Pastime," *Journal of Sport & Social Issues* 26 (November):337–359.

King, C. Richard, and Charles Fruehling Springwood. 2001. *Beyond the Cheers: Race as Spectacle in College Sport* (Albany: State University of New York Press).

Pells, Eddie. 2002. "NASCAR Hopes to Diversify," Associated Press (December 26).

Verducci, Tom, 2003. "Blackout: The African-American Baseball Player Is Vanishing. Does He Have a Future?" *Sports Illustrated* (July 7):56–66.

PART TEN

Structured Inequality: Sport and Gender

Traditionally, gender role expectations have encouraged girls and women to be passive, gentle, delicate, and submissive. These cultural expectations clashed with those traits often associated with sport, such as assertiveness, competitiveness, physical endurance, ruggedness, and dominance. Thus, young women past puberty were encouraged to bypass sports unless the sport retained the femininity of participants. These "allowable" sports had three characteristics: (1) they were aesthetically pleasing (e.g., ice skating, diving, and gymnastics); (2) they did not involve bodily contact with opponents (e.g., bowling, archery, badminton, volleyball, tennis, golf, swimming, and running); and (3) the action was controlled to protect the athletes from overexertion (e.g., running short races, basketball where the offense and defense did not cross half-court).

In effect, these traditional expectations for the sexes denied women equal access to opportunities, not only to sports participation but also to college and to various occupations. Obviously, girls were discriminated against in schools by woefully inadequate facilities—compare the "girls' gym" with the "boys' gym" in any school—and in the budgets. The consequences of sexual discrimination in sport were that: (1) the femininity of those who defied the cultural expectations was often questioned, giving them marginal status; (2) approximately one-half of the population was denied the benefits of sports participation; (3) young women learned their "proper" societal role (i.e., to be on the sidelines supporting men who do the actual achieving); and (4) women were denied a major source of college scholarships.

Currently, quite rapid changes are occurring. Unquestionably, the greatest change in contemporary sport is the dramatic increase in and general acceptance of sports participation by women. These swift changes have occurred for several related reasons. Most prominent is the societal-wide women's movement that has gained increasing momentum since the mid-1960s. Because of the consciousness raising resulting from the movement and the organized efforts to break down the cultural tyranny of gender roles, court cases were initiated to break down sexual discrimination in a number of areas. In athletics, legal suits were successfully brought against various school districts, universities, and even the Little League.

In 1972 Congress passed Title IX of the Education Amendments Act. The essence of this law, which has had the greatest single impact on the move toward sexual equality in all aspects of schools, is: "No person in the United States shall, on the basis of sex, be excluded from taking part in, be denied the benefits of, or be subjected to discrimination in any educational program or activity receiving federal financial assistance."

Although the passage of Title IX and other pressures have led to massive changes, discrimination continues. The first selection, by D. Stanley Eitzen, provides an overview of gender issues in sport. The second, by Donna Lopiano, head of the Women's Sports Foundation, presents a strong argument that men's football is the reason why minor men's sports programs are cut. The final selection, by sociologist Michael A. Messner, answers the question "What is the relationship between participation in organized sports and a young male's developing sense of himself as a success or failure?"

30

Sport and Gender

D. Stanley Eitzen

Sport in its organization, procedures, and operation serves to promote traditional gender roles, thus keeping order (order, however, is not always positive). Sport advances male hegemony in practice and ideology by legitimating a certain dominant version of social reality. From early childhood games to professional sports, the sports experience is "gendered." Boys are expected to participate in sports, to be aggressive, to be physically tough, to take risks, and to accept pain. Thus sport, especially aggressive physical contact sport, is expected for boys and men but not for girls and women. These expectations reproduce male domination in society.

Lois Bryson has argued that sport reproduces patriarchal relations through four minimalizing processes: definition, direct control, ignoring, and trivialization.[1] "When we take a critical look at dominant sport forms in many societies around the world, we see that they often involve actions highlighting masculine virility, power, and toughness —the attributes associated with dominant ideas about masculinity in those societies.'"[2] Male standards are applied to female performance, ensuring female inferiority and even deviance. As sport sociologist Paul Willis has observed, "[The ideal description of sport] is a male description concerning males. Where women become at all visible, then the terms of reference change. There is a very important thread in popular consciousness which sees the very presence of women in sport as bizarre."[3]

Sports participation is expected for men. Sport is strongly associated with male identity and popularity. For women, though, the situation is entirely different. As

Source: D. Stanley Eitzen, *Fair and Foul: Beyond the Myths and Paradoxes of Sport,* 2nd edition (Lanham, MD: Rowman and Littlefield, 2003), excerpts from pp. 81–83, 97–100.

Willis has stated, "Instead of confirming her identity, [sports] success can threaten her with a foreign male identity . . . The female athlete lives through a severe contradiction. To succeed as an athlete can be to fail as a woman, because she has, in certain profound symbolic ways, become a man."[4] Superior women athletes are suspect because strength and athletic skill are accepted as "masculine" traits.

Women's sport is minimized when it is controlled by men. This is demonstrated in the gender composition of leadership positions in the International Olympic Committee, various international and national sports bodies, the National Collegiate Athletic Association, and the administrative and coaching roles in schools and professional leagues.[5]

Women in sport are minimized (and men maximized) when women's activities are ignored. The mass media in the United States have tended to overlook women's sports. When they are reported, the stories, photographs, and commentary tend to reinforce gender role stereotypes. Studies of television coverage indicate that men's sports receive about 92 percent of airtime. Moreover, 97 percent of the athletic figures employed in television commercials are males.[6]

Women's sports are also ignored when cities and schools disproportionately spend enormous amounts on men's sports. As writer Mariah Burton Nelson has noted,

> We live in a country in which the manly sports culture is so pervasive we may fail to recognize the symbolic messages we all receive about men, women, love, sex, and power. We need to take sports seriously—not the scores or the statistics, but the process. Not to focus on who wins, but on who's losing. Who loses when a community spends millions of dollars in tax revenue to construct a new stadium and only men get to play in it, and only men get to work there? Who loses when football and baseball so dominate the public discourse that they eclipse all mention of female volleyball players, gymnasts, basketball players, and swimmers?[7]

Women are also minimized when they are trivialized in sport. As noted earlier, the media framing of the female athlete reinforces gender stereotypes. Considering photographs of women and men athletes, scholar Margaret Carlisle Duncan[8] found that these images emphasized gender differences: (1) female athletes who are sexy and glamorous are most common; (2) female athletes are often photographed in sexual poses; (3) in the framing of photos, male athletes are more likely to be photographed in dominant positions and female athletes in submissive positions; (4) camera angles typically focus up to male athletes and focus down on female athletes; and (5) female athletes are more likely to be shown displaying emotions. As Michael A. Messner has argued, "The choices, the filtering, the entire mediation of the sporting event, is based upon invisible, taken-for-granted assumptions and values of dominant social groups, as such the presentation of the event tends to support corporate, white, and male-dominant ideologies."[9]

Another example of the trivialization of women's sports activities is the naming of their teams. A study comparing the unifying symbols of women's and men's teams found that more than half of colleges and universities in the United States employ names, mascots, and/or logos that demean and derogate women's teams.[10] As elaborated in chapter 12, some schools name their men's teams the Wildcats and their women's teams the Wildkittens. Or the men are the Rams and the women, the Lady Rams (an oxymoron if there ever was one). Thus the naming of women's teams tends to define women athletes and women's athletic programs, as second class and trivial.

The secondary treatment of women in sport that defines and characterizes them as inferior also defines them, by extension, as less capable than men in many other areas of life. Scholar Lois Bryson asserts that "each cultural message about sport is a dual one, celebrating the dominant at the same time as inferiorizing the 'other,'"[11] in this case, celebrating the masculine and inferiorizing the feminine.

Although this dominant ideology is perpetuated in many ways, it is also challenged and contested with some success in all institutional areas, including sport.[12] Pioneering women have broken down the "men-only" rules in such traditionally unlikely areas as automobile racing (Janet Guthrie became the first woman to race in the Indianapolis 500 in 1977), men's locker rooms (women sportswriters now routinely conduct interviews there), high school wrestling against boys,[13] and refereeing men's games (in 1997 the NBA hired two women, Dee Kantner and Violet Palmer, as referees, the first women to officiate in a major professional all-male sports league). In 2002, we witnessed the first woman to referee in the NCAA's men's basketball championship tournament.

The traditional conception of femininity as passive and helpless is challenged today by the fit, athletic, and even muscular appearance of women athletes. Women now engage in pumping iron to sculpt their bodies toward a new standard of femininity that combines beauty with taut, developed muscles. Similarly, women are now rejecting traditional notions of femininity by pushing the limits in endurance events in running, cycling, swimming, and mountain climbing and by engaging freely in strength sports such as bodybuilding, weight lifting, and throwing weights.

• • •

GENDER INEQUITIES

Until the 1970s high school, college, and professional sports in the United States were, with few exceptions, male activities. The barriers were breached finally by court cases (for example, a legal decision to open Little League baseball to girls) and by federal legislation (Title IX in 1972). With these changes, sports opportunities for girls and women have increased manyfold.

> However, prejudices are not altered by courts and legislation, and culturally conditioned responses to gender ideology are ubiquitous and resistant to sudden changes. Therefore, laws may force compliance in equality of opportunity for females in the world of sport, but inequities in sport continue, albeit in more subtle and insidious forms, as has been the case with racism.[14]

Major gender inequities remain, despite the tremendous gains generated by Title IX. An assessment of the situation at big-time schools discloses the following disparities by gender:[15]

- Men coach women's teams but women rarely coach men's teams. Fewer than 2 percent of coaching positions in men's programs are held by women, and most of those were coaches of combined men's and women's teams in cross-country, tennis, and swimming.
- Men outnumber women (56 percent to 44 percent) as coaches of women's teams. Of the 361 new head coaching jobs from 2000 to 2002, women were hired for only 35.
- Head coaches of women's teams in 2001 were paid 75 cents for every dollar earned by coaches of men's teams (not including the many more extras the coaches of men's teams receive).
- Only 18 percent of women's intercollegiate programs are administered by women.
- The higher the level of competition and the better paying the positions, the more likely men will be head coaches and top administrators of women's teams and programs.
- African American women, facing the double jeopardy of minority race and gender, are very underrepresented among coaches (2.6 percent of the head coaches of women's teams and 0 percent of athletic directors in Division I).[16]
- Women's collegiate sports are controlled by the NCAA, a male-dominated organization.
- In 2000, while female students at Division I universities were 53.2 percent of the student body, only 42.3 percent of the athletes were female.
- Despite being a majority of college students, women receive only 41 percent of the athletic scholarships.
- Operating expenses for women's teams are 33 percent of the total operating expenses at Division I-A universities.
- Spending for recruiting was skewed 70 percent to 30 percent in favor of males.
- Two-thirds of the budget for operating expenses for basketball went to men's teams and one-third to women's teams.
- From 1996 to 2001 for every three new dollars (increases in budgets) going into college athletic programs, two dollars went to men's sports and only one dollar to women's sports.[17]
- It is not uncommon for a school with a big-time football program to spend *twice as much on its football team as it spent on all women's sports.*

At the professional level, women have many fewer opportunities than men, and the monetary rewards are considerably less (with the exceptions of ice skating and women's tennis). In professional basketball, for example, there are more teams for men within the United States and abroad. Moreover, the pay is highly skewed with top men receiving in excess of $20 million a year, while only a few women superstars approach $100,000. The women's professional basketball league is the

WNBA, operating under the auspices of the NBA. The WNBA salaries average $55,000, compared to the average salary of $3,170,000 in the NBA (the male organization), and the coaches in the WNBA are typically male (ten of the sixteen head coaches were male in 2001). The prize money for PGA tournaments (for male professional golfers) is many times more than for women professionals playing in the LPGA (the L stands for Ladies, by the way, which connotes elegance, a decidedly unathletic trait). In 2000 the total prize money for the LPGA tour was $36.2 million, far short of the $157 million for the men's tour and the $50 million for the PGA's Senior Tour (this tour is exclusively for men; there is no senior tour for women). Very few women have been able to make it in automobile racing and only then on the fringes, since they have been unable to generate the corporate sponsorships that men drivers receive and that are required to cover the huge expenses involved.

Most significant, while men have the chance for careers as relatively highly paid professional athletes in a number of sports, women do not have these opportunities in sports such as baseball, hockey, and football.

For ancillary positions in sport women again have many fewer opportunities than men. Some examples, using data from 2000:[18]

- Every professional team retains one physician as the primary doctor for its players. The NBA had one woman with that responsibility, and the WNBA had two female physicians.
- There were two female head trainers for men's professional teams (both for soccer teams), and 88 percent of the head trainers in the WNBA were women (the one exception to male dominance in professional athletics).
- As for referees and umpires, women were 3 percent of the referees in the NBA and 43 percent in the WNBA, but 0 percent in the NFL and major-league baseball.
- Radio and television announcing positions are dominated by males, with women holding 3 percent of those positions in the NFL, 2 percent in the NBA and major-league baseball, and 1 percent in the NHL.
- At the college level, only 9.6 percent of full-time sports information directors at Division I schools were women; 26 percent of full-time head athletic trainers were women.[19]

Historically, the International Olympic Committee (IOC) has restricted the number and type of women's sports that were part of the Olympic Games. For example, there were no women athletes at the 1896 Games, and only 14 percent of the athletes in the 1968 Summer Games were women. By 2000 women had gained in participation but were still only 38 percent of the athletes at the Games in Sydney (there were 168 men's events, 120 women's events, and twelve events where women and men competed). The gender composition of the IOC was exclusively male until the 1980s and now only about 10 percent of this powerful administrative body are women.[20] The U.S. Olympic Committee is better represented by women, but they were still a decided minority in 2001, comprising only 26 percent of the Board of Directors and 23 percent of the voting members of the Executive Committee.[21]

The data show that women in sport are second-class citizens. Women have fewer sports participation and career opportunities, fewer resources devoted to their programs, and they are given less media attention than men's sports. Added to this is the discrediting of women athletes by trivializing or marginalizing their accomplishments (nonathletic team names, as noted in chapter 12), focusing on their sexiness or the possibility of their deviant sexuality (the whisper charge of lesbianism). Sport sociologist Mary Jo Kane puts it this way:

> Sport is one of the most powerful institutions in this culture, because of its status and economic and political clout. There's a great deal at stake in sports participation, and the group that has monopolized sport doesn't want to give that up. They know that the best way to maintain control is to trivialize or marginalize their accomplishments. . . . After all, if females are great athletes, then it's harder to say as a society that they shouldn't get press coverage, money, scholarships. But if they are portrayed as people who do sports in their spare time, or as merely pretty girls, it's much easier to deny them access and to maintain the status quo. . . . [The University of Minnesota's Tucker Center for Research on Girls and Women in Sport] 1998 research found that because of the notion that sport belongs to men, there remain deep-seated and persistent barriers to girls in sport: gender stereotyping, sexism, and homophobia.[22]

NOTES

1. Lois Bryson, "Sport and the Maintenance of Masculine Hegemony," *Women's Studies International Forum* 10 (1987): 349–360.

2. Jay J. Coakley, *Sport in Society: Issues and Controversies,* 7th ed. (New York: McGraw-Hill, 2001), p. 227.

3. Paul Willis, "Women in Sport Ideology," in *Sport, Culture and Ideology,* ed. Jennifer Hargreaves (London: Routledge and Kegan Paul, 1982), p. 121.

4. Willis, "Women in Sport Ideology," p. 123.

5. R. Vivian Acosta and Linda J. Carpenter, "Women in Intercollegiate Sport: A Longitudinal Study—Twenty-Five Years Update, 1977–2002" (West Brookfield, Mass.: Carpenter/Acosta, 2002).

6. Edward Turner et al., "Television Consumer Advertising and the Sports Figure," *Sport Marketing Quarterly* 4 (March 1995): 27–33.

7. Mariah Burton Nelson, *The Stronger Women Get, the More Men Love Football: Sexism and the American Culture of Sports* (New York: Harcourt Brace, 1994), p. 8.

8. Margaret Carlisle Duncan, "Sports Photographs and Sexual Difference: Images of Women and Men in the 1984 and 1988 Olympic Games," *Sociology of Sport Journal* 7 (March 1990): 22–43.

9. Michael A. Messner, "Sports and Male Domination," pp. 204–205.

10. D. Stanley Eitzen and Maxine Baca Zinn, "The De-athleticization of Women: The Naming and Gender Marking of Collegiate Sport Teams," *Sociology of Sport Journal* 6 (1989): 362–370.

11. Bryson, "Sport," pp. 349–360.

12. Messner, "Sports and Male Domination."

13. Jeffrey Blackwell, "Girls Grapple with Breaking Tradition," *USA Today,* February 14, 1997, p. 9C; Dylan B. Tomlinson, "Grappling with a Dilemma," *Denver* Post, June 16, 1998, p. 8D.

14. D. Stanley Eitzen and George H. Sage, *Sociology of North American Sport,* 7th ed. (New York: McGraw-Hill, 2002), p. 282.

15. R. Vivian Acosta and Linda J. Carpenter, *Women in Intercollegiate Sport: A Longitudinal Study-Twenty-Five Year Update* (West Brookfield, Mass.: Carpenter/Acosta, 2002); Welch Suggs, "Female Athletes Thrive, but Budget Pressures Loom," *Chronicle of Higher Education,* May 18, 2001, pp. A45–A48.

16. Richard E. Lapchick with Kevin J. Matthews, *2001 Racial and Gender Report Card* (Boston: Center for the Study of Sport in Society, Northeastern University, 2001), pp. 34, 40.

17. Donna Lopiano, "The Real Culprit in the Cutting of Men's Olympic Sports" (New York: Women's Sports Foundation, 2001). www.womenssportsfoundation.org/cgi-bin/iowa/issues/opin/article.html? record=776.

18. Lapchick with Matthews, *2001 Racial and Gender Report Card,* pp. 53–57.

19. Acosta and Carpenter, "Women in Intercollegiate Sport," p. 1.

20. Jay J. Coakley, *Sport in Society: Issues & Controversies,* 7th ed. (New York: McGraw-Hill, 2001), pp. 214, 219.

21. Lapchick with Matthews, 2001 *Racial and Gender Report Card,* p. 27.

22. Mary Jo Kane, "Can Women Save Sports? An Interview by Lynette Lamb," *Utne Reader* 97 (January/February 2000): 57.

31

The Real Culprit in the Cutting of Men's Olympic Sports

Donna Lopiano

Why are the richest athletic programs cutting men's Olympic sports? They're pitting the "have-nots" against each other and unfairly blame Title IX. Donna Lopiano exposes the "Division I football/basketball arms race" as the true culprit of these program cuts.

Division II and III schools, the poorest colleges and universities, are not dropping men's sports. It's the richest Division I athletic programs that are cutting men's swimming, gymnastics, and wrestling programs (Olympic sports). Whenever a men's sport is eliminated, these educational institutions blame Title IX and women's sports. They say they can't afford to add new women's sports programs as required by federal gender equity laws and keep men's Olympic sports. What's wrong with this contention is the fact that there are plenty of new dollars going into Division I college athletic programs that could fund both women's sports and men's Olympic sports. What the public doesn't know is that these new moneys are being used to fuel the arms races being fought in men's football and basketball. NCAA research shows that for every three new dollars going into college athletic programs over the last five years, two are going to men's sports and only one to women's sports. The $1 to women's sports is not closing the significant expenditure gap and the majority of the new money allocated to men's sports is pumping up the already bloated budgets of men's football and basketball.

Source: Donna Lopiano, "The Real Culprit in the Cutting of Men's Olympic Sports," Women's Sports Foundation (March 26, 2002). Online: http://www.womenssportsfoundation.org/cgi-bin/iowa/issues/opin/article.html?record=776.

The problem is not Title IX. The problem is college presidents not putting a stop to the embarrassing waste of money occurring in men's football and basketball. Alumni of private colleges and state legislators of public institutions should be calling for investigations of misuse of funds. Just because the football or basketball team brings in money at the gate, doesn't mean they have a right to spend it however they wish. All revenues generated by institutional activities are institutional funds and it is the fiduciary responsibility of the Boards of Regents and Boards of Trustees to insure the public that these nonprofit educational institutions are fiscally responsible.

For example, the following are true stories of practices at Division I institutions that have recently dropped men's sport programs:

- A university spent $300,000 on lights for a practice football field that was never used for football practice. The football coach wanted to show his recruits how many practice fields had lights. In his four years at the institution, he never used the field.
- A football team was housed in a hotel during preseason football camp instead of the university dormitories, because the team would have to move out of the dorm rooms two days prior to the end of training camp in order to allow regular students to move in for the semester. The coach didn't want the disruption. The snack bill alone at that hotel during that training camp was $86,000.
- A football team spent more than $50,000 last summer to have their meals catered during training camp. The entire travel budget for a women's team sport at the institution was $22,000.
- A university dropped their men's swimming and diving program citing economics. That same university found the means to (1) renovate the outdoor track, (2) renovate the indoor track, including the installation of hydraulic banked turns, (3) build a multi-field baseball complex with heating elements under the soil to keep the grass growing year round, (4) add a new row of skyboxes to the football stadium, and (5) install new state-of-the-art turf in the football stadium.
- One private Division I institution spends 31 percent of its institutional budget on athletics.
- A football team pays for nearly 50 hotel rooms on the night before home games, so that the coaches can babysit their players. Players are fed as if they are on the road, and have been known to rent out entire movie theaters for entertainment purposes. Three charter buses are hired for two days to transport the team to and from the football field, which is three miles from campus—for all home games.
- During spring workouts, which occur during regular classes, football players are fed three meals a day because they are practicing. Yet the baseball team at this same institution is only allowed to spend $15 a day per player on road trips while the sport is in season.
- Following a football season in which a football team won seven games, the head coach treated his entire staff and their wives to a trip to the Bahamas.

These expenditures are simply not prudent. In addition, 300 NCAA Division I schools pay their men's basketball coaches $1 million or more per year while there are only 48 athletic programs among the 900+ NCAA member institutions that operate at a profit.

Schools should be expected to retain all men's sports programs while they bring women's sports into compliance with Title IX. Remedying discrimination does not mean bringing formerly advantaged men's sports down to where women's sports were—with no opportunities to play. Affording current men's sports programs and new women's sports programs requires belt-tightening in Division I. However, colleges should be willing to do whatever it takes to make sure that male athletes in Olympic sports have programs. If necessary, the NCAA must legislate across-the-board expenditure limits and insist on a cessation of the arms race to make this happen. Neither the NCAA nor its member institutions currently show any signs of doing either.

If our institutions of higher education are going to act irresponsibly; continuing to discriminate against women's sports, dropping Olympic sports and operating select teams like professional franchises with million dollar coaches and excessive expenditures, then the IRS should remove their nonprofit status and treat them like commercial sports enterprises. Maybe this is the kind of legislative pressure that must be brought to bear in order to force educational institutions to control their expenses. It's about time the media did some good investigative reporting to reveal the real extent of financial waste and put pressure on college presidents to clean up their acts before the government does so.

Title IX is a good law. We need to keep steady on the course of ensuring that our sons and daughters are treated equally in all educational programs and activities, including sports. We also have to protect sports participation opportunities for our sons by making it clear to high school principals, superintendents, and college presidents that excessive expenditures on one or two priority men's sports and failure to control spending in all sports is unacceptable for educational institutions accorded nonprofit tax status.

32

The Meaning of Success

The Athletic Experience and the Development of Male Identity

Michael A. Messner

Vince Lombardi supposedly said, "Winning isn't everything; it's the only thing," and I couldn't agree more. There's nothing like being number one.

—Joe Montana

The big-name athletes will get considerable financial and social remuneration for their athletic efforts. But what of the others, the 99% who fail? Most will fall short of their dreams of a lucrative professional contract. The great majority of athletes, then, will likely suffer disappointment, underemployment, anxiety, or perhaps even serious mental disorders.

—Donald Harris and D. Stanley Eitzen

What is the relationship between participation in organized sports and a young male's developing sense of himself as a success or failure? And what is the consequent impact on his self-image and his ability to engage in intimate relationships with others? Through the late 1960s, it was almost universally accepted that "sports builds character" and that "a winner in sports will be a winner in life." Consequently, some liberal feminists argued that since participation in organized competitive sports has served as a major source of socialization for males' successful participation in the

Source: "The Meaning of Success: The Athletic Experience and the Development of Male Identity" by Michael A. Messner. From *The Making of Masculinities: The New Men's Studies,* by Harry Brod. Copyright © 1987 by Michael Messner. Reprinted by permission.

public world, girls and young women should have equal access to sports. Lever, for instance, concluded that if women were ever going to be able to develop the proper competitive values and orientations toward work and success, it was incumbent on them to participate in sports.[1]

In the 1970s and 1980s, these uncritical orientations toward sports have been questioned, and the "sports builds character" formula has been found wanting. Sabo points out that the vast majority of research does *not* support the contention that success in sports translates into "work success" or "happiness" in one's personal life.[2] In fact, a great deal of evidence suggests that the contrary is true. Recent critical analyses of success and failure in sports have usually started from assumptions similar to those of Sennett and Cobb and of Rubin: [3] the disjuncture between the *ideology* of success (the Lombardian Ethic) and the socially structured *reality* that most do not "succeed" brings about widespread feelings of failure, lowered self-images, and problems with interpersonal relationships.[4] The most common argument seems to be that the highly competitive world of sports is an exaggerated reflection of advanced industrial capitalism. Within any hierarchy, one can actually work very hard and achieve a lot, yet still be defined (and perceive oneself) as less than successful. Very few people ever reach the mythical "top," but those who do are made ultravisible through the media.[5] It is tempting to view this system as a "structure of failure" because, given the definition of *success,* the system is virtually rigged to bring about the failure of the vast majority of participants. Furthermore, given the dominant values, the participants are apt to blame themselves for their "failure." Schafer argues that the result of this discontinuity between sports values/ideology and reality is a "widespread conditional self-worth" for young athletes. [6] And as Edwards has pointed out, this problem can be even more acute for black athletes, who are disproportionately channeled into sports, yet have no "social safety net" to fall back on after "failure" in sports.

Both the traditional "sports builds character" and the more recent "sports breeds failures" formulas have a common pitfall: Each employs socialization theory in an often simplistic and mechanistic way. Boys are viewed largely as "blank slates" onto which the sports experience imprints values, appropriate "sex-role scripts," and orientations toward self and the world. What is usually not taken into account is the fact that boys (and girls) come to the sports experience with an *already gendered* identity that colors their early motivations and perceptions of the meaning of games and sports. As Gilligan points out, observations of young children's game-playing show that girls bring to the activity a more pragmatic and flexible orientation toward the rules—they are more prone to make exceptions and innovations in the middle of the game in order to make the game more "fair" and maintain relationships with others.[7] Boys tend to have a more firm, even inflexible orientation to the rules of a game—they are less willing to change or alter rules in the middle of the game; to them, the rules are what protects any "fairness." This observation has profound implications for sociological research on sports and gender: The question should not be *simply* "how does sports participation affect boys [or girls]?" but should add "what is it about a developing sense of male identity that *attracts* males to sports in the first place? And how does this socially constructed male identity develop and change as it interacts with the structure and values of the sports world?" In addition to being a social-psychological question, this is also a *historical* question: Since men have not at all times and places related to sports the way they do at present, it is important to explore just what kinds of men exist today. What are their needs, problems, and dreams? How do these men relate to the society they live in? And how do organized sports fit into this picture?

THE "PROBLEM OF MASCULINITY" AND ORGANIZED SPORTS

In the first two decades of this century, men feared that the closing of the frontier, along with changes in the workplace, the family, and the schools, was having a "feminizing" influence on society.[8] One result of the anxiety men felt was the creation of the Boy Scouts of America as a separate sphere of social life where "true manliness" could be instilled in boys *by men*.[9] The rapid rise of organized sports in roughly the same era can be attributed largely to the same phenomenon. As socioeconomic and familial changes continue to erode the traditional bases of male identity and privilege, sports became an increasingly important cultural expression of traditional male values—organized sports became a "primary masculinity-validating experience."[10]

In the post–World War II era, the bureaucratization and rationalization of work, along with the decline of the family wage and women's gradual movement into the labor force, have further undermined the "breadwinner role" as a basis for male identity, thus resulting in a "problem of masculinity" and a "defensive insecurity" among men.[11] As Mills put it, the ethic of success in postwar America "has become less widespread as fact, more confused as image, often dubious as motive, and soured as a way of life. [Yet] there are still compulsions to struggle, to 'amount to something.'"[12]

How have men expressed this need to "amount to something" within a social context that seems to deny them the opportunities to do so? Again, organized sports play an important role. Both on a personal-existential level for athletes and on a symbolic-ideological level for spectators and fans, sports have become one of the "last bastions" of traditional male ideas of success, of male power and superiority over—and separation from—the perceived "feminization" of society. It is likely that the rise of football as "America's number-one game" is largely the result of the comforting clarity it provides between the polarities of traditional male power, strength, and violence and the contemporary fears of social feminization.

But these historical explanations for the increased importance of sports, despite their validity, beg some important questions: Why do men fear the (real or imagined) "feminization" of their world? Why do men appear to need a separate male sphere of life? Why do organized sports appear to be such an attractive means of expressing these needs? Are males simply "socialized" to dominate women and to compete with other men for status, or are they seeking (perhaps unconsciously) something more fundamental? Just what is it that men really *want*? To begin to answer these questions it is necessary to listen to athletes' voices and examine their lives with a social-psychological perspective.

Daniel Levinson's concept of the "individual life structure" is a useful place to begin to construct a gestalt of the life of the athlete.[13] Levinson demonstrates that as males develop and interact with their world, they continue to change throughout their lives. A common theme during developmental periods is the process of individuation, the struggle to separate, to "decide where he stops and where the world begins." "In successive periods of development, as this process goes on, the person forms a clearer boundary between self and world. . . . Greater individuation allows him to be more separate from the world, to be more independent and self-generating. But it also gives him the confidence and understanding to have more intense attachments in the world and to feel more fully a part of it."[14]

This dynamic of separation and attachment provides a valuable social-psychological framework for examining the experiences and problems faced by the athlete as he gropes for and redefines success throughout his life course. In what follows, Levinson's framework is utilized to analyze the lives of 30 former athletes interviewed between 1983 and 1984. Their *interactions* with sports are examined in terms of their initial boyhood attraction to sports; how notions of success in sports connect with a developing sense of male identity; and how self-images, relationships to work and other people, change and develop after the sports career ends.

BOYHOOD: THE PROMISE OF SPORTS

Given how very few athletes actually "make it" through sports, how can the intensity with which millions of boys and young men throw themselves into athletics be explained? Are they simply pushed, socialized, or even *duped* into putting so much emphasis on athletic success? It is important here to examine just what it is that young males hope to get out of the athletic experience. And in terms of *identity*, it is crucial to examine the ways in which the structure and experience of sports activity meet the developmental needs of young males. The story of Willy Rios sheds light on what these needs are. Rios was born in Mexico and moved to the United States at a fairly young age. He never knew his father, and his mother died when he was only 9 years old. Suddenly he felt rootless, and at this time he threw himself into sports, but his initial motivations do not appear to be based upon a need to compete and win. "Actually, what I think sports did for me is it brought me into kind of an instant family. By being on a Little League team, or even just playing with all kinds of different kids in the neighborhood, it brought what I really wanted, which was some kind of closeness."

Similar statements from other men suggest that a fundamental motivational factor behind many young males' sports strivings is a need for connection, "closeness" with others. But why do so many boys see *sports* as an attractive means of establishing connection with others? Chodorow argues that the process of developing a gender identity yields insecurity and ambivalence in males.[15] Males develop "rigid ego boundaries" that ensure separation from others, yet they retain a basic human need for closeness and intimacy with others. The young male, who both seeks and fears attachment with others, thus finds the rulebound structure of games and sports to be a psychologically "safe" place in which he can get (nonintimate) connection with others within a context that maintains clear boundaries, distance, and separation from others. At least for the boy who has some early successes in sports, some of these ambivalent needs can be met, for a time. But there is a catch: For Willy Rios, it was only after he learned that he would get attention (a certain kind of connection) from other people for being a good athlete—indeed, that this attention was *contingent on* his *being good*—that narrow definitions of success, based on performance and winning, became important to him. It was years before he realized that no matter how well he performed, how successful he became, he would not get the closeness that he craved through sports. "It got to be a product in high school. Before, it was just fun, and having acceptance, you know. Yet I had to work for my acceptance in high school that way, just being a jock. So it wasn't fun any more. But it was my self-identity, being a good ballplayer. I was realizing that whatever you excel in, you put out in front of you. Bring it out. Show it. And that's what I did. That was my protection. . . . It was rotten in high school, really."

This conscious striving for successful achievement becomes the primary means through which the young athlete seeks connections with other people. But the irony of the situation, for so many boys and young men like Willy Rios, is that the athletes are seeking to get something from their success in sports that sports cannot deliver—and the *pressure* that they end up putting on themselves to achieve that success ends up stripping them of the ability to receive the one major thing that sports really *does* have to offer: fun.

ADOLESCENCE: YOU'RE ONLY AS GOOD AS YOUR LAST GAME

Adolescence is probably the period of greatest insecurity in the life course, the time when the young male becomes most vulnerable to peer expectation, pressures, and judgments. None of the men interviewed for this study, regardless of their social class or ethnicity, seemed fully able to "turn a deaf ear to the crowd" during their athletic careers. The crowd, which may include immediate family, friends, peers, teammates, as well as the more anonymous fans and media, appears to be a crucially important part of the process of establishing and maintaining the self-images of young athletes. By the time they were in high school, most of the men interviewed for this study had found sports to be a primary means through which to establish a sense of manhood in the world. Especially if they were good athletes, the expectations of the crowd became very powerful and were internalized (and often *magnified*) within the young man's own expectations. As one man stated, by the time he was in high school, "it was *expected* of me to do well in all of my contests—I mean by my coach and my peers, and my family. So I in turn expected to do well, and if I didn't do well, then I'd be very disappointed."

When so much is tied to your performance, the dictum that "you are only as good as your last game" is a powerful judgment. It means that the young man must continually prove, achieve, and then *re*prove, and *re*achieve his status. As a result, many young athletes learn to seek and *need* the appreciation of the crowd to feel that they are worthy human beings. But the internalized values of masculinity along with the insecure nature of the sports world mean that the young man does *not* need the crowd to feel *bad* about himself. In fact, if one is insecure enough, even "success" and the compliments and attention of other people can come to feel hollow and meaningless. For instance, 48-year-old Russ Ellis in his youth shared the basic sense of insecurity common to all young males, and in his case it was probably compounded by his status as a poor black male and an insecure family life. Athletics emerged early in his life as the primary arena in which he and his male peers competed to establish a sense of self in the world. For Ellis, his small physical stature made it difficult to compete successfully in most sports, thus feeding his insecurity—he just never felt as though he belonged with "the big boys." Eventually, though, he became a top middle-distance runner. In high school, however: "Something began to happen there that later plagued me quite a bit. I started doing very well and winning lots of races and by the time the year was over, it was no longer a question for me of *placing*, but *winning*. That attitude really destroyed me ultimately. I would get into the blocks with worries that I wouldn't do well—the regular stomach problems—so I'd often run much less well than my abilities—that is, say, I'd take second or third."

Interestingly, his nervousness, fears, and anxieties did not seem to be visible to "the crowd": "I know in high school, certainly, they saw me as confident and ready to run. No one assumed I could be beaten, which fascinated me, because I had never been good at understanding how I was taken in other people's minds—maybe because I spent so much time inventing myself in their regard in my own mind. I was projecting my fear fantasies on them and taking them for reality."

In 1956 Ellis surprised everyone by taking second place in a world-class field of quarter-milers. But the fact that they ran the fastest time in the world, 46.5, seemed only to "up the ante," to increase the pressures on Ellis, then in college at UCLA.

> Up to that point I had been a nice zippy kid who did good, got into the *Daily Bruin* a lot, and was well-known on campus. But now an event would come up and the papers would say, "Ellis to face so-and-so." So rather than my being in the race, I *was* the race, as far as the press was concerned. And that put a lot of pressure on me that I never learned to handle. What I did was to internalize it, and then I'd sit there and fret and lose sleep, and focus more on not winning than on how I was doing. And in general, I didn't do badly—like one year in the NCAA's I took fourth—you know, in the *national finals*. But I was focused on winning. You know, later on, people would say, "Oh wow, you took fourth in the NCAA?—you were *that good?*" Whereas I thought of these things as *failures*, you know?

Finally, Ellis's years of training, hopes, and fears came to a head at the 1956 Olympic trials, where he failed to qualify, finishing fifth. A rival whom he used to defeat routinely won the event in the Melbourne Olympics as Ellis watched on television. "That killed me. Destroyed me. . . . I had the experience many times after that of digging down and finding that there was infinitely more down there than I ever got—I mean, I know that more than I know anything else. Sometimes I would really feel like an eagle, running. Sometimes in practice at UCLA running was just exactly like flying—and if I could have carried that attitude into events, I would have done much better. But instead, I'd worry. Yeah, I'd worry myself sick."

As suggested earlier, young males like Russ Ellis are "set up" for disappointment, or worse, by the disjuncture between the narrow Lombardian definition of success in the sports world and the reality that very few ever actually reach the top. The athlete's sense of identity established through sports is therefore insecure and problematic, *not simply* because of the high probability of "failure," but also because *success* in the sports world involves the development of a personality that *amplifies* many of the most ambivalent and destructive traits of traditional masculinity. Within the hierarchical world of sports, which in many ways mirrors the capitalist economy, one learns that if he is to survive and avoid being pushed off the ever-narrowing pyramid of success, he must develop certain kinds of relationships—to himself, to his body, to other people, and to the sport itself. In short, the successful athlete must develop a highly goal-oriented personality that encourages him to view his body as a tool, a machine, or even a weapon utilized to defeat an objectified opponent. He is likely to have difficulty establishing intimate and lasting friendships with other males because of low self-disclosure, homophobia, and cut-throat competition. And he is likely to view his public image as a "success" as far more basic and fundamental than any of his interpersonal relationships.

For most of the men interviewed, the quest for success was not the grim task it was for Russ Ellis. Most men did seem to get, at least for a time, a sense of identity (and even some happiness) out of their athletic accomplishments. The attention of the crowd, for many, affirmed their existence as males and was thus a clear motivating force. Gary Affonso, now 42 years old and a high school coach, explained that when he was in high school, he had an "intense desire to practice and compete." "I used to practice the high jump by myself for hours at a time—only got up to 5'3"—scissor! [*Laughs.*] But I think part of it was, the track itself was in view of some of the classrooms, and so as I think back now, maybe I did it for the attention, to be seen. In my freshman year, I chipped my two front teeth in a football game, and after that I always had a gold tooth, and I was always self-conscious about that. Plus I had my glasses, you know. I felt a little conspicuous." This simultaneous shyness, self-consciousness, and conspicuousness *along with* the strongly felt need for attention and external validation (attachment) so often characterize athletes' descriptions of themselves in boyhood and adolescence. The crowd, in this context, can act as a distant, and thus nonthreatening, source of attention and validation of self for the insecure male. Russ Ellis's story typifies that what sports seem to *promise* the young male—affirmation of self and connection with others—is likely to be *undermined* by the youth's actual experience in the sports world. The athletic experience also "sets men up" for another serious problem: the end of a career at a very young age.

DISENGAGEMENT TRAUMA: A CRISIS OF MALE IDENTITY

For some, the end of the athletic career approaches gradually like the unwanted houseguest whose eventual arrival is at least *known* and can be planned for, thus limiting the inevitable inconvenience. For others, the athletic career ends with the shocking suddenness of a violent thunderclap that rudely awakens one from a pleasant dream. But whether it comes gradually or suddenly, the end of the playing career represents the termination of what has often become the *central aspect* of a young male's individual life structure, thus initiating change and transition in the life course.

Previous research on the disengagement crises faced by many retiring athletes has focused on the health, occupational, and financial problems frequently faced by retiring professionals.[16] These problems are especially severe for retiring black athletes, who often have inadequate educational backgrounds and few opportunities within the sports world for media or coaching jobs.[17] But even for those retiring athletes who avoid the pitfalls of financial and occupational crises, substance abuse, obesity, and ill health, the end of the playing career usually involves a crisis of identity. This identity crisis is probably most acute for retiring *professional* athletes, whose careers are coming to an end right at an age when most men's careers are beginning to take off. As retired professional football player Marvin Upshaw stated, "You find yourself just scrambled. You don't know which way to go. Your light, as far as you're concerned, has been turned out. You miss the roar of the crowd. Once you've heard it, you can't get away from it. There's an empty feeling—you feel everything you wanted is gone. All of a sudden you wake up and you find yourself 29, 35 years old, you know, and the one thing that has been the major part of your life is gone. It's gone."

High school and college athletes also face serious and often painful adjustment periods when their career ends. Twenty-six-year-old Dave Joki had been a good high school basketball player, and had played a lot of ball in college. When interviewed, he was right in the middle of a confusing crisis of identity, closely related to his recent disengagement from viewing himself as an athlete.

> These past few months I've been trying a lot of different things, thinking about different careers, things to do. There's been quite a bit of stumbling—and I think that part of my tenuousness about committing myself to any one thing is I'm not sure I'm gonna get strokes if I go that way. *[Embarrassed, nervous laugh.]* It's scary for me and I stay away from searching for those reasons. . . . I guess you could say that I'm stumbling in my relationships too—stumbling in all parts of life. *[Laughs.]* I feel like I'm doing a lot but now knowing what I want.

Surely there is nothing unusual about a man in his mid-20s "stumbling" around and looking for direction in his work and his relationships. That is common for men of his age. But for the former athlete, this stumbling is often more confusing and problematic than for the other men precisely because he has lost the one activity through which he had built his sense of identity, however tenuous it may have been. The "strokes" he received from being a good athlete were his major psychological foundation. The interaction between self and other through which the athlete attempts to solidify his identity is akin to what Cooley called "the looking-glass self." If the athletic activity and the crowd can be viewed as the *mirror* into which the athlete gazes and, in Russ Ellis's words, "invents himself," we can begin to appreciate how devastating it can be when that looking-glass is suddenly and permanently *shattered*, leaving the young man alone, isolated, and disconnected. And since young men often feel comfortable exploring close friendships and intimate relationships only *after* they have established their separate work-related (or sports-related) positional identity, relationships with other people are likely to become more problematic than ever during disengagement.

WORK, LOVE, AND MALE IDENTITY
AFTER DISENGAGEMENT

Eventually, the former athlete must face reality: At a relatively young age, he has to start over. In the words of retired major-league baseball player Ray Fosse, "Now I gotta get on with the rest of it." How is "the rest of it" likely to take shape for the athlete after his career as a player is over? How do men who are "out of the limelight" for a few years come to define themselves as men? How do they define and redefine success? How do the values and attitudes they learned through sports affect their lives? How do their relationships with friends and family change over time?

Many retired athletes retain a powerful drive to reestablish the important relationship with the crowd that served as the primary basis for their identity for so long. Many men throw themselves wholeheartedly into a new vocation—or a confusing *series* of vocations—in a sometimes pathetic attempt to recapture the "high" of athletic competition as well as the status of the successful athlete in the community. For instance, 35-year-old Jackie Ridgle is experiencing what Daniel Levinson calls a "surge of masculine strivings" common to men in their mid-30s.[18] Once a professional basketball player, Ridgle seems motivated now by a powerful drive to be seen once again as "somebody" in the eyes of the public. When interviewed, he had recently been hired as an assistant college basketball coach, which made him feel like he again had a chance to "be somebody."

> When I say "successful," that means somebody that the public looks up to just as a basketball player. Yet you don't have to be playing basketball. You can be anybody: You can be a senator or a mayor, or any number of things. That's what I call successful. Success is recognition. Sure, I'm always proud of myself. But there's that little goal there that until people respect you, then—[*Snaps fingers.*] Anybody can say, "Oh, I know I'm the greatest thing in the world," but *people* run the world, and when *they* say you're successful, then you *know* you're successful.

Indeed men, especially men in early adulthood, usually define themselves primarily in terms of their position in the public world of work. Feminist literature often criticizes this establishment of male identity in terms of work-success as an expression of male privilege and ego satisfaction that comes at the expense of women and children. There is a great deal of truth to the feminist critique: A man's socially defined need to establish himself as "somebody" in the (mostly) male world of work is often accompanied by his frequent physical absence from home and his emotional distance from his family. Thus, while the man is "out there" establishing his "name" in public, the woman is usually home caring for the day-to-day and moment-to-moment needs of her family (regardless of whether or not she also has a job in the paid labor force). Tragically, only in midlife, when the children have already "left the nest" and the woman is often ready to go out into the public world, do some men discover the importance of connection and intimacy.

Yet the interviews indicate that there is not always such a clean and clear "before-after" polarity in the lives of men between work-success and care-intimacy. The "bread-winner ethic" as a male role *has* most definitely contributed to the perpetuation of male privilege and the subordination and economic dependence of women as mothers and housekeepers. But given the reality of the labor market, where women still make only 62 cents to the male dollar, many men feel very responsible for providing the majority of the income and financial security for their families. For instance, 36-year-old Ray Fosse, whose father left his family when he was quite young, has a very strong sense of commitment and responsibility as a provider of income and stability in his own family.

> I'm working an awful lot these days, and trying not to take time away from my family. A lot of times I'm putting the family to sleep, and working late hours and going to bed and getting up early and so forth. I've tried to tell my family this a lot of times: The work that I'm doing now is gonna make it easier in a few years. That's the reason I'm working now, to get that financial security, and I feel like it's coming very soon . . . but, uh, you know, you go a long day and you come home, and it's just not the quality time you'd like to have. And I think when that financial security comes in, then I'm gonna be able to forget about everything.

Jackie Ridgle's words mirror Fosse's. His two jobs and striving to be successful in the public world mean that he has little time to spend with his wife and three children. "I plan to someday. Very seldom do you have enough time to spend with your kids, especially nowadays, so I don't get hung up on that. The wife does sometimes, but as long as I keep a roof over their heads and let 'em know who's who, well, one day they'll respect me. But I can't just get bogged down and take any old job, you know, a filling station job or something. Ah, hell they'll get more respect, my kids for me, right now, than they would if I was somewhere just a regular worker."

Especially for men who have been highly successful athletes (and never have had to learn to "lose gracefully"), the move from sports to work-career as a means of establishing connection and identity in the world is a "natural" transition. Breadwinning becomes a man's socially learned means of seeking attachment, both with his family and, more abstractly, with "society." What is salient (and sometimes tragic) is that the care that a woman gives her family usually puts her into direct daily contact with her family's physical, psychological, and emotional needs. A man's care is usually expressed more abstractly, often in his absence, as his work removes him from day-to-day, moment-to-moment contact with his family.

A man may want, even *crave,* more direct connection with his family, but that connection, and the *time* it takes to establish and maintain it, may cause him to lose the competitive edge he needs to win in the world of work—and that is the arena in which he feels he will ultimately be judged in terms of his success or failure as a man. But it is not simply a matter of *time* spent away from family which is at issue here. As Dizard's research shows clearly, the more "success oriented" a man is, the more "instrumental" his personality will tend to be, thus increasing the psychological and emotional distance between himself and his family.[19]

CHANGING MEANINGS OF SUCCESS IN MIDLIFE

The intense, sometimes obsessive, early adulthood period of striving for work and career success that we see in the lives of Jackie Ridgle and Ray Fosse often begins to change in midlife, when many men experience what Levinson calls "detribalization." Here, the man "becomes more critical of the tribe, the particular groups, institutions, and traditions that have the greatest significance for him, the social matrix to which he is most attached. He is less dependent upon tribal rewards, more questioning of tribal values. . . . The result of this shift is normally not a marked disengagement from the external world but a greater integration of attachment and separateness."[20]

Detribalization—putting less emphasis on how one is defined by others and becoming more self-motivated and self-generating—is often accompanied by a growing sense of *flawed* or *qualified* success. A man's early adulthood dream of success begins to tarnish, appearing more and more as an illusion. Or, the success that a man *has* achieved begins to appear hollow and meaningless, possibly because it has not delivered the closeness he truly craves. The fading, or the loss, of the dream involves a process of mourning, but, as Levinson points out, it can also be a very liberating process in opening the man up for new experiences, new kinds of relationships, and new dreams.

For instance, Russ Ellis states that a few years ago he experienced a midlife crisis when he came to the realization that "I was never going to be on the cover of *Time.*" His wife had a T-shirt made for him with the message *Dare to Be Average* emblazoned on it.

> And it doesn't really *mean* dare to be average—it means dare to take the pressure off yourself, you know? Dare to be a normal person. It gets a funny reaction from people. I think it hits at that place where somehow we all think that we're going to wind up on the cover of *Time* or something, you know? Do you have that? That some day, somewhere, you're gonna be *great,* and everyone will know, everyone will recognize it? Now, I'd rather be great because I'm *good*—and maybe that'll turn into something that's acknowledged, but not at the headline level. I'm not racing so much; I'm concerned that my feet are planted on the ground and that I'm good.

[It sounds like you're running now, as opposed to racing?]

I guess—but running and racing have the same goals. *[Laughs, pauses, then speaks more thoughtfully.]* But maybe you're right—that's a wonderful analogy. Pacing myself. Running is more intelligent—more familiarity with your abilities, your patterns of workouts, who you're running against, the nature of the track, your position, alertness. You have more of an internal clock.

Russ Ellis's midlife detribalization—his transition from a "racer" to a runner"—has left him more comfortable with himself, with his abilities and limitations. He has also experienced an expansion of his ability to experience intimacy with a woman. He had never been comfortable with the "typical jock attitude" toward sex and women,

but I generally maintained a performance attitude about sex for a long time, which was not as enjoyable as it became after I learned to be more like what I thought a woman was like. In other words, when I let myself experience my own body, in a delicious and receptive way rather than in a power, overwhelming way. That was wonderful! *[Laughs.]* To experience my body as someone desired and given to. That's one of the better things. I think I only achieved that very profound intimacy that's found between people, really quite extraordinary, quite recently. *[Long pause.]* It's quite something, quite something. And I feel more fully inducted into the human race by knowing about that.

TOWARD A REDEFINITION OF SUCCESS AND MASCULINITY

"A man in America is a failed boy," wrote John Updike in 1960. Indeed, Updike's ex-athlete Rabbit Angstrom's struggles to achieve meaning and identity in midlife reflect a common theme in modern literature. Social scientific research has suggested that the contemporary sense of failure and inadequacy felt by many American males is largely the result of unrealistic and unachievable social definitions of masculinity and success.[21] This research has suggested that there is more to it than that. Contemporary males often feel empty, alienated, isolated, and as failures because the socially learned means through which they seek validation and identity (achievement in the public worlds of sports and work) do not deliver what is actually craved and needed: intimate connection and unity with other human beings. In fact, the lure of sports becomes a sort of trap. For boys who experience early success in sports, the resulting attention they receive becomes a convenient and attractive means of experiencing attachment with other people within a social context that allows the young male to maintain his "firm ego boundaries" and thus his separation from others. But it appears that, more often than not, athletic participation serves only to exacerbate the already problematic, insecure, and ambivalent nature of males' self-images, and thus their ability to establish and maintain close and intimate relationships with other people. Some men, as they reach midlife, eventually achieve a level of individuation—often through a midlife crisis—that leads to a redefinition of success and an expansion of their ability to experience attachment and intimacy.

Men's personal definitions of success often change in midlife, but this research, as well as that done by Farrell and Rosenberg,[22] suggests that only a *portion* of males experience a midlife crisis that results in the man's transcending his instrumental personality in favor of a more affective generativity. The midlife discovery that the achievement game is an unfulfilling rat race can as easily lead to cynical detachment and greater alienation as it can to detribalization and expanded relational capacities. In other words, there is no assurance that Jackie Ridgle, as he ages, will transform himself from a "racer" to a "runner," as Russ Ellis has. Even if he does change in this way, it is likely that he will have missed participating in the formative years of his children's lives.

Thus the fundamental questions facing future examinations of men's lives should focus on building and understanding of just what the keys are to such a shift at midlife. How are individual men's changes, crises, and relationships affected, shaped, and sometimes contradicted by the social, cultural, and political contexts in which they find themselves? And what *social* changes might make it more likely that boys and men might have more balanced personalities and needs at an *early* age?

An analysis of men's lives that simply describes personal changes while taking social structure as a given cannot adequately *ask* these questions. But an analysis that not only describes changes in male identity throughout the life course but also critically examines the socially structured and defined meaning of "masculinity" can and must ask these questions.

If many of the problems faced by all men (not just athletes) today are to be dealt with, class, ethnic, and sexual preference divisions must be confronted. This would necessarily involve the development of a more cooperative and nurturant ethic among men, as well as a more egalitarian and democratically organized economic system. And since the sports world is an important cultural process that serves, partly to socialize boys and young men to hierarchical, competitive, and aggressive values, the sporting arena is an important context in which to begin to confront the need for a humanization of men.

Yet, if the analysis presented here is correct, the developing psychology of young boys is predisposed to be attracted to the present structure and values of the sports world, so any attempt *simply* to infuse cooperative and egalitarian values into sports is likely to be an exercise in futility. The need for equality between men and women, in the public realm as well as in the home, is a fundamental prerequisite for the humanization of men, sports, and society. One of the most important changes that men could make would be to become more equally involved in parenting. The development of early bonding between fathers and infants (in addition to that between mothers and infants), along with nonsexist child rearing in the family, schools, and sports would have far-reaching effects on society: Boys and men could grow up more psychologically secure, more able to develop balance between separation and attachment, more able at an earlier age to appreciate intimate relationships with other men without destructive and crippling competition and homophobia. A young male with a more secure and balanced personality might also be able to *enjoy* athletic activities for what they really have to offer: the opportunity to engage in healthy exercise, to push oneself toward excellence, and to bond with others in a challenging and fun activity.

NOTES

1. J. Lever, "Sex Differences in the Games Children Play," *Social Problems* 23 (1976).

2. D. Sabo, "Sport Patriarchy and Male Identity: New Questions about Men and Sport," *Arena Review* 9, no. 2, 1985.

3. R. Sennett and J. Cobb, *The Hidden Injuries of Class* (New York: Random House, 1973); and L. B. Rubin, *Worlds of Pain: Life in the Working Class Family* (New York: Basic Books, 1976).

4. D. W. Ball, "Failure in Sport," *American Sociological Review* 41 (1976); J.J. Coakley, *Sports in Society* (St. Louis: Mosby, 1978); D. S. Harris and D. S. Eitzen, "The Consequences of Failure in Sport," *Urban Life* 7 (July 1978): 2; G. B. Leonard, "Winning Isn't Everything: It's Nothing," in *Jock: Sports and Male Identity*, ed. D. Sabo and R. Runfola (Englewood Cliffs, NJ: Prentice Hall, 1980); W. E. Schafer, "Sport and Male Sex Role Socialization," *Sport Sociology Bulletin* 4 (Fall 1975); R. C. Townsend, "The Competitive Male as Loser," in Sabo and Runfola, eds., *Jock;* and T. Tutko and W. Bruns, *Winning Is Everything and Other American Myths* (New York: Macmillan, 1976).

5. In contrast with the importance put on success by millions of boys, the number who "make it" is incredibly small. There are approximately 600 players in major-league baseball, with an average career span of 7 years. Approximately 6–7% of all high school football players ever play in college. Roughly 8% of all draft-eligible college football and basketball athletes are drafted by the pros, and only 2% ever sign a professional contract. The average career for NFL athletes is now 4 years, and for the NBA it is only 3.4 years. Thus the odds of getting anywhere *near* the top are very thin—and if one is talented and lucky enough to get there, his stay will be brief. See H. Edwards, "The Collegiate Athletic Arms Race: Origins and Implications of the 'Rule 48' Controversy," *Journal of Sport and Social Issues* 8, no. 1 (Winter–Spring 1984); Harris and Eitzen, "Consequences of Failure"; and P. Hill and B. Lowe, "The Inevitable Metathesis of the Retiring Athlete," *International Review of Sport Sociology* 9, nos. 3–4 (1978).

6. Schafer, "Sport and Male Sex Role," p. *50.*

7. C. Gilligan, *In a Different Voice: Psychological Theory and Women's Development* (Cambridge: Harvard University Press, 1982); J. Piaget, *The Moral Judgement of the Child* (New York: Free Press, 1965); and Lever, "Games Children Play."

8. P. G. Filene, *Him/Her/Self: Sex Roles in Modern America* (New York: Harcourt Brace Jovanovich, 1975).

9. J. Hantover, "The Boy Scouts and the Validation of Masculinity," *Journal of Social Issues* 34 (1978): 1.

10. J. L. Dubbert, *A Man's Place: Masculinity in Transition* (Englewood Cliffs, NJ: Prentice Hall, 1979).

11. A. Tolson, *The Limits of Masculinity* (New York: Harper and Row, 1977).

12. C. W. Mills, *White Collar* (London: Oxford University Press, 1951).

13. D.J. Levinson, *The Seasons of a Man's Life* (New York: Ballantine, 1978).

14. Ibid., p. 195.

15. N. Chodorow, *The Reproduction of Mothering* (Berkeley: University of California Press, 1978).

16. Hill and Lowe, "Metathesis of Retiring Athlete," pp. 3–4; and B. D. McPherson, "Former Professional Athletes' Adjustment to Retirement," *Physician and Sports Medicine* (August 1978).

17. Edwards, "Collegiate Athletic Arms Race."

18. Levinson, *Seasons of a Man's Life.*

19. J. E. Dizard, "The Price of Success," in *Social Change and the Family,* ed. J. E. Dizard (Chicago: Community and Family Study Center, University of Chicago, 1968).

20. Levinson, *Seasons of a Man's Life,* p. 242.

21. J. H. Pleck, *The Myth of Masculinity* (Cambridge: MIT Press, 1982); Sennett and Cobb, *The Hidden Injuries of Class;* Rubin, *Worlds of Pain;* and Tolson, *Limits of Masculinity.*

22. M. P. Farrell and S. D. Rosenberg, *Men at Midlife* (Boston: Auburn House, 1981).

* FOR FURTHER STUDY *

Acosta, R. Vivian, and Linda Jean Carpenter (annual report). "Women in Intercollegiate Sport," Department of Physical Education and Exercise Science, Brooklyn College.

Bryson, Lois. 1987. "Sport and the Maintenance of Masculine Hegemony," *Women's Studies International Forum 10* (1987)349–360.

Burstyn, Varda. 1999. *The Rites of Men: Manhood, Politics, and the Culture of Sport* (Toronto: University of Toronto Press).

Chronicle of Higher Education. 2002. "Gender Equity in College Sports: 6 Views," (December 6):B7–B10.

Conniff, Ruth. 1998. "The Joy of Women's Sports," *The Nation* (August 10/17):26–30.

Davis, Laurel R. 1997. *The Swimsuit Issue and Sport: Hegemonic Masculinity in Sports Illustrated* (Albany: State University of New York Press).

Eastman, Susan Tyler, and Andrew C. Billings. 1999. "Gender Parity in the Olympics: Hyping Women Athletes, Favoring Men Athletes," *Journal of Sport and Social Issues* 23 (May):140–170.

Hall, M. Ann. "The Discourse of Gender and Sport: From Femininity to Feminism," *Sociology of Sport Journal* 5 (1988):330–340.

Hargreaves, Jennifer. 2000. *Heroines of Sport: The Politics of Difference and Identity* (London: Routledge).

Higgs, Catriona T., Karen H. Weiller, and Scott B. Martin. 2003. "Gender Bias in the 1996 Olympic Games: A Comparative Analysis," *Journal of Sport & Social Issues* 27 (February):52–64.

Hogan, Jackie. 2003. "Staging a Nation: Gendered and Ethnicized Discourses of National Identity in Olympic Opening Ceremonies," *Journal of Sport & Social Issues* 27 (May): 100–123.

Klein, Alan. 1993. *Little Big Men: Bodybuilding Subculture and Gender Construction* (Albany: State University of New York Press).

Klein, Alan. (ed.). "The Macho World of Sport," *International Review for the Sociology of Sport* 25 (1990): entire issue.

Messner, Michael A. 1990. "Men Studying Masculinity: Some Epistemological Questions in Sport Sociology," *Sociology of Sport Journal* 7:136–153.

Messner, Michael A. 1992. *Power at Play: Sports and the Problem of Masculinity* (Boston: Beacon Press).

Messner, Michael A. 1996. "Studying Up on Sex," *Sociology of Sport Journal* 13:221–237.

Messner, Michael A., and Donald F. Sabo. *Sex, Violence & Power in Sports: Rethinking Masculinity* (Freedom CA: The Crossing Press).

Messner, Michael A. 2002. *Taking the Field: Women, Men, and Sports.* (Minneapolis: University of Minnesota Press).

Miller, Toby. 1998. "Commodifying the Male Body, Problematizing 'Hegemonic Masculinity?'" *Journal of Sport and Social Issues* 22 (November):431–447.

Nelson, Mariah Burton. 1994. *The Stronger Women Get, the More Men Love Football: Sexism and the American Culture of Sports* (New York: Harcourt Brace).

Nylund, David. 2003. "Taking a Slice at Sexism: The Controversy over the Exclusionary Membership Practices of the Augusta National Golf Club," *Journal of Sport & Social Issues* 27 (May):195–202.

Suggs, Welch. 2002. "Title IX at 30," *The Chronicle of Higher Education* (June 21). Online: *http//chronicle.com/free/v48/i41/41a03801.htm.*

Tucker, Lori W., and Janet B. Parks. 2001. "Effects of Gender and Sport Type on Intercollegiate Athletes' Perceptions of the Legitimacy of Aggressive Behaviors in Sport," *Sociology
of Sport Journal* 18 (4):403–413.

Wachs, Faye Linda. 2002. "Leveling the Playing Field: Negotiating Gendered Rules in Coed
Softball," *Journal of Sport & Social Issues* 26 (August): 300–316.

Weistart, John. 1998. "Title IX and Intercollegiate Sports: Equal Opportunity?" *Brookings
Review* 16 (Fall):39–43.

Zimbalist, Andrew. 2000. "Backlash Against Title IX: An End Run Around Female Athletes," *The Chronicle of Higher Education* (March 3):B9–B10.

PART ELEVEN

Structured Inequality: Sport and Sexuality

Previous sections on structured inequality examined categories of people designated as minorities in society because of their race/ethnicity or gender. The members of these social categories suffer from powerlessness, negative stereotypes, and discrimination. This unit looks at another type of minority group. Unlike the other three minorities, which are disadvantaged because of economic circumstances or ascribed characteristics, the distinguishing feature of the minority examined in this section—homosexuality—is the object of discrimination because it is defined by the majority as different and, therefore, deviant. It is important to underscore a crucial point: *Homosexuality is not inherently deviant, but it is defined and labeled as deviant.*[1] Put another way, "Variance from the societal norm of heterosexuality is not a social problem; *the societal response to it is.*"[2]

An estimated 14 million adults in the United States identify themselves as gay or lesbian. Among these are former elite athletes: Glenn Burke (major-league baseball), David Kopay (professional football), Greg Louganis and Tom Waddell (Olympians), and Martina Navratilova (tennis). Athletes who publicly acknowledge their homosexuality, however, are rare because of the extent of homophobia among athletes, coaches, fans, and the sports media.

> The extent of homophobia in the sports world is staggering: manifestations range from eight-year-old boys who put each other down with taunts of "queer," "faggot," or "sissy" to high-school locker-room boasting (and, often, lying) about sexual conquests of females, and to college athletes bonding together with a little Saturday night "queer-bashing." To be suspected of being gay, and to be unable to prove one's heterosexual status in the sports world, is clearly not acceptable—indeed, it can be downright dangerous.[3]

313

Women in sport, more than men, endure intense scrutiny about their sexual identities.[4] This is the subject of the first selection, by Pat Griffin, as she discusses (1) the political functions of homophobia in a sexist and heterosexist culture, (2) the manifestations of homophobia in women's sport, (3) the beliefs that support homophobia in women's sport, and (4) strategies for confronting homophobia in women's sport.

The second chapter, by Brian Pronger, focuses on gay men and sport. Pronger's thesis is that since sport for men is overwhelmingly masculine and heterosexual, gay men are often estranged from sport. Team sports are especially difficult for gay men because of the male bonding rituals including "gay bashing" and contrived machismo with its emphasis on toughness and the sexual conquest of women.

The next chapter, by scholar Peter Dreier, makes the case that by 2010 there will be an openly gay major-league baseball player.

NOTES

1. D. Stanley Eitzen and Maxine Baca Zinn, *Social Problems,* 8th ed. (Boston: Allyn & Bacon, 2000), p. 283.

2. Ibid., p. 290.

3. Michael A. Messner. "AIDS, Homophobia, and Sports." In Michael A. Messner and Donald F. Sabo, *Sex, Violence & Power in Sports: Rethinking Masculinity* (Freedom, California: The Crossing Press, 1994), p. 121.

4. See Debra E. Blum, "College Sports' L-Word," *Chronicle of Higher Education* (March 9, 1994): A35–A36.

33

Changing the Game

Homophobia, Sexism, and Lesbians in Sport

Pat Griffin

Throughout the history of Western culture, restrictions have been placed on women's sport participation. These restrictions are enforced through sanctions that evolved to match each successive social climate. Women caught merely observing the male athletes competing in the early Greek Olympic Games were put to death. When Baron DeCoubertin revived the Olympic tradition in 1896, women were invited as spectators but barred from participation. Even in the present-day Olympic Games, women may compete in only one-third of the events.

Although the death penalty for female spectators was too extreme for the late 19th and early 20th centuries, an increasingly influential medical establishment warned white upper-class women about the debilitating physiological effects of vigorous athleticism, particularly on the reproductive system. Women were cautioned about other "masculinizing effects" as well, such as deeper voices, facial hair, and overdeveloped arms and legs. The intent of these warnings was to temper and control women's sport participation and to keep women focused on their "natural" and "patriotic" roles as wives and mothers (Lenskyj, 1986).

During the 1920s and 1930s, as the predicted dire physical consequences proved untrue, strong social taboos restricting female athleticism evolved. Instead of warnings about facial hair and displaced uteruses, women in sport were intimidated by fears of losing social approval. Close female friendships, accepted and even idealized in the 19th century, became suspect when male sexologists like Freud "discovered"

Source: Reprinted by permission from P. Griffin, 1992, "Changing the Game: Homophobia, Sexism, and Lesbians in Sport" *Quest* 44(2), pp. 251–265.

female sexuality in the early 20th century (Faderman, 1981, 1991; Katz, 1976). In the 1930s, as psychology and psychiatry became respected subfields in medicine, these doctors warned of a new menace. An entire typology was created to diagnose the "mannish lesbian," whose depraved sexual appetite and preference for masculine dress and activity were identified as symptoms of psychological disturbance (Newton, 1989). Social commentators in the popular press warned parents about the dangers of allowing impressionable daughters to spend time in all-female environments (Faderman, 1991; Smith-Rosenberg, 1989).

As a result, women's colleges and sports teams were assumed to be places where mannish lesbians lurked. Women in sport and physical education especially fit the profile of women to watch out for: they were in groups without men, they were not engaged in activities thought to enhance their abilities to be good wives and mothers, and they were being physically active in sport, a male activity. Because lesbians were assumed to be masculine creatures who rejected their female identity and roles as wives and mothers, athletic women became highly suspect.

The image of the sick, masculine lesbian sexual predator and her association with athleticism persists in the late 20th century. The power of this image to control and intimidate women is as strong today as it was 60 years ago. What accounts for the staying power of a stereotype that is so extreme it should be laughable except that so many people believe it to be accurate? Whose interests are served by stigmatizing lesbians and accusing women in sport of being lesbians? Why does sport participation by women in the late 20th century continue to be so threatening to the social order? How have women in sport responded to associations with lesbians? How effective have these responses been in defusing concern about lesbians in sport?

The purpose of this chapter is to discuss the issue of lesbians in sport from a feminist perspective that analyzes the function of socially constructed gender roles and sexual identities in maintaining male dominance in North American society. I share the perspective taken by other sport feminists that lesbian and feminist sport participation is a threat to male domination (Bennett, Whitaker, Smith, & Sablove, 1987; Birrell & Richter, 1987; Hall, 1987; Lenskyj, 1986; Messner & Sabo, 1990). In a sexist and heterosexist society (in which heterosexuality is reified as the only normal, natural, and acceptable sexual orientation), women who defy the accepted feminine role or reject a heterosexual identity threaten to upset the imbalance of power enjoyed by white heterosexual men in a patriarchal society (Bryson, 1987). The creation of the mannish lesbian as a pathological condition by early 20th-century male medical doctors provided an effective means to control all women and neutralize challenges to the sexist status quo.

To understand the social stigma associated with lesbian participation in sport, the function of homophobia in maintaining the sexist and heterosexist status quo must be examined (Lenskyj, 1991). Greendorfer (1991) challenged the traditional definition of homophobia as an irrational fear and intolerance of lesbians and gay men. In questioning how irrational homophobia really is, Greendorfer highlighted the systematic and pervasive cultural nature of homophobia. Fear and hatred of lesbians and gay men is more than individual prejudice (Kitzinger, 1987). Homophobia is a powerful political weapon of sexism (Pharr, 1988). The lesbian label is used to define the boundaries of acceptable female behavior in a patriarchal culture: When a woman is called a lesbian, she knows she is out of bounds. Because lesbian identity carries the extreme negative social stigma created by early 20th-century sexologists, most women are loathe to be associated with it. Because women's sport has been labeled a lesbian activity, women in sport are particularly sensitive and vulnerable to the use of the lesbian label to intimidate.

HOW IS HOMOPHOBIA MANIFESTED IN WOMEN'S SPORT?

Manifestations of homophobia in women's sport can be divided into six categories: (a) silence, (b) denial, (c) apology, (d) promotion of a heterosexy image, (e) attacks on lesbians, and (f) preference for male coaches. An exploration of these manifestations illuminates the pervasive nature of prejudice against lesbians in sport and the power of the lesbian stigma to control and marginalize women's sport.

Silence

Silence is the most consistent and enduring manifestation of homophobia in women's sport. From Billie Jean King's revelation of a lesbian relationship in 1981 to the publicity surrounding Penn State women's basketball coach Rene Portland's no-lesbian policy (Lederman, 1991; Longman, 1991), the professional and college sports establishment responds with silence to eruptions of public attention to lesbians in sport. Reporters who attempt to discuss lesbians in sport with sport organizations, athletic directors, coaches, and athletes are typically rebuffed (Lipsyte, 1991), and women in sport wait, hoping the scrutiny will disappear as quickly as possible. Women live in fear that whatever meager gains we have made in sport are always one lesbian scandal away from being wiped out.

Even without the provocation of public scrutiny or threat of scandal, silent avoidance is the strategy of choice. Organizers of coaches' or athletic administrators' conferences rarely schedule programs on homophobia in sport, and when they do, it is always a controversial decision made with fear and concern about the consequences of public dialogue (Krebs, 1984; Lenskyj, 1990). Lesbians in sport are treated like nasty secrets that must be kept locked tightly in the closet. Lesbians, of course, are expected to maintain deep cover at all times. Not surprisingly, most lesbians in sport choose to remain hidden rather than face potential public condemnation. Friends of lesbians protect this secret from outsiders, and the unspoken pact of silence is maintained and passed on to each new generation of women in sport.

Silence has provided some protection. Keeping the closet door locked is an understandable strategy when women in sport are trying to gain social approval in a sexist society and there is no sense that change is possible. Maintaining silence is a survival strategy in a society hostile to women in general and lesbians in particular. How effectively silence enhances sport opportunities for women or defuses homophobia, however, is open to serious question.

Denial

If forced to break silence, many coaches, athletic directors, and athletes resort to denial. High school athletes and their parents often ask college coaches if there are lesbians in their programs. In response, many coaches deny that there are lesbians in sport, at least among athletes or coaches at *their* schools (Fields, 1983). These denials only serve to intensify curiosity and determination to find out who and where these mysterious women are. The closet, it turns out, is made of glass: People know lesbians are in sport despite these denials.

In some cases, parents and athletes who suspect that a respected and loved coach is a lesbian either deny or overlook her sexual identity because they cannot make sense of the apparent contradiction: a lesbian who is competent, loved, and respected. In other instances, a respected lesbian coach is seen as an exception because she does not fit the unflattering lesbian stereotype most people accept as accurate. The end result in any case is to deny the presence of lesbians in sport.

Apology

The third manifestation of homophobia in sport is apology (Felshin, 1974). In an attempt to compensate for an unsavory reputation, women in sport try to promote a feminine image and focus public attention on those who meet white heterosexual standards of beauty. Women in sport have a tradition of assuring ourselves and others that sport participation is consistent with traditional notions of femininity and that women are not masculinized by sport experiences (Gornick, 1971; Hicks, 1979; Locke & Jensen, 1970). To this end, athletes are encouraged, or required in some cases, to engage in the protective camouflage of feminine drag. Professional athletes and college teams are told to wear dresses or attend seminars to learn how to apply makeup, style hair, and select clothes ("Image Lady," 1987). Athletes are encouraged to be seen with boyfriends and reminded to act like ladies when away from the gym (DePaul University's 1984 women's basketball brochure).

The Women's Sports Foundation (WSF) annual dinner, attended by many well-known professional and amateur female athletes, is preceded by an opportunity for the athletes to get free hairstyling and makeup applications before they sit down to eat with the male corporate sponsors, whose money supports many WSF programs. The men attending the dinner are not offered similar help with their appearance. The message is that female athletes in their natural state are not acceptable or attractive and therefore must be fixed and "femmed up" to compensate for their athleticism.

Femininity, however, is a code word for heterosexuality. The underlying fear is not that a female athlete or coach will appear too plain or out of style; the real fear is that she will look like a dyke or, even worse, is one. This intense blend of homophobic and sexist standards of feminine attractiveness remind women in sport that to be acceptable, we must monitor our behavior and appearance at all times.

Silence, denial, and apology are defensive reactions that reflect the power of the lesbian label to intimidate women. These responses ensure that women's sport will be held hostage to the *L* word. As long as questions about lesbians in sport are met with silence, denial, and apology, women can be sent scurrying back to our places on the margins of sport, grateful for the modicum of public approval we have achieved and fearful of losing it.

NEW MANIFESTATIONS OF HOMOPHOBIA IN WOMEN'S SPORT

In the past 10 years, three more responses have developed in reaction to the persistence of the association of sport with lesbians. These manifestations have developed at the same time that women's sport has become more visible, potentially marketable, and increasingly under the control of men and men's sport organizations. Representing an intensified effort to purge the lesbian image, these new strategies reflect a new low in mean-spirited intimidation.

Promotion of a Heterosexy Image

Where presenting a feminine image previously sufficed, corporate sponsors, professional women's sport organizations, some women's college teams, and individual athletes have moved beyond presenting a feminine image to adopting a more explicit display of heterosex appeal. The Ladies Professional Golf Association's 1989 promotional material featured photographs of its pro golfers posing pin-up style in swimsuits (Diaz, 1989). College sport promotional literature has employed double entendres and sexual innuendo to sell women's teams. The women's basketball promotional brochure from Northwestern State University of Louisiana included a photograph of the women's team dressed in Playboy bunny outfits. The copy crowed "These girls can play, boy!" and invited basketball fans to watch games in the "Pleasure Palace" (Solomon, 1991). Popular magazines have featured young, professional female athletes, like Monica Seles or Steffi Graf, in cleavage-revealing heterosexual glamour drag (Kiersh, 1990).

In a more muted attempt to project a heterosexual image, stories about married female athletes and coaches routinely include husbands and children in ways rarely seen when male coaches and athletes are profiled. A recent nationally televised basketball game between the women's teams from the University of Texas and the University of Tennessee featured a half-time profile of the coaches as wives and mothers. The popular press also brings us testimonials from female athletes who have had children claiming that their athletic performance has improved since becoming mothers. All of this to reassure the public, and perhaps ourselves as women in sport, that we are normal despite our athletic interests.

Attacks on Lesbians in Sport

Women in sport endure intense scrutiny of our collective and individual femininity and sexual identities. Innuendo, concern, and prurient curiosity about the sexual identity of female coaches and athletes come from coaches, athletic directors, sports reporters, parents of female athletes, teammates, fans, and the general public (South, Glynn, Rodack, & Capettini, 1990). This manifestation of homophobia is familiar to most people associated with women's sport. Over the last 10 to 12 years, however, concern about lesbians in sport has taken a nasty turn.

Though lesbians in sport have always felt pressure to stay closeted, coaches and athletic directors now openly prohibit lesbian coaches and athletes (Brownworth, 1991; Figel, 1986; Longman, 1991). In a style reminiscent of 1950s McCarthyism, some coaches proclaim their antilesbian policies as an introduction to their programs. Athletes thought to be lesbian are dropped from teams, find themselves benched, or are suddenly ostracized by coaches and teammates (Brownworth, 1991). Coaches impose informal quotas on the number of lesbians, or at least on the number of athletes they think look like lesbians, on their teams (Brownworth, 1991). At some schools, a new coach's heterosexual credentials are scrutinized as carefully as her professional qualifications (Fields, 1983). Coaches thought to be lesbians are fired or intimidated into resigning. These dismissals are not the result of any unethical behavior on the part of the women accused but happen simply because of assumptions made about their sexual identity.

Collegiate and high school female athletes endure lesbian-baiting (name-calling, taunting, and other forms of harassment) from male athletes, heterosexual teammates, opposing teams, spectators, classmates, and sometimes their own coaches (Brownworth, 1991; Fields, 1983; Spander, 1991; Thomas, 1990). Female coaches thought to be lesbians endure harassing phone calls and antilesbian graffiti slipped under their office doors. During a recent National Collegiate Athletic Association (NCAA) women's basketball championship, it was rumored that a group of male coaches went to the local lesbian bar to spy on lesbian coaches who might be there. Another rumor circulated about a list categorizing Division I women's basketball coaches by their sexual identity so that parents of prospective athletes could use this information to avoid schools where lesbians coach. Whether or not these rumors are true doesn't matter: The rumor itself is intimidating enough to remind women in sport that we are being watched and that if we step out of line, we will be punished.

Negative recruiting is perhaps the most self-serving of all the attacks on lesbians in sport. Negative recruiting occurs when college coaches or athletic department personnel reassure prospective athletes and their parents not only that there are no lesbians in this program but also that there *are* lesbians in a rival school's program (Fields, 1983). By playing on parents' and athletes' fear and ignorance, these coaches imply that young women will be safe in their programs but not at a rival school where bull dykes stalk the locker room in search of fresh young conquests.

Fears about lesbian stereotypes are fueled by a high-profile Christian presence at many national championships and coaches' conferences. The Fellowship of Christian Athletes, which regularly sponsors meal functions for coaches at these events, distributed a free antihomosexual booklet to coaches and athletes. Entitled *Emo-*

tional Dependency: A Threat to Close Friendships, this booklet plays into all of the stereotypes of lesbians (Rentzel, 1987). A drawing of a sad young woman and an older woman on the cover hints at the dangers of close female friendships. Unencumbered by any reasonable factual knowledge about homosexuality, the booklet identifies the symptoms of emotional dependency and how this "leads" to homosexual relationships. Finally, the path out of this "counterfeit" intimacy through prayer and discipline is described. The booklet is published by Exodus, a fundamentalist Christian organization devoted to the "redemption" of homosexuals from their "disorder."

By allowing the active participation of antigay organizations in coaches' meetings and championship events, sport governing bodies like the NCAA and the Women's Basketball Coaches' Association are taking an active role in the perpetuation of discrimination against lesbians in sport and the stigmatization of all friendships among women in sport. In this intimidating climate, all women in sport must deal with the double burden of maintaining high-profile heterosexual images and living in terror of being called lesbians.

Preference for Male Coaches

Many parents, athletes, and athletic administrators prefer that men coach women's teams. This preference reflects a lethal mix of sexism and homophobia. Some people believe, based on gender and lesbian stereotypes, that men are better coaches than women. Although a recent NCAA survey of female athletes (NCAA, 1991) indicated that 61% of the respondents did not have a gender preference for their coaches, respondents were concerned about the images they thought male and female coaches had among their friends and family: 65% believed that female coaches were looked upon favorably by family and friends whereas 84% believed that male coaches were looked on favorably by family and friends.

Recent studies have documented the increase in the number of men coaching women's teams (Acosta & Carpenter, 1988). At least part of this increase can be attributed to homophobia. Thorngren (1991), in a study of female coaches, asked respondents how homophobia affected them. These coaches identified hiring and job retention as problems. They cited examples where men were hired to coach women's teams specifically to change a tarnished or negative (read *lesbian*) team image. Thorngren described this as a "cloaking" phenomenon, in which a team's lesbian image is hidden or countered by the presence of a male coach. Consistent with this perception, anecdotal reports from other female head coaches reveal that some believe it essential to hire a male assistant coach to lend a heterosexual persona to a women's team. The coaches in Thorngren's study also reported that women (married and single) leave coaching because of the pressure and stress of constantly having to deal with lesbian labels and stereotypes. Looking at the increase in the number of men coaching women's teams over the last 10 years, it is clear how male coaches have benefitted from sexism and homophobia in women's sport.

SUSPICION, COLLUSION, AND BETRAYAL AMONG WOMEN IN SPORT

The few research studies addressing homophobia or lesbians in sport, as well as informal anecdotal information, have revealed that many women have internalized sexist and homophobic values and beliefs (Blinde, 1990; Griffin, 1987; Guthrie, 1982; Morgan, 1990; Thorngren, 1990, 1991; Woods, 1990). Blinde interviewed women athletes about the pressures and stress they experienced. Many talked about the lesbian image women's sport has and the shame they felt about being female athletes because of that image. Their discomfort with the topic was illustrated by their inability to even say the word *lesbian.* Instead, they made indirect references to it as a problem. Athletes talked in ways that clearly indicated they had bought into the negative images of lesbians, even as they denied that there were lesbians on their teams. These athletes also subscribed to the importance of projecting a feminine image and were discomforted by female athletes who didn't look or act feminine.

Quotes selected to accompany the NCAA survey and the Blinde study illustrate the degree to which many female athletes and coaches accept both the negative stigma attached to lesbian identity and the desirability of projecting a traditionally feminine image:

> The negative image of women in intercollegiate sport scares me. I've met too many lesbians in my college career. I don't want to have that image. (NCAA, 1991)

> Well, if you come and look at our team, I mean, if you saw Jane Doe, she's very pretty. If she walks down the street, everybody screams, you know, screams other things at her. But because she's on the field, it's dykes on spikes. If that isn't a stereotype, then who knows what is. (Blinde, p. 12)

> Homosexual females in this profession [coaching] definitely provide models and guidance in its worst for female athletes. I'd rather see a straight male coach females than a gay women. Homosexual coaches are killing us. (NCAA, 1991)

> I don't fit the stereotype. I mean the stereotype based around women that are very masculine and strong and athletic. I wouldn't say I'm pretty in pink, but I am feminine and I appear very feminine and I act that way. (Blinde, p. 12)

These attempts to distance oneself from the lesbian image and to embrace traditional standards of femininity set up a division among women in sport that can devastate friendships among teammates, poison coach-athlete relationships, and taint feelings about one's identity as an athlete and a woman. Some women restrict close friendships with other women to avoid the possibility that someone might think they are lesbians. Other women consciously cultivate high-profile heterosexual images by talking about their relationships with men and being seen with men as often as possible. As long as our energy is devoted to trying to fit into models of athleticism, gender, and sexuality that support a sexist and heterosexist culture, women in sport can be controlled by anyone who chooses to use our fears and insecurities against us.

UNDERLYING BELIEFS THAT KEEP WOMEN IN SPORT FROM CHALLENGING HOMOPHOBIA

The ability to understand the staying power of the lesbian stigma in sport is limited by several interconnected beliefs. An examination of these beliefs can reveal how past responses in dealing with lesbians in sport have reinforced the power of the lesbian label to intimidate and control.

A Woman's Sexual Identity Is Personal

This belief is perhaps the biggest obstacle to understanding women's oppression in a patriarchal culture (Kitzinger, 1987). As long as a women's sexual identity is seen as solely a private issue, how the lesbian label is used to intimidate all women and to weaken women's challenges to male-dominated institutions will never be understood. The lesbian label is a political weapon that can be used against any woman who steps out of line. Any woman who defies traditional gender roles is called a lesbian. Any woman who chooses a male-identified career is called a lesbian. Any woman who chooses not to have a sexual relationship with a man is called a lesbian. Any woman who speaks out against sexism is called a lesbian. As long as women are afraid to be called lesbians, this label is an effective tool to control all women and limit women's challenges to sexism. Although lesbians are the targets of attack in women's sport, all women in sport are victimized by the use of the lesbian label to intimidate and control.

When a woman's lesbian identity is assumed to be a private matter, homophobia and heterosexism are dismissed. The implication is that these matters are not appropriate topics for professional discussion. As a result, the fear, prejudice, and outright discrimination that thrive in silence are never addressed. A double standard operates, however, for lesbians and heterosexual women in sport. Although open acknowledgment of lesbians in sport is perceived as an inappropriate flaunting of personal life (what you do in the privacy of your home is none of my business), heterosexual women are encouraged to talk about their relationships with men, their children, and their roles as mothers.

Magazine articles about such heterosexual athletes as Chris Evert Mill, Florence Griffiths Joyner, Jackie Joyner Kersey, Joan Benoit, Nancy Lopez, and Mary Decker Slaney have often focused on their weddings, their husbands, or their children. Heterosexual professional athletes are routinely seen celebrating victories by hugging or kissing their husbands, but when Martina Navratilova went into the stands to hug *her* partner after winning the 1990 Wimbledon Championship, she was called a bad role model by former champion Margaret Court. Although heterosexual athletes and coaches are encouraged to display their personal lives to counteract the lesbian image in sport, lesbians are intimidated into invisibility for the same reason.

Claiming to Be Feminist Is Tantamount to Claiming to Be Lesbian

Claiming to be feminist is far too political for many women in sport. To successfully address the sexism and heterosexism in sport, however, women must begin to understand the necessity of seeing homophobia as a political issue and claim feminism as the unifying force needed to bring about change in a patriarchal culture. Part of the reluctance to embrace the feminist label is that feminists have been called lesbians in the same way that female athletes have and for the same reason: to intimidate women and prevent them from challenging the sexist status quo. Women in sport are already intimidated by the lesbian label. For many women, living with the athlete, lesbian, and feminist labels is stigma overload.

By accepting the negative stereotypes associated with these labels, women in sport collude in our own oppression. Rather than seeking social approval as a marginal part of sport in a sexist and heterosexist society, we need to be working for social change and control over our sport destinies. The image of an unrepentant lesbian feminist athlete is a patriarchal nightmare. She is a woman who has discovered her physical and political strength and who refuses to be intimidated by labels. Unfortunately, this image scares women in sport as much as it does those who benefit from the maintenance of the sexist and heterosexist status quo.

The Problem Is Lesbians in Sport Who Call Attention to Themselves

People who believe this assume that as long as lesbians are invisible, our presence will be tolerated and women's sport will progress. The issue for these people is not that there are lesbians in sport but how visible we are. Buying into silence this way has never worked. Other than Martina Navratilova, lesbians in sport are already deeply closeted (Bull, 1991; Muscatine, 1991). This careful camouflage of lesbians has not made women's sport less suspect or less vulnerable to intimidation. Despite efforts to keep the focus on the pretty ones or the ones with husbands and children, women in sport still carry the lesbian stigma into every gym and onto every playing field.

Women in sport must begin to understand that it wouldn't matter if there were no lesbians in sport. The lesbian label would still be used to intimidate and control women's athletics. The energy expended in making lesbians invisible and projecting a happy heterosexual image keeps women in sport fighting among ourselves rather than confronting the heterosexism and sexism that our responses unintentionally serve.

Lesbians Are Bad Role Models and Sexual Predators

This belief buys into all the unsavory lesbian stereotypes left over from the late 19th-century medical doctors who made homosexuality pathological and the early 20th-century sexologists who made female friendships morbid. In reality, there are already numerous closeted lesbians in sport who are highly admired role models. It is the perversity of prejudice that merely knowing about the sexual identity of these admired women instantly turns them into unfit role models.

The sexual-predator stereotype is a particularly pernicious slander on lesbians in sport (South et al., 1990). There is no evidence that lesbians are sexual predators. In fact, statistics on sexual harassment, rape, sexual abuse, and other forms of violence and intimidation show that these offenses are overwhelmingly heterosexual male assaults against women and girls. If we need to be concerned about sexual offenses among coaches or athletes, a better case could be made that it is heterosexual men who should be watched carefully. Blinde (1989) reported that many female athletes, like their male counterparts, are subjected to academic, physical, social, and emotional exploitation by their coaches. When men coach women in a heterosexist and sexist culture, there is the additional potential for sexual and gender-based exploitation when the unequal gender dynamics in the larger society are played out in the coach-athlete relationship.

It is difficult to imagine anyone in women's sport, regardless of sexual identity, condoning coercive sexual relationships of any kind. Even consensual sexual relationships between coaches and athletes involve inherent power differences that make such relationships questionable and can have a negative impact on the athlete as well as on the rest of the team. This kind of behavior should be addressed regardless of the gender or sexual identity of the coaches and athletes involved instead of assuming that lesbian athletes or coaches present a greater problem than others.

Being Called Lesbian or Being Associated with Lesbians Is the Worst Thing That Can Happen in Women's Sport

As long as women in sport buy into the power of the lesbian label to intimidate us, we will never control our sport experience. Blaming lesbians for women's sports' bad image and failure to gain more popularity divides women and keeps us fighting among ourselves. In this way, we collude in maintaining our marginal status by keeping alive the power of the lesbian label to intimidate women into silence, betrayal, and denial. This keeps our energies directed inward rather that outward at the sexism that homophobia serves. Blaming lesbians keeps all women in their place, scurrying to present an image that is acceptable in a sexist and heterosexist society. This keeps our attention diverted from asking other questions: Why are strong female athletes and coaches so threatening to a patriarchal society? Whose interests are served by trivializing and stigmatizing women in sport?

Women in sport need to redefine the problem. Instead of naming and blaming lesbians in sport as the problem, we need to focus our attention on sexism, heterosexism, and homophobia. As part of this renaming process, we need to take the sting out of the lesbian label. Women in sport must stop jumping to the back of the closet and slamming the door every time someone calls us dykes. We need to challenge the use of the lesbian label to intimidate all women in sport.

Women's Sport Can Progress without Dealing with Homophobia

If progress is measured by the extent to which we, as women in sport, control our sporting destinies, take pride in our athletic identities, and tolerate diversity among ourselves, then we are no better off now than we ever have been. We have responded to questions about lesbians in sport with silence, denial, and apology. When these responses fail to divert attention away from the lesbian issue, we have promoted a heterosexy image, attacked lesbians, and hired male coaches. All of these responses call on women to accommodate, assimilate, and collude with the values of a sexist and heterosexist society. All require compromise and deception. The bargain struck is that in return for our silence and our complicity, we are allowed a small piece of the action in a sports world that has been defined by men to serve male-identified values.

We have never considered any alternatives to this cycle of silence, denial, and apology to the outside world while policing the ranks inside. We have never looked inside ourselves to understand our fear and confront it. We have never tried to analyze the political meaning of our fear. We have never stood up to the accusations and threats that keep us in our place.

What do we have to pass on to the next generation of young girls who love to run and throw and catch? What is the value of nicer uniforms, a few extra tournaments, and occasional pictures in the back of the sports section if we can't pass on a sport experience with less silence and fear?

STRATEGIES FOR CONFRONTING HOMOPHOBIA IN WOMEN'S SPORT

What, then, are the alternatives to silence, apology, denial, promoting a heterosexy image, attacking lesbians, and hiring male coaches? How can women in sport begin confronting homophobia rather than perpetuating it? If our goal is to defuse the lesbian label and to strip it of its power to intimidate women in sport, then we must break the silence, not to condemn lesbians but to condemn those who use the lesbian label to intimidate. Our failure to speak out against homophobia signals our consent to the fear, ignorance, and discrimination that flourish in that silence. If our goal is to create a vision of sport in which all women have an opportunity to proudly claim their athletic identity and control their athletic experience, then we must begin to build that future now.

Institutional Policy

Sport-governing organizations and school athletic departments need to enact explicit nondiscrimination and anti-harassment policies that include sexual orientation as a protected category. This is a first step in establishing an organizational climate in which discrimination against lesbians (or gay men) is not tolerated. Most sport governing organizations have not instituted such policies and, when asked by reporters if they are planning to, avoid taking a stand (Brownworth, 1991; Longman, 1991). In addition to nondiscrimination policies, professional standards of conduct for coaches must be developed that outline behavioral expectations regardless of gender or sexual orientation. Sexual harassment policies and the procedures for filing such complaints must be made clear to coaches, athletes, and administrators. As with standards of professional conduct, these policies should apply to everyone.

Education

Everyone associated with physical education and athletics must learn more about homophobia, sexism, and heterosexism. Conferences for coaches, teachers, and administrators should include educational programs focused on understanding homophobia and developing strategies for addressing homophobia in sport.

Athletic departments must sponsor educational programs for athletes that focus not only on homophobia but on other issues of social diversity as well. Because prejudice and fear affect the quality of athletes' sport experience and their relationships with teammates and coaches, educational programs focused on these issues are appropriate for athletic department sponsorship and should be an integral part of the college athletic experience.

Visibility

One of the most effective tools in counteracting homophobia is increased lesbian and gay visibility. Stereotypes and the fear and hatred they perpetuate will lose their power as more lesbian and gay people in sport disclose their identities. Although some people will never accept diversity of sexual identity in sport or in the general population, research indicates that, for most people, contact with "out" lesbian and gay people who embrace their sexual identities reduces prejudice (Herek, 1985).

The athletic world desperately needs more lesbian and gay coaches and athletes to step out of the closet. So far only a handful of athletes or coaches, most notably Martina Navratilova, have had the courage to publicly affirm their lesbian or gay identity (Brown, 1991; Brownworth, 1991; Bull, 1991; Burke, 1991; Muscatine, 1991). The generally accepting, if not warm, reaction of tennis fans to Navratilova's courage and honesty should be encouraging to the many closeted lesbian and gay people in sport. Unfortunately, the fear that keeps most lesbian and gay sports people in the closet is not ungrounded: Coming out as a lesbian or gay athlete or coach is a risk in a heterosexist and sexist society (Brown, 1991; Brownworth, 1991; Burton-Nelson, 1991; Hicks, 1979; Muscatine, 1991). The paradox is that more lesbian and gay people need to risk coming out if homosexuality is to be demystified in North American society.

Another aspect of visibility is the willingness of heterosexual athletes and coaches, as allies of lesbian and gay people, to speak out against homophobia and heterosexism. In the same way that it is important for white people to speak out against racism and for men to speak out against sexism, it is important for heterosexual people to object to antigay harassment, discrimination, and prejudice. It isn't enough to provide silent, private support for lesbian friends. To remain silent signals consent. Speaking out against homophobia is a challenge for heterosexual women in sport that requires them to understand how homophobia is used against them as well as against lesbians. Speaking out against homophobia also requires that heterosexual women confront their own discomfort with being associated with lesbians or being called lesbian, because that is what will happen when they speak out: The lesbian label will be used to try and intimidate them back into silence.

Solidarity

Heterosexual and lesbian women must understand that the only way to overcome homophobia, heterosexism, and sexism in sport is to work in coalition with each other. As long as fear and blame prevent women in sport from finding common ground, we will always be controlled by people whose interests are served by our division. Our energy will be focused on social approval rather than on social change, and on keeping what little we have rather than on getting what we deserve.

Pressure Tactics

Unfortunately, meaningful social change never happens with tension and resistance. Every civil and human rights struggle in the United States has required the mobilization of political pressure exerted on people with power to force them to confront injustice. Addressing sexism, heterosexism, and homophobia in women's sport will be no different. Taking a stand will mean being prepared to use the media, collect petitions, lobby officials, picket, write letters, file official complaints, and take advantage of other pressure tactics.

CONCLUSION

Eliminating the insidious trio of sexism, heterosexism, and homophobia in women's sport will take a sustained commitment to social justice that will challenge much of what has been accepted as natural about gender and sexuality. Addressing sexism, heterosexism, and homophobia in women's sport requires that past conceptions of gender and sexuality be recognized as social constructions that confer privilege and normalcy on particular social groups: men and heterosexuals. Other social groups (women, lesbians, and gay men) are defined as inferior or deviant and are denied access to the social resources and status conferred on heterosexual men.

Sport in the late 20th century is, perhaps, the last arena in which men can hope to differentiate themselves from women. In sport, men learn to value a traditional heterosexual masculinity that embraces male domination and denigrates women's values (Messner & Sabo, 1990). If sport is to maintain its meaning as a masculine ritual in a patriarchal society, women must be made to feel like trespassers. Women's sport participation must be trivialized and controlled (Bennett et al., 1987). The lesbian label, with its unsavory stigma, is an effective tool to achieve these goals.

If women in sport in the 21st century are to have a sport experience free of intimidation, fear, shame, and betrayal, then, as citizens of the 20th century, we must begin to reevaluate our beliefs, prejudices, and practices. We must begin to challenge the sexist, heterosexist, and homophobic status quo as it lives in our heads, on our teams, and in our schools. A generation of young girls—our daughters, nieces, younger sisters, and students—is depending on us.

REFERENCES

Acosta, V., & Carpenter, L. (1988). Status of women in athletics: Causes and changes. *Journal of Health, Physical Education, Recreation & Dance, 56* (6), 35–37.

Bennett, R., Whitaker, G., Smith, N., & Sablove, A. (1987). Changing the rules of the game: Reflections toward a feminist analysis of sport. *Women's Studies International Forum, 10* (4), 369–380.

Birrell, S., & Richter, D. (1987). Is a diamond forever? Feminist transformations of sport. *Women's Studies International Forum, 10* (4), 395–410.

Blinde, E. (1989). Unequal exchange and exploitation in college sport: The case of the female athlete. *Arena Review, 13* (2), 110–123.

Blinde, E. (1990, March). Pressure and stress in women's college sports: Views from athletes. Paper presented at the annual convention of the American Alliance for Health, Physical Education, Recreation and Dance, New Orleans.

Brown, K. (1991). Homophobia in women's sports. *Deneuve, 1* (2), 4–6, 29.

Brownworth, V. (1991, June 4). Bigotry on the home team: Lesbians face harsh penalties in the sports world. *The Advocate,* pp. 34–39.

Bryson, L. (1987). Sport and the maintenance of male hegemony. *Women's Studies International Forum, 10* (4), 349–360.

Bull, C. (1991, December 31). The magic of Martina. *The Advocate,* pp. 38–40.

Burke, G. (1991, September 18). Dodgers wanted me to get married. *USA Today,* p. 10C.

Burton-Nelson, M. (1991). *Are we winning yet?* New York: Random House.

Diaz, J. (1989, February 13). Find the golf here? *Sports Illustrated,* pp. 58–64.

Faderman, L. (1981). *Surpassing the love of men: Romantic friendship and love between women from the Renaissance to the present.* New York: Morrow.

Faderman, L. (1991). *Odd girls and twilight lovers: A history of lesbian life in twentieth-century America.* New York: Columbia University Press.

Felshin, J. (1974). The triple option . . . for women in sport. *Quest, 21,* 36–40.

Fields, C. (1983, October 26). Allegations of lesbianism being used to intimidate, female academics say. *Chronicle of Higher Education,* pp. 1, 18–19.

Figel, B. (1986, June 16). Lesbians in the world of athletics. *Chicago Sun-Times* p. 119.

Gornick, V. (1971, May 18). Ladies of the links. *Look,* pp. 69–76.

Greendorfer, S. (1991, April). Analyzing homophobia: Its weapons and impacts. Paper presented at the annual convention of the American Alliance for Health, Physical Education, Recreation and Dance, San Francisco.

Griffin, P. (1987, August). Lesbians, homophobia, and women's sport: An exploratory analysis. Paper presented at the annual meeting of the American Psychological Association, New York.

Guthrie, S. (1982). *Homophobia: Its impact on women in sport and physical education.* Unpublished master's thesis, California State University, Long Beach.

Hall, A. (Ed.) (1987). The gendering of sport, leisure, and physical education [Special issue]. *Women's Studies International Forum,* 10 (4).

Herek, G. (1985). Beyond "homophobia": A social psychological perspective on attitudes toward lesbians and gay men. In J. DeCecco (Ed.), *Bashers, baiters, and bigots: Homophobia in American Society* (pp. 1–22), New York: Harrington Park Press.

Hicks, B. (1979, October/November). Lesbian athletes. *Christopher Street,* pp. 42–50.

Image lady. (1987, July). *Golf Illustrated,* p. 9.

Katz, J. (1976). *Gay American History.* New York: Avon.

Kiersh, E. (1990, April). Graf's dash. *Vogue,* pp. 348–353, 420.

Kitzinger, C. (1987). *The social construction of lesbiansim.* Newbury Park, CA: Sage.

Krebs, P. (1984). At the starting blocks: Women athletes' new agenda. *Off our backs,* 14 (1), 1–3.

Lederman, D. (1991, June 5). Penn State's coach's comments about lesbian athletes may be used to test university's new policy on bias. *Chronicle of Higher Education,* pp. A27–28.

Lenskyj, H. (1986). *Out of bounds: Women, sport, and sexuality.* Toronto: Women's Press.

Lenskyj, H. (1990). Combatting homophobia in sports. *Off our backs,* 20 (6), 2–3.

Lenskyj, H. (1991). Combatting homophobia in sport and physical education. *Sociology of Sport Journal,* 8 (1), 61–69.

Lipsyte, R. (1991, May 24). Gay bias moves off the sidelines. *New York Times,* p. B1.

Locke, L., & Jensen, M. (1970, Fall). Heterosexuality of women in physical education. *The Pod,* pp. 30–34.

Longman, J. (1991, March 10). Lions women's basketball coach is used to fighting and winning. *Philadelphia Inquirer,* pp. 1G, 6G.

Messner, M., & Sabo, D. (Eds.) (1990). *Sport, men, and the gender order—Critical feminist perspectives.* Champaign, IL: Human Kinetics.

Morgan, E. (1990). *Lesbianism and feminism in women's athletics: Intersection, bridge, or gap?* Unpublished manuscript, Brown University, Providence.

Muscatine, A. (1991, November/December). To tell the truth, Navratilova takes consequences. *Women's Sports Pages,* pp. 8–9. (Available from Women's SportsPages, P.O. Box 151534, Chevy Chase, MD 20825)

National Collegiate Athletic Association. (1991). *NCAA study on women's intercollegiate athletics: Perceived barriers of women in intercollegiate athletic careers.* Overland Park, KS: NCAA.

Newton, E. (1989). The mannish lesbian: Radclyffe Hall and the new woman. In M. Duberman, M. Vicinus, & G. Chauncey (Eds.), *Hidden from history: Reclaiming the gay and lesbian past* (pp. 281–293). New York: New American Library.

Pharr, S. (1988). *Homophobia: A weapon of sexism.* Inverness, CA: Chardon Press.

Rentzel, L. (1987). *Emotional dependency: A threat to close friendships.* San Rafael, CA: Exodus International.

Smith-Rosenberg, C. (1989). Discourses of sexuality and subjectivity: The new woman, 1870–1936. In M. Duberman, M. Vicinus, & G. Chauncey (Eds.), *Hidden from history: Reclaiming the gay and lesbian past* (pp. 264–280). New York: New American Library.

Solomon, A. (1991, March 20). Passing game. *Village Voice,* p. 92.

South, J., Glynn, M., Rodack, J., & Capettini, R. (1990, July 31). Explosive gay scandal rocks women's tennis. *National Enquirer,* pp. 20–21.

Spander, D. (1991, September 1). It's a question of acceptability. *Sacramento Bee,* pp. D1, D14–15.

Thomas, R. (1990, December 12). Two women at Brooklyn College file rights complaint. *New York Times*, p. 22.

Thorngren, C. (1990, April). Pressure and stress in women's college sport: Views from coaches. Paper presented at the annual convention of the American Alliance for Health, Physical Education, Recreation and Dance, New Orleans.

Thorngren, C. (1991, April). Homophobia and women coaches: Controls and constraints. Paper presented at the annual convention of the American Alliance for Health, Physical Education, Recreation and Dance, San Francisco.

Woods, S. (1990). The contextual realities of being a lesbian physical education teacher: Living in two worlds (doctoral dissertation, University of Massachusetts, Amherst, 1989). *Dissertation Abstracts International 51* (3), 788.

34

Sport and Masculinity

The Estrangement of Gay Men

Brian Pronger

Athletics is a traditional theater for the acting out of myths. The ancient Olympic Games were religious celebrations in which the central myths of Hellenic culture were dramatized. Class and patriarchy, as well as the religious belief that fame (which can be achieved by winning at the Olympics) bestows immortality, were the cultural focus of the ancient games. The similarity between the ancient Olympics and modern-day athletics is limited to the more abstract fact that both are dramatizations of myth. Notions that we take for granted, such as fair play, the virtue of participation in sport for its own sake, and the importance of personal bests, were unknown to the ancients. The ancient games could be quite violent, sometimes being fought to the death, and winning was the only thing that mattered. In fact, if an athlete could intimidate his opponents to the point of their withdrawing from the competition, he was considered successful without even participating in the event.

Sport in contemporary Western culture also dramatizes myths; preeminent among them is the myth of masculinity. One of the men I interviewed said:

> Our culture has definitely rewarded those who are very masculine and perform well, and men over women. Male tennis players, male golf players make more money than female golfers do. So there is a reward for masculinity and a punishment, in some way, for femininity. . . . I think also there's an intimidating factor to

Source: "Rookies and Debutantes: Estranged Athletes" by Brian Pronger. From *The Arena of Masculinity: Sports, Homosexuality and the Meaning of Sex,* by Brian Pronger. Copyright © 1990 by St. Martin's Press. Reprinted by permission.

athletics and the way the program's run: gym teachers calling kids sissies if they can't run laps.

Another, who likes lifting weights and wrestling, said:

> The way it's currently constituted in terms of the commercial basis that most sport depends on, and certainly the way it was taught to me in school, sport as it exists now parallels closely the individual, aggressive qualities that are seen as masculine by most people today, so I think that the connection is quite clear. And in team sports, it's not a feminist quilting-bee type group, but rather a bunch of behemoths who, instead of not being aggressive and choosing to be cooperative, are in fact simply pooling their collective aggressiveness and channeling it in one way. So I think there's quite a clear connection between sports and masculinity.

For boys, sport is an initiation into manhood, a forum in which they can realize their place in the orthodoxy of gender culture. Sport gives them a feel for masculinity, a sense of how they are different from girls. For those who wish to emphasize their masculine sense of place, the masculinity of sport is a happy discovery, a way of expressing and exploring an important sense of themselves. But not all boys are comfortable with this rookie masculinity. For some, becoming adult men is more a matter of learning how they are estranged from masculine culture than it is one of becoming snug in its orthodoxy. For these boys, the sporting rights of masculine passage make them poignantly aware of their unease. Sport is a masculine obligation that they may fulfill, sometimes at great psychic and physical cost. And there are some boys who just see sports as a hostile world that is to be avoided. One of my interviewees said:

> My experience was that there was no place for me in the conventional sports structure, either ones that my peers had devised for playing ball hockey in the streets, or in the standard high-school of junior-high-school structure.

Athletics, as an expression of orthodox masculinity, can be typified in three categories: violence, struggle, and aesthetics. The most masculine sports are the violent ones—boxing, football, and hockey. Less masculine are those in which struggle is a dominant characteristic: one struggles with one's opponents and with oneself without perpetrating violence. Baseball, wrestling, tennis, swimming, and track are sports in which nonviolent struggle with one's opponent(s) is integral to the sport. Typical sports where the struggle is primarily with oneself are field events, golf, archery, and weight lifting. The least masculine sports are those where success is determined by the marriage of skill and aesthetic expression. Such sports are figure skating, diving, gymnastics, and body building. These aesthetic sports are the least masculine because they involve the lowest degree of aggression. . . .

Contrary to the popular opinion that aggressive combative sports like football and hockey are an outlet for the diffusion of natural aggressive energies, it has been found that these sports actually contribute to the development of aggressive behavior. "Research with high-school and college athletes finds they are more quick to anger than nonathletes and that those who participate in combative sports, such as hockey and football, respond to frustration with a greater degree of aggression when compared to athletes in noncontact sports and nonathletes."[1] Combative sports are really a training ground for aggressive violent masculinity.

The physical and psychic pain that is at the heart of this kind of masculinity is an imposition. According to Gary Shaw, Dave Meggyesy, and other commentators on football, vulnerable young men are pushed to the limits of physical and psychic abuse by coaches and athletic bureaucracies whose only interest in winning, regardless of the long- and short-term damage it may cause the athletes.[2] Shaw points out that Darrell Royal, the famous head coach of the University of Texas Longhorns, was successful because of his ability to manipulate "the fears of boys in their late adolescence. Their fears of masculinity, their fears of acceptance, their fears of not being good enough—in short, their need to feel like acceptable men."[3] I interviewed a national track coach (who is heterosexual) who said:

> I played football and hockey because it was masculine. My fear that I would be discovered being afraid was greater than my fear of being hurt, and I was getting hurt all the time because I was much smaller than most everyone else. It hurt a lot to hit and get hit. But I was aggressive. It was part of being male and defining your masculinity and toughness. It's a dehumanizing process.

He also described the perverse attitude that one learns to take to injury and pain, not only that that one experiences oneself, but also among one's teammates.

> When I was coaching high-school football one of the kids broke his leg; he was screaming in pain; his femur was sticking out through his pant leg. We carried him off in a stretcher and went on with the game. It was terrible; a human tragedy had happened there and no one let on that anything bad had happened. They just pushed down their emotions and went on with the game.

Boys and men who are willing to put themselves through such violence do so out of an attachment to the meaning of orthodox masculinity. The pain is worth it because masculinity is worth it. Stressing the importance of masculinity, Vince Lombardi said, "When a football player loses his supreme confidence in his super-masculinity, he is in deep trouble."[4] Homosexual boys can be quite apprehensive about the status of their masculinity. Some may go through the horrors of football in an attempt to counteract suspicions of their extremely vulnerable masculinity. The former American pro football player David Kopay said: " [Football] also provided a convenient way for me—and who can say how many of my teammates?—to camouflage my true sexual feelings for men."[5] Others, and I think the majority, avoid violent sports because they feel no need to pursue an inappropriate world of masculinity.

Homosexual men and boys often feel estranged from sport because of its masculinity. Said one man:

> I didn't have a great predilection for sports. I didn't like competition. I really felt uncomfortable with my male peers. Even before I knew I was homosexual, I knew that I had sexual feelings for men. I was also aware that people were categorizing me as nelly or sissy. And I knew that I just wouldn't enjoy going out and playing football in that kind of atmosphere. I was more comfortable reading.
>
> I very often saw myself as less masculine than the boys who were doing [sports]. I suffered a lot because of that; I really think I undervalued myself because of that and never really felt comfortable being a gentle person, which I feel is the best way to categorize the way I was then.
>
> I was very intimidated by sports then; I felt it was very ungentle. I'm not so intimidated anymore. The moment I was able to drop athletics as a subject, I did, and I didn't go near a gym again until university.

The estrangement that many homosexual boys and men feel can be very intense in team sports, especially those characterized by violence and aggression. Of the thirty-two gay men I interviewed, two had played some football in high school and three had played hockey as children—none had continued playing hockey after puberty. That they did not play hockey after puberty is significant, for it is at puberty that hockey playing becomes truly violent[6] and a serious manifestation of masculinity. Although there is evidence that some particularly ambitious parents encourage their prepubescent boys to play a rough game of hockey, it is at puberty and the onset of adolescence that some boys play rough on their own initiative and take it as an expression of their masculinity. (I personally remember well the difference between older adolescent boys and myself—they would hit and roughhouse in earnest; you could tell that it meant something important to them. Whereas it struck me as an unpleasant and alien kind of behavior.) Only one of the men I interviewed found these sports satisfying. He lived on an air force base where everyone played hockey and his father was the coach. His sisters and even his mother played hockey. When his father was transferred to another base, where hockey was not the major social institution, he stopped playing. Another, who became a competitive swimmer, came from a hockey-playing family—his uncle was in the NHL. He said, "My father's idea of sports is very traditional—camaraderie between the men, the physical contact. . . . I gave up hockey; I did it for a few years. I pretended I was going to block people. I went through the motions but didn't believe in what I was doing, so I walked away from it. I got involved in swimming and really enjoyed it." One man who played football quit because "they always want you to play when you're injured and tough it out. 'It doesn't hurt that much.' After sophomore year, when I broke my foot playing football, I lost my trust in playing football anymore after that. It wasn't worth it. My big event was track, and the broken foot put my track career back, so I said, 'It's not worthwhile for me in the long run.'"

Not one of the men I spoke to had laudatory things to say about football. Regarding football and hockey, one said:

> I would say that there's something masculine about certain sports. Football and hockey. I think these sports are much more red-necked because they are violent. I don't like them as sports, they are noisy, boisterous, based on the desire to see people hit, be hit, and if that's masculine, I don't want any part of it.

A competitive swimmer said:

> Homosexuality and football just do not mix—I don't know why. Maybe it's the homophobic tendency of men that they are not comfortable with the idea of doing anything else but massacring one another on the football field.

Many of the men I interviewed said they were uncomfortable with team sports. As a member of a team it's important that one identify with the team, that one see one's goals as being in common with the team. Now, if team goals were simply athletic, then homosexual men and boys would probably have no problem identifying with them. But athleticism is often not the only theme in team sports; orthodox masculinity is usually an important subtext if not *the* leitmotif. Coaches demand that their athletes play like men, even if they are just boys; it's boys' concern about masculinity that is played upon to motivate more aggressive performances. Team dynamics depend on a common commitment to orthodox masculinity. With that commitment go assumptions, not the least of which is the heterosexuality of team members. In such a setting where heterosexuality is assumed, homosexuality is more of an insult than a sexual disposition—football coaches are well known for berating their players with insults: "ladies," "faggots," "pansies." Such childish pejoratives are effective because there is a tacit understanding on the team that no one is homosexual or would want to be known as such. Needless to say, gay men or boys who do not share this contempt for homosexuality will feel uncomfortable with its use as a "motivating" insult. More importantly, because they may not share the same view of orthodox masculinity as others on the team, they will feel estranged from its role in sport and find it difficult to join in the chorus of its masculine leitmotif. Consequently, gay men often avoid team sports. Comments from gay men, such as "I had to play baseball and soccer in school and I didn't like team sports," are not uncommon.

Adding to their estrangement in athletics is the not exceptional experience of gay men being the last picked for teams. One man recalled field day at his public school.

> They divided each class into teams and there were six kids on each team. We all stood there and the team leaders decided who they wanted. Finally, I was the last one standing and I had to join a team. When the teacher asked the team leaders how many they had, my leader said, "Five and a half, 'cause we have Palmer."

Rather than an intrinsic lack of physical ability, this athletic ineptitude is probably a reflection of the indifference some homosexual boys feel toward sports because of its orthodox masculine leitmotif.

> There's the whole nightmare about baseball—trying to be as far out in left field as you could possibly get and then every now and then a ball coming your way and having to pick it up, throw it, run after it, pick it up again, throw it until it finally got back to the starting post, or whatever it is in baseball.

A man who is now quite muscular and a good swimmer said:

> I was a real klutz. I was always the last one picked to be in anything. You didn't throw the ball right, you couldn't skate properly, and you were afraid of playing hockey. You didn't want to play hockey. I would say that a lot of gays would be in that category. Mostly, I hated going to [gym classes in high school]. I couldn't stand it. Volleyball, basketball—I didn't understand the rules and [had] no desire to do any of that either.

Even gay men who were in fact fine athletes in individual sports would sometimes be the last picked for teams. Myles Pearson, who swam as an international competitor, recalls how he felt in gym class.

> I was a little sissy kid, so in gym classes you'd be the last one chosen on the team to play soccer or dodge ball, or whatever, and the same in high school. I went to a private boy's high school where the ultimate insult was "you faggot." And I didn't fit in well there. I don't remember high school warmly. It was the worst time.

Most athletic activities, with the exception of those that are by nature violent, have little or no *intrinsic* connection with orthodox masculinity. But orthodox masculinity often becomes associated with athletics nonetheless. Gay men and boys who are involved in athletics are often aware of the orthodox masculine leitmotif that can make them feel that they are outsiders in sports. Pearson, the swimmer, said he felt like an outsider

> in the locker room, but not in the pool. In the pool everyone was friends, and swim meets were fine. In the locker room, I think maybe I pulled away rather than was pushed away. Just because locker rooms are a boisterous kind of place; they were telling dirty jokes and talking about the girls in the locker room next to them, and I wasn't interested in participating. I would just be on the sidelines.

His experience emphasizes the fact that from a purely athletic point of view, the experience of homosexual men and boys in sports cannot always be distinguished from their heterosexual counterparts. But when the orthodox masculine, and therefore heterosexual, leitmotif comes into play in the athletic environment, a sense of not being part of the action, of being outside, of estrangement, is amplified for homosexual men and boys.

While uncomfortable in team sports, many gay men and boys find individual athletic activity more satisfying.

> Being from the north, certain kinds of physical activity were very central and very enjoyable to me—canoeing, rowing, hiking, backpacking, snowshoeing, skiing, these were all part of the regular activity. And I think I've always enjoyed individual performance. I've always got a great deal of enjoyment of this kind out of paddling, being able to do so many miles a day, and doing a real long portage, and the great physical satisfaction of the whole thing, and the sense of well-being. But it's always been individual sports, or sports of that kind, that I shared with two or three other people, I never enjoyed team sports very much. I never enjoyed hockey, I liked skating. I never enjoyed baseball. I liked hitting the ball. The game at which I was best was tennis. I liked fencing too. These were things that I did by myself as opposed to being a member of a team.

This man found the physical activities themselves, for example, skating and hitting the ball, enjoyable, but it was the team dynamics he found distasteful.

A university-level competitive swimmer said that, unlike his friends, he didn't play team sports much.

> I never did play hockey or baseball, which is what all my friends were doing. I swam; started when I was eight. In school, I was very into sports—track—I excelled in sports. Volleyball, badminton, gymnastics. I wasn't seriously into basketball, even though I'm tall. The only team sports were volleyball and curling.

Eilert Frerichs, who grew up on a farm and enjoyed the hard physical labor of farming, hated team sports.

> [Team sports] scared me. It may have had to do with comparison with other children, and then in organized sports, in athletics at school, marks were assigned, which is gross. I probably could work in the fields longer than most boys who weren't from the farm, but no marks are assigned to that kind of activity.

And Myles Pearson:

> I can remember when we played team sports in elementary school and maybe high school. If you did something wrong the whole team would turn on you, sometimes it was your fault, sometimes it wasn't. That really pissed me off. But I found with track (which I did for one year too), and with swimming, it's a lot more individual. I was a lot more proud of individual medals than I was of relay medals. That's part of why I didn't like team things when I was younger. But later on, I was never really

interested in team sports because the boys grew up and were tougher and it was this macho thing that I didn't fit in with and that didn't feel a part of me.

One of the reasons Pearson didn't like team sports was that he was aware of the orthodox masculine or "macho" leitmotif that at adolescence becomes the métier for boys in sports. Sensing this leitmotif in team sports, some gay men, even though they are participating on a team, prefer to think of the sport as individual. John Goodwin, once an internationally competitive oarsman, said he thought of rowing as an individual sport even if he was rowing in sixes or eights. "It's a team sport only because you are together in the boat, but you have to go beyond that."

Commenting on the seeming predilection that gay men have for individual sports over team sports, former runner Jim Pullen said:

> I think there are more gay people who are swimmers, runners, and skaters than there are football players and baseball players, partly because it's something you can do on your own. I think if you are uncomfortable being part of the mainstream heterosexual thing, if you are a little different, if you are a little effete, shall we say, and you're interested in sports or you're led to sports, then it's easier to do something on your own, where you don't have eighty people in the locker room together, which is intimidating anyway, I would think. When I talk to my gay friends now, for them, gym class was always a dreaded thing. They would always find some illness or something, anything to avoid going to gym and going through this team thing and playing ball and playing football. So if you were athletically talented you probably got into figure skating or swimming. I think that there are probably more natural things than football where you have to learn to knock people over. You can just go out for a run or a swim. If you are insecure, even the slightest bit, about being involved in any big group thing, especially with a bunch of heterosexual men thumping each other, then, at the very first practice when you've got eighty of them all doing it [trying to make the team] you'd probably avoid it. You'd have to really want to do it in order to suffer through that.

A former varsity swimmer, John Argue, said, "The difference between running, skiing, and swimming and team sports is that you are dealing with your own body in order to get it in to as good shape as possible in order to excel, so that it is between you and nature, so to speak. It's an expression of pleasure and well-being. Whereas in team sports, the point is domination over others. . . . In team sports it is quite frightening; one wins by fighting, beating, and pummeling—I don't like that." A university phys ed instructor said, "The gay men I know around here are swimmers, divers, gymnasts. I don't know any gay football players."

*   *   *

The orthodox masculine leitmotif can also be heard in sports that fall into the "struggle" category. The volume at which the leitmotif is played depends not so much on the nature of the sport as it does on the attitude of the athletes and coaches. Some gay men think of swimming and similar sports as very masculine. A varsity-level swimmer told me:

> I think swimming is a very masculine sport. I think people who swim are some of the hardest-trained athletes, just because of the element of water. I think your body goes through more. You have to be tough mentally. . . . Swimmers aren't bulky so some people may tend to think they aren't as masculine, but I'm biased. I guess the most masculine to me are the sports like running . . . anything by itself . . . biking, track.

Another man, a volleyball player, agreed,

> I think, probably, athletes in individual sports like skiing would be more masculine, only because the challenge is so much greater and nobody relies on other people, you're doing it all yourself.

These men consider the attributes of strength, mental toughness, and independence, which are required in the individual sports, to be masculine and, therefore, see these sports as more masculine than violent team sports. But this equation of toughness and masculinity is unsatisfactory because it ignores the importance of violent aggression as the quintessential expression of masculine power. The desire to cast less violent sports as equally masculine as more violent ones reflects a wish to maintain a sort of masculine credibility, a credibility that, ultimately, is dubious.

A swimmer, Gerry Oxford, said he sees nothing particularly masculine about his sport.

> Swimming isn't up there with football; it isn't associated in most people's minds with a traditional masculine kind of image. Being a good swimmer just earns you scorn in the weight room of Hart House [a university athletic facility]. You are probably a faggot if you are a good swimmer. They'd have trouble saying about a football team, 'You don't play with that *fag* football team, do ya?' Swimming is not a butch enough sport to discredit accusations that you're queer. Athletes, however, wouldn't have this attitude about swimming because they know how hard it is to swim. People have more trouble with a football player being queer; there's something gentle about swimmers—they don't go around beating each other up.

The swimming world was horrified when at the Commonwealth Games, in the presence of the Queen, the world record holder in breast stroke, Victor Davis, kicked over a chair because he was upset that his relay team had been disqualified from a race. Such masculine expression of anger pales next to football players breaking each other's legs or hockey players smashing each other into the boards, knocking themselves unconscious.

Another competitive swimmer said he thought orthodox masculinity was expressed in sports not so much through the sport itself but through a more peripheral machismo. "The camaraderie that borderlines on macho, the bum patting sort of locker-room stuff, is macho. There's a lot of contrived machismo as the trappings of the sport—the image goes with the sport but it's not in the sport. . . . There's nothing particularly macho about swimming; both men and women do it and they do it the same way." He thinks the level of orthodox masculinity depends on the coach and other athletes. "The coach didn't try to motivate the team by references to fags. . . . My coach was a professor of child psychology—so that he was concerned about the development of his athletes as people, not just as swimmers. There were a couple of assholes [on the team] but I think that everyone thought they were ridiculous brutes."

Being in the midst of the machismo of sports can be estranging. One man said, "Doing basic jock stuff with the guys in the swim club, the 'all-for-one-and-one-for-all' sort of thing, I felt that I was a hypocrite, that I was playing along, doing the team, macho thing, talking about women, and you know it's not your natural thing, and you really are different, and you think absolutely nobody understands me."

The social side of athletics, especially for teenagers and college athletes, is overwhelmingly heterosexual. For most boys, their relationship with girls is a preoccupation of their adolescence. One's teammates form a boys-wanting-girls club. Weekend nights, the club goes out together in Dad's car. With the radio blaring, they cruise the town's main drag, looking for girls. There is a lot of hooting, and many rude comments are hurled at the female passersby. Boys "hanging moons" is de rigueur on such occasions. To most of the boys in the car, this playful baring of posteriors is both funny and "kinda gross." Who, after all, would want to look at a guy's ass? For the homosexually inclined, this teenage experience may be read in several ways. Out with their friends, they are members of the boys-wanting-girls club. But secretly, often unconsciously, they are more interested in the boys than the girls. And when one of the guys "hangs a moon," the homosexually inclined teenager's laughter is probably a response to more than one interpretation of the significance of a boy's bared bum. But he knows that he must not let on that he is aware of any other significance. And so he hides behind the facade of being a member of the club. The others boys in the club, unaware of the homosexually inclined boy's inclinations, assume that everyone is a member in good standing. That experience of seeming to belong when one senses that one really does not, the experience of keeping one's life a secret, amplifies the feeling of estrangement.

The athletic world is organized under the ironic assumption that everyone is heterosexual. It's a setup that few in that world question. Males and females, for example, are always given separate change and shower facilities; the assumption being, if they were to change and shower together, their heterosexual desires would overwhelm their sense of propriety. Women's teams that have male coaches do not allow them in the showers or changing rooms with the athletes. A male coach of a men's or boy's team, on the other hand, is automatically accorded the privilege of seeing his athletes naked in the locker room and showers.

Frequently, boys on the team will go out together on dates with girls. While the other boys have their arms around the girls, feeling this to be advantageous to the fulfillment of their sexual destiny, the homosexual boy is aware that the situation has somewhat less potential. John Goodwin told me that he remembered such dates:

> And girls, although I liked them, weren't doing the same to me that boys were doing. So there'd be a gang that was going out on dates and I'd be with my girlfriend and this boy who I had a crush on and his girlfriend, and what I really wanted was to be with him, not the girl. It got to be awkward at that point.

In situations such as this, a young homosexual man knows that as far as everyone else in concerned he is like them. It makes him poignantly aware, however, that he is not.

The irony of being with girls when one is interested in boys can be intense. Novelist John Fox writes of a young swimmer who, while dancing with a girl at a high-school dance, finds himself fantasizing about having sex with a man in a movie he had seen.

> I liked this brother of Paul Newman in this sort of western movie I saw that took place in the present. There I was dancing this slow dance with Sue, thinking about this guy in the movie and my head was on her neck and I could smell perfume but in my mind this guy is on a rumpled bed in his underwear in the ranch house that's in the movie and it's late in the morning. I, also in my underwear, sit on the bed and reach out, put my hand on his crotch and his cock jumps into my hand and he smiles out one side of his mouth and I have a hard-on and I tried to grind up against Sue but there was nothing *down* there to grind up *against* and her tits were all mushed up against my chest. I lifted my head, looked up at the band playing on the stage and kind of choked, "I'm thirsty."[7]

Having had girlfriends all through high school, wanting to be a member in good standing of the boys-wanting-girls club, when I went to university I thought it was appropriate to continue doing so. Several months into a relationship with a woman, whom I was seeing almost daily, we still hadn't had sex; we hadn't even kissed each other. She was getting frustrated. One night when we were out drinking with the gang, she decided to show her dissatisfaction with my seemingly inactive libido: she put her arms around one of the other fellows at the table and he responded gratefully to her advances. It hit me like a ton of bricks. I was jealous. But it was *my girlfriend* I was jealous of. For weeks, I had had a crush on the guy she was coming on to, although until that moment I hadn't realized it. I remember I couldn't take my eyes off his strong, hairy forearms. My girlfriend was watching me. When she realized what was going on, she started to laugh. Still watching me, she ran her fingers up and down his arms, playing with those brown hairs. Then, with an incredibly devious look in her eyes, she turned her attention from me, said something to him I couldn't hear, and deep-kissed him. I was devastated. My girlfriend was getting the man I wanted. I looked around our table; everyone was drunk. It was boy/girl all the way around and they were all over each other. I couldn't stand it; I grabbed my coat and ran out of the bar.

As time passes, membership in the boys-wanting-girls club becomes more of a strain; it becomes more difficult to reconcile with one's homosexual desires. Eventually some men with homosexual desires, but by no means all of them, relinquish their membership. While they are in the club, they find themselves in a heterosexual world, a world in which they don't belong. Some homosexual boys make a point of avoiding the club, one manifestation of which is the social world of athletics. Others live with the duality of being outsiders on the inside.

The experience of being a "sissy," or at least being known as one, is not uncommon for gay boys and men. A sissy is a man or boy who does not subscribe to the orthodox myth of masculinity; he doesn't think like a "real man." Sissiness isn't necessarily the description of behavior; it's a personal disposition. The word "sissy" is derived from "sister" *(Concise Oxford Dictionary)*, hence the "girlish" connotation. "Sissy" is usually considered a pejorative expression, especially when it is hurled as an accusation. But when employed by gay men as self-description, its perjorative sense is undermined. Gay men who have eschewed orthodox masculinity have no problem considering themselves as sissies—they do not, after all, subscribe to orthodoxy in gender and don't, therefore, feel compelled to establish a nonsissy status for themselves. One exercise club very popular with gay men in Toronto was well known as "Sissy Fitness." Certainly, not all gay men welcome the application of sissiness to themselves— some are uncomfortable with their estranged place in gender culture; they prefer to think of themselves as just as masculine as their heterosexual counterparts. Like David Kopay, they may go out of their way to "prove" their orthodox masculinity.

Whereas one might behave in a certain way because one is a sissy, one is not confined to that behavior; a sissy may behave effeminately or masculinely. A number of the men I interviewed, even though some of them were fine high-performance athletes, referred to themselves and their gay teammates as "sissies." One man talked about the juxtaposition of fine athletic ability and markedly gay self-expression.

> In gay sports, the sports I play, there are some athletes that are absolutely superb. These people could have played on any state university team and they are in fine physical shape. So it's a very competitive sport, especially the North American Gay Volleyball Association, but those wonderful, superb athletes are the most outrageous screamers you've ever seen and they'll do it right there on the court.[8]

A very fashionable young man, who used to be a gymnast and a certified gymnastics coach, joined a gay baseball team. Although many of the men on the team were very good baseball players, many of them did not behave in the traditionally masculine manner of baseball players.

> In baseball this summer I've never seen so many nelly boys. There's a lot of nelly boys and they can be just amazing athletes. They may not have a masculine bone in their bodies but put a baseball bat in their hands and they'll show you how to play baseball. I think that surprises a lot of people—it surprised me. But I surprised a lot of people too. They expected this trendy little fag to not know what to do with a

baseball bat; but, you know, I got up there and did a good job and I helped my team. . . . Everyone always associates sports with being a butch man and the idea of fags playing baseball. . . . Playing baseball with gay people was really interesting; it was a lot of fun.

Commenting on the juxtaposition of fine athletic ability and sissy-like effeminate manners, a former college basketball player said:

I have friends who are effeminate, and athletically speaking, I know of some very good volleyball players, who are among the best in North America, who are very effeminate, drag-queen types, and that opened my eyes a long time ago. How could this person possibly be better than me when they have long hair, long finger nails, every time he gets a spike he screams, and then I realized that your level of masculinity or femininity really doesn't have a hell of a lot to do with your athletic ability.

It's important to note that these three examples referred to the experience that these men had with gay community sports. When gay men are involved in mainstream sports organizations, they usually do not feel free to express sissy sensibilities. The orthodox masculine leitmotif, although it is most severely expressed in violent team sports, reverberates throughout the athletic world, albeit in varying degrees.

Not surprisingly, it is the aesthetic sports that are the most gay sports. A gymnast I spoke to said that being a gymnast in high school made his peers suspect that he was gay. Figure skating is dominated by gay men. A former figure skater who is now a policeman told me:

Figure skating was called "fairy skating." Figure skating is very close to ballet; it's a feminine sport. I was a figure skater. Everyone automatically assumed you were gay if you were a figure skater. Straight men were so far in a minority in figure skating—I can remember sitting at the 1980 national men's championship, and of the eight senior men at the national level, seven of them were gay. And that's probably a fairly accurate projection of the numbers in figure skating. Eighty or ninety percent of the men in figure skating are gay. My suspicion is that it's because of the artistic component in figure skating. I've also heard that there are a lot more gay men in gymnastics than there are in other sports. I don't know whether it's overgeneralizing to say that gay men are attracted to a sport that involves some sort of artistic expression, but it seems to be that there are more gay gymnasts and figure skaters than football players.

Although figure skating is dominated by gay men on the ice, the rules and traditions of the sport belie that fact somewhat. The pairs competition is the only sport that requires the competitors to ape heterosexual relations—it is ironic indeed that the sport with the highest proportion of homosexual men employs the most blatantly heterosexual signs. Even in football men don't have to feign an interest in women in order to score points The rules do not allow two men to skate the pairs event together. Most of the time, the men wear pseudo-masculine outfits—tight-fitting little military uniforms are de rigueur on the ice. But these uniforms are not without irony; invariably their masculinity is elegantly undermined by glittering accents in sequins and gold lamé.

Because most male figure skaters are gay, the sport can feel like home for gay men and boys. Nevertheless, there are at least shadows of the experience of estrangement in this sport. The inherently romantic heterosexual significance of the pairs competition is at odds with the proclivities of gay men and boys. And famous figure skaters try to keep their homosexuality a secret. Whereas most sports heroes like to feature their wives and children when the media do personal profiles, gay figure skaters hide their "significant others" from the press. So, hiding homosexuality and the sense of estrangement that comes with it is a feature of even the most homosexual (mainstream) sport.

*   *   *

By showing that homosexual men tend to gravitate to individual, nonviolent sports, I am not suggesting that there are no homosexual men and boys in violent team sports. There certainly are homosexual men who pursue these sports, David Kopay being a well-known case in point. In fact, that there are homosexual men in such sports, given the overwhelmingly orthodox and heterosexual significance of those sports, is very important; it speaks of the multifaceted nuances of homosexuality. . . .

Sports for homosexual men is a place of estrangement. It is an orthodox masculine world that emphasizes the unusual relationship homosexuals have with our culture in general.

NOTES

1. J. Goldstein, "Sports Violence." in D. S. Eitzen (Ed.), *Sport in Contemporary Society: An Anthology,* 2nd ed. (New York: St. Martin's Press, 1984), p. 92.

2. Gary Shaw, *Meat on the Hoof: The Hidden World of Texas Football* (New York: St. Martin's Press, 1972). See also sports psychologist Thomas Tutko, *Winning Is Everything and Other American Myths* (New York: Macmillan, 1976).

3. Shaw, op. cit., p. 207.

4. David Kopay with P. Young, *The David Kopay Story: An Extraordinary Self-Revelation* (New York: Donald I. Fine, 1977), p. 152.

5. Ibid., p. 53.

6. See Edmund Vaz, "The Culture of Young Hockey Players: Some Initial Observations." In Albert W. Taylor (Ed.), *Training: Scientific Basis and Application: A Symposium* (Springfield, Illinois: Charles C. Thomas, 1972), pp. 222–234.

7. John Fox, *The Boys on the Rock* (New York: St. Martin's Press, 1984), pp. 19–20.

8. "Screamers" refers to "screaming queens," which is an expression for gay men who make a point of their gayness by behaving in blatantly effeminate ways—it often entails a lot of shrieking.

35

Is Baseball Ready for a Gay Jackie Robinson?

Peter Dreier

Richard Greenberg's *Take Me Out,* which won this year's Tony award for best Broadway play, tells the story of a celebrated New York City baseball hero who announces that he's gay. In reality, no gay major-league player has ever publicly acknowledged his homosexuality while still in uniform. How close are we to real life imitating art?

The U.S. Supreme Court's June ruling in *Lawrence v. Texas* is one indication that Americans are increasingly accepting of homosexuals. Out-of-the-closet gays and lesbians have been elected to Congress and are prominent in the entertainment industry, business, journalism, and the clergy. Many big cities and suburbs have openly gay schoolteachers. TV sit-coms have openly gay characters and the *New York Times* now includes same-sex wedding announcements.

Certain spheres of American life, however, have resisted change. The military has infamously clung to its code of "don't ask, don't tell." Professional sports leagues may not enforce such a policy overtly, but in practice its force is equally felt, especially for male athletes.

It is easier for athletes in individual sports—like tennis star Martina Navratilova and diver Greg Louganis—to come out of the closet than players on team sports. According to conventional wisdom, a gay teammate would threaten the macho camaraderie that involves constant butt-slapping and the close physical proximity of the locker room. So while there are no doubt homosexuals currently playing in the

Source: Peter Dreier, "Is Baseball Ready for a Gay Jackie Robinson?" *In These Times* (September 15, 2003), pp. 19–20.

National Football League, National Basketball Association, and Major League Baseball, they are deep in the closet.

Three former NFL players have come out after they retired. David Kopay, who hid his homosexuality while playing as an NFL running back for nine years in the '60s and '70s, came out in 1975 and was the first major athlete to do so. Roy Simmons, an offensive guard for the Giants and the Redskins from 1979 to 1983, revealed his sexual orientation during an appearance on *The Phil Donahue Show* in 1992. Esera Tuaolo, a 280-pound defensive lineman who played nine years in the NFL, came out last year, three years after he retired. Revealing his secret on HBO's *Real Sports* and in *ESPN Magazine,* he acknowledged that while playing in the NFL he lived with his partner, with whom he now has two adopted children, but felt compelled to keep it a secret. His teammates routinely told gay jokes in the locker room, he explained. "They made me go further and further into depression, further and further into shame."

Only two gay former major-league baseball players, Glenn Burke and Billy Bean (not to be confused with former player and current Oakland A's General Manager Billy Beane), have come out of the closet. Burke, who played for the Dodgers and Oakland A's from 1976 to 1979, came out to family and friends in 1975 but lived in fear that his teammates and managers would discover his sexual orientation.

In his autobiography, *Out at Home,* published posthumously, Burke revealed that the Dodgers' management offered to pay for a luxurious honeymoon if he would agree to a "marriage of convenience" to conceal his homosexuality. When he refused, he was traded to the A's. The A's manager Billy Martin made public statements about not wanting a homosexual in his clubhouse, a clear reference to Burke.

Frustrated, Burke retired and kept his homosexuality secret until he cooperated for a 1982 article in *Inside Sports* magazine. Burke continued to play competitive sports. He won medals in the 100- and 200-meter sprints in the 1982 Gay Games and played basketball in the 1986 Gay Games. Later, Burke struggled with drug abuse, homelessness, and AIDS, from which he eventually died in 1995.

While Bean played for the Tigers, Dodgers, and Padres from 1987 to 1995, he pretended to date women, furtively went to gay bars, and hid his gay lover from teammates and fans. In his recently published memoir, *Going the Other Way,* Bean recounts how Dodgers manager Tommy Lasorda constantly made homophobic jokes, even as Lasorda's gay son was dying from AIDS.

Bean quit when he could no longer stand living a double life. When he came out publicly in 1999, his story made front-page news in the *New York Times.* Like Kopay, since coming out, he has become active in gay rights causes.

In his autobiography, *Behind the Mask,* Dave Pallone—a major-league umpire who was quietly fired in 1988 after rumors about his sexual orientation circulated in the baseball world—contends that there are enough gay major-league players to create an All-Star team. Indeed, because everyone assumes that there are gay ballplayers, the game of trying to identify them sometimes leads to bizarre rumors and denials. Last year, for example, *Details* magazine quoted New York Mets manager Bobby Valentine as saying that professional baseball is "probably ready for an openly gay player," adding, "the players are diverse enough now that I think they could handle it."

Then, *New York Post* gossip columnist Neal Travis speculated that Valentine's comments were a "pre-emptory strike" meant to pave the way for one of his players to come out. "There is a persistent rumor around town," Travis wrote, "that one Mets star who spends a lot of time with pretty models in clubs is actually gay and has started to think about declaring his sexual orientation."

The rumors focused on the Mets' star catcher Mike Piazza, who felt compelled to hold an impromptu press conference. "I'm not gay," Piazza announced. "I'm heterosexual." But he also said he believed that players were ready to accept an openly gay teammate. "In this day and age," Piazza told reporters, "it's irrelevant. I don't think it would be a problem at all."

Perhaps not. But at least one team and one player has to be willing to break the barrier, just as the Brooklyn Dodgers and Jackie Robinson did more than 50 years ago.

The breaking of baseball's color line was not simply an act of individual heroism on Robinson's part. As historian Jules Tygiel recounts in *Baseball's Great Experiment,* it took an inter-racial protest movement among liberal and progressive activists, as well as the Negro press, who had agitated for years to integrate major-league baseball before Dodgers General Manager Branch Rickey signed Robinson to a contract in 1945, then brought him up to the majors two years later.

Rickey, aware of the many great black ballplayers in the Negro Leagues, believed that the integration of baseball would improve the overall level of play. He also believed—correctly, it turned out—that black baseball fans would flock to Ebbets Field to watch black athletes play on the same field as whites.

Robinson did more than integrate major-league baseball. The dignity with which he handled his encounters with racism among fellow players and fans—on the diamond as well as in hotels, restaurants, trains, and other public places—drew public attention to the issue, stirred the consciences of many whites, and gave black Americans a tremendous boost of pride, paving the way for the civil rights movement a decade later. Indeed, Martin Luther King once told pitcher Don Newcombe—who along with Roy Campanella followed Robinson from the Negro Leagues to the Brooklyn Dodgers—"You'll never known what you and Jackie and Roy did to make it possible for me to do my job."

Major-league sports and the military were two of the first national institutions to be racially integrated, but they are among the last to openly accept gays into their ranks. Some managers, fellow players, and sportswriters know the identity of at least a few gay major leaguers, but so far no gay player has been involuntarily outed.

No doubt a few of the MLB's gay players have considered coming out publicly while still in uniform. Certainly there are gay players in college or in the minor leagues who fantasize about being the gay Jackie Robinson. But so far they have calculated that the personal or financial costs outweigh the benefits. They fear being ostracized by fellow players, harassed by fans, and perhaps traded—or dropped entirely—by their team's management. There is a strong fundamentalist Christian current within major-league baseball, which could make life uncomfortable for the first "out" player. That, in turn, could affect his ability to play to his potential.

And, initially at least, an openly gay player might lose some of his commercial endorsements.

Of course, if several gay ballplayers came out simultaneously, no single player would have to confront the abuse (as well as bask in the cheers) on his own, as Robinson did.

In 1947, Rickey feared that if Robinson turned out to be a bust as a major-league player, it would set back the cause of ending baseball apartheid for at least several years. The same may be true today in terms of the first out-of-the-closet ballplayer. A player of All-Star stature would make things easier for everyone who followed.

Asked about the likelihood of a gay player coming out of the closet, Philadelphia Phillies manager Larry Bowa told the Associated Press: "If it was me, I'd probably wait until my career was over. I'm sure it would depend on who the player was. If he hits .340, it probably would be easier than if he hits .220."

Baseball executives certainly recognize that there are plenty of gay—or otherwise sympathetic—baseball fans who would spin the turnstiles to cheer for a homosexual player. Lesbians now constitute a significant segment of the audience for women's pro basketball.

In 2001, ESPN conducted a poll, asking: "If a player on your favorite professional sports team announced he or she was gay or lesbian, how would this affect your attitude towards that player?" Only 17 percent said they would turn against the player, 63 percent said it would make no differences, and 20 percent said they would become a bigger fan.

Although baseball no longer has the monopoly on fans' affections that it did in Robinson's day, it still plays a central role in our culture. As Robinson showed, once that barrier is shattered, it will have profound ripple effects, not only in sports but in many aspects of American society.

However it happens, expect to see an openly gay major-league baseball player by the end of the first decade of the twenty-first century.

✳ **FOR FURTHER STUDY** ✳

Blum, Debra E. 1994. "College Sports' L-Word." *The Chronicle of Higher Education* (March 9):A35–A36.

Broad, K. L. 2001. "The Gendered Unapologetic: Queer Resistance in Women's Sport," *Sociology of Sport Journal* 18 (2):181–204.

Dworkin, Shari Lee, and Faye Linda Wachs. 1998. "'Disciplining the Body': HIV-Positive Male Athletes, Media Surveillance and the Policing of Sexuality," *Sociology of Sport Journal* 15(1):1–20.

Fusco, Caroline. 2000. "Lesbians and Locker Rooms," in *Taking Sport Seriously: Social Issues in Canadian Sport,* Peter Donnelly (ed.), (Toronto: Thompson Education Publishing), pp. 91–94.

Griffin, Pat, 1998. *Strong Women, Deep Closets: Lesbians and Homophobia in Sport* (Champaign, IL: Human Kinetics).

Jacobson, Jennifer. 2002. "The Loneliest Athletes," *The Chronicle of Higher Education* (November 1): A36–A38.

Lipsyte, Robert. 2000. "An Icon Recast: Support for Gay Athlete," (April 30). Online: http://nytimes.com/library/sports/other/043000oth-lipsyte.html.

Lynch, Eamon. 2003. "Having a Gay Old Time," *Sports Illustrated* (June 16): G8–G12.

Messner, Michael A. 1996. "Studying Up on Sex." *Sociology of Sport Journal* 13: 221–237.

Price, Michael, and Andrew Parker. 2003. "Sport, Sexuality, and the Gender Order: Amateur Rugby Union, Gay Men, and Social Exclusion," *Sociology of Sport Journal* 20 (2): 108–126.

Sykes, Heather. 1998. "Turning the Closets Inside/Out: Towards a Queer-Feminist Theory in Women's Physical Education," *Sociology of Sport Journal* 15 (2): 154–173.

Tomlinson, Dylan B. 1998. "Fear and Loathing," *Denver Post* (April 28): 10D.

PART TWELVE

Expanding the Horizons:
Sport and Globalization

Globalization, according to Joseph Maguire, refers to transnational economics and technological exchange, communication networks, and migratory patterns resulting in interconnected world patterns.[1] Globalization, then, involves, among other things, markets, production, finance, the movement of people, and cultural homogenization. There has been a global economy for 500 years. In the sport realm the cultural imperialism employed by the British colonists of the nineteenth and twentieth centuries brought their sport (soccer, rugby, cricket) to their colonies (e.g., India). The Olympic movement spread around the globe during the twentieth century, and this, too, has been interpreted by some observers as a reflection of the colonial dominance of the West,[2] but in the last twenty-five years or so, it has accelerated rapidly.

While globalization is not new, the pace has quickened rapidly with the transportation and communications revolutions of the late twentieth century. Maguire states:

> These globalization processes . . . appear to be leading to a form of time-space compression. That is, people are experiencing spatial and temporal dimensions differently. There is a speeding up of time and a "shrinking" of space. Modern technologies enable people, images, ideas and money to criss-cross the globe with great rapidity.[3]

The following are some examples of the globalization phenomenon in sport, using 2003 data for the National Basketball Association:[4]

- In 1973 only two NBA players were from other countries. In 2003 there were 65 representing 34 different countries.

- 15 percent of the league's $900 million in annual television revenues (excluding local broadcasts) was derived from its 148 television partners in 212 countries and territories.
- 40 percent of the visitors to NBA.com (which includes sites in Spanish, Japanese, and Chinese) log on from outside the United States.
- About 20 percent of all NBA merchandise is sold overseas ($430 million in annual revenues).

The two selections in this section provide information on the global dimensions of sport in today's world. The first selection, by Jay Coakley, provides an overview of the phenomenon. The second, by George Sage, focuses not only on the global reach of the Nike Corporation, the major worldwide producer and marketer of sports materials, but also the sordid history of the exploitation of workers in low-wage economies. Most significant, Sage chronicles the success of various social movements to change policies of the Nike Corporation.

NOTES

1. Joseph Maguire, "Sport and Globalization," in *Handbook of Sports Studies,* Jay Coakley and Eric Dunning (eds.), (London: Sage, 2000), p. 356. For more on the defining characteristics of globalization, see Jeremy Breecher, Tim Costello, and Brendan Smith, *Globalization from Below: The Power of Solidarity* (Cambridge, MA: South End Press, 2000), pp. 1–4; and Robert K. Schaeffer, *Understanding Globalization: The Social Consequences of Political, Economic, and Environmental Change,* 2nd ed. (Lanham, MD: Rowman & Littlefield, 2003), pp. 1–18.

2. H. Eichberg, "Olympic Sport: Neocolonialism and Alternatives," *International Review for the Sociology of Sport* 19: 97–105.

3. Maguire, op. cit., p. 356.

4. Daniel Eisenberg. "The NBA's Global Game Plan," *Time* (March 17, 2003), pp. 59–63.

36

Globalization and Sports
Issues and Controversies

Jay J. Coakley

NEW POLITICAL REALITIES IN AN ERA OF TRANSNATIONAL CORPORATIONS

Today, international sports are less likely to be scenes for nationalistic displays than scenes for commercial displays by large and powerful transnational corporations. This was clearly evident in Atlanta (1996), Nagano (1998), Sydney (2000), and Salt Lake City (2002), and it will be evident in future locations.

Global politics have changed dramatically over the past decade. Nation-states have been joined by powerful transnational organizations in global power relations. In fact, about half of the largest economies in the world are corporations, *not* nation-states. As nation-states have lifted trade restrictions, decreased tariffs, and loosened their internal regulations to promote their own capitalist expansion, transnational corporations have become increasingly powerful players in global politics. Many of them are now more powerful in economic terms than the nations in which their products are manufactured. This, of course, gives them political power as well.

Therefore, instead of focusing just on international relations when we study sports and political processes, we must broaden our focus to consider *transnational relations*. This enables us to acknowledge that nation-states are now joined by

Source: Jay J. Coakley, *Sport in Society: Issues and Controversies,* 8th ed. (New York: McGraw-Hill, 2004), pp. 460–469.

major corporations and other powerful transnational organizations as global political players.

Nationalism still exists in connection with international sports, especially those played in regions where political and economic issues call attention to national differences and interests. However, in the case of many sport events, the differences between national interests and identities and corporate interests and identities are becoming increasingly blurred. This was highlighted by Phil Knight, the CEO of the U.S.-based Nike corporation, as he explained the basis for his team loyalty during the 1994 World Cup:

> We see a natural evolution . . . dividing the world into their athletes and ours. And we glory ours. When the U.S. played Brazil in the World Cup, I rooted for Brazil because it was a Nike team. America was Adidas.

Knight's point was that he identified teams and athletes in terms of corporate logos, not nationalities. He knew that Nike's markets were not limited to the United States. They were and continue to be worldwide, and this was why Nike gave Brazil's national sport teams $200 million for the right to use the Brazilian soccer team to market Nike products around the world through the year 2005. Knight sees logo loyalty as more important than national loyalty when it comes to international sports; he sees consumerism replacing patriotism when it comes to identifying athletes and teams; he sees international sports events as sites for Nike and other corporate sponsors to deliver advertising messages promoting their companies' interests, and promoting general global capitalist expansion. Furthermore, he and fellow executives from other powerful corporations see this as good for the people of the world. Their conclusion would be similar to conclusions made by those using functionalist theory: Sport contributes to economic expansion, and this is good for everyone in the world.

To the extent that corporate sponsors influence sport events and media coverage, international sports televised around the world are used as vehicles for presenting to massive audiences a range of messages promoting the interests of corporate capitalism (Donnelly, 1996). These messages are directed to spectator-consumers, not spectator-citizens. Instead of focusing on patriotism or nationalism, the messages that come with international sports now focus on status consciousness and individual consumption. Sports that don't enable corporations to deliver their messages to consumers with purchasing power are not sponsored. If spectators and media audiences are not potential consumers, corporations see little reason to sponsor events, so, unless the media are publicly owned, they are not likely to cover events viewed by those who have little purchasing power.

Of course, the power of corporations is not unlimited or uncontested, as conflict theorists would have us conclude. Figurational research has identified cases in which local populations use their own cultural perspectives to interpret and apply the images and discourses that come with global sports and global advertising. However, those who use critical theories note that global media sports and the commercial messages that accompany them often cleverly fuse the global and the local through thoughtfully and carefully edited images of local traditions, sport action, and consumer products (Jackson and Hokowhitu, 2002; Jackson and Scherer, 2002). They argue that these fused images tend to "detraditionalize" local cultures by presenting local symbols and lifestyles in connection with consumer products.

Nike has been especially clever in this regard. As cultural theorist David Andrews points out, Nike commercials that aired in connection with global sport events during the late 1990s masterfully presented images from numerous localities around the world. These local images were "reassembled"and situated in connection with Nike products, such as soccer apparel worn by players from many nations as they kicked a soccer ball in numerous locations around the globe. Andrews argues that Nike captures local traditions and wraps its branded jerseys around them until there is little else to be seen or discussed. This has now become a common advertising strategy.

The conclusions made by critical theories have not been explored sufficiently in research, but it is clear that, as corporations join or replace nation-states as sponsors of athletes and teams around the world, sports do become framed in new political terms. According to John Horan, the publisher of *Sporting Goods Intelligence,* "It's not the Free World versus Communism anymore. Now you take sides with sneaker companies. Now everybody looks at the Olympics as Nike versus Reebok" (in Reid, 1996, p. 4BB). Horan's conclusion is probably distorted by his hope that global sports are perceived in this way. However, despite some distortion and exaggeration, Horan expresses the intent of transnational corporations as they spend billions of dollars to sponsor sports around the world.

The late Roone Arledge, former president of ABC News and director of ABC Sports, noted that this intent was becoming a reality in connection with sport events. He observed that the Olympic Games are "basically a commercial enterprise that tries every four years to make as much money as it possibly can," and that the games don't have "much to do with the heroic words that we use to describe them" (in Reid, 1996, p. 4BB). Reaffirming Arledge's conclusion, Dick Ebersol, president of NBC Sports, explained that NBC paid over $3.5 billion for the U.S. rights to televise all Olympic Games from 2000 to 2008, because the Olympics "has this amazing ability to put the whole family in front of the television together, which is what advertisers are grabbing at" (in Steinbreder, 1996, p. 38).

These statements, made only thirteen years after Peter Ueberroth, president of the Los Angeles Olympic Organizing Committee, described the Olympics as an athletic-*political* event, illustrate the power of corporate capitalism. In just over a decade, the characterization of the largest sport event in the world changed from athletic-*political* to athletic-*economic.*

Representatives from many major corporations around the world have come to see the potential of sports to establish new commercial markets and to promote the ideology of consumerism, which drives those markets. Although the sponsorship money coming from these corporations is welcomed by those who benefit from it, the primary goal of those who own and control the corporations is to make profits.

Coca-Cola may sponsor the Olympics because it wants to bring people together, but it is primarily interested in selling as many Cokes as possible to 6.3 billion people around the world. This is also why the Mars candy company pays millions to be the official snack food of the Olympics and why McDonald's uses the Olympics and nearly fat-free athletes' bodies to market hamburgers and fries around the world.

According to Sut Jhally, a noted communications profession from the University of Massachusetts, transnational corporations pay billions of dollars to sponsor global sports in an effort to become "global cultural commissars." Jhally says that if you listen closely and critically to the advertisements of these sponsors, you'll discover that, in addition to their products, they are selling a way of life based on consumption. They use sports to present images and messages emphasizing individual success through competition, production, and consumption. They know that elite competitive sports are ideal vehicles for presenting these images and messages, because such sports have become primary sources of entertainment around the world. When people are being entertained while watching these sports in person or on television, they are emotionally primed to hear what the sponsors have to say.

Of course, many people ignore the images and messages emphasized by sponsors, or they redefine them to fit local and personal circumstances. But this does not prevent large corporations from spending billions to deliver them. Advertisers understand that sooner or later the images and messages associated with sources of pleasure and entertainment in people's lives will in some form enter the imaginations and conversations of a proportion of those who see and hear them. Commercial images and messages do not dictate what people think, but they certainly influence what people think about, and, in this way, they become a part of the overall discourse that occurs in cultures around the globe.

We should not interpret this description of the new politics of sports to mean that sports around the world somehow have fallen victim to a global conspiracy hatched by transnational corporations. It means only that transnational organizations have joined nation-states in the global political context in which sports are defined, organized, planned, promoted, played, and presented, and given meaning around the world (Jackson and Scherer, 2002).

OTHER GLOBAL POLITICAL ISSUES

As sports have become increasingly commercialized, and as national boundaries have become less relevant in sports, an increasing number of athletes have become global migrant workers. They go where their sports are played, where they can be supported or earn money while they play, or where they can have the cultural experiences they seek. This global migration of athletes has raised new political issues in connection with sports.

Another global political issue is related to the production of sporting goods. As the demand for sports equipment and clothing has increased in wealthy nations, transnational corporations have cut costs for those products by manufacturing them in labor-intensive poor countries, where wage costs are extremely low. The result has been a clear split between the world's haves and have-nots when it comes to sports: Those born into privilege in wealthy nations consume the products made by those born into disadvantaged circumstances in poor nations. This is not a new issue, but it ties sports to global politics in yet another way.

Athletes as Global Migrant Workers

Human history of full of examples of labor migration, both forced and voluntary. Industrial societies, in particular, have depended on mobile labor forces responsive to the needs of production. Now that economies have become more global, the pervasiveness and diversity of labor migration patterns have increased. This is true in sports as well as other occupational categories (Maguire et al., 2002). Athletes frequently move from their hometowns when they are recruited to play elite sports, and then they may move many times after that, as they are traded from team to team or seek continuing opportunities to play their sports.

As geographer John Bale and sociologist Joe Maguire have noted in a book on athletic talent migration (1994), athletes move from state to state and region to region within nations, as well as from nation to nation within and between continents. They have noted also that each of these moves raises issues related to the following: (1) the personal adjustment of migrating athletes, (2) the rights of athletes as workers in various nations, (3) the impact of talent migration on the nations from and to which athletes migrate, and (4) the impact of athlete migration on patterns of personal, cultural, and national identity formation.

Some migration patterns are seasonal, involving temporary moves as athletes travel from one climate area to another to play their sports. Patterns may follow annual tour schedules, as athletes travel from tournament to tournament around a region or the world, as they may involve long-term or permanent moves from one region or nation to another.

The range of personal experiences among migrating athletes is great. They vary from major forms of culture shock and chronic loneliness to minor homesickness and lifestyle adjustments. Some athletes are exploited by teams of clubs, whereas others make great amounts of money and receive a hero's welcome when they return home in the off-season. Some encounter prejudice against foreigners or various forms of racial and ethnic bigotry, whereas others are socially accepted and make good friends. Some cling to their national identities and socialize with fellow athletes from their homelands, whereas others develop more global identities unrelated to one national or cultural background. In some cases, teams and clubs expect foreign athletes to adjust on their own, whereas others provide support for those who need to learn a new language or become familiar with new cultural settings (Klein, 1991).

Athletic talent migration also has an impact on the nations involved. For example, many Latin American nations have their best baseball players recruited by Major League teams in the United States. This not only depletes the talent the Latin American nations need to maintain professional baseball in their local economies but also forces them to depend on U.S.-based satellite television companies even to watch the players from their nations. As Major League Baseball teams in North America recruit stars from professional teams in Japan, some Japanese people worry that this trend could destroy professional baseball in their country. At the same time, they are proud that Japanese players excel on Major League teams. As they watch Major League games on satellite television, attendance and television ratings for Japanese baseball decline.

Furthermore, as people in other countries and continents watch sports based in the United States and Canada, they often are exposed to images and messages consistent with the advertising interests of corporations headquartered in the United States. Similar patterns exist in connection with European soccer teams that recruit players from around the world. In fact, soccer has higher rates of talent migration than other sports, although hockey, track and field, and basketball have high rates as well. The impact of this migration on national talent pools and on the ability of local clubs and teams to maintain economically viable sport programs is complex. Talent migration usually benefits the nation to which athletes move more than it benefits the nation from which athletes come, but this is not always the case.

The impact of global migration by athletes on how people think about and identify themselves in connection with nation-states is something we know little about. Many people appreciate athletic talent regardless of the athlete's nationality. At the same time, many people have special affections for athletes and teams representing their nations of citizenship or their nations of origin. Leagues such as the NHL are open to athletes from all nations. In fact, even though most of the teams are located in U.S. cities, less than 20 percent of the players are U.S.-born; about 60 percent are from Canada, and nearly 30 percent are from European nations. In Major League Baseball, over one-fourth of the players on Major League teams and over 40 percent of the players at all levels of professional baseball in North America were not born in the United States. Among the 416 players on 29 NBA teams at the start of the 2002–2003 season, 67, or 16 percent, were born outside the United States.

These trends have been worrisome to some people. This is why some leagues have quotas that limit the number of foreign-born or foreign-nationality players that teams may sign to contracts. For example, in the early 1990s, Japan banned U.S. women basketball players from its professional league. At the same time, professional leagues in Italy, Spain, and France allowed their teams to have up to two foreign players, many of whom were from the United States. In 1996, England lifted all quotas for both men's and women's pro basketball teams; during the same year, the new MLS (Major League Soccer) in the United States limited the number of non–U.S. players to four per team. Currently, some people in the United States are calling for limits on the number of foreign athletes who can play on intercollegiate teams. At the same time, many athletic departments are recruiting more athletes from outside the United States.

As commercial sport organizations expand their franchise locations across national borders, and as they recruit athletes regardless of nationality, talent migration will increase in the future. The social implications of this trend will be important to study and understand.

Global Politics and the Production of Sports Equipment and Apparel

Free trade agreements (for example, GATT and NAFTA), signed by many new nations in the mid-1990s, have created a new global economic environment. In this environment, it is cost-effective for large corporations selling vast amounts of goods to people in wealthy nations to locate production facilities in labor-intensive poor nations. These corporations are taxed at much lower rates when they move products from nation to nation, so they can make products in nations where labor is cheap and regulations are scarce and then sell them in wealthy nations, where people can afford to buy them.

These political-economic changes mean that, through the 1990s, most athletic shoes costing well over $100 a pair in the United States were cut and sewn by workers making less than 25 cents per hour in China and Indonesia, less than 75 cents per hour in Thailand, and less than $2.25 per hour in South Korea (Enloe, 1995; Kidd and Donnelly, 2000).

Similar patterns existed in connection with the production of clothes bearing patriotic-looking red, white, and blue NFL and NBA logos sold in the United States. Soccer balls sanctioned by FIFA, the international soccer federation, often were hand-sewn by child laborers making far less than poverty-level wages in poor nations, where people were desperate for any kind of work. And, while Nike athletes were making millions of dollars on their shoe endorsements, Nike shoes were being made mostly by young women in Southeast Asia working ten to thirteen hours a day, six days a week under oppressive conditions for 13–20 cents per hour (U.S. dollars)— far below a living wage in China, Vietnam, and Indonesia.

This exploitation attracted worldwide attention among religious, human rights, and labor organizations, as well as other activist groups. Sport sociologist George Sage has described the international Nike transnational advocacy network, which emerged during the mid-1990s. This network of dozens of organizations from many countries gradually mobilized consciousness and various forms of political action, which influenced various government policies on labor and human rights issues and Nike's relationship with production contractors in Southeast Asia. The network was so effective that the Nike logo became associated with sweatshops and unfair labor practices in the minds of many consumers. Nike's earnings declined, and its executives began to take responsibility for making changes in its production facilities; they even downsized the swoosh logo and converted the print logo to *nike* with a small *n* because they wanted to understate their presence and avoid negative attention among potential consumers.

Sage's case study of the Nike transnational advocacy network is heartening, because it documents the power of people to make change. The Internet and other global communications technologies make it possible for people around the world to mobilize in response to human rights violations and other important social issues. Of course, many factors influence the formation of a transnational advocacy network, but, when issues resonate across many groups of people, a network of organizations and individuals can organize, take action, and have an impact on global political processes. If this were not possible, what would stop transnational corporations, which are accountable to nothing but a generally underregulated global marketplace, from pursuing their interests in whatever ways they wish?

In November 2001, the University of North Carolina signed a contract with Nike, contingent on the sporting goods company following an anti-sweatshop code for all equipment and apparel provided to university teams. For the university, a primary goal of this $28 million contract was to force Nike to end its exploitive child labor practices. Representatives of the campus saw this as one step in dealing with the general exploitation of labor in poor nations where there are few or no laws protecting workers or regulating the conditions under which they work.

Other universities have considered taking or have taken similar steps. In the case of Nike, this type of action can be effective because it has contracts with 200 college and university athletic departments. But exploitation continues to exist as corporations seek the cheapest labor they can find to manufacture their products. This exploitation will end only when consumers in wealthy nations take collective social actions that demand changes in public and corporate policies around the world. Human rights and social justice groups have fought these battles for many years, but they need help.

MAKING SENSE OF TODAY'S POLITICAL REALITIES

It's not easy to explain all the changes discussed in this chapter. Are sports simply a part of general globalization processes through which various sport forms come together in many combinations? Are we witnessing the modernization of sports? Are sports being Americanized? Europeanized? Asianized?

Are we seeing sports simply being diffused throughout the world, with people in some countries emulating the sports played in other countries, or are sports being used in connection with new forms of cultural imperialism and colonization?

Are sports tools for making poorer nations dependent on wealthier ones, or are they tools for establishing cultural independence and autonomy in emerging nations?

Is it accurate to say that sports are becoming commercialized, or should we say that corporations are appropriating sports for the purpose of global capitalist expansion?

Are traditional and folk sports around the world being destroyed by heavily publicized sports based in wealthy nations, or do people take sport forms from other cultures and creatively adapt them to their own circumstances?

Are sports becoming more democratic, or have new forms of sponsorship actually restricted people's choices about when and how they will play sports?

Those who study sports as social phenomena now are devoting more of their attention to these questions. The best work on these issues involves data collected at global *and* local levels (Donnelly, 1996). This work calls attention to the fact that powerful people do not simply impose certain sport forms on less powerful people around the world. Even when sports from powerful nations are played in other parts of the world, the meanings associated with them are often grounded in the local cultures in which they are played. It is important to understand global trends, but it is also important to understand the local expressions of and responses to those trends. Power is a process, not a thing; it is always exercised through social relations, so the study of power must focus on how people agree and disagree with one another as they attempt to live their lives in meaningful terms. This is true in connection with sports, as it is in other dimensions of social life.

REFERENCES

Donnelly, P. 1996. "Prolympism: Sport Monoculture as Crisis and Opportunity." *Quest* 48, 1:25–42.

Enloe, C. 1995. "The Globetrotting Sneaker." *Ms.* 5,5:10–15.

Jackson, S. J., and B. Hokowhitu. 2002. "Sport, Tribes, and Technology: The New Zealand All Blacks *Haka* and the Politics of Identity." *Journal of Sport and Social Issues* (2):125–39.

Jackson, S. J., and J. Scherer. 2002. *Screening the Nation's Past: Adidas, Advertising and Corporate Nationalism in New Zealand.* Paper presented at the annual conference of the North American Society for the Sociology of Sport, Indianapolis (November).

Klein, A. 1991. *Sugarball: The American Game, the Dominican Dream.* New Haven, CT: Yale University Press.

Kidd, B., and P. Donnelly. 2000. "Human Rights in Sports." *International Review for the Sociology of Sport* 35 (2):131–48.

Maguire, J., G. Jarvie, L. Mansfield, and J. Bradley. 2002. *Sports Worlds: A Sociological Perspective.* Champaign, IL: Human Kinetics.

Reid, S. M. 1996. "The Selling of the Games." *The Denver Post,* July 21:4BB.

Steinbreder, J. 1996. "Big spender." *Sky* (Delta Airlines magazine), July:37–42.

37

Corporate Globalization and Sporting Goods Manufacturing
The Case of Nike

George H. Sage

The sporting goods industry, like other major business industries, can be divided into relatively similar segments for the purpose of analyzing target markets, formulating marketing and positioning strategies, and identifying consumer groups. According to Brenda Pitts and her sport-management colleagues, the sport industry is composed of three major components: sport performance, sport promotion, and sport production. Sport performance consists of involvement in sport as a participant (athlete) or as a spectator; sport promotion encompasses various modes that promote sports—promotional merchandising, the media, sponsorships, endorsements, and so forth. The sport production segment of the sport industry comprises those products necessary or desired for the production of or to influence the quality of sport performance. Sporting goods—especially equipment, apparel, and footwear—are major products within this segment.[1]

The Sporting Goods Manufacturers Association (SGMA) defines this industry as "a composition of manufacturers of athletic footwear, sports apparel, and sporting goods equipment, as well as manufacturers of accessory items to the sports and recreation market." An essential segment of the sport industry, sporting goods constitute a $150 billion global industry; in the United States alone, sporting goods industry sales (at wholesale) were nearly $50 billion in 2003. Thus the production of sporting goods is a key component in the sport industry.

Although there are three components in the sport industry, there are only two ingredients that are indispensable. Regardless of where sporting activities take place, one is the participants, the other is the apparel and footwear that are worn and the equipment—the sporting goods—that is used: uniforms, T-shirts, sneakers, balls, bats, gloves, protective equipment, and so forth that are necessary for playing sports. In many cases, these are required and regulated by the rules.

But sporting goods and equipment are not gifts of nature; all sporting apparel, footwear, and equipment are made by people, who, except for a random chance of nature that has put them where they are and us where we are, are just like us—they are human beings. It is their labor that allows all of us to play, watch, coach, and administer sports. Their labor, in effect, is the very foundation of our sporting experience.

What about those who toil in factories all over the world to make sporting experiences satisfying and pleasant for athletes, fans, coaches, and sport administrators? They are rarely the subject of the sports pages of newspapers and magazines, nor are they part of the daily network radio and television sports reports. Athletes, coaches, teams, leagues, and so forth are the focus of media sports. Sports sections in newspapers and radio and TV sports news daily report the minute details of individual athlete's performances, teams' performances, league standings, and they also provide "lead-up" stories of coming sports events. Entire television and radio networks are devoted to reporting the same information, in addition to broadcasting sports events. But there is virtually nothing—a huge silence, as it were—about those who labor in factories all over the world to manufacture the apparel and equipment necessary for the sporting events that drive the sport industry.

THE GLOBAL ECONOMY AND SPORTING GOODS MANUFACTURING

Foreign commerce, even direct investment between countries, has been a part of the national economies of industrialized countries for over a century. It has only been in the past 40 years that the production, distribution, and consumption of products and services of most corporations has taken place between countries. That expansion of what is now called the global economy can be seen by the increase in cross-border trade, which grew from $629 billion in 1960 to $7.43 *trillion* in 2002. Transnational corporations (TNCs) increased in number from 7,000 in the 1960s to 65,000 today, and they control over 850,000 foreign affiliates worldwide.[2] TNCs are huge, powerful economic enterprises. Economically, they exceed the size of most governments; indeed, of the world's 100 largest economies, 66 are transnational corporations and only 34 are nations. In his State of the Union address in January 2000, President Bill Clinton declared that "globalization is the central reality of our time."

Product manufacturing is the major driving force of globalization, as advanced capitalist and developing countries seek to increase their shares of the wealth of nations, and a key aspect of the global economy is a capital system and division of labor known as the "export-processing system." In this system, product research, design, development, and marketing take place in industrially developed countries while the labor-intensive, assembly-line phases of product manufacture are relegated to developing (aka Third World) nations. The finished product is then exported for distribution in developed countries of the world. Because manufactured goods from developing countries have increased sharply in the past 25 years, over one-third of the earnings of the 200 largest U.S. TNCs are now from their export-processing operations.

The prevailing organizational pattern used by TNCs in export-processing manufacturing is to either establish factories, or contract with foreign manufacturing firms, in countries with authoritarian governments, where production costs are cheaper, labor protections are not enforced, workers are most repressed, there is a non-union workforce, and weak or nonexistent safety and environmental laws prevail. This process is widely known throughout the world as the "race to the bottom," which refers to shifting production to the lowest-wage countries. The most dramatic shift of this kind in the past decade has been to China, where average wages are just 2.1 percent of U.S. average wages.[3]

One of the consequences of the export-processing system for workers in developed countries is that manufacturing employment in the United States has plummeted. TNCs have closed factories in industrialized countries and moved the jobs to people in developing countries throughout the world. As Figure 37-1 illustrates, manufacturing now accounts for only 11 percent of employment in the United States compared with roughly 28 percent 40 years ago. Just between 2000 and 2003—three years—American manufacturing lost 2.7 million jobs.[4] Thus, corporate layoffs in the United States are at a pace of about half a million jobs per year. For workers and their communities in developed countries, the consequences of export-processing industrialization have been grim: closed plants, replacement jobs paying minimal wages, and a variety of physical and mental worker afflictions, as well as community disintegration linked to the global economy.

Consequently, in the United States the number of imported manufactured goods has risen sharply in the past 25 years. Between 1970 and 1980 the percentages of imported and exported manufactured goods were about the same. But by 2000 imports had skyrocketed to 80 percent and exports had sunk to 20 percent. With China alone, the United States had a trade deficit of over $100 billion trade deficit in 2002.[5]

The consequences of export-processing industrialization in developing countries has been dreadful. Although this system has provided employment for many workers, there have been adverse consequence as well: wages so low that workers cannot provide for their basic needs, unjust and inhuman working conditions, prohibition of union organization, and environmental devastation. Add widespread child labor to these conditions. According to International Labor Organization estimates released in 2002, some 352 million children aged 5 to 17 are engaged in some form of economic activity in the world, with the Asian-Pacific region having the largest number of child workers.[6]

In spite of claims by TNCs, numerous economists, and governments that globalization tends to equalize economic equality between developed and developing countries, there has actually been increasing *inequality* between those countries. Ac-

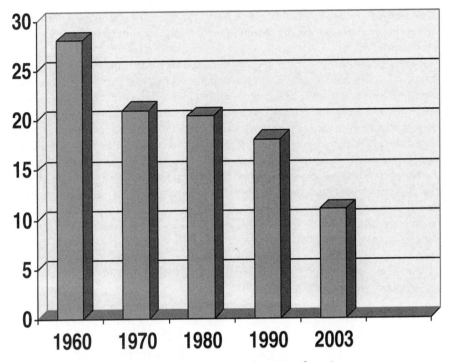

Figure 37-1 Percentage of U.S. Workers Employed in Manufacturing

Source: U.S. Bureau of Labor Statistics

cording to the United Nations Development Programme, the income gap between the 20 percent of the world's people living in the richest countries and the 20 percent in the poorest countries was 74 to 1 in 1997, up from 60 to 1 in 1990 and 30 to 1 in 1960. In other words, the economic gap between rich and poor countries *widened* dramatically. More recently this trend has been confirmed in the *United Nations Human Development Report 2003.* Fifty-four countries grew poorer, and 21 saw a decline in their human development indicators. Furthermore, gaps are widening both between and within countries.[7]

SPORTING GOODS MANUFACTURING IN THE GLOBAL ECONOMY: THE CASE OF NIKE

Sporting goods manufacturing is one of the most flourishing export-processing industries. Indeed, sporting goods manufacturers that produce all of their products domestically are now a minority because many of them have "run away" to various low-wage export-processing countries across the world. Over 90 percent of the sneakers and other sporting goods sold in the United States are imports made in foreign countries. China alone, arguably the country with the most abhorrent working conditions in the world, accounts for approximately 65 percent of global sporting goods production.[8]

The focus of this chapter is on a single sporting goods manufacturing firm—Nike—but it is important for readers to understand that there are 6,500 other sporting goods product manufacturers many of whose products are made in developing countries. Nike was chosen to illustrate how sporting goods firms have transferred their productive operations from the country in which they are incorporated to foreign export-processing operations in developing countries because it is the exemplar, the "poster boy" of this practice. In fact, the editors of the *Far Eastern Economic Review* even called the global economy "The New Nike Economy." Two writers for the *Washington Post* agreed, stating, "No company symbolizes the mobilization of American companies overseas more than Nike. Its 30-year history in Asia is as close as any one company's story can be to the history of globalization, to the spread of dollars . . . into the poor corners of the earth. . . . [I]t is a story of restless and ruthless capital, continually moving from country to country in search of new markets and untapped low-wage labor."[9]

The corporation that is now Nike was founded in 1964 by its current CEO, Philip Knight, and Bill Bowerman, then the University of Oregon track and field coach. The original name of the company was Blue Ribbon Sports. Nike was adopted as the name for a new style of running shoes in 1971; the corporate name was changed to Nike later. Its corporate headquarters is located in Beaverton, Oregon.

At first, the sneakers sold by Blue Ribbon Sports were made in Japan, at that time a low-wage country. But by the time the corporate name Nike, Inc., was adopted, Japanese labor wages had become more expensive, so over the next few years Nike management opened footwear manufacturing plants in New Hampshire and Maine. But Philip Knight's thinking was well ahead of the curve with respect to understanding the profitability potential of manufacturing in developing countries, and in 1977 the first factory in South Korea was opened. By the early 1980s nearly 90 percent of Nike's sports footwear was produced by South Korean and Taiwanese shoe manufacturers. By then Knight was considering closing Nike footwear manufacturing in New Hampshire and Maine and shifting production to South Korea and Taiwan, because both were low-wage countries with cooperative governments for export-processing plants.

Nike's American shoe factories were closed in the mid-1980s. Productive operations in Asia were carried out through subcontracting with local manufacturers, thus eliminating the need for Nike to build plants, hire workers, and carry out the day-to-day tasks of production. Product research, design, promotion, and distribution became the main functions of the Nike corporation itself. As Phil Knight said, "We grew this company by investing our money in design, development, marketing and sales, and asking other companies to manufacture our products."[10]

In the late 1980s, democratic reforms came to South Korea and Taiwan; wages increased dramatically, and labor movements won the right to form independent unions and to strike. Responding to these developments, Nike began persuading its contractors to shift much of their Nike footwear operations out of these two countries into politically autocratic, military-dominated countries like Indonesia and Thailand and later to China and Vietnam, in a relentless drive for a favorable political climate and the lowest-cost labor to make its shoes and apparel.

In an interview with *Harvard Business Review,* Phil Knight explained the strategy underlying the series of moves from one Asian country to another: "We were . . . good at keeping our manufacturing costs down. . . . Puma and Adidas were still manufacturing in high-wage European countries. But we knew that wages were lower in Asia, and we knew how to get around in that environment."[11] Knight also knew that political leaders in these countries were attracting foreign corporations with promises of weak or poorly enforced labor and environmental standards, and unions were outlawed or state controlled.

By 1998 about 40 percent of all Nike shoes were produced in Indonesia, with China and Vietnam the other major Asian Nike footwear manufacturing nations. Currently, Nike has around 450,000 workers making Nike products in Southeast Asia; over 50 Nike footwear and apparel factories in China employ more than 120,000 workers. None of Nike's footwear is manufactured within the United States. Nike does not own its factories; it contracts with foreign manufacturers, mostly located in cheap labor countries in Asia, to supply it with shoes.

Nike's Asian Factories: Not a Pretty Sight

In the late 1980s, when Nike shifted footwear production from Taiwan and South Korea, the primary country of relocation was Indonesia, a nation led by a brutal dictator who was aggressively courting TNC investments in order to build up exports for Indonesia. From the beginning, Nike contractors in Indonesia engaged in what one writer called "management by terror." The minimum wage in the shoe factories was 83 cents per day, which was only 56 percent of the wage the government considered as meeting the "minimum physical needs" level—a wage governments use as a subsistence level for a single adult worker in a given country.[12]

Horrendous working conditions, extremely long working days, mandatory overtime, and abusive behavior by supervisors quickly led to strikes and protests in the Indonesian sport shoe factories, and later in Nike factories in Vietnam and China. These actions resulted in increased scrutiny of Nike's factories, at first by the Indonesian press. Then the foreign media and nongovernmental organizations (NGOs) began to focus on wages and conditions in Nike factories. Throughout the 1990s labor problems arose in every Asian country where Nike contractors were located.

During the decade of the 1990s sixteen major investigations were made of factories producing Nike footwear in Indonesia, China, and Vietnam. Investigations were carried out by a variety of organizations—academic, religious, labor, human rights, and development—from various countries. The length of time collecting data, expertise of the investigators, and methodology of data collection varied considerably, but the investigations revealed similar patterns and conditions in Nike's Asian shoe factories.

The reports can be summarized as follows: Appalling labor conditions were essentially the same in all of Nike's factories. Seventy-five to 80 percent of Nike workers were women—mostly under the age of 24—who regularly put in 10 to 13 hour days, worked six days a week, and were forced to work overtime two to three times per week. The typical worker was paid 13 to 20 cents (in U.S. dollars) an hour—which was $1.60 to $2.20 per day. This wage was below the "minimum physical needs" figure. Worker abuse was widespread in the Nike factories.

Local industrial safety laws were nearly useless in practice in all of the Nike Asian factories because Nike contractors simply ignored the rules and regulations set out in the laws. Not surprisingly, the investigations found that the results of cutting costs on safety and the health of the mostly women workers were alarming.

Several of the reports found that Nike's record on workers' rights in these countries was deplorable. Independent unions were not permitted in the factories. Where Nike workers attempted organizing to fight for their rights, Nike's contractors called in the police or military, and workers were arrested and subjected to torture and beatings.

Such conditions existed in these countries because the political leaders were blatantly corrupt; they could be paid off and they, in turn, made sure police and military units maintained vigilance for signs of labor activism. A Stanford University professor who studied Nike's Indonesian factories said: "Nike's got business in Indonesia because the workers are docile by virtue of government repression and they can't protest. The world that Nike and Philip Knight represent is the opposite of human rights and civilized values."[13]

At the same time as the investigations of Nike factories were being reported, and the abysmal workers' wages and working conditions were revealed, the Nike corporation was expanding rapidly and recording record-breaking revenue almost annually. Moreover, Nike was spending lavishly on promoting its products, paying out 1.13 *billion* on advertising alone in 1998.

As the reports from these investigations were published, and each largely corroborated the results of the others, mass media throughout the world began to report the findings of these investigations. Between 1992 and 1996, as global understanding and consciousness grew, it struck a collective chord of horror and outrage, spurring collective actions by workers in Nike's Asian factories, and launching what ultimately became the Nike social movement. This movement was composed of a coalition of organizations, each with its own maze of affiliates, members, friends, and allies. As it grew, it became so dense and diverse, with so many interlocking links, that the organizational matrix became difficult to identify clearly. Figure 37-2 illustrates the types of organizations that became part of the Nike social movement.

It was actually Nike workers in Indonesia who initiated the struggle against the low wages, unsafe and unhealthy working conditions, and abusive treatment in the factories. Worker complaints escalated to work stoppages and then to strikes against Nike contractors. For example, in 1992, 6,500 workers at the Sung Hwa Dunia factory in Indonesia began a one-day strike, demanding better wages and working conditions. These actions incited many NGOs throughout the world to take up the

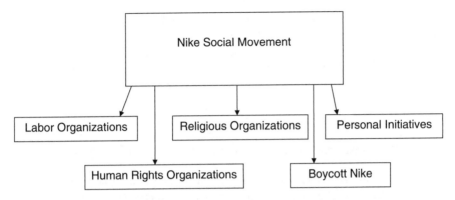

Figure 37-2 Types of Organizations Composing the Nike Social Movement

Source: Adapted from George H. Sage, "Justice Do It! The Nike Transactional Advocacy Network: Organization, Collective Actions, and Outcomes," *Sociology of Sport Journal* 16, no. 3 (1999).

workers' cause, thus forming the broad structure for a Nike social movement, which then organized a variety of campaigns against Nike. Those campaigns, which took the form of demonstrations, protests, op-ed columns, TV spots, sit-ins, and marches, were devoted to making the public aware of Nike's labor practices.

The Nike social movement was the first global social movement to widely employ Internet communication. Literally dozens of Web sites connected the various organizations and served to inform the general public about Nike campaigns—announcing times, places, and purpose of future ones, and reporting the outcomes of previous ones. Cultivating the media by packaging information about workers in Nike factories in a timely and dramatic way, the social movement organizations were quite successful in attracting both electronic and print mass media coverage. For example, two hour-long programs about Nike factories were shown on the CBS program *48 Hours,* one in 1993 and the other in 1996. ESPN's *Outside the Lines* carried an hour-long documentary titled *Made in Vietnam: The Sneaker Controversy* that revealed unsafe and abusive working condition inside Nike factories.

The Nike social movement and its campaigns quickly agreed upon the most important objectives they were organized to accomplish. Those were:

- A subsistence wage for Nike workers
- Safe working conditions for Nike workers
- Freedom to organize for Nike workers
- Respect for the human rights of Nike workers

Their ultimate goal was to create enough public outrage against Nike that governments, business organizations, unions, religious organizations, and human rights groups would bring pressure on Nike to change its labor practices and move forcefully to improve conditions in the factories.

Through a loose system of networking, the Nike social movement was about to mobilize a multitude of mostly civil initiatives to respond to the various reports of Nike's factories documenting Nike's below subsistence wages, abysmal working conditions, employment of very young girls, abuse of workers, and antiunion practices. All of these campaigns portrayed Nike as a repressive, abusive, unjust, and inhuman corporation. Between 1993 and 1998 the Nike social movement reached its peak of actions and influence.

Nike's Responses to Factory Reports and the Social Movement

From its beginnings, Nike management carefully crafted the image of a company with an "attitude"—one journalist referred to it as a swagger—thus appealing to the "cool," "hip," and savvy side of the teenage and young adult populations, the major consumer groups for sports footwear. Its famous slogan, "Just Do It!" wordlessly asserts a "no excuses" viewpoint. Nike's advertising images have consistently communicated an irreverence and rebellious posture, which also reflected in some of its endorsers, such as Dennis Rodman, John McEnroe, and Charles Barkley. Nike CEO Philip Knight himself admitted: "What we are all about is being against the establishment."[14]

At the same time, Nike had scrupulously honed a rhetoric of social responsibility, suggesting a socially conscious global corporate citizen with a sensitivity to racial, gender, and disability discrimination, as well as a concern for the environment. This was accompanied by its engaging in a variety of promotional ventures designed to illustrate Nike's support for empowering minority and disadvantaged groups.[15]

With such a corporate perspective, it is perhaps not surprising that Nike's initial response to the reports about its Asian factories was overwhelmingly denial, resentment, and anger. At first, Nike management denied responsibility for conditions in the Asian factories, arguing that Nike merely contracted with suppliers, who actually manufactured the shoes, and therefore Nike could not control what went on in the factories. Nike's vice president for production argued: "We don't set policy within the factories; it is their business to run."[16] This is, of course, absurd; Nike always had overall control of its productive operations through the power it had over its contractors. In all its contracts with suppliers Nike specified very precisely all of the quality standards that had to be met in the manufacture of their products. There is no reason at all that Nike management could not also specify labor standards with regard to the workers in the factories.

In response to some of its workers' unrest and mounting critical reports of its Asian footwear factories, Nike developed a Code of Conduct and Memorandum of Understanding in 1992 for its suppliers. Every factory employee was to receive a copy of the Code of Conduct, or the Code was to be placed where every worker could read it. However, several of the investigations of Nike factories found that many Nike workers had no knowledge of the existence of the Code and that the Code was flagrantly violated by Nike's contractors. Interviews with Nike's workers about the Code suggested that it was chiefly an instrument of damage control rather than a mechanism for worker protection in Nike factories.

Another form of response Nike made to the reports about conditions in its factories was to employ its own factory investigators. Nike hired the accounting firm Ernst & Young in 1994 to conduct audits of labor and environmental conditions inside its contractors' factories to determine whether the factories were in compliance with Nike's corporate code of conduct. In 1997 Nike commissioned former American United Nations Ambassador Andrew Young and his GoodWorks International company to go to Asia and investigate its factory operations in Indonesia, China, and Vietnam. Later in the same year Nike released a summary of an investigation of its Asian factories it had funded, which had been done as a class project by a group of MBA students at the Amos Tuck School of Business at Dartmouth.

All three reports were prepared and paid for by Nike; none were independent inspections of Nike factories. Nevertheless, Ernst & Young reported numerous violations of labor laws on maximum working hours, inadequate safety equipment and training, and a series of hazardous and abusive working conditions inside the plants, including widespread worker exposure to hazardous chemicals. Andrew Young's review of Nike factories was silent on the issue of health and safety; did not address the use of hazardous chemicals, and made no mention of corporal punishment, except to acknowledge "there have been problems." Young totally avoided the most obvious and controversial issue—whether Nike paid its workers fair wages—saying that it was beyond the "technical capacity" of his investigation. For all intents and purposes, the Dartmouth Tuck Business School study was worthless. Analysts found the methodology of the study to be totally inadequate and questioned the validity of results obtained by students untrained for this type of research and paid for by Nike. Thus, all three reports came under scathing criticism from international human rights, labor, and religious organizations, as well as a number of journalists.

Meanwhile, in the mid-1990s Nike initiated a public relations blitz—including press conferences, letters to the editor, and so forth—to defend its corporate reputation and mute the mounting criticism of its labor practices. Ironically, the outcome was more negative public relations. For example, in 1998 Marc Kasky, a California consumer activist, sued Nike under the state's false advertising laws, claiming Nike was making false and misleading public statements. Nike countered that it was engaging in protected free speech. The California Supreme Court ruled 4 to 3 in favor of Kasky, holding that Nike's statements were commercial speech and thus could be regulated as advertising. Nike appealed to the U.S. Supreme Court; in 2003 that Court returned the case to California. In September 2003 Nike announced that it would pay Kasky $1.5 million to settle the case, thus staving off what could have been an unflattering court fight.

Perhaps the most consistent and persistent response Nike management made during the 1990s to the reports about its Asian factories was: "Why is Nike being singled out when the Asia factories of other sports footwear and apparel manufacturers are very similar to Nike's?" One of Nike's public relations spokespersons posed the question this way: "Why . . . are we the sole target of all this interest" in foreign sport footwear production operations?

Several types of replies were made by the Nike social movement organizations: They argued that because Nike had been the industry pioneer in moving its productive operations overseas, complaints about its labor practices were the first to surface in the Asian sports footwear industry. It was also pointed out that a basic principle of labor collective actions is to go after the market leader, and that Nike was far and away the market leader in the sports footwear industry, with a 40 percent share of the market; moreover, by Nike's own research, its corporate icon—the swoosh brand—is recognized by 97 percent of Americans. As the "corporation marquée" in the sports footwear and apparel industry, other corporations in the industry looked to Nike for leadership. Even Nike CEO Philip Knight acknowledged: "Our competitors just follow our lead." Therefore, there was reason to believe that when Nike agreed to the demands of the Nike social movement, other companies in that industry would follow. As the founder of a Nike campaign called "Justice. Do It Nike" put it: "Nike is . . . the largest company [in the sport shoe industry] and has set the precedent for . . . [the] race to the bottom. If Nike reforms, they will trumpet the change and other manufacturers will have to follow."

Unspoken, but clearly one reason that Nike was being targeted, was an arrogance and hypocrisy in Nike's management and corporate culture that many Nike social movement organizers and supportive media journalists perceived. For Nike critics, CEO Phil Knight was viewed as contemptuous, insensitive, and iconoclastic in his public actions. As one leader of the Nike movement noted: "The company and its founder have always had a reputation for being aggressive and unconventional, the 'bad boys' of the shoe industry, built on an irreverence for the sporting establishment and for any authority which might cramp the individual's style." Nike's advertising seemed to take pride in communicating an in-your-face hipness and a win-at-all-cost image.[17]

Nike Social Movement Outcomes

The Nike brand name and reputation were severely damaged for millions of people throughout the world by the reports about conditions in Asian Nike factories and the campaigns of the Nike social movement. For many, the Nike swoosh became associated with sweatshops and the oppression of workers. Indeed, in a speech Philip Knight gave in May 1998 he admitted this, saying, "The Nike product has become synonymous with slave wages, forced overtime and arbitrary abuse." He also said, "I truly believe that . . . [consumers do] not want to buy products made in abusive conditions."

The Nike campaigns won sympathy and support for their objectives. They helped to change governmental policies in several foreign countries, such as the establishment of or increases in minimum wages, reforms in working-condition standards, and limitations on hours worked per day and week. Several governments adopted new public policies to permit independent union organization.

Nike campaigns also brought their message about Nike's Asian factories to American university campuses. Many students were moved to organize and campaign in a variety of ways to show their support for the movement. This led to the founding of the United Students against Sweatshops (USAS) in the summer of 1998.

Nike had a 49 percent decline in its 1998 fiscal net income compared to 1997. The company lost $68 million the last quarter (May–August 1998), the first time in 13 years the company had a quarterly loss. In the first quarter of 1999 (June–August 1998) revenue fell 9 percent; net income dropped 35 percent. These trends in earnings suggest that the Nike campaigns were likely adversely affecting Nike's revenues. However, the collapse of several Asian economies was affecting revenues of many TNCs between 1997 and 1998, and this may have also been a factor in Nike's revenue declines.

Nike Changes Course

Speaking before the National Press Club luncheon in Washington, D.C., on May 12, 1998, Nike CEO, Philip Knight, announced plans for a substantially new course for the company. This course—what he called "New Labor Initiatives"—was Nike's plan for significant reforms in the company's labor practices. The most notable of the new initiatives were:

- Nike was increasing the minimum age of footwear factory workers to 18, and the minimum age for all other light-manufacturing workers (apparel, accessories, equipment) to 16.
- Nike was adopting U.S. Occupational Safety and Health Administration (OSHA) indoor air quality standards for all footwear factories.
- Nike was expanding education programs, for workers in all Nike footwear factories.
- Nike was expanding its current monitoring program.

Organizations of the Nike social movement viewed these initiatives as an admission by Nike that there were serious problems in its Asian factories, and they also believed that these reforms came about as a direct result of the years of Nike campaigns that brought Nike labor practices to the awareness of world consumers. The feeling throughout these Nike social movement organizations was that Nike would not have taken these steps had it not been for the various Nike campaigns. In his book about international social activism, Randy Shaw said this about the Nike movement: "The growth of the anti-Nike campaign . . . demonstrates not only the power of activists acting nationally to rewrite the rules of the global economy, but the triumph of the activists' vision of what is possible over prevailing, mainstream assumptions that have too often deterred social change efforts in all fields."[18] The Nike social movement showed that popular struggles can improve the plight of workers who labor under oppressive and unjust conditions in the global economy.

The Debate over Monitoring Sporting Goods Manufacturing Factories

Following Knight's announcement of the "New Initiatives" reforms, a vice president for corporate responsibility was employed, and shareholders at the 1998 Nike annual meeting were informed that by the end of the year the company would have an independent monitoring system underway. That same year, under the threat of a National Livable Wage Campaign, Nike announced it was raising wages of its Indonesian workers by 25 percent (where wages were raised, they did not keep up with the rapid inflation in Indonesia). Finally, as predicted by the Nike social movement organizers, after Nike's "New Initiatives" announcement, other sporting goods manufacturers promised to reform their foreign-manufacturing operations, conform to codes of conduct, and agree to independent monitoring of their factories.

With Nike and other sporting goods companies promising labor reforms, attention turned to issues of independent monitoring of factories to assure that the corporations' promises could actually be verified through inspections by independent monitors. Over the following five years, vigorous and prolonged debate took place about the issue of independent factory monitoring. Sporting goods manufacturers supported the use of monitoring organizations that were "business friendly" and had weak labor and human rights representation. On the other side, labor and human rights, as well as the United Students Against Sweatshops, lobbied for monitoring organizations that would more likely be sensitive to the interests of workers.

Before discussing the problems associated with monitoring, it is necessary to comment on the role that university campus organizations played in the factory monitoring issue. In the mid-1990s the Nike social movement was reaching its peak of influence and reports about Nike's Asian factories became a popular topic on many American university campuses. Students began to raise questions about their own university's affiliations with Nike. As they did this, they demanded that their university take responsibility for the labor conditions under which its licensed and university-logo products were made by adopting Codes of Conduct to regulate the labor practices of the manufacturers of those licensed products. The idea behind the students' campaign was this: They opposed their colleges and universities supporting the appalling sweatshop system, and they did not want their institution profiting from the exploitation of the children, men, and women around the world who make the products that carry the university logo.

In July of 1998, student activists from over 30 different colleges and universities active in the anti-sweatshop movement formed USAS, the purpose of which was to be a cohesive coalition of students on campuses working on antisweatshop and Code of Conduct campaigns. One of the main goals of the USAS was to coordinate student participation and action around the development of manufacturers' Codes of Conduct and monitoring systems.

In less than one year, USAS spread to over 100 campuses across the United States and Canada (in 2003 USAS had chapters at over 200 university campuses), raising an awareness about the sweatshop issue to unprecedented levels. Students at Duke University took the lead in winning a commitment from the Duke administration to require full public disclosure of its licensees and in securing the university's approval of a Code of Conduct for all licensees who make products carrying the Duke name or logos and used by the university's sports teams.

Students at dozens of universities followed the Duke students' lead, winning commitments to full public disclosure by corporations, revealing the location of contractor's plants manufacturing the university's merchandise and athletic equipment, and securing approval of Codes of Conduct for all their licensees and assurances that those plants meet the code of conduct.[19] But on campuses across the country a major debate centered around the question of how these codes would be enforced. The answer, of course, was through a system of independent monitoring of factories where the university's products were made. So a central issue arose over which monitoring organization was the most appropriate.

Between 1998 and 2003 several organizations vied for recognition as the most credible and reputable independent factory monitoring firm. By 2003 two organizations had become the leaders: the Fair Labor Association (FLA) and the Worker Rights Consortium (WRC). The FLA initially gained the upper hand, primarily because it had been created out of the Apparel Industry Partnership that was formed from a diverse group of industry, labor, and human rights leaders that President Clinton brought to the White House in 1996 to discuss industry conditions. The FLA professed to be an independent monitoring organization that protects the rights of workers and holds manufacturers, as well as contractors and suppliers, publicly accountable for their labor practices. According to the FLA's information brochures, it certifies that corporations are in compliance with their Codes of Conduct and serves as a source of information for the public.[20]

The WRC was founded by the USAS in consultation with labor and human rights experts. The WRC Mission Statement on its Web site, asserts that it "is committed to building constructive working relationships with licensees. . . . [W]e recognize the licensees will play a central role in any progress that occurs toward better conditions in production facilities around the world. The WRC's goal is not to embarrass licensees but to promote real improvements in factory conditions."[21]

Despite the FLA's claim to be "independent" it is considered by many NGOs and labor unions to be "business-friendly," and, indeed, it is the preferred monitoring organization for manufacturing corporations as well as many university administrators. In 2003 some 170 colleges and universities were affiliated with the FLA. Major support for the WRC comes largely from labor, religious, and human rights organizations, and thus is considered unacceptable by most manufacturing corporations. According to the WRC, there were over 100 college and university affiliates in 2003.[22]

In 2004 the issue over the "best" monitoring organization for providing independent inspections and objective reporting of findings was still a hotly contested issue. The FLA has the edge in size and resources because it represents a multi-stakeholder coalition of companies, universities, and NGOs, whose foreign manufacturers supply their products. Nike is one of the FLA companies. The WRC was created by college and university administrations, students, and labor rights experts. Its purpose is only to assist in the enforcement of manufacturing Codes of Conduct adopted by colleges and universities. Thus, it has a more limited role in the factory monitoring industry.

Nike's New Initiatives: A Commitment to Reform or a Public Relations Ploy?

When Phil Knight made his "New Initiatives" speech, and then followed up with a number of actions appearing to show that those initiatives were under way, many of the individuals and organizations in the Nike social movement felt they had accomplished most of their objectives and turned to other issues. However, at the time of Knight's announcement he said nothing about the company being committed to paying a living wage for a normal workweek. Because this had been a fundamental demand of the Nike social movement from its beginning, a number of the movement organizations pledged to remain active until Nike committed to this issue. They also vowed to scrutinize Nike's future labor practices to make sure Nike delivered on the promises made in its initiatives. It turns out that their concerns about Nike were well founded. Over the next few years Nike invested substantial resources in public relations promoting its improved labor practices and invoked a corporate responsibility rhetoric for treating workers well, but reports from various labor and human rights organizations consistently told a different story, a story of unfulfilled promises.

A year after the "New Initiatives" announcement, the Urban Community Mission (Jakarta) conducted a survey of Nike's Indonesian workers. That report summarized the findings: "Contradicting claims by Nike to have reformed [its Asian factories], this survey indicated that excessive and compulsory overtime, abusive management practices and inadequate wages are still features of Nike contracted factories in Indonesia."[23] In Indonesian factories of another sport footwear company surveyed by the Urban Community Mission, the management practices were less cruel and the workers were under much less pressure than Nike workers. But low wages were a significant issue in those factories as well.

In the spring of 2000 a group of international labor rights organizations reported on a series of investigations made at various Nike factories in Thailand, Indonesia, Vietnam, and Cambodia during 1999 and 2000. The investigations found consistent evidence of abusive and exploitative working conditions including the following: wages below the level required for meeting basic needs, oppressively long working hours, excessive overtime, violent punishment of workers, and aggressive antiunion activity on the part of factory management. The report concluded: "This leads us to believe that labour abuses are the norm in . . . suppliers' factories and not isolated incidents as Nike has frequently suggested to the media."[24]

In December 1999 and March 2000, the Hong Kong Christian Industrial Committee interviewed workers at Nike's factories in China. The reports disclosed that Nike's workers endured abusive and often illegal conditions. Some of those were: extreme hours of work—up to 12.5-hour days, 7-day workweeks, wages of 11 to 58 cents per hour where a living wage was over 87 cents per hour, cheating workers of their earned wages, and dangerous working conditions.[25]

In February 2001, the Global Alliance for Workers and Communities, formed by a consortium of companies and groups—including Nike—to study workplace experiences and life opportunities for workers in developing countries, released a 106-page report on the labor conditions at nine Nike factories in Indonesia. Nike had commissioned the project and spent $7.8 million to fund it. The report was titled *Workers' Voices: An Interim Report on Workers' Needs and Aspirations in Nine Nike Contract Factories in Indonesia;* many of the findings from interviews and focus groups involving more that 4,200 workers, confirmed what investigations of Nike Asian factories had been reporting for over 10 years. Even Nike management found the report findings "disturbing," and in a press release admitted that "no worker should be subject to some of the working conditions reported in this assessment."

The Global Alliance assessment process did not examine workplace conditions in depth, but a series of questions were included on workplace conditions. In the report, over half the workers said that basic monthly wages were not adequate to meet workers' subsistence living expenses. Forty-five percent were not satisfied with health facilities at the factories, workers at all nine factories reported experiencing or seeing various forms of harassment and abuse, and workers were forced to work overtime.[26]

In response to the Global Alliance report, Nike drew up a "remediation plan" that addressed compensation, terms of work, harassment, conditions of work, and reporting a worker's death, the most significant problems that were identified in the report. For each problem area, a plan of action was described.[27] Three months after the Global Alliance report, Global Exchange, an international human rights organization, published a 115-page report titled *Still Waiting for Nike to Do It.* The report revealed that three years after Phil Knight's speech to the National Press Club Nike workers were still forced to work excessive hours, were not earning a livable wage, and were subject to harassment and dismissal if they attempt to form unions. The report concluded: "Nike has misled consumers and let down the workers who make its products and who continue to suffer extreme injustice while Nike touts itself as an 'industry leader' in corporate responsibility." The Global Exchange corporate accountability organizer said, "Over the last three years, Nike has treated this issue as a public relations inconvenience rather than a serious human rights issue."[28]

In the same month that the Global Exchange report was published, a National Labor Committee (NLC) delegation left for Bangladesh. They went to study labor conditions in Bangladesh because it is the third largest export-processing country for apparel exported to the United States. In a booklet published in 2002 titled *Bangladesh: Ending the Race to the Bottom,* the NLC delegation reported on labor conditions in seven factories that produce logoed apparel for American universities, three of which produced Nike products, while the other four produced products for other sporting goods firms, such as Reebok, Pro Sports, and Wilson Sporting Goods.

In the Nike factories studied, the average hours of work per week at the three plants were 66, 78, and 80 hours; below-subsistence wages were paid at all the factories; health and sanitary conditions in the plants were appalling; workers were abused in a variety of ways; and attempts to organize a union were met with firing. (The right to organize and bargain collectively are guaranteed legal rights by Bangladesh labor law. However, the law does not apply in the country's Export Processing Zones, where all these factories are located.) In one Nike factory, no worker had ever heard of the Nike Code of Conduct. Conditions in the four factories not producing Nike products were very similar to those in Nike factories, confirming the point that I made earlier in this chapter.[29]

Also in 2002 a report titled *We Are Not Machines* was published by a coalition of labor rights organizations based on interviews with about 35 Indonesian workers from four sport shoe factories producing Nike and Adidas. This report was actually a follow-up of a report released in 2000 titled, *Like Cutting Bamboo, Nike and Indonesian Workers' Right to Freedom of Association,* which detailed abuse of workers' human rights—verbal abuse, humiliation in front of other workers, excessively long work week, below-subsistence wages, and lack of respect for freedom of association and collective bargaining rights. When that report was published, Nike promised it would investigate, but it never published anything about the investigation.

The *We Are Not Machines* report was an attempt to assess whether any progress had been made in improving conditions in the factories since the first report was released. According to the new report, despite some small steps forward, poverty and fear still dominated the lives of Nike and Adidas workers in Indonesia, so any measures that Nike took fell well short of ensuring that workers were able to live with dignity. Fundamental wage inadequacies, working conditions, and lack of freedom of association were still present.[30]

These reports add to what has become a long list of factories that make products for Nike where serious labor violations have been found. The findings of the various studies of Nike's Asian factories in the five years after Knight's "New Initiatives" announcement convincingly show that many of Nike's factories continue to have many of the same conditions that have been reported for over 10 years. As one Nike social movement organizer remarked, "Persuading Nike to reform its factories is like pulling a reluctant tomcat across a carpet."

Three important points need to be made about Nike at this point: First it is important to note that Nike has over 450 factories in Asia, and not all of them have been part of the factories' reports. So it is possible that workers at some of Nike's factories do not suffer the conditions of those that have been studied. That seems unlikely, however. Second, most of the recent reports acknowledge that some of the conditions in Nike's factories have improved. For example, in the Global Alliance study, the majority of workers said they were satisfied with the health facilities at their respective factory as well as their work relationships with their direct supervisors and factory management. Nike has also prepared reports outlining how it proposes to address the findings of various reports. As mentioned above, it developed a "remediation plan" as a response to the Global Alliance release. In the fall of 2001, Nike published a detailed 56-page "Corporate Responsibility Report" that described its efforts toward understanding and managing global labor compliance and its commitment to diversity, and pledged its support for environmental sustainability. Still, Nike did not commit to a living wage for its workers in any of its documents.[31] Third, Nike has contributed substantial amounts of money to educational programs, community youth programs (e.g., Participate in the Lives of America's Youth [PLAY]), and promoted race and gender empowerment in various ways.

In spite of these actions, the contradiction between what Nike has claimed about its factories and what study after study has reported about those factories has continued because Nike persistently projected a corporate image of concern for the working conditions in its factories and a commitment to reform them, but the company's basic strategy relied on damage control and public relations.

Extraordinary resources have been expended by Nike deflecting blame and disparaging the findings in the reports about the company's factories. Simultaneously Nike has integrated high-profile public relations initiatives while touting a wide-ranging social consciousness and a commitment to corporate responsibility, such as the educational, youth, and racial and gender projects mentioned above, all of which were designed to portray the company in a positive light. This strategy has preserved Nike's core company policies that have allowed it to profit from sweatshop labor.

In some ways this strategy has served Nike well, especially with its stockholders and those loyal to its brand name. But in other ways it has not served well. While the company has been able to ameliorate some of the damage to its reputation with this strategy, it has opened itself to credibility problems. According to two Canadian sociologists, it "has created an image problem . . . by setting the company's self-identity at odds with a growing public reputation for sweatshop practices. Activist criticism has been able to question Nike's credibility by exposing the gap between the company's social responsibility claims and its . . . labor practices." They also note that "The motivation of the anti-sweatshop movement is a belief that Nike is hypocritical in the way it lays claim to social responsibility as an instrument of commercial promotionalism yet continues to exploit young, migrant, female workers in the developing world."[32]

Nike has been successful at creating wealth for its owners and shareholders, but while doing this it has also been a corporate leader in the race to the bottom, in seeking the lowest wage countries for its productive operations. But low wages have only been part of the story. The other part has been the miserable working conditions that its workers have had to endure. Reports over the past 10 years have consistently shown that Nike is a leader in exploitation of workers, not in the protection of workers. The evidence has shown that labor abuses have been central to the way Nike runs its business.

To be sure, Nike is not the only company that has followed this global economy model. Nike has received extensive public criticism not because it is the worst, but because it has had the largest share of the sports footwear market and the accompanying profits, and can therefore most easily afford to lead a change in corporate direction. Some researchers who have studied Nike's promotional strategies believe that "Nike faces the dual problem of making substantive improvements to working conditions, wages, and workers' rights and restoring its public credibility as a company whose claims to social responsibility are seen as sincere."[33]

Globalization is inevitable, and transnational corporate power and privilege will surely continue, but TNCs like Nike can play a very positive role in developing countries. Private sector investment can be an important driver for global economic growth and poverty reduction. TNCs can provide stable, long-term, decently paying jobs. They can ensure that workers' basic rights are respected in the workplace. Unfortunately, up to this point, many have not. But organizations and networks of the new civil globalism, like the Nike social movement, are determined to challenge the oppressive and exploitative power and practices of the transnational corporate global economy. The hopes for a better future throughout the world rest on a cooperative relationship and mutual respect between corporations and their workforce.

NOTES

This chapter has been prepared for publication in D. Stanley Eitzen (ed.) *Sport in Contemporary Society: An Anthology* (7th edition). Any other use of this chapter is prohibited without the permission of George H. Sage.

1. Brenda G. Pitts, Larence F. Fielding, and Lori K. Miller, "Industry Segmentation Theory and the Sport Industry: Developing a Sport Industry Segment Model," *Sport Marketing Quarterly* 3, no. 1 (1994): 15–24.

2. United Nations Conference on Trade and Development, *World Investment Report 2002* (New York: United Nations, 2002); see also Tony Schirato and Jen Webb, *Understanding Globalization* (Thousand Oaks: Sage, 2003); Michael Veseth (ed.) *The Rise of the Global Economy* (Chicago: Fitzroy Dearborn, 2002).

3. Michael D. Yates, *Naming the System: Inequality and Work in the Global Economy* (New York: Monthly Review Press, 2003); see also David Zweig, *Internationalizing China: Domestic Interests and Global Linkages* (Ithaca: Cornell University Press, 2002); Tony Schirato and Jen Webb, *Understanding Globalization* (Thousand Oaks: Sage, 2003).

4. Alan Levenson, "As U.S. Economy Adapts to Change, Manufacturing Takes a Back Seat," *T. Rowe Price Report* (Fall 2003), pp. 13–14; see also Barbara Hagenbaugh, "U.S. Manufacturing Jobs Fading Away Fast," *USA Today,* 13 December 2002, pp. 1B–2B; Robert J. S. Ross, "The 'Race to the Bottom' in Imported Clothes," *Dollars and Sense* (January/February 2002), pp. 46–47.

5. Sue Kirchhoff, "U.S. Manufacturers vs. China," *USA Today,* 1 July 2003, p. 4B.

6. International Labour Office, *Every Child Counts: New Global Estimates on Child Labour* (Geneva, ILO, 2002).

7. United Nations Development Programme, "Overview," *Human Development Report 1999* (New York: Oxford University Press, 1999), p. 3; United Nations Development Programme, *Human Development Report 2003* (New York: Oxford University Press, 2003); see also J. Cox, "Poor Nations Just Getting Poorer," *USA Today,* 13 September 2000, p. 5B; Yates, *Naming the System.*

8. National Labor Committee, *No More Sweatshops!* (New York: NLC, 2002), p. 2; Maria Stefan, "Greetings from China," *SportsEdge* (October 2001), p. 30; for a brief history of the history of the sporting goods industry, see George H. Sage, "The Sporting Goods Industry: From Struggling Entrepreneurs to National Business to Transnational Corporations," in *The Commercialisation of Sport,* ed. Trevor Slack (London: Frank Cass, in press).

9. Anne Swardson and Sandra Bugawara, "Asian Workers Become Customers," *The Washington Post,* 30 December 1996, pp. A1, A16.

10. Nike, Inc., "CEO Philip H. Knight's letter: Nike and Corporate Responsibility," *Corporate Responsibility Report* (October 2001), p. inside cover; for accounts of Nike's early history, see J. B. Strasser and Laurie Becklund, *Swoosh, the Unauthorized Story of Nike and the Men Who Played There* (New York: Harper Business, 1993); Donald Katz, *Just Do It: The Nike Spirit in the Corporate World* (New York: Random House, 1994).

11. Geraldine E. Willigan, "High Performance Marketing: An Interview with Nike's Phil Knight," *Harvard Business Review* 70 (July 1992), p. 92.

12. Jeff Ballinger and Claes Olsson, (eds.) *Behind the Swoosh: The Struggle of Indonesians Making Nike Shoes* (Global Publications Foundation, 1997).

13. Quoted in M. Mohtashemi, "Knight Defends Firm's Asian Wages," *Global Exchange Campaigns* (1997). http://www.globalexchange.org/watch/campaigns/gophilgo5.8.htm; see also George H. Sage, "Justice Do It! The Nike Transactional Advocacy Network: Organization, Collective Actions, and Outcomes," *Sociology of Sport Journal* 16, no. 3 (1999): 206–235.

14. Timothy Egan, "The Swoon of Swoosh," *New York Times Magazine,* 13 September 1998, p. 69.

15. Graham Knight and Josh Greenberg, "Promotionalism and Subpolitics: Nike and Its Critics," *Management Communication Quarterly* 15 (May 2002): 541–570; see also Carol A. Stabile, "Nike, Social Responsibility, and the Hidden Abode of Production," *Critical Studies in Media Communication* 17 (June 2000): 186–204.

16. Quoted in Donald Katz, *Just Do It: The Nike Spirit in the Corporate World* (New York: Random House, 1994), p. 191.

17. Robert Goldman and Stephen Papson, *Nike Culture: The Sign of the Swoosh* (Thousand Oaks: Sage, 1998); see also Walter LaFeber, *Michael Jordan and the New Global Capitalism* (New York: W. W. Norton, 1999).

18. Randy Shaw, *Reclaiming America: Nike, Clean Air, and the New National Activism* (Berkeley: University of California Press, 1999), p. 16.

19. See M. B. Marklein, "Colleges Apply Conduct Codes to Logo Sweatshops," *USA Today,* 1 June 1998, p. 1D; Thad Williamson, "Who Wants to Be a Cheerleader for a Sweatshop?" *Dollars and Sense* (July/August, 2002): 24–26; see also Chapter 7,"The Student Anti-Sweatshop Movement," in Jay R. Mandle, *Globalization and the Poor* (Cambridge: Cambridge University Press, 2003).

20. Fair Labor Association, Homepage, http://www.fairlabor.org. (2003).

21. Worker Rights Consortium, Homepage. http://workersrights.org. (2003).

22. David Moberg, "Too Cruel for School: Students Stand Up for Workers Rights," *In These Times* (27 May 2002): 21–22; see also Dara O'Rourke, "Sweatshop 101," *Dollars and Sense,* (September/October 2001): 14–17, 46.

23. Urban Community Mission Survey Report. "Cruel Treatment Working for Nike in Indonesia," (December 1999). http://summersault.com/~agj/clr/alerts/crueltreatmentworkingfornikeinindonesia.html.

24. Quoted in "UNITE! Report, 'Sweatshops Behind the Swoosh,'" p. 3 (2000). http://www.uniteunion.org/pressbox/nikereport3.html, p. 1.

25. "UNITE! Report, 'Sweatshops Behind the Swoosh,'" p. 2 (2000). http://www.uniteunion.org/pressbox/nike-report2.html, pp. 2–4.

26. See "Workers' Needs Assessment in Nike Contract Factories: A Summary of Findings," *Global Alliance for Workers and Communities: Progress Report* 2 (February 2001).

27. "Nike Releases Remediation Plan for Indonesian Factories," Nike Press Release, 22 February 2001.

28. Global Exchange, *Still Waiting for Nike to Do It* (2001). http://store.globalexchange.org/nike.html; Josh Richman, "Is Nike Still Doing It?" MotherJones.com (16 May 2001), p. 1, retrieve: MotherJones.com; click on "Search" and then type in "Is Nike Still Doing It?"

29. National Labor Committee, *Bangladesh: Ending the Race to the Bottom* (New York: National Labor Committee, 2002).

30. Timothy Conner, *Like Cutting Bamboo: Nike and Indonesian Workers' Rights to Freedom of Association* (2000), http://www.caa.org.au/campaigns/nike/association/report.html; Timothy Connor, *We Are Not Machines* (2002) http://www.caa.org.au/campaigns/nike/reports/machines/index.html.

31. "Corporate Responsibility Report fy01," Nike, Inc. (2001). http://www.nike.com/ nikebiz.jhtml;bsessionid=5WUP5FEFZM3VQCQCGIMCF4YKAIZCQIZ.

32. Knight and Greenberg, "Promotionalism and Subpolitics," pp. 565, 554; see also Stabile, "Nike, Social Responsibility, and the Hidden Abode of Production."

33. Ibid., p. 544.

* FOR FURTHER STUDY *

Baimer, A. 2001. *Sport, Nationalism, and Globalization: European and North American Perspectives*. Albany: State University of New York Press.

Barney, Robert K., Stephen R. Wenn, and Scott G. Martyn. 2002. *Selling the Five Rings: The International Olympic Committee and the Rise of Olympic Commercialism* (Salt Lake City: University of Utah Press).

Cole, C. L. 2002. "The Place of Golf in U. S. Imperialism," *Journal of Sport & Social Issues* 26 (November):331–336.

Harvey, Jean, Alan Law, and Michael Cantelon. 2001. "North American Professional Team Sport Franchises Ownership: Patterns and Global Entertainment Conglomerates," *Sociology of Sport Journal* 18 (4):435–457.

Harvey, Jean, and Maurice Saint-Germain. 2001. "Sporting Goods Trade, International Division of Labor, and the Unequal Hierarchy of Nations," *Sociology of Sport Journal* 18 (2):231–246.

Lafeber, W. 2000. *Michael Jordan and the New Global Capitalism* (New York: W. W. Norton).

Magee, Jonathan, and John Sugden. 2002. "'The World at Their Feet': Professional Football and International Labor Migration," *Journal of Sport & Social Issues* 26 (November):421–437.

Magnusson, Gudmundur K. 2001. "The Internationalization of Sports: The Case of Iceland." *International Review for the Sociology of Sport* 36 (March):59–70.

Maguire, Joseph. 1999. *Global Sport: Identities, Societies, Civilizations* (Cambridge, UK: Polity).

Maguire, Joseph. 2000. "Sport and Globalization." Pp. 356–367 in *Handbook of Sports Studies* Jay Coakley and Eric Dunning (eds.), (London: Sage).

Scherer, Jay. 2001. "Globalization and the Construction of Local Particularities: A Case Study of the Winnipeg Jets," *Sociology of Sport Journal* 18 (2):205–230.

Wong, Lloyd L., and Ricardo Trumper. 2002. "Global Celebrity Athletes and Nationalism," *Journal of Sport & Social Issues* 26 (May): 168–194.

About the Editor

D. Stanley Eitzen (Ph.D., University of Kansas) is professor emeritus of sociology at Colorado State University, where he taught for twenty-one years, the last as John N. Stern Distinguished Professor. Prior to that he taught at the University of Kansas. He was editor of *The Social Science Journal* from 1978 to 1984. Professor Eitzen began his career as a high school teacher and athletic coach. His interest in the sociology of sport has led him to author or co-author numerous books and articles, including *Sociology of North American Sport* (with George H. Sage), seventh edition and *Fair and Foul: Beyond the Myths and Paradoxes of Sport,* second edition. His most recent books on subjects other than sport include *Experiencing Poverty: Voices from the Bottom* (with Kelly Eitzen Smith), *Paths to Homelessness: Extreme Poverty and the Urban Housing Crisis* (co-authored with Doug A. Timmer and Kathryn D. Talley), *In Conflict and Order: Understanding Society* (with Maxine Baca Zinn), tenth edition; *Diversity in Families* (with Maxine Baca Zinn), seventh edition; and *Social Problems* (with Maxine Baca Zinn), ninth edition.